Dismembering
the American Dream

The Life and
Fiction of
Richard Yates

Kate Charlton-Jones

Foreword by DEWITT HENRY
Afterword by MONICA YATES

THE UNIVERSITY OF ALABAMA PRESS
Tuscaloosa

The University of Alabama Press
Tuscaloosa, Alabama 35487-0380
uapress.ua.edu

Typeface: Minion and Helvetica
Manufactured in the United States of America

Cover photograph: Yates looking out the door of the pump house at Babaril in Mahopac,
circa 1958; courtesy of the Richard Yates Estate
Cover design: Mary-Frances Burt / Burt&Burt

∞

The paper on which this book is printed meets the minimum requirements of American
National Standard for Information Sciences—Permanence of Paper for Printed Library
Materials, ANSI Z39.48-1984.

Library of Congress Cataloging-in-Publication Data

Charlton-Jones, Kate, 1959–
    Dismembering the American dream : the life and fiction of Richard Yates / Kate
Charlton-Jones ; foreword by DeWitt Henry ; afterword by Monica Yates.
       pages cm
    Includes bibliographical references and index.
    ISBN 978-0-8173-1825-3 (hardback) — ISBN 978-0-8173-8748-8 (ebook)
    1. Yates, Richard, 1926–1992—Criticism and interpretation. I. Title.
    PS3575.A83Z65 2014
    813'.54—dc23
                                                                    2014002564

For John

"The Americans are funny. You have a funny sense of time—
or perhaps you have no sense of time at all, I can't tell. Time
always sounds like a parade *chez vous*—a triumphant parade, like
armies with banners entering a town. As though, with enough
time. . . . and all that fearful energy and virtue you people have,
everything will be settled, solved, put in its place. And when I say
everything," he added, grimly, "I mean all the serious, dreadful
things, like pain and death and love, in which you Americans do
not believe."

James Baldwin, *Giovanni's Room*

But once that was done she began to find bad places back in the
main part of the story: scenes that went on too long and others
that didn't go on long enough, paragraphs that weren't pulling
their narrative weight . . . and far too many easy, poorly chosen
words. The only truly professional approach now, it seemed,
would be to write the whole damned thing over again.

Richard Yates, *Young Hearts Crying*

Contents

List of Illustrations

Foreword

This admirably thorough and well-balanced critical study is corrective and, more broadly, instructive. Yates and his oeuvre of seven novels and two collections of stories remain underappreciated. Kate Charlton-Jones's work brings to mind two of my favorite studies of novelists: F. R. Leavis's *D. H. Lawrence: Novelist* and Carlos Baker's *Hemingway: The Writer as Artist*. Both argue, as does Charlton-Jones, for reappreciation and better understanding of the art. We once had D. H. Lawrence, the artless prophet (if not pornographer), and Ernest Hemingway, the baby-talking minimalist, and now Yates is portrayed as a pessimist and artistic throwback, obsessively mining the "same half-acre of pain." Charlton-Jones helps us, with her particular cultural distance (as an English reader, as a contemporary of Yates's daughters, and as a feminist), to contextualize Yates and "the prescience of his writing," especially his "insight into marriage, women's rights, gender roles, and social interaction."

She compares the account in Yates's fiction of the American 1950s and 1960s to accounts by sociologists, social historians, film historians, and other commentators, but stops short of recommending Yates primarily for his historical value, as one might Sinclair Lewis on the 1920s. While Yates has much to say about his times, she argues, he has more to say about life in general.

In her exemplary reading, Charlton-Jones is more sensitive than earlier critics to the "careful system of narrative layering," "authorial ironies," and "subtly inflected descriptions" in Yates; in fact, her appreciation of "ironic realism"—something rarely discussed this side of Wayne C. Booth's *Rhetoric of Irony*—may be her strongest contribution. Baker sought to teach us about Hemingway's art, but Yates's is a difficult, high art.

She also proves as a reader to be as well informed and perceptive about such postmodern contemporaries of Yates as John Cheever, Kurt Vonnegut, and John Barth as she is of J. D. Salinger and John O'Hara. She makes the significant point that Yates "helped to modernize the realist novel and, to an extent, helped to narrow the gap between the metafictionalists and traditionalists." In addition, she explores the comparison of Yates to his professed masters, Fitzgerald, Hemingway, and Flaubert. She makes apt use of quotes from Yates's letters, interviews, and other sources in his own words.

Charlton-Jones organizes her discussion by such key topics as "performative selves," "gender roles," and "parental control and sexuality," and on each topic she ranges gracefully among Yates's major and minor texts, early and later. She also brings the history of film to bear on Yates's use of movies for his characters; it is the analogue of Don Quixote's absorption with medieval romances.

She is able to criticize Yates's flawed art as well as his successes. Even though "Yates's fiction challenges the bigoted views of the era," she finds that his narrative perspective falters in the later novels when it comes to mother figures and women's sexuality. Echoing feminist critiques of Hemingway, she speculates about "the work of a man who fears women's sexuality because he does not fully understand it and because he fears what it will reveal about him."

Surely Yates himself would have flinched at this suggestion, but he would have been proud overall and gratified by the accuracies of Charlton-Jones's reading of his art. After her attentive and perceptive study, lesser readings of Yates will no longer prove acceptable.

—DeWitt Henry, Emerson College

Acknowledgments

I've had long enough to think about what to say here but, even so, it isn't an easy task when so many people have contributed, directly or indirectly, to my work. Years ago, at the University of Cambridge, the late Margot Heinemann taught me to value words and have confidence in my opinion; I've always tried to honor her advice. Many thanks must go to Professor Richard Gray, who taught me and encouraged me when I started on this journey. Alongside him, and also attached to the University of Essex, I want to thank the late Dr. Joe Allard, Dr. Owen Robinson, Dr. Theophilus Savvas, Dr. Bright Molande, Penny Woollard, Dr. John Cant, and Jane Thorp. I am grateful to the staff at the Albert Sloman Library (University of Essex) and those at Cambridge University Library for their work in assisting me. I would also like to acknowledge the part Sharon Monteith (University of Nottingham) played in sharpening my thoughts. In addition, I would like to thank the editors of the *Icfai Journal of American Literature*, *Literature Compass*, and *The Literary Encyclopedia* for publishing early versions of my work.

My friend Athena is responsible for my first reading of Richard Yates, having handed me *Revolutionary Road* through my kitchen window in 2005; a bizarre introduction to Yates's work, but true nevertheless. This was a real example, if ever there was one, of what Richard Ford describes in his introduction to *Revolutionary Road* as a "cultural-literary secret handshake" among readers who would appreciate the quality of Richard Yates's work. Another example is the relationship I built up, through a shared love of Yates's work, with Alex Siskin in Los Angeles. Blogging was our medium; Richard Yates was our subject. My friends have been wonderfully supportive, despite having to listen to many a dull tale about the work in progress. The Causerie, made up of a wonderful group of like-minded people, demands special thanks for giving constant encouragement; thank you to them all, Nella Probert in par-

ticular. In addition, my friend Guy Martin must be credited with always being on hand to give very helpful advice.

In 2008 I went to Boston and spent a happy week reading and rereading the Yates papers in the Howard Gotlieb Archival Center for Research at Boston University. I would like to thank the staff very much indeed for being so enthusiastic about what I was doing, Sean Noel and Laura Russo in particular. While in Boston, I met DeWitt Henry. He has been the most wonderful mentor throughout this whole process, partly because he holds his old friend's work in such high esteem and wants it to have greater recognition and partly because he has always supported my approach. DeWitt Henry has been tireless in his quiet, unobtrusive assistance.

On that same trip, I met Yates's biographer, Blake Bailey. He has never failed to answer a question I have suddenly thrown at him from across the pond. Thank you, Blake, not just for that, and the admirable *A Tragic Honesty*, but also for introducing me to Monica Yates. I have been extraordinarily lucky to have regular contact with Monica and through her with her sister Sharon. Monica, in particular, has been so helpful in her direct way; she can be relied upon—like her father—to sniff out falsehood at a considerable distance. I am honored and hugely grateful for the support of Richard Yates's family. I must thank them, Grace Schulman, and the Wylie Agency for the use of photographs of Richard Yates.

Finally, to thank the most important people beginning with Dan Waterman, editor-in-chief at the University of Alabama Press, and those who worked with him, Joanna Jacobs and Dawn Hall. They were brave enough to take this on. Furthermore, I would like to thank Martin Halliwell (University of Leicester) and Steve Yarborough (Emerson College, Boston). My sister and brother-in-law, Fiona and Simon Pearson, have given practical advice and warm encouragement, as have Julie Charlton-Jones and Anna Blunt. My three children, Edward, Olivia, and Finn, have been patient, encouraging, usually interested, and *always* my most devoted supporters. Wiser than their years, all three can be relied upon for leveling advice. This book would not have happened without the love, constancy, conviction, and irrepressible good humor of their father, my best friend, John. It is dedicated to him.

The Published Works of Richard Yates
(1926–1992)

Revolutionary Road (1961)
Eleven Kinds of Loneliness (short stories) (1962)
A Special Providence (1969)
Disturbing the Peace (1975)
The Easter Parade (1976)
A Good School (1978)
Liars in Love (short stories) (1981)
Young Hearts Crying (1984)
Lie Down in Darkness (screenplay) (1985)
Cold Spring Harbor (1986)
The Collected Stories of Richard Yates (2001)

Introduction

1. Yates in the little pump house at Babaril in Mahopac where the Yates family rented a house from 1956 to 1961. Yates used a small room in the main house as his writing room until Monica was born in 1957, when he moved to the pump house. Courtesy of the Richard Yates Estate.

Every sensibility has its canon of indelible encounters, perhaps more deeply personal than explicable. My own list includes *The Secret Garden*, the poems of Robert Frost, *Jane Eyre*, *Pride and Prejudice*, *Anna Karenina*, *King Lear*, *Middlemarch*, "Sunday Morning" by Wallace Stevens, and *Revolutionary Road*. I've spared my reader the full list of what constitutes my literary awakening and, of course, it doesn't stop with *Revolutionary Road*. Alice Walker's *The Color Purple*, Elizabeth Strout's *Olive Kitteridge*, Edmund de Waal's *The Hare with the Amber Eyes*, and Colm Tóibín's *The Master* follow on; the list will always continue.

What unites such literary encounters over time, language, and culture is the reader's heightened awareness of highly accomplished writing; in different ways, they are judged to be masterpieces that the reader feels compelled to pass on. As with the other foundation stones of my education, having finished Richard Yates's first novel, I wanted to share it immediately and discuss it with others; my mind was racing with the many thoughts it provoked. I wanted to read everything he had ever written, there and then, but, paradoxically perhaps, more than that I wanted to sit in a quiet place and contemplate the story I had just read. Yates makes his own reference to such feelings of awakening after having read *The Great Gatsby*, which, like some of Keats's poetry, left him "with a stunning illumination of the world."[1] However, my enthusiasm for Yates's work has not blinded me to some of the weaknesses that occur in his novels. I address these as they emerge and as I find fault lines across his oeuvre. Nevertheless, I make no apology for the fact that *Dismembering the American Dream* is above all else an extended appreciation of Yates's work.

Richard Yates's writing, particularly his first novel and first book of short stories, forms a significant contribution to American literature, but it is one that has been largely overlooked. This is all the more puzzling when one considers his economy of style, his narrative layering and robust antisentimentality, all of which combine to create writing of the highest quality. His fictions are powerful, memorable, affecting, and original. Despite a recent surge of interest in Yates's writing following the release of Sam Mendes's film *Revolutionary Road* (2008),[2] there is still a defensive job to be done. Asked why I have chosen to write about the fiction of a man whose take on life is so deeply miserable, my response is always the same two questions: have you read *Eleven Kinds of Loneliness*? Have you read *Revolutionary Road*? To read Yates's tales of disordered lives is to uncover not misery (though the lives he describes are sad and profoundly lonely), but an insightful, enriching, and often-humorous understanding of human weakness and vulnerability. Yates's narratives absorb his readers so entirely, and mirror their own emotional highs and lows so skillfully, that the act of reading becomes an act of recognition. His work demonstrates his ability to tease powerful human drama out of the most quotidian moments. At the same time, Yates's fiction displays an object lesson in the art of fine prose writing; it is not incidental that so many early Yates enthusiasts were established writers.

The general task of this book, therefore, is to provide an extended critical examination of the novels and short stories of this author and to address their neglect. My work explores how Yates extends the realist form when many of his contemporaries (with several notable exceptions) had moved away from seeking to imitate the real. It investigates the dominant theme of all his work; ideas about performative behavior are at the heart of all his fictions. Within that broad framework, Yates looks in some detail at the writer's role in society and examines the development of social and sexual relationships in mid-twentieth-century America. In addition to exploring these different features of his writing, I illustrate how Yates not only incorporates within his work some of the concerns and methods of postmodernist writers but also how, nevertheless, he resists their ontological challenges. I should point out that throughout this book I refer to the generic writer as male to aid fluency and because all the writers I examine are male. While it might seem odd to take such a one-sided view of the literature of the period, I want my comparisons of Yates's work to be as evenhanded as possible. For this reason I also ignore the drama and poetry of the era and only make literary comparisons with the work of other novelists.

While many of his contemporaries went on to achieve both status and renown, Yates battled to stay solvent and healthy and to follow up the relative success of his first novel, *Revolutionary Road*. He was a temperamental man who inspired great devotion from those who knew him well, but he struggled throughout his life with illness, alcoholism, two failed marriages, and a string of affairs that etched their way both into his view of the world and of himself. With the exception of his love and dedication toward his three daughters, it was only writing that sustained him. *Revolutionary Road*, published in 1961, both Yates's first novel and first published work, and *Eleven Kinds of Loneliness*, published in 1962, were initially well received, but they did not sell well. Writers such as Tennessee Williams, Kurt Vonnegut Jr., Richard Ford, and Andre Dubus were vocal in their admiration of Yates's fiction, but fewer than twelve thousand copies of *Revolutionary Road* were sold in his lifetime. His later novels and short stories fared even less well and, though reissued, are still given scant critical attention. In January 2009, at the time of the United Kingdom release of Sam Mendes's cinematic version of *Revolutionary Road*, well over three million copies of this novel had been sold in the United States. It reached number one on the *New York Times* best-seller list by what would have been his eighty-third birthday, February 3, 2009.

Richard Yates was born into a lower middle-class American family in Yonkers in 1926. He died in Alabama in 1992 with seven novels and two collections of short stories to his name. In addition, he wrote three screenplays: *Lie Down in Darkness*, from the novel of the same name by William Styron, *Iwo Jima*, and *The Bridge at Remagen*. Only the last script was filmed, but he had hated the whole process of writing it and was fired from the project when he refused to make extensive revisions: "the movie was finally released in 1969—though Yates had disowned it so completely that he even refused to list *Remagen* on his otherwise all-encompassing resumé of 1973. He told friends he was appalled to have his name associated with such a 'dog,' and claims the final version was an almost total rewrite."[3] Highly self-critical, Yates frequently bemoaned the fact that he had not produced more. But each novel and each story was written and rewritten exhaustively as he honed his art and demanded perfection in every written word. In the first ten years of his writing life, he had an enormous struggle to get published. Furthermore, he was hampered by severe bouts of manic depression; he had to endure this condition throughout his adult life.

The issue of timing was not insignificant for Yates and the reception of his work; his early 1960s publications (his first novel and first book of short stories) were published at a point when the literary fashion was toward both postrealist fiction and the New Journalists' particular form of realism. New fiction celebrated diversity, instability, change, and, above all else, it somehow upheld the notion that anything was possible. It was exciting, experimental, and it looked forward not backward. The editors and critics of the time seemed to see not just social realist fiction but also fiction that concerned itself with life in the 1950s as passé (unless it gave voice to emerging minorities). Yates's work only dwells on the contemporary postwar mood toward celebrating change and experimentation in order to undercut it. Moreover (and for many this is still a critical weakness of his work), Yates's sad stories offer no redemption or possibility of redemption.

The voice of this writer is unashamedly WASPish, as are the voices of the predominantly white middle-class characters he creates. At a time when literature began celebrating authors from other races and social backgrounds, this is a further indication that Yates missed his time and his mark. The short stories in *Eleven Kinds of Loneliness* (1962) were all, with the exception of the last story, "Builders," written in the 1950s, so that superficially the lives he was describing seemed to be out of date. Nick Fraser comments on this as he assesses Yates's early unpopularity in the light of the recent resurgence of interest in his work: "Yates's problem wasn't just blackness of vision, but persistently bad timing. His books appeared either passé when they dealt with the time in which he was growing up or dangerously at odds with prevailing wisdom. . . . To imply that, far from pursuing the approved dream, executives in corporations didn't really do much work, was something not even Jack Lemmon could have conveyed to the American public in Yates's heyday."[4] Steeped in 1950s settings, Yates's work was, therefore, seen as "historical" and as being *about* the 1950s, so that the prescience of his writing was overlooked. The American reading public appears not to have seen beyond those settings and, as a consequence, failed to appreciate the universality of his fictional dramas. With the exception of a collection of devoted readers, often writers themselves,[5] his insights into marriage, women's rights, and gender roles, alongside his mordant observations about social interaction generally, were, in the main, disregarded. In addition, Yates's style and technique give the highly misleading impression of being simple and arrived at without much effort. It seems that such simplicity was regarded pejoratively set against the playful ironies, the metaphysical questioning, and the uncertain landscapes of "new" fiction. How ironic that Yates's clarity of expression, alongside the moral ambiguities he relished creating (the very thing that today's readership applauds), were regarded by many notable contemporary editors as unexceptional. The editor of a then-new magazine called *Discovery*, Vance Bourjaily, wrote to Yates's agent about one of Yates's short stories. He bemoaned the fact that it was so difficult to tell "whether tragedy's involved or simply animal pathos."[6]

Not polemical but voicing liberal social concerns, not comic but often funny and usually ironic, Yates's work was underappreciated and written off as the product of a misanthrope's unrelentingly negative worldview. Whereas writers such as Philip Roth, John Updike, and Saul Bellow insisted on the intellectual and emotional audacity of their characters, and found readers in great numbers, literary critics seemed to find no such insistence in Yates's work; gripped by inertia, self-doubt, and sexual impotence, Yates's figures lacked both intellectual and emotional courage. One *Harper's* editor's letter of rejection sounds almost plaintive: "*Why* does he have to write so unpleasantly that one feels there's just no good in anybody?"[7] Often seen sidestepping challenges and failing at every kind of domestic or social hurdle, the protagonists limp off into a murky distance at the end of a typical Yatesian tale. To a middle-class reader in the mid-twentieth century, therefore, the appeal of their constraints was limited.

Yates's characters are dreamers who envisage a better, richer, more successful and more romantic life. As Dan DeLuca suggests, his dreamers can be defined as "those whose self-confidence is misplaced and those who don't even have the faith to believe in themselves."[8] While the latter type seems to be exclusively filled by female characters such as the Grimes sisters in *The Easter Parade* or Rachel Drake in *Cold Spring Harbor*, the men of his fiction are self-deluded, deeply flawed individuals who either show determined optimism while all about them things are going wrong or wallow in despair and look for others to blame. Michael Davenport, the protagonist of *Young Hearts Crying*, for instance, is a writer who resents others for not accepting his work rather than attempting a critical self-appraisal of his work's weaknesses. Similarly self-absorbed, Evan Shepard (*Cold Spring Harbor*) feels that his married life has become dull, but instead of looking for ways to improve life for his wife Rachel and himself, he seeks out his former lover—the mother of his first child—in order to have fun. Running away from responsibility is almost always an attractive option for Yates's male characters.

Ridiculed by others, or by a narrative voice that exposes them, Yates's protagonists ensnare the reader as they feel the discomfort of disillusionment.

It is frequently only the reader, however, who appreciates the self-delusion or hypocrisy being depicted. Through a careful system of narrative layering, Yates describes the selfish impulse behind his protagonists' dreams of a better life. Small details may infiltrate a narrative that imitates the aspirational thoughts of an individual. These facts disturb the fluency of their versions of themselves, and they often provoke the reader to look askance at the characters' assessment of the past, or of what is happening to them in the present of the story. The inevitable result of this is that the reader looks back with some concern at a reliable version of events being ignored. The way Yates creates characters—and the way they interact—suggests that he regards people as being incapable of a trustworthy version of their own history; he indicates that egos, dreams, and a self-aggrandizing tendency will always distort memory.

Within his fiction, therefore, Yates picks apart his characters' idealized versions of themselves and dismembers their dreams entirely. These dreams have acquired a substance and three-dimensionality that is missing in the ordinariness of their day-to-day lives. So much more powerful and, indeed, dangerous, than just a series of wistful imaginings, the dreams of Yates's characters become a blueprint for the way they seek to live. In addition, the emphasis on each character's physical mannerisms, and their often-grotesque bad habits, ensures that the collapse of a romanticized version of selfhood and society is physical, visceral, and painful. Beyond gently implying that the character in question may be deluded, Yates employs a variety of methods of exposure to indicate the serious implications for society if such delusions go unchecked. For many readers, curiously, this is not depressing but edifying. Through a mimetic process, such readers "live" the lives Yates describes, but, with the restrained use of an ironic tone, the author, almost imperceptibly, inserts a whisper of distance. Moving to Paris, publishing a successful novel, holding a relationship together, being sober in the morning, writing a hundred coherent words: these are the way Yates's protagonists downwardly adjust their scale of dreaming, and it is what David Castronovo and Steven Goldleaf in their monograph *Richard Yates* call Yates's tendency toward "rewriting Fitzgerald's winter dreams of love and social ambition in a minor key."[9]

In April 1961, at the time of *Revolutionary Road*'s release, the *New Yorker* published a stinging review of the novel and referred to Yates's work as "flimsy."[10] In spite of such a review, the recognition and praise *Revolutionary Road* received in other publications raised Yates's expectations for further plaudits. To his dismay, the acclaim his work received thereafter was muted at best. His quiet tales of domestic lives in disarray did little to inspire hope and confidence; more to the point, they strongly implied that very little was possible at all. While this was exactly how he intended people to respond to his work, Yates was unprepared for the corollary. The low sales figures of each publication meant that he lived in a constant state of anxiety about money and debts unpaid, that he drank heavily to help cope with such anxiety, and that his self-esteem was always precarious. As a result, striving, and subsequently disappointment, became a way of life and informed many of his characterizations.

However, set against the pervasive difficulties of his life, there were flashes of real, acknowledged success. Yates was nominated for the National Book Award in 1962 for *Revolutionary Road*, although he was not the eventual winner. That same year he finished writing the film script for William Styron's 1951 novel *Lie Down in Darkness*, which was very well received although never produced, and in 1963 he worked for several months as a speechwriter for the US attorney general, Robert Kennedy. In this role he helped to transform Kennedy's image, reportedly producing brilliant speeches on civil rights that enabled him to publicize his own liberal views. Kurt Vonnegut noted, "He used RFK as a ventriloquist's dummy."[11] In 1976, among the plaudits it received, *The Easter Parade* was nominated for the National Book Critics Circle Award. It didn't win.

Recent criticism has been more consistently admiring of the late novelist's oeuvre. Many reviewers start by alluding to Yates's exceptional writing and go on to suggest the relevance of his work for a contemporary readership. Richard Russo, for instance, makes the point that there is still much that resonates in that "blackness of vision": "The excitement one feels reading these dark stories . . . is the exhilaration of encountering, recognizing, and embracing the truth. It's not a pretty truth? Too bad. That we recognize ourselves in the blindness, the neediness, the loneliness, even the cruelty of Yates's people, will have to suffice."[12] The fact that his work has had more critical notice since the turn of the twenty-first century than it ever had in his lifetime suggests that a new readership has discovered that Yates has much to say, not only about the 1950s and 1960s (and occasionally even the 1970s) but also about life in general. A fan-created website devoted to him is at http://www.richardyates.org/. There is a Facebook page with similar origins, "Richard Yates" (https://www.facebook.com/richardyatesauthor), and I have run a blog since 2009 dedicated to discussion of his work (*kateonyates. wordpress.com*).

Even the briefest glance at Blake Bailey's biography of Yates, *A Tragic Honesty*, confirms that Yates's material is highly autobiographical. Yates's use of his own biography with thinly veiled portraits of its major figures—himself, his parents, and his wives—is a significant feature of his writing and, with the repeated patterns of flawed relationships, is often seen as a major weakness. There was nothing he could do about such criticism except examine it within his writing in order to try and make sense of it; as illustrated in *Young Hearts Crying* by Michael Davenport's bleak self-criticisms, Yates was inclined to take a defensive position as he debated the issue within some of his fictions. All his writer/characters have the same trait—whether male or female—so that their encounters in life are always the starting point for their fictions. For Yates, as for his characters, life's experiences were not so much inspirational as dictatorial.

By contrast, Yates felt the work of many postmodernists was led by intellectual rather than experiential ideas: "it's emotionally empty. It isn't *felt*."[13] The character of Lucy Davenport, appraising the final episode of a story she's been working on for months, illustrates Yates's view of the problem. She hopes it will work but then realizes that "it hadn't really happened, and so it seemed to cast an unhealthy glow of fraudulence over the whole story."[14] Yates's characters, on the whole, inhabit the world he inhabited, whether suburban small towns of East Coast America, dingy rooms of an impoverished family in Manhattan, or pokey apartments on the fringes of Hollywood. Both men and women are caught in the net of his caustic gaze and are frequently heavy drinkers, negligent fathers, poor mothers, talentless artists, and unappealing social climbers. That was the world he knew; that was the world he fictionalized. Figures recur across his work, versions of himself acting out versions of his life.

If writing about dreamers—and writing about aspects of his own life—seems to hark back to the literature of F. Scott Fitzgerald and Ernest Hemingway, there are several aspects of Yates's work that seem "modern" by contrast. Absorbing and exploring some aspects of postmodernism's stylistic and epistemological concerns, his writing is touched by the fashionable ideas and narrative technique of the postwar era. Although he draws little, if any, attention to this in his own comments about his work, it is possible to find those issues without probing too deeply. Perhaps those issues account in part for the resurgence of interest in his work as the 1950s and 1960s are re-examined by a new generation of critical readers fascinated by the era into which they were born. Readers of Yates's fictions discover that his voice and observations have enduring relevance. The emphasis on the dialogic nature of experience, for instance—the way his characters are drawn and encapsulated through dialogue—raises questions that contemporary postmodernists were also investigating.

Similarly, by weaving into his narratives writer/protagonists as central characters, Yates adopts a typically postmodern technique that critiques the thing it describes; he becomes the writer *and* a central character, a chronicler *and* a witness. By splitting the "self" he operates within the text as both writer/character and author/observer. Where consolation is to be found (and, as I suggested earlier, one can never find *redemption* in Yates's work), it is in the role of the writer who attempts to shape and illustrate reality creatively in order to understand it. As he picks apart the dreams of his protagonists, Yates undercuts any resolution his work appears to offer with the use of an ironic narrative voice and by posing, silently, further wider questions for the reader to contemplate.

Equally "modern" are the endings Yates chooses for his fictions. They are both unexpected and challenging and they shy away from the kind of neat, moral outcomes that one might expect from "traditional" realist fiction. To me they suggest further that Yates wants to stretch the boundaries of realism. With his endings Yates suggests that life is a series of struggles pulling us forward, promising us futures, but throwing up problems that drag us relentlessly backward. In the content, mood, and in some aspects of the style of his work, Yates seems to look "over his shoulder" so that one cannot fail to be reminded of those final lines of *The Great Gatsby*: "So we beat on, boats against the current, borne back ceaselessly into the past."[15] This is not nostalgia so much as a sense that there is a stronger undertow than anticipated. Yates looks back to learn about the present, but not out of a sense of longing for a time past; his view of the future is similarly unromanticized. Thus his fiction provides no happy endings. It suggests emphatically that there are no easy answers to the dilemmas of modern life.

Central to Yates's view of life is his sensitivity to the fact that people are blind to the dishonesty of "spin" in the language and imagery of advertising and film; I examine this from a number of different angles. Yates is alert to the manner in which romanticized, glamorized ideals—"stars" such as Laurence Olivier and Alan Ladd—and the films that promote these icons, infect the language and behavior of daily life. A few observers, even then, perceived the culture of celebrity to have a corrosive effect. Yates sees how adulation of an inherently false persona weakens an individual's grasp on reality and creates a pervasive sense of dissatisfaction. I struggle to think of any other novelist writing in the 1950s or 1960s who so powerfully draws attention to an obsession with celebrity and the trappings of fame, an obsession that dominates many people's views of life in the twenty-first century.

In a manner designed to draw attention to insincerity and provoke inquiry into the way individuals interrelate, Yates frequently highlights the performative nature of human behavior, examining the self-conscious way in which roles are adopted to create a particular effect. Inevitably, the roles chosen are those handed down by both big and small screens. Yates wants to expose the way superficial posturing, influenced by motion pictures, creates a barrier to authentic communication. This aspect of life in the 1950s and 1960s is a dominant, recurring, and effective theme in his work; his characters "narrate" themselves as they go along, often unable to distinguish between projected ideals and prosaic truths. A preoccupation with notions of authenticity is characteristic of literature in the late 1950s and early 1960s, and in that respect Yates was very much *of* his time. He developed his own method of inquiry within a broadly realist style. Dark humor and an unflinching eye characterize his realism as he refuses to ignore the fakery of the performative gestures of human experience. Using dramaturgical metaphors, usually drawn from film, Yates focuses attention on the insubstantiality of the self that many other writers, such as J. D. Salinger, also explore and examine.[16]

For Yates, being a writer *is* his performance in life; his work is a detailed investigation into how to manage that role. At the same time, he is constantly considering and refining his thoughts about the forms of his fictions so that they come as close as possible to an artistically shaped version of the truth of life. Blake Bailey notes that in 1950 Yates, age twenty-four, was hospitalized in a tuberculosis ward. At this relatively late stage in life he discovered literature and undertook a great deal of reading that he felt he had missed out on by not going to college. Bailey draws attention to the fact that during this course of autodidactic learning, Yates "particularly . . . read (and reread) Chekhov."[17] From his own reading, therefore, rather than from any formal education, Yates developed literary heroes, and their influence on his fiction can be traced.

Since being a writer is Yates's main performance, it is not surprising that writers feature heavily in his fiction. His interest in creativity and the creative temperament encompasses painters and sculptors as well. None of these creative souls are romanticized, and it is often on them, and their failings, that Yates's gimlet gaze rests longest. Creativity is examined more widely by presenting artists who act as a counterpoint to struggling writers; Yates often chooses the visual arts to demonstrate his views on the move toward postmodernism. In *Young Hearts Crying* (1984), his sixth published novel, this is made particularly clear with several fine artists at the center of the story. The main protagonist is, however, a writer, though perhaps in a weak attempt to shrug off accusations of self-portraiture, Yates's character writes poems and plays but not novels.

The writers of Yates's fiction have mental health problems that are made worse by their dependence on alcohol and cigarettes. Since manic depression, as well as heavy drinking and smoking, were features of Yates's life, they seep into his fictional portraits. This is most obvious in the character of John Wilder, the central character of *Disturbing the Peace*. In his attempt to reflect an accurate portrayal of mental instability in this novel, Yates challenges his readers to accept that any one of them could "fall" as John Wilder does. He is shown to be a very ordinary man who slips into the disturbing underclass of the mentally ill and socially aggressive. Hospitalization for Wilder enables Yates to draw on his own grim experiences at Bellevue and other so-called mental hospitals. He infuses his powerful and disquieting descriptions of such institutions with grim details designed to make his readers feel as uncomfortable as possible. It is clear that Yates's writers struggle to achieve in any area of life, even if they are not mental patients. However, while they are beleaguered individuals, their craft offers a tentative form of rescue or consolation not seen elsewhere.

Yates's depiction of gender roles and relationships is insightful, often ahead of his time, and at the same time problematic. In his novels, Yates's portrayal of marriage—and the infidelities endemic in his view of marriage—provides a caustic impression of the institution. While he claimed he believed in marriage in the *Ploughshares* interview, more often than not his writing suggests otherwise.[18] In his early work, including *Revolutionary Road*, Yates's depiction of the struggles men, and more particularly women, encounter within the home and outside it prefigure some of the concerns the second wave of feminism adopted. He was not alone in doing this, but it was not a generally accepted view of the way the sexes related to each other. The issues he draws attention to did not become part of mainstream thinking until after the publication of Betty Friedan's *The Feminine Mystique* in 1963.

Yates addresses the issue of abortion in his novels, though not in order to have an extensive debate about the morality of the practice. In *The Easter Parade* he confronts the fact that it is both illegal and commonplace but, lest the reader think he is making a feminist point, he links a libidinous lifestyle with the need for terminations. It seems that he wants the reader to empathize with his female protagonist but not admire her. Similarly, Yates writes with clarity about sexual desire in young girls and women, but frequently this develops into a distorting and disturbing presentation of female sexuality. Indeed, throughout his body of work Yates seems to equate sexual liberation with promiscuity and disreputable behavior. He was confused about women in the personal sphere but unequivocal that as far as work and their role in society was concerned, they were held back and diminished by men.

From a feminist perspective, Yates's observations about women often seem impressively ahead of their time, as is the case in his work when writing about

abortions. However, any such feminist perspective is undercut by the greatest weakness of his writing: his ideas about women, in terms of their sexual
desire, show an unusual loss of authorial perspective and are full of contradictions. There is such an uncomfortable, recurring veneer of distaste per-
meating almost all of his allusions to the female sex drive that it is hard not
to link his depictions of such desire to a fear of women or even (possible)
confusion about his own sexuality. I explore this in the full knowledge that
although Yates was always uncertain regarding his manliness and how to
project his masculinity as a sensitive male, he was neither effeminate nor
homosexual. Nevertheless, his repeated references to impotence, alongside
the suppressed homosexuality of many of his male characters, cannot be ignored. The complex and distorted relationship between mothers and sons is
a constant theme within Yates's work, as is the observation that fathers get
a raw deal in the divorce courts. The fathers of Yates's fiction are frequently
outsiders, kept apart from their children, left alone to cope with the emotions
of love, loss, and bitterness. Writing about what he knew and had witnessed,
Yates's observations were at cross-purposes with how America wanted to see
itself: egalitarian, industrious, and the place of opportunity for all, no matter
what his or her race or gender.

By republishing his work at the turn of the century, Random House and
Vintage responded to the demands of a small but vocal group of writers and
readers who recognize Yates as an unacknowledged author of enormous
worth and influence. In addition to those already cited, a new generation of
supporters of Yates's fiction has emerged: Salman Rushdie, Lionel Shriver,
Woody Allen, David Hare, and Nick Hornby—the latter referred to *Revolutionary Road* in one of his books[19]—are forthright in their recommenda-
tion of this writer. Yates, it seems, even without the continuing force of publishing houses and advertising behind him, has long excited in his readers
a loyal and jealously guarded secret society. Richard Ford, writing in the introduction to the 2001 edition of *Revolutionary Road*, describes the deeply
felt enthusiasm for what he terms this "cultish standard."[20] Yates's works have
provoked this kind of devotion not just because they demonstrate such fine
writing but *because* they have never excited the breadth of readership and
the acknowledgment they deserve; people who discover Yates quietly take
on the promotion of Yates.

With the republication of all Yates's works in the past decade, in addition
to Blake Bailey's biography and Sam Mendes's film, a palpable excitement
about this neglected author has been created. Benjamin Lytal expressed this
sense of a Yates revival attendant on Mendes's film when he wrote in the *New
York Sun* that the film will, "put the gist of 'Revolutionary Road' across to

millions who have never heard of Yates. . . . Like his hero F. Scott Fitzgerald, who experienced a posthumous revival mid-century, Yates is getting a second act, and it will be bigger than his first."[21] That second act was bigger than the first (how could it not be?), but the sad truth is that the Mendes film came and went without showering either its director or its cast in the glorious accolades that had been predicted. Therefore, any lasting legacy for the body of Yates's work on the back of many anticipated film awards has eluded it. Undoubtedly the film raised Yates's profile, and many hundreds of thousand copies of his first novel were sold as a result, but to the Yates devotee it was a time of mixed emotion. It was thrilling to see paperbacks of his work everywhere for an all-too-brief few months, but it was a disappointment to see them packaged as movie tie-ins, with the story they contained commercialized by pictures of highly marketable actors on the front. In the light of Yates's views about Hollywood stars, it seemed particularly ironic and misjudged.

Apart from Blake Bailey's biography, the material directly related to Yates is scarce. The Twayne's United States Authors series produced a posthumous monograph in 1996. This gives an indication that he was regarded with some respect by the time he died, although the publishers were perhaps anticipating an interest that has had to wait over a decade to even begin. Jerome Klinkowitz includes a chapter on Yates in his work *The New American Novel of Manners* (1986), and Morris Dickstein devotes several pages in his essay "Fiction and Society, 1940–1970" to an analysis of Yates's work.[22] The year 2001 saw the publication of a new edition of *Revolutionary Road* with an introduction by Richard Ford.[23] *The Collected Stories of Richard Yates*, with an introduction by Richard Russo, was published in 2004.[24] In 2009 Everyman produced an edition that included *Revolutionary Road*, *The Easter Parade*, and *Eleven Kinds of Loneliness* with an introduction by the novelist and journalist Richard Price.[25] The most recent publication is an anecdotal account of Yates's life and work by his friend Marty Naparsteck.[26] Apart from that, there are several interviews and reviews that have enabled me to gain some purchase on Yates's views about his work, on how it was received, and on his ideas about writing in general. For the most part, I am guided by his texts and what they reveal. There is, therefore, a good deal of close analysis of his writing, both to examine Yates's own form of social realism and in order to look in detail at his style.

In conjunction with Yates's fiction, I look at the work of several social historians, critics, and sociologists as a way of seeing how Yates reflected debates of his time. Erving Goffman is among those I refer to, for his sociological perspective and for his work on the performing self. William James's thoughts about behavioral theory in general and performative behavior in particular have also proved relevant and informative. As the social sciences developed in the twentieth century, the theories that were advanced became more specific. The psychologist Mark Snyder, for instance, divides people into low and high self-monitors. Although the division, as I interpret it, may be rather simplistic, it is useful when trying to articulate a basic difference between those who rarely reflect upon their own behavior and those who self-consciously adjust their mannerisms and assess the effect of their performances on those around them.

Susan J. Douglas, writing about the social history of the 1950s and 1960s from a feminist perspective, suggests that the roles the media played have both a positive and negative part in shaping behavior. Ian Burkitt's work, *Social Selves: Theories of the Social Formation of Personality* (1991), focuses on divergent views of man; the Renaissance view of man as unique and a monad is set in opposition to twentieth-century views of man as a socially constructed animal. With societal bonds informing personality, the primary role of language in the formation of self and the ability of the self to look at itself objectively is scrutinized. These arguments are germane to the study of Yates since they enrich an understanding of how the issues he raises sit within a wider social and historical context.

Revolutionary Road is generally regarded as Yates's finest work and has therefore been given the most critical attention in recent university courses. It will come as no surprise, therefore, that as well as a chapter devoted to this novel, discussion of it is threaded throughout my work. However, my critical study, while always aware of the power of Yates's first published work, also includes discussion of many of his short stories and looks in detail at his six other novels. They, too, deserve our close attention. In the course of my book, I will try to suggest how Yates's fiction sits alongside that of other writers, contemporaneous and antecedent, both in the style and content of their writing. This creates an opportunity to look in detail at how the work of Henry James, J. D. Salinger, Nathanael West, John O'Hara, F. Scott Fitzgerald, and Ernest Hemingway, among others, influenced Yates's work.

Now, after the hype of the film, Yates's work might seem to have lost its foothold were it not for the fact that teachers and academics have been promoting it to a new generation of readers. They recognize that his work, quite apart from its considerable literary merit, affords twenty-first-century readers an interesting and incisive view of domestic life in America during the 1950s, a period of history long reexamined and debated. While the predominant role of the writer is to question and subvert, Yates's countercultural stance supplied neither the confidence nor, apparently, the innovation to win a wide readership, even though his first publication suggested otherwise. With his meticulous eye for detail and his uncomfortable accounts of life in suburbia, Manhattan, or Los Angeles, Yates provides a portrayal of American life that while it offers small comfort offers us great insight; perhaps it is only now that America is ready to face the questions Yates raises about life as he knew it. It is my hope that this book will add to the *real* resurgence of interest in Richard Yates's fiction and help to persuade those who have either dismissed it or have yet to read his stories that they have made a grave error of omission.

1
Revolutionary Road

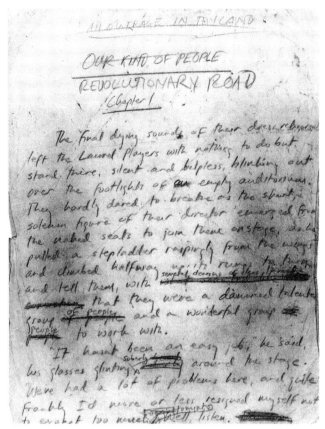

2. The first page of an early draft of *Revolutionary Road*.
Courtesy of the Howard Gotlieb Archival Center for Research
at Boston University.

Revolutionary Road took five years to complete. It is an acute and painful
study of the pretensions of a group of young middle-class couples, and one
couple in particular, living a suburban life with dreams of escape. Richard
Yates's clarity of expression and his understanding of the hidden preoccupations of the human heart are exceptional in this novel. His prose, uncluttered
by verbosity or arcane language, demonstrates remarkable narrative control
as it moves seamlessly from one perspective to another. The fact that it took

Yates five years to complete the novel is a measure of how exacting and precise he was about every sentence he wrote. That this will be a tale about artistic and social pretension, performance in both the domestic and social arena, is left in no doubt as the novel begins at the end of the dress rehearsal of a play.

The Laurel Players wait for the director's verdict on that rehearsal. Here we witness the director's cliché-ridden display of emotion, his performance of "the moved director" that reveals nothing about his true feelings or their acting. Yates presents this display as a sentimental speech designed to draw attention to what he perceives to be his status as the person in control. The narrative tone suggests this, as does the fact that he physically stages himself above his cast. The careful description of the director's preparation to speak includes the way he arranges first the stepladder and then himself: "he climbed halfway up its rungs to turn and tell them, with several clearings of his throat, that they were a damned talented group of people."[1] The throat-clearing detail suggests his self-consciousness and underlines the inauthenticity and vacuity of his "sincere" response. This impression is heightened as Yates describes his hand movements showing, with the precision of a camera, the way mannerism enhances performance: "He let the fingers of one hand splay out across the pocket of his shirt to show what a simple, physical thing the heart was; then he made the same hand into a fist, which he shook slowly and wordlessly, in a long dramatic pause, closing one eye and allowing his moist lower lip to curl out in a grimace of triumph and pride."[2] What he then says to the players is immaterial since his body language has done all the talking necessary to aid our reading of this minor player in Yates's story. Sadly the players themselves do not share our informed perspective.

Yates, writing with the cold eye of the social satirist, can seem unusually mocking of his characters as his narrative revelations about performance continue to imply the possibility of "being" without performance as an integral feature. Perhaps anticipating the work of later sociologists and their awareness of low self-monitors (people who rarely scrutinize their own behavior), Yates deplores the fact that most people perform to hide the truth of who they are and what they feel. Relying on enacted emotions, the people of Yates's fiction are shallow types largely unable to identify honesty in either their own behavior or that of others. He creates characters who reflect his awareness of human indifference to truth; one gets the impression that this is not a perspective Yates relishes but one he feels unable to ignore. Bailey's biography is full of instances where, in a drunken state, Yates railed at the weaknesses of others, and this highly critical perspective is apparent throughout his fiction. It is as if he feels that mankind has had the wool pulled firmly over its eyes and it is his job to raise this romanticizing veil. Erving Goffman explains the root of the critical stance toward forced or inauthentic social interaction that Yates adopted in his fiction: "one finds that the performer can be fully taken in by his own act; he can be sincerely convinced that the impression of reality which he stages is the real reality. When his audience is also convinced in this way about the show . . . only the sociologist or the socially disgruntled will have any doubts about the 'realness' of what is presented."[3] Yates, then, takes on the role of the socially disgruntled writer; perhaps that is *his* best performance.

If exposing performative, socially inauthentic behavior is central to this writer's art, it is wholly appropriate that Yates uses a play as a metaphorical device. His description of *The Petrified Forest* at the beginning of *Revolutionary Road* is masterful and precise in the detail with which he captures the various performances we witness. He leaves the reader in no doubt that it is not only those on the stage who are acting. With narrative layering that is characteristic of Yates at his best, the reader is a member of an audience to an audience as people file in preparing to take their own roles seriously. The reader might feel here the influence of J. D. Salinger's preoccupations. In *The Catcher in the Rye*, Holden Caulfield is sickened as he recalls the theater audience: "You never saw so many phonies in all your life, everybody smoking their ears off and talking about the play so that everybody could hear and know how sharp they were."[4] Both writers highlight how the members of the audience are performing. They want to be seen to be serious, ready to absorb and classify what they witness, ready to observe themselves rising intellectually above the evening's cultural content: "But it was, after all, a fine theater piece with a basic point of view that was every bit as valid today as in the thirties ('Even more valid,' one man kept telling his wife, who chewed her lips and nodded, seeing what he meant; 'even more valid, when you think about it')."[5] In this small extract, the narrative, which begins with the words "The audience, arriving in a long clean serpent of cars,"[6] seamlessly shifts from a third-person stance to mimicry of general conversation before arriving at the particular speech enacted. And with that dialogue this nameless couple is exposed as the wife's chewed lips suggest a nervousness that their confident talk belies. The narrator then steps swiftly back to adopt the third-person observational role again as the play begins and the reader is introduced to April Wheeler.

Blake Bailey observes that "from the beginning [April] is shown as two women (at least), filtered through the mingled perspectives of Frank and the rest of the audience."[7] She is first "the girl who played the heroine, Gabrielle,"[8] who excites warm approval in the audience; then, in imitation of the audience's recognition, categorization and acceptance of the person behind the role, she is the girl who "had attended one of the leading dramatic schools of New York less than ten years before."[9] April then becomes a member of the community: "[she is] a tall ash blonde with a patrician kind of beauty that no amount of amateur lighting could distort."[10] If April can hold all these roles together and convincingly sustain her performance as Gabrielle all will be well; she has to believe in her performance, and the audience has to believe in it too. But almost immediately Yates subtly undercuts the narrative claim that "she seemed ideally cast in the role"[11] by introducing a note of resistance to such belief. The narrator, again mimicking the audience's gaze, notices, "that bearing two children had left her a shade too heavy in the hips and thighs."[12]

The play is a disaster. With just a few details, Yates recreates the squirming embarrassment of the audience and conveys the subsequent tension that arises for all those who had gone expecting a triumph—namely, Frank Wheeler. The narrative switches to Wheeler's perspective, and the different roles he had anticipated playing that night are presented as a series of cinematic scenes: "himself rushing home to swing his children laughing in the air, to gulp a cocktail and chatter through an early dinner with his wife; himself driving her to the high school . . . himself sitting spellbound in pride . . . himself glowing and dishevelled."[13] The cinematic imagining here, which acts as a subtle comment on the pervasive influence of contemporary film, places emphasis on the performative nature of his behavior. With the heavy emphasis of a drumbeat, the narrative rhythm falls on each reiterated "himself," leaving no doubt that Frank Wheeler is the star of his own film and that he had never intended to go out to enjoy his wife's success. If that had been his intention, it was only insofar as it reflected well on him: "Nowhere in these plans had he foreseen the weight and shock of reality."[14] With these words, and a Chekhovian description[15] of the beautiful actress dissolving before his eyes into "the graceless, suffering creature whose existence he tried every day of his life to deny,"[16] it is equally clear that his love for his wife is dependent on her sustaining the role of the "patrician beauty" he first fell in love with. By implication, her performances have proved not only inadequate on the stage but also in marriage as he is forced to recognize and claim her: "[She is] a gaunt constricted woman whose red eyes flashed reproach, whose false smile in the curtain call was as homely as his own sore feet, his own damp climbing underwear and his own sour smell."[17] As we see at the end of the book, Shep Campbell adjusts his perspective of his own wife in a similar way.

With such uncomfortable details, Yates allows his characters to reveal themselves in all their weakness and controls the way they do this with subtlety; it is not April who is most exposed here but Frank. It is almost always the case in Yates's work that his protagonist, usually male and usually a thinly disguised version of himself, is most ruthlessly undercut. The reader cannot fail to notice that what Frank wants here is a fiction, a wife that time and experience hasn't touched, for he wants "the swaying, shining vision of a girl he hadn't seen in years"[18] to remain permanent. Yates makes it clear that his characters are all performing, therefore, but the roles they have set themselves are idealized and romanticized, and they are none of them equal to the roles they have chosen.

It would be an inattentive reader who didn't notice Yates's pervasive observations about social performance and the dishonesty it implies: all of the commentators on his work draw attention to this trait. Jerome Klinkowitz, for instance, writes about Frank's dreams of Europe and notes the way that Frank "performs" those dreams in his everyday behavior: "To sustain the illusion of their promised success, Frank creates a role and loses himself within it, making sure each gesture to cross a room or light a cigarette has the air of rakish romanticism to it that characterized their first courtship, the tone of which these European plans are meant to revive."[19] In addition, and more damaging to the notion of authenticity, is the clearly dramatized idea that humans not only demand but also prescribe the performance of others, just as Frank determines and limits the roles that April can play. This first novel is an extended examination of the way in which men and women battle for control within marriage. Edward Albee explores similar territory in *Who's Afraid of Virginia Woolf?*, first performed ten months after the publication of Yates's novel.[20]

If the control of a situation is cynically manipulated, there are devastating implications, as Erving Goffman suggests, for the potential of relationships: "[the person in control can] lead them to act voluntarily in accordance with his own plan."[21] Of course, the kind of control that this implies is not available to Frank outside the home at a moment when April is literally performing and where the community can witness the success or failure of that performance. After the production of *The Petrified Forest*, his despair and ensuing violent frustration is consequent upon the loss of that power. In the argument that develops between the couple, April indicates that she has always felt constrained by him:

> "Oh, I've always known I had to be your conscience and your guts—*and* your punching bag. Just because you've got me safely in a trap you think you—"
> "*You* in a trap! *You* in a trap! *Jesus*, don't make me laugh!"
> "Yes, me." She made a claw of her hand and clutched at her collarbone.[22]

Just such an awareness causes April to reflect, the morning of her death, that she has handed Frank authority and control by allowing herself to believe in a series of fictions about him and about them as a couple: "all honesty, all truth, was as far away and glimmering, as hopelessly unattainable as the world of the golden people."[23] At one level, by aborting their child, April's final act is a means of asserting power she never had in her marriage.

With the small detail of her clawlike hand grasping at herself, Yates subtly prefigures the damage April will one day do to herself; she knows she is trapped but not how to break free. Self-harm is the inevitable outcome of her desperate situation, and for the reader, her plight is made more wretched by her understanding of its cause. Realizing that the gulf between them is insurmountable, and with no energy left to fight Frank, April gives her greatest and most generous performance on the morning of her death as she encourages her husband to explain the workings of a computer. Attentive to his needs, she gives in to the role Frank has long wanted her to play and acts as the dutiful, submissive wife. She stage-manages all the details of their last breakfast together with careful, chilling precision and eradicates any trace of the violent argument of the night before: "The table was carefully set with two plates for breakfast. The kitchen was filled with sunlight and with the aromas of coffee and bacon. April was at the stove, wearing a fresh maternity dress, and she looked up at him with a shy smile."[24] Using simple but tightly constructed sentences, Yates conveys the sense that April is immersed in her final performance as the compliant, conforming wife. Even the sunlight helps set the "happy" scene, a scene that anyone, and notably Frank, might mistake for perfect harmony.

In his attempts to find methods to highlight how people create a dream of selfhood and then enact and perfect that dream as a performance for others, Yates uses mirrors in ways that comment on the people they reflect. While they provide a tool for the individual to observe and perfect an idealized version of self, Yates's narratives ensure that they are also a means by which the performance is critically observed and rejected. He suggests a subtle gap between the reality of who the individual is and who he wants to be by ensuring his readers take a step back from the activity of the text at the moment the mirror image is observed. As the mirror doubles the image, the reader's response is similarly doubled so that we not only witness a character holding a gaze but look too at the object of their gaze. This makes the questioning of authenticity more explicit.

When Frank visits April in her dressing room following the disastrous performance, Yates describes Frank coming in and catching sight of his reflection: "He looked at himself in the mirror, tightening his jaw and turning his head a little to one side to give it a leaner, more commanding look, the face he had given himself in mirrors since boyhood and which no photograph had ever quite achieved, until with a start he found that she was watching him."[25] Within a sentence, Yates suggests not only the repetitive nature of Frank's search for a "commanding look" but also its failure since it is never there in photographs. In addition, April's gaze, trained on him, briefly becomes the reader's gaze, and with that shift Yates ensures his reader will also catch Frank out as he flexes his vanity. For it is April's silent response that seals how we receive this held moment: "Her own eyes were there in the mirror, trained on his for an uncomfortable moment before she lowered them to stare at the middle button of his coat."[26] So much is implied in that lowering of her eyes that the reader, too, feels like looking away from his solipsistic performance. A similar effect is produced when Frank, having stopped the car on the highway, rages out of control, as Yates contrasts a vivid dramatization of Frank's extravagant anger with April's quiet despair. Hands, feet, and voice are all employed to maximize his angry moment until, frustrated beyond any control, he slams his fist into the roof of their car; "He hit the car four times that way: *Bong! Bong! Bong! Bong!*—while she stood and watched."[27] April's silent observation is the mirror through which the reader witnesses this performance.

The reader cannot help but adopt both April's gaze and her point of view and is, in effect, asked to trust her. In sharp contrast to the way Frank uses mirrors to confirm something about himself, his appearance and his performance, Yates describes April facing her image directly in the scene in the dressing room: "She was alone, sitting very straight at a mirror and removing her make-up."[28] She is stripping away her mask. Ironically, since the reader has been introduced to this woman literally acting, she is implicitly "facing" herself head-on. There is no implied affectation of pose or demeanor; she is both "sitting very straight" and seeing very straight, taking in her reddening eyes and aging face. Crudely put, Yates shows Frank Wheeler looking to confirm an untruth from his mirror image while April searches for honest reflection. Using such small details, Yates manipulates how his reader receives the authenticity, or lack thereof, of his characters.

In addition to the use of mirrors, Yates uses April's silent stare as an eloquent means of expression. How she looks at Frank, whether with a gaze held in a mirror or a face-to-face glare, is the marker by which the reader empathizes more closely with her. The reader momentarily shares her look and thus her emotional and critical stance. In effect, the experience of reading *Revolutionary Road* is one of gathering an accumulation of April's gazes. Although April is the "actress," her determination to look full in the face of reality is evoked by these momentary glimpses of Frank through her eyes. The subtle irony of Yates's prose incorporates more and more of such gazes, encouraging the reader to achieve a distance from Frank's reading of those unflinching looks. This is particularly evident with the irony employed toward the end of the novel when Frank thinks he is most in control: "Soon too—and this was the most encouraging sign of all—he began to be aware at odd moments that she was covertly watching him through a mist of romantic admiration."[29] As the reader is aware, it is Frank who sees things through "a mist of romantic admiration"; for April the mist has finally lifted and the effect is devastating.

In all of his novels Yates is able to show how the performative behavior of his protagonists is revealed at every level of interaction. For characters like Frank, that is to say, for dreamers of a better version of selfhood, always trying to find a way to grasp an authentic performance but without sufficient self-awareness that this is what they are doing, dress is seen as a valid tool. Yates's fiction suggests that in dressing one literally assumes the costume of the desired persona. He consistently draws attention to this small but significant aspect of aspirational behavior and suggests that if the character assuming a role believes his costume indicates its authenticity, he will be unmasked. Lionel Trilling explains the role appearance has to play in a social order dominated by money rather than class: "In a shifting society great emphasis is put on appearance. . . . To appear to be established is one of the ways of becoming established."[30]

In the 1970s Leon Samson developed Trilling's point, suggesting that it is the superficial similarities of dress that assure Americans that they are all the same: "What adds to the unrealism of democracy in America, and at the same time serves to conceal it, is the democratic make-believe that introduces itself in the very dress of the American, which despite the underlying real differences in quality that correspond very strictly to the class distinction nevertheless manages to achieve a surface similarity. The clerk wears the same straw hat as his employer. That it is not really the same straw hat does not matter so long as he wears a straw hat just the same. The generic similarity hides the real dissimilarity, the abstract category takes the place of the concrete, and the American moves in a world of abstract straw hats that all but obliterates the class relation."[31] Yates's focus is on the self-conscious, aspirational attention his characters give to their appearance and the disparity between the garments they might choose to wear with who they actually are.

Just as he uses mirrors to raise questions about identity and authenticity, he frequently uses clothing to draw attention to this disparity and connect it to the pervasive, damaging influence of film.

There is a suggestion at times, however, that certain characters are the stronger for their playful, even frivolous, attitude to dress and costume. Occasionally an individual will demonstrate a freedom in performance that others, who take themselves more seriously, cannot manage. In *Young Hearts Crying*, Yates dramatizes Michael Davenport's discomfort and irritation at Thomas Nelson's lighthearted appropriation of different jackets: "What the hell was Nelson trying to do—be a different kind of war veteran every time he moved to a new town?"[32] Nelson's appropriation of clothes is inextricably linked to his equally playful attitude toward his work and his art. His is an attitude that Davenport doesn't understand since it undermines the seriousness with which he approaches both himself and his craft. Furthermore, the fact that Nelson is both lighthearted *and* successful leaves Davenport resentful and confused.

It would appear that Yates is suggesting that some people can carry off an appropriation of roles with great success. What is equally clear is that his protagonists, his alter egos, do not have this ability; they take themselves too seriously and are manifestly unable to break free of the fetters of their self-centered behavior. Thus while Yates might admire Nelson's self-confidence, Michael Davenport is bewildered by it. However, as with all Yates's political positions, there is another side to this argument, in this case one that makes Davenport's truth seeking seem mature and responsible. The first few pages of *Young Hearts Crying* are an attack on romantic notions about the Army Air Force and on the idea that it was "the luckiest, happiest branch of the service."[33] Indeed, to Davenport his time in the force was "humbling and tedious and bleak."[34] Indirectly critiquing America's understanding of its role in the war alongside false attitudes that fed ideas about American exceptionalism, Yates stands shoulder to shoulder with his often unappealing protagonist.

Goffman explains that "we must be prepared to see that the impression of reality fostered by a performance is a delicate, fragile thing that can be shattered by very minor mishaps."[35] Performances, if inexpertly executed, can lead to the type of humiliation Yates often explores in his fiction. In *Revolutionary Road*, Frank Wheeler finds that the school hall where April is on stage evokes memories of his fourteen-year-old self planning a trip by freight train to the West Coast. The memory of how he carefully chose his costume, creating an effect that is a mixture of the pioneer and the cowboy, gives this scene dramatic and nostalgic force: "Levi jacket and pants, an army-type khaki shirt with shoulder tabs, high-cut work shoes with steel caps at heel and toe. An old felt hat of his father's . . . would lend the right note of honest poverty to the outfit."[36] At age fourteen Frank saw himself as a tough guy and planned to dress to suit the idealized image. Frank remembers that the trip never happened because of a derisive comment by the one person he tells: "Where do you get these weird ideas, anyway? The movies or someplace?"[37] The reader suspects, and later knows, that this is exactly where Frank will have found his template; for his ideas are rarely original. His performances are not only "borrowed" but also do not suit his character; as Krebs puts it, "you're a jerk."[38] This memory guides the reader to see that the roles Frank tries to assume in the present of the narrative remain equally inauthentic. As Frank appears to bathe in the warm afterglow of his recollections, while mentally skirting over the humiliation of Krebs's remarks, the reader has had much revealed about Frank in a very minor incident. Yates uses his narrator both to mirror Frank's thoughts and to expose Frank through them.

In *Cold Spring Harbor*, Yates describes a very similar moment but shifts the narrative empathy. The Yatesian character, Phil Drake, who puts down his weaker friend's desire to lie about his age and join the Marines, seems, at one level, harsh and insensitive for the same reasons that Krebs appeared so in the first novel. However, the reader is more inclined to accept Drake's dismissal of fanciful dreaming because the narrative is filtered through his perspective. In the episode in *Revolutionary Road*, Krebs lays the blame for these unrealistic dreams of manliness at the door of Hollywood; Phil Drake is equally clear about their origin: "You didn't get this out of the papers, you dummy; you got it outa the fucking movies. . . . You wouldn't even pass for *fif*teen."[39]

Yates, therefore, makes an implied distinction between types of performances; to be authentic, they should be organically born out of and fused with character. However, Yates rarely gives his characters access to undiminished interior thought. Frank, remembering his childhood dream of escape, is the closest the reader gets to Yates's form of interiority. It is a mimicry of a thought process that never loses the objective, controlling, and ironic voice of the narrator. Yates uses such moments of interiority to display the gap Goffman suggested between the intended performance and the actuality of that personality as the reader receives it and as the writer intended it. In his work, many voices collide to create the picture of the fractured "subject" at work on his chosen role.

Using the "objective correlative"[40] to add depth to the way in which the reader understands his characters and their emotional complexity, Yates borrows a technique from one of his literary heroes. In a feature article, he describes the moment when T. S. Eliot's phrase finally made sense to him:

> I had never understood what Eliot meant by the curious phrase "ob-
> jective correlative" until the scene in "Gatsby" where the most comi-
> cally sinister Meyer Wolfshiem . . . displays his cufflinks and explains
> that they are "the finest specimens of human molars."
>
> Get it? Got it. *That's* what Eliot meant.[41]

The description of the path that Frank tries to build from his house to the
road is an objective correlative for his idealized version of home. The path,
which is never completed, remains a comment upon his ideals just as his
struggle to build it becomes a distilled image of his performance as a man.
Metaphorically speaking, it is the means by which Frank tries to control how
the Wheelers will both be seen and approached, that is to say, by the front
door and not by the kitchen: "The idea was to lay a long, curving walk from
the front door to the road, to divert visitors from coming in through the
kitchen."[42] By implication, the work that goes on in a house will be shielded
from any visitor's view, and the Wheelers can receive their guests assuming
a grander air. The path is intended to provide a literal means by which the
Wheelers' friends will cross their threshold, a literal means by which the
Wheelers' suburban performances can be enacted. Thus the incomplete path,
which gives rise to an outburst against his children, is a highly charged objective correlative and another narrative indicator of the tense and fractured
nature of the Wheeler home.

   In his layering of narratives, Yates is able to combine the seriousness of
this "scene" with a lightness of touch. He highlights Frank's attire for this
tough work as a costume that echoes his boyhood dream: "He spent the afternoon in an old pair of army pants and a torn shirt, working on his stone
path."[43] The narrative moves through a range of perspectives. Yates begins
with the third person narrator who tells the reader that "He spent the afternoon in an old pair of army pants." The narrative then slides into a mode
of reporting his thoughts that, with the continued use of the second person
pronoun, resists the full mimetic process: "It had seemed simple enough last
weekend, when he'd started it."[44] Finally, and with dramatic force to emphasize his assertion of masculinity, the narration becomes an imitation of his
thoughts with no distancing, objective comment as those thoughts alone reveal the idealization of his project: "At least it was man's work. At least, squat-
ting to rest on the wooded slope, he could look down and see his house the
way a house ought to look on a fine spring day, safe on its carpet of green, the
frail white sanctuary of a man's love, a man's wife and children."[45] But it is not
only his labor and his family life that he sees in romantic terms; the greatest
focus is again on his idealization of a masculine self: "Lowering his eyes with

the solemnity of this thought, he could take pleasure in the sight of his own flexed thigh, lean and straining under the old O.D., and of the heavily veined forearm that lay across it and the dirty hand that hung there . . . so that his temples ached in zeal and triumph as he heaved a rock up from the suck of its white-wormed socket and let it roll end over end down the shuddering leafmold, because he was a man."[46] With the heavy repetition of "man" and "man's," and with a style that appears to parody D. H. Lawrence's *Sons and Lovers* (1913), Yates leaves the smiling reader in no doubt of his sardonic tone. Central to all his fiction is an interrogation of what it means to be a man in a world where advertising, magazines, and films have appropriated how masculinity is to be defined.

Frank Wheeler's performances seamlessly follow one another until the very end of the novel when he thinks, despite the appalling fight of the night before, that perhaps he has "rescued" his life from a headlong rush to disaster. The reader, however, is aware of the fact that April is now the one in control; she has slipped not only into her "fresh maternity dress," but also into her "shy smile."[47] There is a subtle and disturbing irony in the connection Yates draws between April's newly discovered control and her well-honed perfor-mance; April knows that such control is dependent on her maintaining a facade. Although Frank is aware that there is a "strange, elaborate pretense that nothing had happened yesterday,"[48] he does not have the imaginative capacity to see beyond and behind her performance. To do so would be to recognize how totally he has failed in his marriage and how inadequate he is as a man. Frank's awareness of this pretense does however add a tentative-ness and hesitancy to his performance that renders it genuine in the eyes of the reader. Without posturing or affectation, his remarks are stuttered and uncertain: "'It certainly is a—nice morning out, isn't it?' he said."[49]

Yates encourages his readers to feel that they are witnessing an authentic performance, that Frank is revealing his true self at breakfast by emphasiz-ing his innocent enthusiasm as he draws a description of the workings of a computer. The sincerity of his behavior is all the more striking, coming as it does straight after the explosive argument of the night before where all his instruction on how to behave is from the movies: "he wondered what he ought to do. In the movies, when women got hysterical like this, men slapped them until they stopped."[50] However, the movies, Frank finds, are not always able to supply him with a version that mirrors his experience. More accu-rately, his experience does not imitate the movie version of reality, and he is, therefore, at sea, knowing no other version and being unaccustomed to recognizing an authentic performance when it confronts him: "Finally she sank into a chair, still laughing, and he waited for what he guessed would be a transition from laughter to weeping—that was what usually happened in the movies—but instead her subsiding was oddly normal."[51] Yates's wry use of the phrase "oddly normal" draws attention to Frank's inability to process the normality of April's response. She is laughing at him and at his dismissal of John Givings because she has recognized, as Frank has not, that Givings, with his acerbic commentary, is right. The reader is therefore attuned to the fact that the gap between April and Frank's understanding of themselves and their relationship is now an enormous chasm as Frank delivers what he believes to be his "perfect exit line."[52] He storms out of the room. The calm and apparently peaceful atmosphere of the next morning has a sinister quality for the reader as April hones her skills as a dutiful wife, all the while planning her cataclysmic, potentially suicidal act. We receive Frank's joy and relief at the possible happy future they will have together, therefore, acutely aware of the vein of irony that runs through Yates's description: "At first he was too bashful to eat. It was like the first time he'd ever taken a girl out to dinner."[53] As Frank's confidence grows and intensifies, Yates skillfully manipulates the narrative so that the reader's assurance slips away.

In his work on multiple selves, William James draws specific attention to the potency of the performance we reserve for those we love. This is our most deeply felt role, and its success or failure moves us more profoundly than other performances we might give.[54] During their final breakfast Frank has convinced himself that he has rescued their relationship and, after their row, that they have a future together. Although he may be more relieved than loving, Yates quietly suggests the shift from despair to elation of a man whose feeling of relationship is about to be reinstated. As Frank gains confidence he reveals his authentic self, but with subtlety and a gently placed ironic tone, Yates ensures that the reader is more in step with the artifice of April's taut execution of her role. He intensifies the unbearable poignancy of this scene as Frank, thinking his wife is truly interested, bashfully and carefully explains the workings of the computer to her. The reader is aware that April's polite inquiries are those of a person who has removed her *self* and given up not just on the relationship but also on life. The interplay between these two vastly differing perspectives of this chronotopic moment lends this scene its dreadful tension. While Frank considers saying what is on his mind at their parting, he is too afraid to break the spell of their rapprochement, and his genuine self once again disappears behind a recognized and comforting performance: "And then it was easy to decide what to do next: without touching her he began as slowly as any movie actor, to bend toward her lips."[55]

Richard Yates exposes pretension in *Revolutionary Road* with microcosmic precision and leaves his reader gasping at the accuracy of his intimate observations. By depicting the ordinary men and women of the American middle classes, Yates's gimlet eye turns on all Americans; this may have alienated his potential readership. His vision of humanity was perceived to be unrelentingly negative and deeply misanthropic. Many notable contemporaries such as Tennessee Williams were effusive in their praise of his first novel,[56] and Yates himself was quietly proud of what he had achieved. It is typical of his style to include his thoughts about his first novel in his penultimate novel, *Young Hearts Crying*. The writer Carl Traynor outlines Yates's thoughts: "I think it's good. Fact is, I think it's a whole lot better than good. It may not set the world on fire or anything swell like that, but people are gonna pay attention."[57] He was right, though it took many years before that "attention" was paid. At the time of publication, the critics' views were usually tempered by disapproval of the negativity of his vision. Orville Prescott, writing in the daily London *Times*, spoke of the book as "brilliantly dismal" and concluded his review by damning Yates's efforts: "No fair-minded reader could finish *Revolutionary Road* without admiration for Mr. Yates's impressive skill; but whether the mentally ill Wheelers deserve the five years of hard labor Mr Yates has lavished upon them is another question."[58] To dismiss the Wheelers as "mentally ill" is to dismiss their concerns, ambitions, and evasions. Yates's great achievement is in making our most uncomfortable selves recognizable. His individual characters are exposed, but nowhere are they, or we as readers, allowed the comfort of assuming that their foibles are idiosyncratic. They are rendered as a generalized tableau of human weakness and as sharply perceived individuals at the same time.

2
Richard Yates and Hollywood

3. Richard and Sheila
Yates, Paris, circa 1952.

How Richard Yates related to Hollywood demands more than just a few cursory phrases; it was a difficult relationship and reflected the complexity of the role Hollywood played in relation to the nation. Throughout his fiction Yates makes ample use of cinematic metaphor as a way of pointing out the influence film had on the society in which he lived. The era in which he grew up and first experienced the power of the movies was the 1930s and early 1940s. This era of filmmaking most closely influenced his views on the power and significance of Hollywood and on the representation of the social realities Hollywood disseminated. As a youth, and a youth who was not a keen reader, the cinema was the main source of entertainment. Divorced, on her own, and averse to housework, Yates's mother used to take her two young children, when they were still young and out of school, to watch films in order to pass the time: "The three of them were together constantly, and their principal way of killing time was going to the movies . . . he often startled friends with detailed and rather emotional accounts of the movies he'd seen in the thirties."[1] Fascinated by the cinema, Yates acknowledges it as a spur to his very early writing: "It must have been the movies of the 1930s more than any other influence that got me into the habit of thinking like a writer. I wasn't a bookish child; reading was such hard work for me that I avoided it wherever possible."[2] In several novels, Yates invokes film and an

obsession with cinematic storytelling as an indicator of a character's immaturity and as a signal to the reader that the character in question is prepared
to absorb make-believe (film) over reality (literature). Undoubtedly enticed
by the promise of wealth and fame that Hollywood might offer an impoverished writer, this is, nevertheless, Yates's way of charting his own and his
characters' intellectual development.

In *Disturbing the Peace*, for instance, the narrative makes reference to John
Wilder's life-long obsession with movies. As the character tells his friend Paul
Borg within the first few pages of the novel, "All my life, I've never been realistic. I ever tell you how I wanted to make movies?"[3] Later, he tells his ther-
apist, "I'm a very, very slow reader. Guess that's the main reason I've spent
most of my life watching movies."[4] Yates, too, was a very slow reader and
was similarly fascinated by film, even if to his mind it was not an art form
and could not be compared to literature.

Despite his early fascination with film, Yates was dismissive of cinematic
narratives throughout his "mature" life: "I almost never go to a movie now . . .
because movies are for children."[5] From this position of maturity, his fictional
characters are repeatedly undercut by film metaphors to indicate the models
by which the dream of the good life in 1950s America was sustained. In the
"roles" they provide, films are an updated version of medieval romances for
Don Quixotes desperate to perform. Therefore, in a manner similar to J. D.
Salinger, Yates ridicules movies as unreliable, distorted, sentimentalized versions of reality in whose heroes and reassurances people are too ready to believe. Holden Caulfield, for instance, is explicit about how his writer brother,
a brother whose stories he greatly admires, has "sold out." He used to go to a
nightclub in Greenwich Village, he says, "before he went out to Hollywood
and prostituted himself."[6] For Yates, despising phoniness as much as Salinger does, the fear of selling out was very real.

In the interwar years, films were produced that were in part stimulated
by contemporary political issues such as Prohibition and racketeering. Similarly, the Great Depression provided fertile ground for films about families
overcoming hardship. Writing about this era, Ian Scott talks of Hollywood as
offering "its own version of exceptionalism and manifest destiny."[7] He goes
on to argue that in the 1930s "this was of course predicated upon a very
vital need; the United States was fighting an ideological battle, a battle for
the hearts and minds of a people who had begun to suspect that America's
great democratic experiment was, in the face of the Depression, all washed
up. Political films during the decade countered this in a way that was part
triumphalist, part nationalistic, but almost wholly recognisable as a fragment
of the mythic landscape upon which American history had been built."[8] Seen

in this context, it is therefore not surprising that two of the most successful films of this era, and ones that are popular to this day, were *The Wizard of Oz* (1939)[9] and *Gone with the Wind* (1939).[10]

In 1934, the Motion Picture Producers and Distributors of America established the Production Code Administration to counteract the effects of what was seen by some in Washington as Hollywood's dangerously liberal attitude toward American culture and its politics.[11] Mark Wheeler describes how films made in the 1920s, before the code was adopted, "attracted the wrath of Christian organisations, temperance associations, anti-Semitic groups and local censors who believed the studio's Jewish entrepreneurs were corrupting the nation's morals."[12] The Motion Picture Production Code, therefore, had the effect of sanitizing the image the United States portrayed to its own citizens and to an international audience: "The sanctity of marriage and the home were upheld, and adultery or illicit sex, though sometimes necessitated by the plot, could not be made explicit. The code prohibited nudity, suggestive dances and the ridicule of religion, while forbidding depictions of drug use, venereal disease, childbirth and miscegenation. The criminals were not to inspire sympathy, murders had to avoid imitation and brutal slayings should not be shown."[13] As Wheeler indicates, the strict enforcement of the code ensured that Hollywood's power was reinforced: "Hollywood's status in political affairs demonstrated its growing importance as a purveyor of popular dreams throughout the interwar years."[14]

In common with most artists, Yates abhorred the inauthenticity the code seemed to promote and wanted to correct the way Americans and American lifestyles were represented. He registered the effect of the code and realized that it had important implications for how writers such as himself situated their critical representations of society. By removing all that was a threat to the way Washington wanted its citizens to see themselves, the movie industry and the political elite became more apparently unified: "Hollywood became a significant force in reflecting and informing the societal debates which existed throughout American life."[15] The fact that subtle political and social messages are contained in, for example, Frank Capra's *Mr. Deeds Goes to Town* (1936)[16] or *It's a Wonderful Life* (1946),[17] did not alter the fact that they were not the dominant impressions audiences received; happy endings were a necessary part of the enforcement of what was essentially a code of well-being.[18]

Richard Yates was immersed in cinematic narratives, therefore, at a time when films were often romantic, epic, and populist and gave rise to even bigger stars than those hitherto seen. The concept of stardom had become big business in Hollywood in the early part of the century, and it was intrinsically linked to glamorizing life itself. Stars were promoted, and the ideals they represented were sold as a way of extending Hollywood's economic influence. Hollywood might have always been something of a propaganda machine for America, but after the Second World War, in the 1950s, Hollywood remained an important tool in the promotion of this newly ascendant nation and helped endorse the idea (and ideal) of America as an egalitarian, classless society where the little guy could see his dreams of wealth, status, and stability realized, *and* get the girl *and* get the house *and* the two children:[19] dream big, and on the whole the dreams were rewarded. With stars promoting such ideals, the individual citizen had a face and a character to identify with, albeit carefully packaged. Cinematically projected promises added powerful dimensions to what was understood by the term the *American Dream*. Although by no means all films of the 1940s and 1950s projected an ideal version of life and happiness in postwar America, Yates's critical attention was drawn to the influence of those romantic films.

Since Yates had been brought up in movie theaters, there is some inevitability in the fact that his narratives mirror his interest in film. In an article for the *New York Times*, he referred to the "movie-haunted stories" he'd write for his teachers and reflected that "movies filled a double need: They gave me an awful lot of cheap story material and a good place to hide."[20] Perhaps it was experiencing the vast gap that existed between the circumstances of his young life and the sentiment and glamorization films offered that drove Yates's desire to represent a more honest view of life for the American middle classes. The happy endings of Hollywood productions are never replicated in Yates's dark, sometimes tragic, fictional conclusions. In addition, his work provides a detailed critique of the kind of exceptionalism and individualism that Hollywood was promoting. As he explores the romantic, conservative tradition of individualism, he suggests that the individual lacks the insight and the power to counteract the effects of the Hollywood machine. He suggests that the behavior it glamorizes and the ideals it promotes infiltrate the lives of Americans at every level as they search for ways to conform and better themselves. Ronald Sukenick neatly sums up much of what Yates's work implies: "The electrosphere has taught us, has required us, to narrate ourselves as we go along. We imagine ourselves as if we were on film or TV . . . and that image of ourselves in the media gives authority to our experience, makes it real. . . . All media induce schizophrenia, increasing the need for feedback, in order to determine where between self and reflection the reality lies."[21]

"A Glutton for Punishment" was published as part of Yates's first book of short stories, *Eleven Kinds of Loneliness*.[22] In this curious story of a man addicted to the role of loser or victim, Yates showed an early, if somewhat unpolished, interest in the idea of performance, whether it be in the office or in the home; as in all his fiction, the life of the ordinary, unexceptional individual interests him most. The basic premise of this story is that Walter Henderson, the protagonist, is addicted to the only performance in which he has ever managed to succeed: that of the loser or victim. This is a role he perfected as a child playing cops and robbers with his friends when the skill of dying an authentic and dramatic death became the whole game: "It became a matter of individual performance, almost an art."[23] As the narrator moves back and forth between an omniscient position and one that mimics Walter's viewpoint, the reader is brought closer to his performance. That his protagonist is called Walter is an indicator to a readership, aware of James Thurber's Walter Mitty stories, that this man may be something of a fantasist. The name is used ironically, of course, since his fantasy is not of fame, fortune, or power, but is of losing. Yates shows that "art" at its inception when Walter is a child but then goes on to show how his friends have shed their childish skins, whereas Walter has not. The point that Yates is making in this story is that there are those who never progress from that initial performance. While Walter's friends grow up, Walter, a "slight, poorly coordinated boy"[24] has learned that he is good at one thing, and he relishes it: "Nobody could match the abandon with which he flung his limp body down the hill, and he reveled in the small acclaim it won him."[25]

The narrative of "A Glutton for Punishment" leaps forward from childhood games to Walter's last day in the office. He is sure he is about to be fired, and he is. With an unnecessarily heavy hand Yates underscores the connection with Walter's childish success: "There was certainly no denying that the role of a good loser had always held an inordinate appeal for him."[26] Emphasizing the pivotal point in this way detracts from the power of the story, and nowhere more glaringly than at its ending when Walter finally confesses to his wife that he has been fired: "It was the most graceful thing he had done all day. 'They got me,' he said."[27] The cliché may be entirely in keeping with Walter's idiom, but it serves as a trite ending to the story. However, it should be noted that when he wrote this story Yates was writing with magazine publication in mind. That being the case, the story falls down in the same way his hero Fitzgerald's late short stories fall down; both volumes of *The Price Was High*[28] contain stories with a similarly clunking lack of subtlety. It was a style that sold well for immediate, throwaway consumption and earned Fitzgerald money. Yates, always desperate for money, adopted a similar strategy for similar purposes; he did not want to alienate his imagined readership of middle-class housewives with elliptical or obscure messages. There were, however, some compromises Yates refused to make.

With that same magazine readership in mind, Yates's agent, Monica McCall, hated the ending of "A Glutton for Punishment" for its bleakness and lack of resolution and presumably for its cartoonish quality. According to Blake Bailey's biography of Yates, McCall wanted something Yates would never be able to produce: "She wanted a happy ending, in short, or if nothing else a bit of normal character development—but of course nothing could be more inimical to Yates's basic view of humanity and Walt in particular."[29] McCall had not been working for Yates long enough to know that he would never compromise his reluctance to provide "happy endings" because that was not his experience of life; he refused to change it. As Yates explained in an interview: "Easy affirmations are silly and cheap, of course; but when a tough, honest writer can look squarely at all the horrors of the world, face all the facts, and still come up with a hard-won, joyous celebration of life at the end, in spite of everything, that can be wonderful."[30]

The "joyous celebration of life" that Yates refers to must not be confused with a happy ending. He strives for honesty and truth that may taste and smell bad but is truthful nevertheless. The ending of this story might be weak but it adheres to the character in question in the sense that his essential childishness is apparent. Cinematic in its detail, it also coheres with Walter's sense that he is acting in some kind of a movie: "'Well, darling—' he began. His right hand came up and touched the middle button of his shirt, as if to unfasten it, and then with a great deflating sigh he collapsed backward into the chair, one foot sliding out on the carpet and the other curled beneath him."[31] The narrative energy and pace of the story is slowed as the narrator, adopting Walter's viewpoint with characteristic hyperbole, makes clear in every carefully noted detail how self-conscious this "dying" act is.

In the Yatesian view, Walter's impoverishment is not merely in having only one performance of self to draw on but in having no authentic idea of selfhood. He has just one successful version of the person known as Walter Henderson, and it is utterly self-conscious. The tension I would suggest Yates would like the reader to feel at the end (the fact that he does not succeed is due to an oversigning of the impending situation) is the tension Walter feels in his desperate attempt to hang on to his conception of himself as a hero who will earn his wife's respect. He reaches out unsuccessfully for another possible self, a self that could restrain him from burdening his wife and one with which he could maintain an inner strength: "He poured a tiny bit more for her and a full glass for himself. His hand was shaking and he spilled a little of it, but she didn't seem to notice. Nor did she seem to notice that his replies grew more and more strained as she kept the conversation going. . . . But holding on grew less and less easy as the children's splashing bath-noises floated into the room."[32] He is not trying to be heroic, but stoic, not triumphant but dignified, but even these "diminished" qualities, or performances, elude him, as they always have.

Walter has not been able to sustain his desire to protect his wife from the truth of the situation and can no longer maintain the fiction. He had anticipated his wife's response to his carefully timed news with all its attendant emotions present in his conception of it: "He knew just how she would look at him when he told her—in blank disbelief at first and then, gradually, with the dawning of a kind of respect he hadn't seen in her for years."[33] Jerome Klinkowitz points out that Walter, who has conceived his own "perfect fiction," writes the scene in his head, "in terms of language and rhythms, all appropriate not to her gestures in actual life but to their existence on the page. For that is what Walter's life has become, a short story, novel, or screenplay."[34] In my view, Walter's perfect fiction is, like the ending, primarily cinematic in the visual details of its narrative.

The conclusion of this story might be awkward, but Yates is successful in his ability to create the basic self-consciousness of social performance. To do this he is proficient in his use of cinematic metaphors that take in not just the sense of an individual acting but also refer to the technical know-how of camera work. Klinkowitz, in his assessment of Walter's perfect fiction, seems not to have noticed this. Using technical details, Yates is able to add depth to the individual's illusory confidence while at the same time drawing the reader's attention to the mechanics of the "game." After Walter has been fired, Yates reproduces Walter's thoughts. The narrative moves with ease and fluency and emphasizes that he is acutely aware of the performances being enacted around him. These roles are heightened by the metaphor Yates, mimicking Walter, employs to describe them, a metaphor sustained until the end of the story: "It was as if the whole thing were a scene in a movie. The camera had opened the action from Crowell's viewpoint and dollied back to take the entire office as a frame for Walter's figure in lonely, stately passage; now it came in for a long-held close-up of Walter's face, switched to other brief views of his colleague's turning heads . . . and switched again to Walter's viewpoint."[35] The vocabulary Yates employs underscores the preoccupation with image and performance in general.

It is striking that the film being made in Walter's head has Walter in the center of the frame almost the whole time. With careful narrative control, Yates indicates how his protagonist is attuned to performances around him but only has a partial appreciation of his own. For the reader, a bigger picture emerges: "(Joe Collins looking worried, Fred Holmes trying to keep from looking pleased)."[36] These observations of the minor players in Walter's "film" are parenthetical because they barely register for him (but it is the parentheses that make them stand out for the reader). Nor does the prosaic nature of Walter's final encounter at a water cooler diminish his sense of grandeur at this moment: "The next part of the scene was at the water cooler, where Joe Collins's sober eyes became enriched with sympathy as Walter approached him."[37] The use of the word "approached" deftly draws attention to his deliberate, and deliberately slow, advance.

Yates's characters are unable to look beneath the surface of their performances to bring some critical weight to bear on their own inauthenticity. According to James Howard Kunstler, this failure was a feature of postwar life, albeit one that he locates firmly in suburbia. He indicates how the new reliance on the screen, and the indulgence in a celebratory culture, encourages superficiality. It reflects the propensity toward self-satisfaction in a prosperous nation that believed in the dream life it was creating for its citizens: "The creation of a suburban culture and all its trappings, along with our fortunate position vis-à-vis other nations, augured an era of boundless prosperity, security, comfort, and ease. It is no wonder that the pop culture artifacts of that day—the movies, early TV shows, and magazines—reflect a smug uncritical optimism about American life that seems rather cretinous now—Mom, Dad (puffing on a pipe), Skippy, and Sis driving up the parkway in the new DeSoto to look at the new model homes out in Lazy Acres."[38] With a few name changes, this sardonic description of the American family echoes Yates's creations of family life, for he wrote to expose the lies such models perpetrated.

Yates's use of film metaphor indicates that when characters are ill at ease with themselves and the world, they reach for the movies as a way of confirming something (in a manner reminiscent of the way they use mirrors, as discussed in the previous chapter). In other words, and the authorial irony is always apparent, they reach for something substantial by looking to the insubstantial, ephemeral world of film. Thus, in a similar way to Walter, Rachel Drake (*Cold Spring Harbor*) "began to feel like an exceptionally pretty girl. She felt almost like a girl in the movies, because meeting Evan Shepard had given her the opening episode of a movie she could play over and over in her mind whenever she felt like it."[39] And when she hears that the draft board has summoned her husband for a physical examination, "Rachel tried to be brave about it because that was how young wives were shown to be in the movies."[40] Her feelings are sidelined in favor of borrowed cinematic reactions; real emotion is buried under the model and weight of synthetic, glossy, predetermined Hollywood responses. These responses do, at one level, help instruct the girl from the 1940s and 1950s who is kept ignorant and repressed by the demands society makes of her. But at the same time they contribute to how limited her understanding of her own behavior can be when there is little to encourage her to know herself.

Commentators such as Susan Douglas suggest that the media played both a positive and negative role in shaping behavior,[41] yet Yates's view is more disapproving of the unrealistic expectations the film and advertising industries set up. Rachel Drake appears to refer to the movies in order to process her experiences. While there is the suggestion that she derives some comfort from finding she is replicating a well-worn Hollywood trope, the stronger implication is that she is deeply, naively, unrealistic. The dichotomy is made more explicit later when, borrowing the idiom of the Drake family, Yates writes, "The movies were wonderful because they took you out of yourself, and at the same time they gave you a sense of being whole."[42] Movies, he makes clear, are a wonderful escape for people whose lives are dull and riven by poverty and disappointment, but they also act like a narcotic, preventing those same people from facing their problems.

What is difficult about "A Glutton for Punishment" overall is that there is some slippage in the narrative view. Yates adopts Walter's limited viewpoint in the present day of the text but sometimes suggests a greater intelligence in the protagonist. On the one hand the narrative voice mimics the naive, chatty thoughts of this rather simple man: "And the amazing thing, he thought—the really amazing thing"[43] and, in response to his firing, "The funny part was that it came as a shock."[44] On the other hand, the distance sometimes collapses between the naive character, wrapped up in himself with no ability to digest or make sense of the signs he sees, and the savvy narrator who draws attention to the essence of the story: "This bright cocktail mood was a carefully studied effect, he knew. So was her motherly sternness over the children's supper. . . . The orderly rotation of many careful moods was her life, or rather, what her life had become. She managed it well, and it was only rarely, looking very closely at her face, that he could see how much the effort was costing her."[45] Walter's careful observations here do not sound like the thoughts of the man who rushed out into the street having lost his job, realizing, "how completely he had enjoyed himself."[46] This summary of the wife's mood and behavior reads like the viable perception of an author who has dropped his guard rather than something his character might have observed. Yates had not yet worked out how to employ narrative voice subtly and skillfully, both as eyes and ears *and* as commentator; he has tried to weave his cynical viewpoint of human behavior into the viewpoint of a character not blessed with such critical powers. By the time he wrote his first novel, *Revolutionary Road*, this problem had all but disappeared.

Yates's deep-rooted interest in role-playing, or performative behavior, seems to have been driven in part by three dominant ideas. Firstly, that we all have a "true" self; secondly, that we shy away from revealing our true selves. While this may be innate, it is more likely a consequence of upbringing and informs how we relate to others as well as how we see ourselves. For reasons about which one cannot generalize, we may find it impossible to present ourselves without any kind of a mask. The mask, or performance enacted, becomes both a refuge and a reality; it is the reality of how we want to *seem*. Thirdly, Yates's interest was driven by the understanding that Hollywood, and the phenomenon that was Hollywood, exerted enormous, fundamentally negative influences over the lives of ordinary American men and women. The synthetic aspect of Hollywood has, Yates suggests, seeped into small communities everywhere. He implies this "infection" in his description of the newly emergent Route Twelve in *Revolutionary Road*: "a long bright valley of colored plastic and plate glass and stainless steel—KING KONE, MOBILGAS, SHOPORAMA, EAT—."[47] Yates implicitly criticizes the people who spring from this environment and seem more comfortable in it than they do among the decaying old houses and broken roads of a former, more organically evolved community; life as it used to be is juxtaposed with life as it is now, in 1955. Now, as represented by a world of giant plastic, capitalized signs, and with crass, distinctly *un*funny spellings, seems both phony and manufactured.

In Yates's work, Hollywood, the iconic, glamorous, much-talked-about haven, is hard to find. In *Disturbing the Peace*, for instance, John Wilder and Pamela Hendricks arrive at the Los Angeles airport and are immediately disorientated by the vast sprawl of the city: "It went on for miles in all directions without ever becoming a city, and the part of it called Hollywood was the most elusive of all."[48] The movies produced in postwar America depicted a glamorous world of romance and longing, of consumerism as a healthy "activity" and of beauty that was intrinsically linked to power and material goods, as evinced by smart clothes and expensive cars and houses. Simple binary oppositions were set up and took root: beautiful people were morally good people; ugly people were unsuccessful at best, villainous at worst. These dreams of material success, and the marital harmony that went with them, propelled Americans, Yates suggests, toward goals that were ephemeral, short-term, self-interested, and, most importantly, false.

Notions of performative behavior take on added meaning as Yates critiques the role Hollywood and cinema play in the aspirations and dreams of specifically white middle-class Americans trying to rebuild and reaffirm a positive worldview. If the ability to reinvent the self, carve out a new identity and shake off old ties, is an integral part of the American Dream, life as a sophisticated Hollywood star is the apotheosis of that aspect of the dream. In Yates's fiction, there are no stars but only seedy individuals characterized by their greed and ruthlessness. By focusing on individual success and individual portraits of a glamorous, exciting lifestyle, Hollywood endorses the ideal of stardom and, as Brian Neve indicates, suggests it is something to which all can aspire: "By presenting the primarily WASP Hollywood stars as role models and generally downplaying ethnicity in the social rituals and practices portrayed on the screen, the cinema arguably played a key role in promoting and even defining a new national culture, at a time, in the late thirties, when more young 'ethnics,' low income and rural Americans were joining the urban middle classes in the cinemas."[49]

Scattered throughout Yates's work are characters aping the behavior of characters in films. In *The Easter Parade* Yates suggests how Hollywood impinges on the lives of ordinary American citizens who want to emulate the fantasy world of the movies (and in this novel female citizens are shown to be particularly vulnerable to such desires). Toward the beginning of the story, Emily listens to her hopelessly romantic, inadequate mother say that she and the girls' father are "coming to a new understanding."[50] Emily's narrative comment, which reads like an aside to the reader to look askance at the mother, makes clear Yates's distaste: "It was like something a divorced mother in the movies might say, just before the music comes up for the fadeout."[51] The mother's words and manner are seen as morally suspect for their association with the fakery of the cinematic world they impersonate, and the inclination toward relying on the movies for information as to how to behave is intensified as the story develops. This is particularly apparent in the behavior of the older sister, Sarah Grimes, whose opinions, mannerisms, and fatal choices are all rooted in film. Yates is clear that Sarah Grimes is a *victim* of the pervasive power of the movie culture that has raised her. When dating her first boyfriend, Donald Clellon, she can only answer Emily's query as to what she sees in him with the whimsical, imitative gesture and idiom of a Hollywood romance: "'I don't know, I just like him.' She paused and lowered her eyes like a movie star in a close-up. 'I think I may be in love with him.'"[52]

Sarah Grimes, in common with most Yatesian characters, does not learn from her mistakes. Her subsequent boyfriend, and future husband, presents himself as ideal because of his movie-star looks, as is made clear by her breathless enthusiasm: "And Sarah had to sit down in one of their motheaten easy chairs to catch her breath. 'Oh, Pookie,' she said. 'He looks—he looks just like Laurence *Oliv*ier."[53] Yates makes his condemnation of that culture silently clear as he juxtaposes the moth-eaten chair and all the grime and grease of their existence with their determined insistence that lives like theirs can mirror Hollywood. He suggests that the line between a grim reality and a celluloid fantasy has become dangerously blurred for this young woman. Defying her mother, who realizes Clellon is a fraud, Sarah continues to be courted by him. She bases the decisions she makes about staying with her boyfriend on a cocktail of social expectations and a simulation of film behavior: "The heroines of all the movies she had ever seen made clear that she couldn't do otherwise; besides, what about all the people to whom she'd introduced him as 'my fiancé'?"[54]

While Yates's fiction criticizes what Hollywood is, as well as what it represents, he does not absolve himself from a susceptibility to its promises. Like several of his protagonists, Yates sought work in Hollywood, so his critical view is compromised by his own economic need and by the fact that like so many others, Yates bought into the promises Hollywood offered. He eagerly awaited the news that *Revolutionary Road* might be made into a film, as his biographer, Blake Bailey, makes clear: "Yates half-heartedly cast about for work while hoping that Hollywood's interest in his novel would soon amount to more than occasional teasing."[55] He recognized that through Hollywood he might not only make money to support his two (and later three) daughters, but he might also make a name for himself. When at the end of 1961 the plans for a film version of *Revolutionary Road* were shelved but replaced with a suggestion that he write the screenplay for William Styron's novel *Lie Down in Darkness*, Yates was "almost equally excited and nervous," for it was a job that "would buy my freedom for the next two years."[56]

To begin with this project proceeded smoothly enough and Yates wrote an excellent screenplay of Styron's novel. In his introduction to the script George Bluestone notes how swiftly Yates produced the work.[57] However, the screenplay was never filmed; the suggestion of an incestuous relationship frightened off the intended star, Natalie Wood, and her agent.[58] Yates admits in his letters that he found the glamour of Hollywood alluring and as if to play the role properly, "rented a sporty white convertible"[59] in which he could get around. However, he felt reassured that he had not also sold his soul since he and the director had the same attitude to the project: "both he and [John] Frankenheimer agreed on a rigorously faithful adaptation of Styron's novel, with due emphasis on its incest theme and damn the censors."[60] The ultimate failure of the project was an enormous blow both financially and psychologically because his expectations for its success had been allowed to rise to great heights. What was typical for Hollywood struck deep at the heart of a man who was already unstable.

Like Fitzgerald before him, Yates was courted, rebuffed, and disappointed by the film industry, but in the process he was able to examine Hollywood as a phenomenon. More importantly, he was able to store up a new set of individuals to write about as he met producers, directors, writers, and agents with increasing regularity.[61] Years later these individuals emerged in his fiction; works such as *Disturbing the Peace* and "Saying Goodbye to Sally" draw heavily on Yates's time in Los Angeles. Such connections suggest to me how deeply he felt both the collapse of the *Lie Down in Darkness* project and at the same time how much he felt like an outsider in Tinseltown.[62]

Jack Fields, the protagonist of "Saying Goodbye to Sally," leaves his life in New York's Greenwich Village in order to "write a screenplay based on a contemporary novel that he greatly admired."[63] Both the portrait Yates paints of the director and the name he gives him, Carl Oppenheimer, provide a recognizable fictionalized version of John Frankenheimer, the man who was to have directed his screenplay. Writing fictional accounts that interpret events from his own life was Yates's way of ensuring that he adhered to the truth of an experience. On the one hand, the process of writing provides a means by which to objectify and make sense of experiences, and, on the other, it means he can give flesh more faithfully to the emotions those experiences generated. It is primarily the human condition that Yates is illuminating; his exposé of Hollywood is secondary.

In "Saying Goodbye to Sally" Yates openly addresses the connection between his dreamers and those of Fitzgerald. As Jack Fields flies to Los Angeles he considers the fact that he might be about to have "a significant adventure: F. Scott Fitzgerald in Hollywood."[64] Yates's experience of Hollywood, like that of many writers, was very different from the world he'd imagined, as he makes clear in this story. Although other people seem invariably to find a luxurious home, Fields lives in a shabby little beach house. Like Yates himself, Fields finds that the cockroaches of his Greenwich Village apartment appear to have moved with him: "He didn't realize until after moving in—and after paying three months' rent in advance—that the place was very nearly as dismal and damp as his cellar in New York."[65] Such ironic touches within this novel are at the expense of Jack Fields's view of himself, at the expense of Yates, and at the expense of the Hollywood machine.

Yates's presentation of Hollywood fuses a mixture of direct references to places and the activity of movie making with metaphor and symbol that enriches his creative, and critical, perspective. Using the metaphor of Jill Jarvis's house, Hollywood is presented as a decadent place of irresponsible behavior, drink-fueled and careless. While that might sound tame enough, Yates makes it clear that it is also a place where people are ultimately cruel, playing practical jokes that are always at the expense of an innocent. There are, for instance, suggestions of child neglect in the portrait of Jill's son "Kicker." Indicating that all may not be as it seems in this house, Yates sets his description of this child in stark counterpoint to the opulence of the furnishings: "An arrangement of leather-padded wrought-iron benches was built around the hearth, and on one of the benches sat a pale, sad boy of about thirteen, facing away from the fire and holding his clasped hands between his thighs, looking as though he had come to sit there because there was nothing else to do."[66]

The mansion is as decadent and iconic as Gatsby's house: they are both central to the stories being told but are disquieting to the reader as their glamorous surfaces barely conceal darker truths. In Yates's story, descriptions of the house are subtly woven into the narrative so that it becomes both intoxicating and repellent. In an early description through Jack's eyes, it is a striking home, a place filled with light, space, and warmth with its "lofty portico" and the "great many sun-bright windows."[67] However, as Jack becomes familiar with the Jarvis house and the lifestyle therein, his view shifts, but with his view of the house complicated by his view of Sally, the shift he makes is not as great as the one the reader makes. Yates achieves this whisper of a distance between author and protagonist with scarcely perceptible details. When Sally is showing him around the house Jack notices a Japanese lacquered table in her bedroom and asks whether she ever uses it: "I just thought you might call up five or six very close friends once in a while, get 'em all up here in their socks and sit 'em cross-legged around this thing, turn down the lights and break out the chopsticks and have yourselves a swell little evening in Tokyo."[68] His mocking irony greatly annoys her. At this point, the artificiality of the home is clear to Jack; he realizes what he is looking at is akin to a film set, and he ridicules it. Later that night, lying in bed and musing on Fitzgerald's affair with Sheilah Graham, Jack decides that Fitzgerald, unable to drink and trying to write "must have been humbly grateful just to have her there."[69] The innocuousness of the thought belies its importance: Jack is desperately lonely and by implication is prepared to compromise in order to stay with Sally. The house therefore becomes an object of derision for the author/narrator/reader but no longer for the protagonist, as Yates, enforcing the distance by the use of his protagonist's full name, relates how "Jack Fields became, briefly, a resident of that Greek Revival mansion in Beverly Hills."[70] While it has become a "Greek revival mansion" for the reader, it has not for Jack. Implicitly, in becoming a temporary resident, and desirous of sustaining his relationship with Sally, he has had to abandon his habitual critical stance.

With barely visible distaste, Yates suggests that the money used to build this house had its origins in slavery, further relegating it morally and inten-sifying the sense of it as a place of darkness. The initial description excites no alarm: "It was a vast white mansion of the Old South, with at least six columns rising from its porch to its lofty portico."[71] The impression one re-ceives is of grandeur and opulence, and one barely registers the connection with "the Old South." However, when Sally later suggests the origin of the Jarvis money in vague, careless terms, the reader reaches beyond her unques-tioning languor to examine the author's suggestion of money earned from slavery: "'Well, I don't really *know* where all the money comes from,' she said. 'I know she gets an awful lot of it from her father, someplace in Georgia, and I know his family's had an awful lot of it down there for an awful long time, but I don't really know where it *comes* from. Cotton or something, I guess.'"[72] Suddenly the phrase "of the Old South" has a historical specificity: this is not a mansion built *in the style of* the South; it is *of* the South. Furthermore, the only visible working person in the house is the stalwart housekeeper, "the plump uniformed Negro maid named Nippy."[73] Yates spells out her pivotal role as each night she encourages them to move from their alcoholic suste-nance to the table to eat; she is often ignored. Yates leaves it to the reader to decide how far to take the metaphorical association between Hollywood and this house. He carefully constructs the connection of slave-earned wealth, deliberately but delicately building it up until the reader registers the stark image of the maid, Nippy, standing in the doorway. It would be wrong to conclude that Yates saw Hollywood as a place funded by, and constructed by, slave-earned money. He was well aware that entrepreneurs who largely financed Hollywood happened to be Jewish, but I think he wanted to sug-gest the moral dubiousness of the place without appearing to be anti-Semitic.

As the story draws to its conclusion, Fields's position as an outsider look-ing in on a world he neither likes nor understands is reaffirmed. Sally asserts, for instance, that the dress Fields has admired so much might help her "trap the *next* counterfeit F. Scott Fitzgerald who comes stumbling out to Movie-land."[74] She reveals, therefore, not just her intention to move on but also sug-gests she always knew about his rather immature, idolatrous worship of the late writer. This exposes Fields completely as it comes immediately after his silent, narrative confession as to why he is buying her an expensive last meal: "He had thought too that it might be the kind of thing F. Scott Fitz-gerald would have done at a time like this, but he kept that part of it to him-self. He had tried for years to prevent anyone from knowing the full extent of his preoccupation with Fitzgerald."[75] Jack Fields is last seen standing on the outside looking into the mansion where his ex-girlfriend lives. This is a powerful image because the house appears to swallow her up as room after room is lit at her entrance, symbolically suggesting her move further and further away from him: "He stood watching until after she'd gone inside, and until the tall windows of one room after another cast their sudden light into the darkness. Then more lights came on and more, room upon room, as Sally ventured deeper into the house she had always loved."[76] At this point we are reminded that "light" plays an uncertain role in Yates's work; while providing warmth and clarity, light also assaults the protagonists by highlighting their flaws and weaknesses. The Yatesian writer can only operate in the shade and half-light. Similarly, the house, like the Hollywood it represents, is an ambiguous place. Fields is literally out in the cold, staring at something he cannot be part of, but the house is also a place that seems to devour its inhabitants.

For all that this mansion is held up for criticism, it holds an allure as a place of possibility and activity; morally questionable yet full of energy, relationships are carelessly discarded there, but it is nevertheless a place where new relationships are made and intensified. It is an environment where men and women quite literally play, but, as with the joke at Woody Starr's[77] expense, play becomes cruel very quickly. Women are seen primarily as beautiful objects, but this house is also a place where women have some control, even if through the use of their bodies. "Saying Goodbye to Sally" takes a hard look at the falsity and precariousness of life in Hollywood, its shallow relationships, careless parenting, and pursuit of wealth, but it also critiques the naïveté and cynicism of those who work there; the young writer from outside this world, who briefly gets sucked in, is not excluded. However, I would suggest that by keeping Jack Fields a "failure" in Hollywood terms and by presenting him as an outsider looking in on a world that no longer holds any place for him, Yates suggests, as he often does, some small consolation in the role of the writer; the writer wrests back some perspective from events that have nearly engulfed him. In the darkness, or half-light, he is protected.

With *Disturbing the Peace* Yates produced a more biting indictment of Hollywood. As John Wilder and his girlfriend, Pamela, arrive in Los Angeles, Yates creates the strong sense that they are outsiders. In order to find their way through the machinery of Hollywood they are totally at the mercy of individuals they have never met. The tenuousness of Pamela's one connection is made plain but is also made to sound ordinary, as if it is through such circuitous routes that deals are made: "Edgar Freeman was their only 'contact,' a producer-director at Columbia Pictures whose uncle was an acquaintance of her father's."[78] They have gone to LA full of burning zeal to make this picture of "Bellevue" happen but with no sense of the difficulties involved, thus every knock leaves bruises; drink is the sustaining force as they ricochet through the institution. It transpires that Freeman's Hollywood is built on exploitation cinema, what he describes as, "Beach pictures and bike pictures, right. Also horror pictures."[79] Driving back disconsolate from that first meeting, Wilder notes "the grubby white edifice of the Hollywood Palladium."[80] With such small details, Yates charts the grim progression from the ideal to the real for his protagonist since both the people and the geography are disappointing. While the Hollywood Hills are pretty, "the canyons led too quickly into the enormous suburban waste of the San Fernando Valley,"[81] and while they reassure themselves that the best parts of the city must lie to the west, when they get there, they find "only sandy, weatherbeaten slums."[82]

The biggest blow for Wilder, and a cause of his subsequent breakdown, comes from the careless voice of a man who is interested above all else in whether their film can be made into "a commercially viable property."[83] Carl Munchin, a producer, suggests that what they have is an art house project and that if he were to get involved it would have to be changed substantially. With no idea that this is Wilder's own story, Munchin sallies forth with a lack of sensitivity that Yates makes painful for the reader. He is explicit about what those changes should be: "Just as a guideline I'd say build him up for another breakdown—a real breakdown—in part two, and then in part three let him have it. Pull out all the stops. . . . I say let him go crazy. Wipe him out."[84] The reader has experienced the visceral account of mental breakdown in the course of this novel (and has also stored up the grotesque reality of a place such as Bellevue) and knows too the degree of desperation and instability in the protagonist, but Munchin is blithely unaware of such details and becomes openly exploitative. He knows he holds their project in the palm of his hand and is only concerned about "what's of interest to me."[85] Yates's dramatic irony places clear emphasis on the fact that there is never any doubt that money is the *only* currency here, and one cannot ignore the fact that truth plays a very small part in what sells as a narrative.

Novels that are structurally cinematic, as Yates's often are, are easily confused with novels written with film productions in mind. In the 1960s, Norman Podhoretz criticized Edmund Wilson's views on the sterility of the literature of the 1930s and in doing so suggested what drove writers such as Yates. He made the point that while money was a huge draw toward the writing of a cinematic novel, it was not the only one: "His explanation of this anomaly is the influence of Hollywood—all these writers are unconsciously trying to produce novels that can be translated to the screen with a minimum of difficulty. . . . Wilson's rather lazy-minded attempt to refer the problem, in good 20's style, to the lure of filthy lucre constitutes a failure on his part to recognize the existence of a crucially important new phenomenon in American culture: the middlebrow writer."[86] At first glance it might seem that Yates was writing, as Wilson suggests other writers were, with movies in mind. This assumption is compounded by the fact that Yates often addressed the phenomenon of Hollywood in his work. However, his high hopes for his work suggest this was not true. Although he wrote very cinematic fictions where one "scene" seems to follow another "scene," with dialogue as the means of narrative development, Yates did not see himself as a middlebrow writer. He had high aspirations to be recognized and applauded by the literary reviewers of his time.

In interviews and in Yates's fictions, literature is always privileged over film as if a movie could never compete with a book: "They're two different art forms, that's all, and there's plenty of room for both. I like a good movie, but I like a good novel better—possibly because when you read you can let the narrative pictures create themselves in your mind as you go along, rather than having them arbitrarily flashed at you, and that seems a more rewarding experience."[87] In the uncut version of this interview, Yates was far more explicit and hard-hitting in his criticism of film: "when you read a good novel what you do is run off a movie in your mind. You're reading printed words on a page, but they make pictures in your head, and they're *your* pictures and you bring to them what you can depending on how smart you are and how sensitive you are, but when you watch a movie all you're watching is some body [*sic*] else's pictures and they're not yours. When you get a verbal image going on a page that's given to you to make of what you can, then the picture is all yours, but when you watch a movie it's somebody else's; it's just an easy way of absorbing art."[88] Yates requested that this "rant" of his be removed from the published version, presumably because it would, in all likelihood, alienate him from the few contacts he had made in Hollywood and in so doing make it even more difficult for him to earn money there.

Ironically, with Sam Mendes's film of *Revolutionary Road*,[89] the winner of several awards, and with talk of a film of *The Easter Parade*, Yates's stock in Hollywood might well be rising. Yates's daughter, Monica Yates, wrote of a visit she paid with her older sister Sharon to the Mendes film set. Calling the casting "brilliant" and noting that the screenplay seemed "to have left well enough alone," she applauds what Hollywood, at its best, *can* give to the literary world: "It is impossible for me to imagine only knowing the film version of a book, and I can't help hoping everybody wants the experience to be available both ways; but how miraculous is it, that an artist's great lifelong desire should be granted; that people should listen to him, and continue to know the people he gave voice to, forever. That is what Hollywood can do for literature."[90] But Sam Mendes's film of Yates's first novel did not reverberate through the film world in the same way that the written work affected the literati of the 1960s. Yates's multilayered narrative could not be replicated in film despite Justin Haythe's excellent screenplay and a cast of very impressive actors giving strong, even memorable, performances. Perhaps Yates was right when he spoke of the act of reading as akin to running "a movie in your mind" as distinct from watching something where all the work is done for you. So much of the success of the novel, and this is largely true of all Yates's work, is dependent on the reader being completely engaged, engaged enough to imagine every nuance of every conversation. By handing the visual images to you, by editing the narrative to fit the demands of cinema, Mendes diminishes what is required of his audience and produces something digestible and safe (but the DVD of the film does include many superb deleted scenes and reinforces the point that commercial interests, not aesthetic ones, dictated what was left in). What Yates produced was never "safe." Nevertheless, it is a measure of how seriously Yates's work is now taken that Stewart O'Nan's comment in 1999 seems both prescient and, in spite of the delay, a touch ironic: "A good biography could spark a re-evaluation of his achievement, though at present there does not appear to be one on the horizon. Likewise, the movie possibilities are nil."[91] Blake Bailey reminds us what place the longed for but ever-escaping film of *Revolutionary Road* held in Yates's life: "For the rest of Yates' life, the lucrative prospect of *Revolutionary Road*—the movie—shimmered like a mirage in the middle distance."[92] Of course it was the money and its attendant security that he was after above all else, but he also knew his first novel deserved more attention. However, resisting sentimentality and the ephemera of the Hollywood world, Yates was articulate in his diagnosis of the place in a strikingly similar fashion to Holden Caulfield's exasperated cry as he considers how films have cheapened his own responses: "The goddam movies. They can ruin you. I'm not kidding."[93]

Using a mixture of paraphrase and quotation from Yates's personal papers, and adopting the same kind of mimetic narrative that Yates uses so often, Bailey makes clear Yates's distaste, and his passion: "As for the movies themselves, as for The Industry: 'Don't get me started,' he'd say, but by then he was already started. 'The goddamn movies' had a malignant effect on society; they were made by greedy, dishonest, untalented, manipulative bastards, and created a wholly false version of reality that made people think love or success or whatever was right around the corner, when in truth (as they were soon reminded) it wasn't. 'I used to *like* the movies,' he'd sigh."[94] Richard Yates always fought the place, but he kept going back.

3

Theories of Selfhood

4. Richard Yates in Fahnestock State Park, New York, 1962 or 1963. Courtesy of Grace Schulman.

It is axiomatic that we all perform all of the time, whether onstage, in a social situation, or even in the home; we invent a version of ourselves not just once but to suit every situation we encounter. Performance is routinely understood to be part of human existence. We shield ourselves behind masks, know-ingly or unknowingly, we project "fictional" images of ourselves, sometimes innocently, as part of our aspirational inclinations or as a devious means of shirking our responsibilities, and we are routinely amused, horrified, or be-guiled by the performances of others. The pervasive use of social networking sites in contemporary life has only added to the sense that people can choose how to project themselves as they routinely change their "profile picture" and carefully edit what information about their lives is released.

However, it should be said at the outset that this idea that humans wear masks or choose different performances to suit their moods and the context in which they find themselves is a relatively recent view of the way humans interact. For the modernists and postmodernists it became a preoccupation and a paradigm; their investigation of the notion of selfhood continually drew attention to its instability. Yates absorbs some of their preoccupations but suggests, as is demonstrated by the narrative view of his characters' performances—generally such performances are undercut or highlighted by the use of an ironic voice—that there was an authentic self to be uncovered. His literary craft, grounded in the implicit notion that reality can be transcribed onto the page, nevertheless challenges the privilege of the author and suggests, with its narrative layering and constantly shifting perspective, a more complex view of the reality of human interaction.

In his book *Social Selves: Theories of the Social Formation of Personality* (1991), Ian Burkitt traces the shift from Renaissance thought (based on the work of, among others, René Descartes and Immanuel Kant), whereby man was seen as a solitary individual, a monad, "separate, distinct and unique,"[1] to thought informed by the work of sociologists in the twentieth century that suggested the *social bonds* that inform personality. Burkitt argues that by and large modern thought is still informed by the Renaissance view of man as monad and has been slow to absorb the work of social scientists such as George Herbert Mead, whose theory of "social behaviorism" provides a more reliable, if more complex, model by which to investigate and understand human performance: "The basic thesis that Mead propounded was that the 'mind' and 'self' are formed within the social, communicative activity of the group. He was therefore one of the first theorists to explore the notion that personality develops within discourse."[2] Burkitt stresses the two most important aspects of Mead's theory that are necessarily interconnected: the primary role of language in the formation of self and the ability of the self to look at itself objectively. Burkitt argues: "the responses of the self can only enter awareness when the individual gains an objective view of their own self. This can only be attained through language, by taking the attitude of others towards the self. Even when we are alone, our introspective thinking takes place in the form of an internal conversation with our own self, mediated by social language and meanings."[3] Only very particular Yatesian figures demonstrate any ability to look at themselves and their actions objectively.

In Yates's work, it is the inability of the characters to examine their inclinations and behavior objectively that is at the root of their social breakdowns. Crudely put, the performances his characters adopt consistently show that they maintain a view of selfhood that is essentially one of the monad. Burkitt outlines the dangers of this way of thinking for the self: "To think of the personality as a monad, a pre-sealed primary reality out of which emerges social relations, is to cling to a supernatural notion of the self."[4] I would suggest, however, that Yates has a more complex view of selfhood that is perhaps subconsciously informed by the likes of Mead and Erving Goffman (I say subconsciously because it seems unlikely that Yates will have delved into the work of such theorists; he expresses an aversion to all theorizing). With a central dramaturgical metaphor for behavior, Goffman's work is important when considering the mid-twentieth century and in particular the work of Yates. His study, *The Presentation of Self in Everyday Life*, was published in 1959, when Yates was revising a draft of his first novel. We cannot know whether Yates ever read Goffman's work, but his understanding of performative behavior (that is, intrinsically false behavior that emerges from a desire to be seen in a particular way), as depicted in his fiction, may be read as a creative interpretation of Goffman's views. As David Castronovo and Steven Goldleaf express it: "In analyzing the underlying structure of public behavior—how people make impressions, what routines they follow in projecting themselves—Goffman draws a floor plan of Yates's America."[5]

In *The Presentation of Self in Everyday Life*, Goffman makes a significant contribution to the understanding of the human propensity for social "performance." He strives to pick apart the face from the mask, or at least to look behind it, at the "given" reason for the wearing of that mask from the actual reason. As part of that aim, Goffman characterizes an important difference in the expressiveness of the individual as that between two different types of sign activity: "the expression that he *gives*, and the expression that he *gives off*."[6] The former involves the verbal symbols he uses to convey information; this is communication in the traditional and narrow sense. The latter "involves a wide range of action that others can treat as symptomatic of the actor, the expectation being that the action was performed for reasons other than the information conveyed in this way."[7] This area, this gap between these two modes of expressive behavior, interested Goffman most. The implication of his work is that there is no true self without the adoption of roles. As a result of the gap Goffman identifies between the individual and his or her performance, many of the social problems of communication and understanding not only arise but also are nurtured, as the novelists, dramatists, and poets of the mid-twentieth century illustrate in the fictional lives they portray.

Lionel Trilling, writing in 1948, saw, as Yates did later, that it was part of the novelist's task to investigate the performative conduct of individuals: "The characteristic work of the novel is to record the illusion that snobbery generates and to try to penetrate to the truth which, as the novel assumes, lies hidden beneath all the false appearances."[8] Like Yates, Trilling saw such behavior as masking the truth of a person, and even if nuanced slightly differently, Yates's characterizations pursue a similar line. The performative nature of human behavior is not so much a theme within any one Yatesian story as it is the ontological starting point for *all* his work. In that respect, like J. D. Salinger's and John O'Hara's work, and though realistic in style, his fiction shifts toward similarities with that of the postmodernists as it draws attention to ideas about the insubstantiality of the self.

Throughout his life and throughout his work, Yates was highly attuned to the performative nature of human experience and the adoption of personae and masks that accompanied it. Building on a discourse that can be traced back to Chaucer and which, of course, includes the Elizabethans (Shakespeare's *Hamlet* in particular), Yates transforms what was a tragic preoccupation with appearance and reality into an examination of the prosaic preoccupations of the American middle classes. His interest lies not just in the grandiloquence of the loud and exuberant, or conversely in the timid gestures of the cowed, but is always focused on the minutiae of the various signals that give ordinary human performance its richness, subtlety, and complexity. The fact that individuals assume different roles for different situations fascinates Yates, and he questions, by implication, how an authentic version of selfhood is represented. Jerome Klinkowitz reinforces this idea: "In all these works the characters are creatures of their age and interested in sign systems themselves. When choosing to act, they often consult models from literature, film, or national politics, and when sorting out their identities they are challenged by the catalog of models which a self-conscious awareness of their culture provides."[9] As a young man growing up in the eastern states of America, Yates observed the lives of those around him closely. The perceptive characterizations of his fictions demonstrate that he is particularly sensitive to the nature of an individual's performance within a wider social group. His interrogations of human conduct suggest at the same time both the complex, psychological origins of any one performance and the simplicity of its designs. The masks and disguises any one of his fictional characters wears are laid bare for the reader, and even if the narrative suggests the psychological origin of such disguises, they nevertheless act as a biting commentary on the character's self-awareness and maturity.

The many complex reasons behind a chosen performance interested this author greatly. With his depiction of Shep Campbell (*Revolutionary Road*) the reader is given a clear illustration of the propensity to perform in order to hide a truth. Shining his shoes, singing lustily as he works, swigging his beer and snapping his rag, Campbell relishes the image he is projecting. However, as the narrator points out, the tough-guy persona is one he rarely has access to nowadays. Campbell is in possession of an uncommon human trait, for, unlike most of Yates's characters, this man is able, occasionally, to be self-reflective. However, his ability to assess his own performativity is limited by the way in which he replaces one dream or untruth with another. He has, as a married, middle-aged adult in suburbia, learned to put aside the "stolid peasant's look"[10] and save it for shoe shining and tire changing. It might have suited his social politics as a young man but he now recognizes that it is a long way from the truth of who he is. His yearning to be "insensitive and ill-bred"[11] is undermined by "the most shameful facts of his life: that he'd been raised in a succession of brownstone and penthouse apartments . . . schooled by private tutors . . . [and was dressed by his mother] in 'adorable' tartan kilts that came from Bergdorf Goodman."[12]

Yates is at pains to make his reader see that although Shep thinks he has escaped the foolhardiness of his youthful inverted snobbery, he has not. The East offers a new kind of dream for Shep: "Bright visions came to haunt him of a world that could and should have been his, a world of intellect and sensibility that now lay forever mixed in his mind with 'the East.' In the East, he then believed, a man went to college not for vocational training but in disciplined search for wisdom and beauty, and nobody over the age of twelve believed that those words were for sissies."[13] As part of this new dream, his clothes will change into "rumpled tweeds and flannels" and the girls of the East will be "marvelously slim and graceful."[14] What is critical about this passage is Yates's insertion of the words "he then believed." In a sense, while this novel has the Wheelers at its center, it also charts the passage of Shep Campbell's final awakening as all his romantic idealizations are picked apart. In the present of the narrative, he is in the process of learning just how ordinary life is for everyone, even in the East. The final lessons he has to learn are centered on the demystification of those he thought he knew: Frank and April Wheeler, and, more importantly, his own wife, Milly.

Heavily reliant on dialogue, Yates's novels and short stories show his characters performing so that performance is not so much described as enacted through dialogic exchange. Communication and meaning are conveyed by language actively bartered between individuals, and thus the reader recognizes meaning is a social construction as Mikhail Bakhtin and many Russian theorists described it,[15] not individual, or monologic, as Yates might have been educated to think. Although Yates was quite probably uninterested in theories about language, his writing is informed by modern thought and pivots around an intuitive sense of the dialogization of language and the instability of linguistic performance.

Displaying a keen insight into the way mannerisms, dialogue, and the affectations of dress operate in normal social interaction, Yates seems to want to get as close as possible to the naked, unadorned experience of being human and to investigate the way a person, whatever his or her age, gender, or class, emerges into a social scene with a variety of performances. It is, perhaps, for this reason that early readers of his work often saw it as misanthropic. Yates's focus on the fakery in human behavior without the understanding, then becoming prevalent, that we are always and everywhere performing, was depressing and an irritant. Unlike his contemporaries, many of whom worked the perennial notion of performance into their work, Yates seemed to believe he could *unmask* his characters in order to expose them and uncover an underlying truth. With the work of late twentieth-century sociologists in mind, we now have a more complex view of performance than Erving Goffman provided. Partly as a result of this, Yates's work can be read in a new light.

In American fiction the propensity to reinvent the self, and the adoption of masks with that aim in mind, is part of a cultural inheritance of a society where there is a far greater social fluidity than in Europe where, until the mid-twentieth century, one's role in society was assigned at birth. In Nathanael West's *Miss Lonelyhearts*, for instance, invention *is* existence. John Barth's defamiliarizing novel *The End of the Road* takes this a step further, suggesting existence is invention. In F. Scott Fitzgerald's *The Great Gatsby*, Jay Gatsby's life's work has been a process of reinvention, of becoming the wealthy East Coast host and of shedding his midwestern roots. He literally dedicates his life to pursuing a dream of another self with a new name and invented background; it is a dream that ultimately destroys him. Martin Halliwell draws attention to the repetition of this dream of self-reinvention and escape in the literature of the 1950s: "One of the strongest themes of the decade was that of authenticity, the difficulty of preserving genuine experience in the face of commercial and ideological pressures. . . . The image of the 'phoney' runs through 1950s literature: from Holden Caulfield's concerns about the lack of authenticity in *The Catcher in the Rye* (1951) and Norman Mailer's exposure of shallow culture in *The Deer Park* (1955). . . . Other texts such as Jack Kerouac's *On the Road* (1957) and Robert Frank's photographic study *The Americans* (1958) attempted to rediscover the possibility of genuine experience in a decade where everything was open to salesman's spin and Madison Avenue repackaging."[16] Many American writers who influenced Yates's work explored the process of self-invention, or reinvention, and new beginnings. Yates viewed the process as an integral part of performative behavior and a facet of the search for an elusive dream of a better life.

Yates's mission is to puncture misplaced dreams, to suggest by implication that the dream, and the behavior that gives expression to that dream, does not usually sit well with the aspirational man or woman. He sets about replacing such ideas with disturbing and uncomfortable truths; what is interesting is how this implicates him as much as it does his characters. Frank Wheeler's happy description of himself as "an intense, nicotine-stained, John-Paul-Sartre sort of man"[17] suggests a degree of levity in Yates's exposure of performative behavior. However, beyond that levity, there was, for Yates, a serious issue to explore. As already observed, and in ways that are similar to Ernest Hemingway's characterizations, one notes how many times the individual being scrutinized is a writer in Yates's fiction, and this includes Wheeler;[18] the critical gaze is designed deliberately to penetrate the author's own facade. Yates's obsession with exposing inauthentic behavior is, it seems, an obsession with finding his own authentic self. As his friend David Milch expressed it: "The ordeal of inauthenticity—what was real versus feigned—was a drama enacted in every gesture of his. Dick had this punitive self-consciousness: Had he integrated the *idea* of being a writer with being a writer?"[19] But "what was real versus feigned" is not always a simple choice for people. Yates also negotiates the way inauthenticity can be demanded of certain individuals to satisfy a societal need. This is particularly true for women in postwar America. Emily Grimes, savoring the idea of being an intellectual, for instance, muses on the way performative behavior is required in order to mask the fact that she is bright and female: "You had to be serious, but—this was the maddening paradox—you had to seem never to take anything very seriously."[20]

The stability or sincerity of our performance is one way in which others will be able to judge us as people. As Goffman expresses it, "We often expect . . . a confirming consistency between appearance and manner."[21] We expect that consistency in order to have a stable view of another person affirmed, but it is Yates's premise that more often than not such consistency is disrupted. The reader sees that his work abounds with individuals whose behavior is affected and insincere and who cynically manipulate others for their own gain. Frank Wheeler (*Revolutionary Road*), John Wilder (*Disturbing the Peace*), Michael Davenport (*Young Hearts Crying*), and Evan Shepard (*Cold Spring Harbor*) all have a propensity toward manipulation and selfishness that the reader cannot fail to register. By contrast, Shep Campbell's faltering attempts to scrutinize and assess his own behavior engage the reader's empathy.

The older women in Yates's fiction, the mothers in particular, are not able to learn about the value of sincerity, nor do they have any clear and honest sense of self. They lack the ability to examine their own rather shallow, often pathetic, performances, as Castronovo and Goldleaf assert: "Yates's characters typically get through most of their lives without knowing what's wrong."[22] More problematic than how others might see us is how we see ourselves and what we learn about ourselves from the performances we give; this too was an abiding interest for Yates. With a dearth of figures that regularly question their behavior, Yates, in his characterization of April Wheeler, indicates how catastrophic it can be when there is a sudden application of honest self-reflection and scrutiny of past performances. As she says to Shep Campbell, she has lived her life on the premise that she would one day live among "heroic super-people" but has now realized that "it's the most stupid ruinous kind of self-deception there is."[23]

In Yates's work, his characters' inability to be objective about their behavior has been interrupted or curtailed long before the reader meets them, thus we are always cringing at their socially inept gestures or remarks and what Klinkowitz refers to as their "misreading" of manners: "In *Young Hearts Crying*, Yates presents a couple who court, marry, and divorce amid the signs of their culture, often basing their decisions on a reading or misreading of the manners which surround them."[24] An example of this social blindness occurs when Michael Davenport, drunk and trying desperately to impress his host and hostess, and deaf to their protestations, decides to move their rug to play soldiers:

> "So whaddya say we set up a few companies right here. Now. In this room."
> "Naw, the carpet's no good, Mike," Nelson said. "You need a wood floor to get 'em to stand right."
> "Well, hell, can't we roll the carpet back? Just until I get a little artillery practice?"
> He was dimly aware of Nelson saying "Naw, look, it's—" but he had already lunged off. . . . when he heard Nelson call "Naw, I mean wait—it's tacked down."
> Too late. A hundred carpet tacks flew and danced in shuddering clouds of house dust.[25]

Michael not only wrecks the evening but also reveals his social ineptitude, and this in turn severely damages the other characters' opinion of him.

When Michael Davenport jerks aside Tom Nelson's carpet he may merely be judged to be insensitive, but later in the story his confused notion of what constitutes male strength is revealed; he sees aggression and power as synonymous. He initiates a macho punching game with a man at a party who he perceives as weak and whose point of view he dislikes. Unwillingly the man, Al Damon, agrees to punch Davenport, who then reciprocates: "Michael's fist traveled only a short distance but it was fast, it connected in just the right way, and Al Damon lay unconscious on the rug."[26] There is no narrative comment, just the stark depiction of the act. But Yates's authorial silence only underscores the stupidity of Davenport and his performance. The writer's moral standpoint is suggested but not emphasized; it is as if Yates feels too acutely the iniquity and hypocrisy of taking a judgmental position over another's failings, especially when the complex notion of masculinity is being considered.

Yates's fascination with "misreadings" such as Davenport's is visible throughout his work and is often related to his male protagonists' inability to reconcile their masculinity with their social responsibility. They want to display and flaunt their maleness without realizing that to do so is to reveal a fundamental weakness in their understanding of how intelligent society views male strength; that is to say, it should be evident in an implicit rather than explicit manner. Yates primarily uses misunderstandings such as these to suggest that his protagonists poorly understand the codified behavior that determines whether one is accepted or rejected by others. Just occasionally, however, the novelist uses "misreadings" to cast a critical glance over the codes themselves and appears not only to be criticizing individuals who misread social cues but also to be highlighting a societal confusion about what is expected of men. That his male protagonists so often "get it wrong" is partly a result of the wider social confusion that Yates observed in postwar America. In "Saying Goodbye to Sally," for example, the artist Woody Starr is the only character, with the exception of the maid, to pay any attention to the young boy, Kicker. The boy's negligent mother spends her time drinking with her friends and all but ignores him. Yates draws attention to Starr's compassionate nature, but at the same time he makes it clear that his gentleness is the reason for Starr's later isolation in a society that sees such a caring nature in a man as a weakness.

From the mid-nineteenth century onward the nature of scientific inquiry accelerated. The growth of interest in the sciences of psychology and sociology was part of a broader pattern; much greater significance was accorded to the sciences in general and, specifically, to the study of how human beings function as social animals.[27] At the end of the nineteenth century William James, in his work *The Principles of Psychology* (1890), noted that "*a man has as many social selves as there are individuals who recognize him* and carry an image of him in their mind. To wound any one of these his images is to wound him. . . . From this there results what practically is a division of the man into several selves; and this may be a discordant splitting, as where one is afraid to let one set of his acquaintances know him as he is elsewhere; or it may be a perfectly harmonious division of labour."[28] James's scientific inquiry into notions of selfhood expresses, in language that will be plain, not merely to other psychologists, an observation that informs most of the literature written thereafter: man has "several selves," and it is this idea that Goffman later developed.[29]

It would seem, therefore, that the "normal" individual can adopt a variety of masks, as William James has indicated, and as later sociologists agreed. This assessment of human behavior was qualified by psychologists of the twentieth century who found a more complex system of behavior at work, finding that there are those who have the power and the confidence to adhere rigidly to their own conception of themselves. In 1987 Mark Snyder wrote about James's opinion: "He was correct but only for some people—it is only the high self-monitors of the world who, properly speaking, may be said to have not one, but many social selves. For low self-monitors, the public appearances and private realities of the self seem to be one and the same."[30] Snyder asserts that there are those who "regard themselves as rather adaptive creatures who shrewdly choose selves that fit their situations"[31] and those who "feel that they must not compromise their identities for other people and should not bend to the will of circumstance."[32] Thus Snyder, in opposition to Goffman, suggests that performative behavior is not common to all; this is an important idea to consider in relation to Yates's fiction.

Castronovo and Goldleaf claim that Yates, like Goffman, adopts an uncritical stance toward the performative behavior he uncovers: "Nevertheless, mere phoniness is not the theme of either Goffman or Yates: working with the facts of social survival, both writers deal with low-level deception only incidentally. Their fundamental concern is the struggling social self, and ridicule and social satire are thus only incidental to their work. The 'how' of impression management, rather than its morality, is the central concern in Goffman and Yates."[33] Goffman's and Yates's interest in human interaction was undoubtedly of a similar nature, and was a driving force behind their output as writers, but the written products—one a scientific study, the other a novel—were utterly distinct and reflected their differing standpoints. Burkitt argues that Goffman "does not distinguish between true and false selves,"[34] but Yates, I would suggest, makes this distinction clear.[35] Sociologists may attach no moral coloring to the observation of high self-monitors, that is to say, people who display a variety of selves, and low self-monitors, people who value consistency and do not alter their presentational self, but Yates's work does. His fiction abounds with people who adopt different roles and whose adoption of those roles is ironically undercut, and, by implication, criticized by the narrative voice. Exposing the diversity of roles male and female protagonists adopt, Yates's narrative position usually finds these people unstable, at the very least. More often, the protagonists are found to be fickle and insincere.

To claim that Yates was not interested in the morality of his characters' behavior is to miss the authorial irony behind his portraits of the socially ambitious, inauthentic, and misguided people he creates. What is true, however, is that Yates obfuscates rather than asserts a moral position. His moral compass is not firmly fixed in any one direction; rather, he explores the complexities of human interaction illustrating how first one position, seen from a particular perspective, elicits our empathy, but then, as the perspective changes, how our empathetic engagement shifts. Moral coloring informs all his work, but the authorial intention is centered on preventing simplistic, judgmental, and reductive assessments. The moral thrust of his work is, therefore, closely linked to the ability, or lack of ability, his characters show in objectifying and assessing their behavior. Yates doesn't write about perfect people anymore than he depicts moral vagrants. He is interested in ordinary people and in the various shades of gray that characterize their conduct.

The initial unfavorable portrait of Gloria Drake (*Cold Spring Harbor*), for instance, leaves the reader in no doubt as to her hopelessness: "Her very way of sitting suggested an anxious need to be heard and understood, and to be liked if possible . . . her clasped hands writhing to the rhythms of her own talk."[36] Her talkativeness is the dominant characteristic as she prattles on interminably, unaware of the inappropriateness of her behavior: "She was ready to give her heart away to total strangers off the street."[37] However, the reader, finding the portrait amusing, cannot dismiss her out of hand and cannot laugh out loud, for Yates determines that her loneliness and excitement are easy to recognize. This is typical of Yates's ironic humor; at the point of laughter, the inclination to scoff or smile is arrested by the introduction of a small detail that would make such a reaction inappropriate.

The reader might want to dismiss Gloria Drake, and certainly as the novel progresses it becomes harder not to, but Yates makes his portrait vibrate with her very human failings. Just as Evan, Gloria's future son-in-law, is ready to amuse his father with repeated impersonations of this unfortunate woman, Charles Shepard arrests the moment with portentous ceremony. The narrative slows in the manner of a cinematic still and, in a way that includes the reader, he rebukes his son: "He swirled the ice in his drink, took a sip, and put it back on the bar. Then he stood straighter and settled the fit of his suit coat with several smart tugs at the hem of it, as if it were a military tunic. 'As a matter of fact,' he said again, 'there's never been anything funny about a woman dying for love.'"[38] Yates's moral standpoint is clearly compassionate toward human weakness, and condescension of any kind is repeatedly exposed. In a similar vein to the bustling, well-meaning nosiness of Mrs. Givings in *Revolutionary Road* (a woman who has struggled with a psychopathic son who has attacked her), Gloria Drake must be accepted; to dismiss her is to be without any heart. Yates may set up his characters for mockery, but, as if he catches himself doing that, he will then arrest and challenge that view.

"Doctor Jack-o'-Lantern," from *Eleven Kinds of Loneliness*, illustrates moral complexity that is typical of Yates's style. A young zealous schoolteacher has her ideals for social integration and fairness—ideals that any reader might share—challenged by the behavior of a new arrival in her class. Vincent Sabella is an orphaned boy who, by his poverty and upbringing, is set apart from her middle-class charges. It is clear that Sabella excites Miss Price's "sense of mission."[39] The use of this rather self-important phrase is a gentle indication from Yates that her dedication and imagination may be overenthusiastic and misplaced. Despite Miss Price's well-intentioned attempts to integrate the child and promote him to his classmates—"I know we'll all do our best to make him feel at home"[40]—the reader squirms at her patronizing comments, knowing, in a way that she clearly does not know, that this will only make matters worse for Sabella. She is culpable of not listening to who and what Vincent Sabella is, a fact made abundantly clear in the task of establishing what he would like to be called. In answer to her question, what name would he like to be known by, he asks her to call him Vinny, and she persists in hearing only Vincent:

> "Vinny, I said," he said again, squirming.
> "Vincent, is it? All right, then, Vincent." A few of the class giggled, but nobody bothered to correct her; it would be more fun to let the mistake continue.[41]

The naïveté of Miss Price's kindness, and her albeit well-intentioned interventions, have made life at the school impossible for this boy: "he was well on the way to becoming the worst kind of teacher's pet, a victim of the teacher's pity."[42] While Miss Price thinks she is being encouraging in her warm and friendly overtures to this boy, Yates suggests that she is confusing him by singling him out. More than this, Yates implies her behavior is dangerous. Miss Price fails to register how damaged Sabella is, and while hoping to inspire loyalty, her words and actions will inevitably be interpreted by him in a sexual way, as they are by the reader. Through Sabella's eyes the reader witnesses a lunchtime chat between teacher and pupil and cannot fail to pick up on the sensuality of her movements: "Miss Price sat back more comfortably on the desk top, crossed her legs and allowed one slim stockinged foot to slip part of the way out of its moccasin."[43] And at the end of their talk, she "stood up and smoothed her skirt over her long thighs."[44] The fact that Yates merges these third person descriptions with Miss Price's conversational overtures suggests a degree of awareness on her part as to the effect she is having. She wants to be liked and uses her body to assist her in this aim. This is, Yates's narrative implies, perilously naive.

Sabella's subsequent sexualized behavior, as is revealed by chalk drawings on a wall, suggests that life has been complicated and tough for him. He has been subjected to experiences that don't accord with her ideal of childhood. Sabella is reproved for his deed, but the way he is punished makes matters even worse for him. Thinking that he doesn't understand the moral code her other pupils live by, she tries to befriend him further. She doesn't chastise him, as a new boy, as a welfare boy, in the same way as she would have treated her other pupils. Instead, she continues to personalize the relationship between them: "I almost wish I could be angry—that would make it much easier—but instead I'm hurt. I've tried to be a good friend to you, and I thought you wanted to be my friend too."[45] It is only when his fellow classmates think that Vincent has been kept behind to be told off that Vincent feels briefly accepted, a facade then destroyed as the teacher is so overtly friendly and so gushingly thrilled that finally these boys are "friends." For all that Sabella's actions are seen to be out of the norm, Yates's narrative suggests that Miss Price is the one most at fault. Without any malice, but with too much emphasis on her idea of *self* and what Yates refers to as her "well-intentioned groping in the shadows,"[46] Miss Price has sealed the fate of Vincent Sabella.

In his short story "A Compassionate Leave,"[47] Yates provides a master class in writing that explores moral uncertainty with its shifting perspectives and changing idioms. The soldier, Private First Class Paul Colby, whose actions and thoughts dominate the narrative, is young, American, virginal, and ill at ease with himself. The war is over but the occupying forces still have much to do before they can return home. Following a three-day pass to Paris with a fellow soldier, Colby takes compassionate leave from their camp near Rheims in order to visit his mother and sister, Marcia, in London; such are the bare bones of this story. Yates deftly shifts the reader's view of Colby as, with each new event, another aspect of his immature character and his background is revealed. Yates deliberately plays with reader empathy and deftly shifts the moral coloring of the narrative in order to show how extraordinarily complex it is for a young man, for anyone, in fact, to know themselves.

The reader might feel critical of Colby for the various roles he adopts—sneering at a fellow soldier, for instance, or lampooning the French and thinking all French women are available for sexual encounters with American soldiers—but a more empathetic response is encouraged when the details of his parents' careless behavior are revealed. The suggestion that Colby's mother's tears are fake when they finally meet up situates the painful fallout from his parents' divorce firmly in the present of Colby's story: "she seemed to be weeping but he couldn't be sure" and "having apparently dried her tears"[48] are phrases mimicking Colby's thoughts that indicate an unbridgeable distance between him and his mother. The reader is left pondering how any young man can learn the value of honest self-criticism with parents who rely on inauthentic performances themselves. In a manner similar to the presentation of Miss Price, it is never overtly suggested that Colby is any worse than anyone else—he could be any nineteen-year-old 1940s American soldier—but, as his weaknesses *and* his vulnerabilities are exposed, they create a composite, finely textured portrait of an inexperienced young man desperately trying, and failing, to live up to an ideal version of himself.

Yates highlights Colby's self-consciousness as he attempts to assess what impression he is creating when he meets up with his sister. The suggestion is that such self-awareness is partly the result of the unfamiliarity that has arisen between two siblings who have lived apart since they were young; it is also, more emphatically, indicative of Colby's character and his desperation to perform in the right way: "he kept secretly congratulating himself on how well he was doing."[49] Yates skillfully blends narrative that seems objective ("He rushed forward and enwrapped her in a great hug"[50]) with narrative that mimics Colby's interior thoughts ("and he brought it off well"[51]); this technique creates descriptive fluidity while at the same time adding depth and texture. However, Colby does register one mistake when he takes his sister for a drink and orders her a beer without asking her first what she might like. The narration, using his idiom, states, "apart from that he couldn't find anything the matter with his performance."[52] He has attempted to judge his own behavior by merely glancing at the superficial aspect of interaction, and therein lies the moral thrust of Yates's writing. Colby's actions are not malicious but are entirely wrapped up in self; it is this self-centeredness and the desire to hone "performance" that keep people poor in terms of self-knowledge and relationship.

Colby's sister, on the other hand, appears to encapsulate the kind of moral outlook that Yates would have his readers admire. Direct and brave as she evidently was in childhood, she is similarly forthright and bold as a young adult when she corrects the myths about herself. She admits to having given a false picture of her behavior: "God, I was *terrified* of boys at sixteen."[53] Furthermore, with the description of her boyfriend, she offers a challenge to clichéd, romanticized versions of masculinity—"He's sort of small and funny-looking"[54]—and offers an account of relationship that is based on solid rather than superficial values. Marcia's is a tender narrative that involves some measure of compromise: "I may not go to the States at all next year; I may go to Heidelberg because that's where Ralph wants to go."[55] Faithfully attempting to record the dynamics of social relationships in the mid-1940s, Yates is careful to show that the element of "sacrifice" is one-sided.

As far as Colby's behavior is concerned, the moral perspective of this story is framed by two fairly routine moments, and in the handling of these events Yates adds depth to his characterization of his protagonist. The narrative focuses initially on the shame a fellow soldier, Myron Phelps, is made to feel for giving voice to his relief at being away from the complexities of life, army or civilian: "We got fresh air, we got shelter, we got food, we got discipline. This is a *man's* life."[56] The camp is immediately filled with the sound of derisory laughter, Colby's included, and Phelps is made to feel ashamed and ostracized. Privately Colby recognizes that "he too had come to like the simplicity, the order and idleness of life in these tents in the grass. There was nothing to prove here."[57] His unspoken recognition of the truth of Phelps's remark, while all around him laugh at the man, encourages the reader to limit the sphere of their expectations for Colby. However, by the end of the story, Colby has been through so much that elicits reader empathy. Without telegraphing the purpose, Yates brings him full circle to a point where he is happy to be returning to camp and his evident relief mirrors Phelps's earlier remark: "Tomorrow he would telephone his mother and say he'd been called back to France, 'for duty,' a phrase she would neither understand nor ever question; then all that would be finished."[58] What Yates leads the reader to understand is that "all that" refers to the complex, messy, and frustrating business of being a man.

The reader is in no doubt that this young man has been through difficult experiences that have left him vulnerable and disappointed. However, by the end of the story we are told, "He walked a great distance alone after that, and there wasn't anything devil-may-care about it. The heels of his boots came down in a calm, regular cadence."[59] Yates leaves his reader to work out the metaphorical resonance of this prosaic description, but it is clear that Colby has abandoned the performative behavior that limited his potential in every sphere of his life. With characteristic understatement, Yates sounds the beat of a man slowly gaining self-knowledge.

4

Disrupting the Facade

5. Richard Yates, 1962. Taken to promote *Eleven Kinds of Loneliness*. Reproduced courtesy of Grace Schulman.

In sharp contrast to the number of inauthentic and self-absorbed individuals in Richard Yates's work—the high self-monitors, as Mark Snyder refers to them[1]—the reader only rarely encounters a low self-monitor, and they stand out as people apart. However, such characters are not exempt from the caustic gaze of this author and could not be described as heroic. Yates is always unsentimental in his portraits so that these figures also display unfavorable qualities, but they have an integrity lacking in the dominant Yatesian figure. John Givings in *Revolutionary Road* and Sergeant Reece in the short story "Jody Rolled the Bones" are a couple of notable examples of the obdurate low self-monitor in Yates's fiction. In ways that are distinct, both characters play critical roles in shaping the moral coloring of the stories we read.

As an institutionalized mental patient, John Givings has a freedom from the constraints of what is perceived as normal social conduct. Like the fool in King Lear he speaks with often-impeccable logic as he punctures a fragile social atmosphere by asking questions no one wants to address because to do so is to admit to the fact that there are performances being enacted. His uncomfortable truths act as a counterpoint to other views being expressed, ensuring that the reader remains outside looking in at the Wheelers and their friends with his bewilderment and his critical eye. His very presence causes a disturbance and he *appears* to be blithely unaware of this, but the reader gradually becomes more certain that the disturbance he causes is deliberate and constructed: "He was making a slow, stiff-legged circuit of the living room, still wearing his cap, examining everything."[2] His brazen speech and unpredictable movements, unconstrained by acceptance of the codes of politeness, mean that he is a dangerous presence, but not because he is mad; on the contrary, he seems to be ruthlessly sane and prone to wrong-footing everyone. The point is that no one knows how to read this apparently unselfconscious individual, and the tension he excites is palpable.

In response to April Wheeler's polite request that her guests sit down, Givings's behavior is bizarre and simple, threatening and childlike: "John removed his cap and laid it on one of the bookshelves; then he spread his feet and dropped to a squat, sitting on his heels like a farmhand, bouncing a little, reaching down between his knees to flick a cigarette ash neatly into the cuff of his work pants. When he looked up at them now his face was free of tension; he had assumed a kind of pawky, Will Rogers expression that made him look intelligent and humorous."[3] His behavior is de-stabilizing, and deliberately so. Yates describes him as having "assumed a . . . Will Rogers expression," not as "having" one, creating the impression, therefore, that Givings is playing a game that mocks them all. Perceiving that life is full of such shallow performances, Givings adopts his own. He is always several steps ahead of those who take their performances seriously, people such as his mother and the Wheelers.

Givings's hosts, as well as his mother, sense they are being derided, but they neither understand it nor do they know how to undercut it; he is too quick for them. They are variously described in poses of acute discomfort as Givings attempts to puncture the social facade and feeds back distorted versions of comments his mother had made earlier about the Wheelers. A comment such as "the nice young revolutionaries on Wheeler Road,"[4] for instance, captures the tone of her prattling idiom without being exactly what she will have said. He uses the phrase, giving the words a deliberately patronizing, sarcastic inflection, to ensure it disturbs the fragile social equilibrium. He repeats his mother's inane chatter and asks them implicitly to recognize his description of it: "You know how she is? How she talks and talks and talks and never says anything?"[5] To ensure that the reader understands the effect this man is having on the group, Yates depicts Givings's audience in various poses of awkwardness and embarrassment. April is seen later, "twisting her fingers at her waist,"[6] and at the earlier meeting between the two families, his mother is described as "sitting tense as a coiled snake on the edge of the sofa."[7]

Mrs. Givings tries to cut off John's rude remarks and intrusive questioning with gushing politeness and exclaimed observations that seem desperate and designed to distract and divert attention from her son: "Oh, and look at this magnificent *food*!"[8] and "Oh, *look*, the sun's coming out!"[9] To the dismay of those he is with, John Givings disrupts the performances they have carefully nurtured. Thus whenever he appears in the novel, there is always the same ghastly tension, as he cuts through the codified behavior. As Morris Dickstein observes, "He is brilliantly mad: grievously damaged but lucid, dysfunctional but clairvoyant . . . he is the tragic demon the suburbs are designed to repress, the bad news no one welcomes in this pastoral utopia."[10] For the reader the perspective of the author, who seems complicit with his "villain" because he too abhors the social performances required of him, complicates that tension. The point about John Givings is that he does not give a damn; he is not going to play their games, unless for his own amusement. In a society where affectation and performance form an integral part of what it is to be a success, a fact Givings knows only too well, he is seen as a failure. He is seen as such a threat to all the social codes that he must be locked away.

John Givings's attitude toward self-presentation is an interesting aspect of his resistance to the accepted social mores. His mother bemoans the fact that he will not wear the clothes she provides, for they are the clothes of the average middle-class man: "Week after week she brought him clothes of his own to wear—good shirts and trousers, his fine old tweed jacket with the leather elbows, his cashmere sweater—and still he insisted in dressing up in these hospital things. He did it for spite."[11] The irony is, of course, that if John Givings put on the middle-class uniform of American suburbia he *would be* dressing up, hence his insistence on presenting himself authentically. Toward the end of the novel the Givingses make another disastrous visit to the Wheelers' house. Emerging from the hospital for the trip, John Givings, as before, insists on wearing the uniform of a mental patient; his parents watch him adjust his appearance with deliberation and precision: "He carefully placed the cap dead-center on his head, and the picture of the public charge was complete. 'Let's go.'"[12] Again, Yates's use of the phrase "the picture of the public charge" suggests that Givings is completely alert to the image he has perfected. He *is* a public charge and so must appear as one, even if, for his parents, this is socially embarrassing.

The Wheelers have had a massive row and are completely unprepared for the family's visit. Everyone works extra hard to cover embarrassment—everyone, that is, except Givings. He has no patience with social niceties and cuts through the chitchat with his aggressive questioning: "'Listen,' John said, and all the other talk stopped dead. 'What's the deal, anyway? I mean I hear you people changed your minds. How come?'"[13] As the fact of the pregnancy is revealed, and it is generally accepted that they cannot go to Europe if April is pregnant, Givings arrests a conversation that has only just found its footing: "'Hold it a second, Ma,' he said, standing up. 'Hold it a second. I don't get this.' And he fixed on Frank the stare of a prosecuting attorney. 'What's so obvious about it? I mean okay, she's pregnant; so what? Don't people have babies in Europe?'"[14] The reader's experience of the exquisite logic and humor of this (why, indeed, can't she have a baby in Europe?) is swiftly forgotten as Givings's questioning becomes both more intrusive and more aggressive. The party breaks up when he is forcibly removed by his parents, but not before he has burrowed underneath the Wheelers' facade of marital harmony and outraged them all: "I wouldn't be surprised if you knocked her up on purpose, just so you could spend the rest of your life hiding behind that maternity dress."[15] Like the writer who created him, John Givings wants to disrupt false performances and expose inauthenticity. He smells Frank's duplicity and is determined to outwit someone who outwits others. Givings provides what Goffman calls "destructive information": "Given the fragility and the required expressive coherence of the reality that is dramatized by a performance, there are usually facts which, if attention is drawn to them during the performance, would discredit, disrupt, or make useless the impression that the performance offers."[16]

At the end of the novel, Givings's parents' visits to the hospital have diminished to one a month. It appears as though he has been replaced in his mother's life by a puppy. The implication is that society in general, and his parents in particular, can only function by giving him minimal attention. He is locked away not to protect himself but to protect a society that cannot deal with its illusions being destroyed. However, Yates refuses to sentimentalize Givings's position as an outcast and is at pains to present him as a thoroughly unlikeable character in order to avoid this. Castronovo and Goldleaf explain this important character's dual function: "he becomes a critic of weak people, as well as a part of the destructive chain of relations in the novel."[17]

Like many of his predecessors, Yates makes it clear that he never wanted to apportion blame or ascribe evil to any one character. Attuned to the moral ambiguity of life, his purpose is to reveal uncertainty, and by dramatizing it in his fictions, to show how life is far more complex than the binary opposition of good and evil suggests. Referring to two of his favorite novels, he draws attention to this in "Some Very Good Masters": "Another thing I have always liked about both 'Gatsby' and 'Bovary' is that there are no villains in either one. The force of evil is felt in these novels but is never personified—neither novelist is willing to let us off that easily."[18] And in an interview a few years earlier, he explains what he feels to be the reader's role in this: "I much prefer the kind of story where the reader is left wondering who's to blame until it begins to dawn on him (the reader) that he himself must bear some of the responsibility because he's human and therefore infinitely fallible."[19] While noting the audaciousness of including a character such as Givings in a novel written in the 1950s, Dickstein puts forward the idea that it "shows us how much even realist fiction has changed since the start of the decade. The mad seer is really a figure from the Laingian counterculture of the sixties."[20] There are several aspects to Yates's work that indicate that he was ahead of his time in the 1950s; giving validity to the utterances of a psychiatric patient is just one of them. In addition, he continually draws attention to the fact that discussions about the complexity of human behavior have to take place in an ethical gray area.

In "Jody Rolled the Bones" Yates depicts a further similarly unattractive and utterly ruthless individual who, like Givings, carries with him the air of authenticity. In a manner that prefigures the later story, "A Compassionate Leave," Yates's narrative style draws attention to the isolate, the person who speaks a truth the group doesn't want to hear. This story is an extended portrait of a platoon sergeant called Reece through the eyes of a young soldier. Reece is a stickler for detail, does not befriend the men in his charge, and keeps himself to himself. Discipline is everything to him, and he exerts a constant pressure on the men in his charge to do exactly as they are told, without argument: "He alienated us on the first day by butchering our names."[21] Reece is interested in them as part of a fighting machine rather than as individuals; for him as the consummate soldier, they are only as strong as their weakest man. Since he is so uncompromising in his attitude to the men, their respect for him, and understanding of him, is only arrived at slowly.

It is 1944, the men are doing basic training in a Texas army camp, and they fully expect that they will have to go to war. Reece begins to ease up on the men only as they learn to conduct themselves better. As their discipline improves and they value their individual selves less, they learn to like the framework he has insisted on: "But with our new efficiency at marching we got so that we *almost* enjoyed it, and even responded with enthusiasm to Reece's marching chant. . . . But now the chant seemed uniquely stirring, an authentic piece of folklore from older armies and older wars, with roots deep in the life we were just beginning to understand."[22] Yates understands how group mentality is a force unto itself, and this is an interesting feature of the story. The need to lose individual concerns is a necessary by-product. The soldiers cohere and are efficient, and, as the ending suggests, safe, as long as they work as a group and as long as they are in Reece's care. This is something that Reece alone understands: "It was *almost* a disappointment when he gave us route step on the outskirts of the camp and we became individuals again, cocking back our helmets and slouching along out of step, with the fine unanimity of the chant left behind."[23] The use of the word "almost" in both the sentences indicates Yates's unwillingness to sentimentalize the situation. These are seventeen- and eighteen-year-old boys, after all, and their reluctance to give in wholeheartedly is what makes this depiction seem so authentic.

The men learn to respect and even admire Sergeant Reece, and they become a good platoon as a result. The lieutenant in command, however, does not think highly of Reece, and toward the end of the story the men learn that Reece is to be transferred. A man who is his opposite in every way takes his place; that man befriends the men and is "a slack drill master."[24] Yates draws a careful distinction here between Reece's uncompromising presentation of himself, his honest performance, and the new platoon sergeant's more affected chameleon nature. Sergeant Ruby changes how he presents himself to suit the time and the context, so that when the lieutenant comes to talk to the men, Ruby adopts an authoritative and sycophantic attitude. He borrows the idiom of his troops in order to demonstrate how close they are: "I think I can speak fa yez all as well as myself when I say, Lieutenant, we're *gonna* play ball wit'you, like you said, because this here is one platoon that knows a Good Joe when we see one."[25]

Comedic though the narrative is, the reader cringes as Yates shows how Sergeant Ruby *displays* his authority over his men while ingratiating himself with the lieutenant; Yates's humorous moments are always swiftly followed by such uncomfortable realizations. For this shameless falsehood, Sergeant Ruby earns the derision of his troops, who "all began to make loud retching noises"[26] as soon as the lieutenant has withdrawn. His defense of his actions is the key to Yates's view of performative behavior: "'Whatsa matta?' he demanded. 'Whatsa matta? Don'tcha think he does it to the captain? Don'tcha think the captain does it up at Battalion? Listen, wise up, will yez? *Evvybody* does it! *Evvybody* does it! What the hellya think makes the Army *go*?'"[27] Although the men can now relax and even enjoy their new sergeant's company, they leave the army sloppy and unfit for fighting. The narrator makes it clear that they leave their training "a bunch of shameless little wise guys to be scattered and absorbed into the vast disorder of the Army, but at least Reece never saw it happen, and he was the only one who might have cared."[28]

Richard Russo writes about "Jody Rolled the Bones" in the introduction to *The Collected Stories of Richard Yates*, but he omits an important element in his analysis of it: "The young soldiers in the story may believe they've been unlucky to be drafted and even unluckier to be in the hated Sergeant Reece's platoon, but at least in the latter they couldn't have been luckier, because it's Reece who will make men of them, something these boys want without knowing it. What they *think* they want—an easier life at boot camp— could be deadly where they're headed, a fact they're blind to."[29] The point that Russo glosses over is that the narrator is no longer blind to this point of view. His present-day narration, reflecting on his experiences in the army, draws attention to his own naïveté as well as to that of the other young soldiers. In this way Yates subtly distances the reader's experience of Reece from that of the soldiers: "We were pretty naïve, and I think we'd all expected more of a Victor McLaglen—burly, roaring and tough, but lovable, in the Hollywood tradition. Reece was tough, all right, but he never roared and we didn't love him."[30]

While the narrator makes clear that the young soldiers are "shameless little wise guys"[31] and that "Reece bore the brunt of [their cockiness],"[32] the story's apparent focus is on the portrait of Reece as "a dumb Rebel bastard."[33] Through the narrator, Yates draws attention to the way a socially acceptable performance is expected, almost prescribed, and is based on recognizable models led by Hollywood images. That Reece never smiled "except in cruelty,"[34] and that he resisted all familiarity but was very much his own man, is something the young soldiers cannot adjust to. The older narrator, however, is dismayed by the realization of how immature they all were as young soldiers. The description of Reece's authoritarian regime and his demanding, even cruel manner is fairly straightforward, but the reader receives it with that word "naive" (from the first paragraph) lodged firmly in the mind; it sets up the expectation that a process of maturation has already taken place for the now older narrator.

Both Sergeant Reece and John Givings are obdurate, hard-hitting individuals, but they each have an authenticity about them that the narrator draws to the reader's attention; their honesty is derived from their self-confidence and the consistency of their sense of self. To achieve that solidity of character, Yates's narrative strategy is to avoid giving them interior thoughts, the implication being that they are as they seem since any such interior life would suggest self-consciousness and self-questioning not apparent in either man. They are, in effect, what they *say*, and there is no interior perspective to disrupt that impression. Their apparent strength is also derived from the weaknesses of those they operate among.

Yates sees the opposition between the authentic and inauthentic in the performance of individuals very starkly and in that sense creates characters whose lack of self-scrutiny suggests this contrast. J. D. Salinger took an opposite approach to a similar mode of inquiry in his novel *The Catcher in the Rye* (1951). While in Yates's work there are few authentic characters capable of self-criticism, Salinger's story is narrated, and dominated, by Holden Caulfield's sensitive, subjective, questioning voice. He is consumed not only by the inauthenticity of almost all those he describes but is also plagued by the sense that he too might have to adopt the phoniness he despises if he is to survive. Both writers, with their different modes of expression, adhere to the belief that there is such a thing as an authentic self, and both show how that "self" is under attack. Like Holden Caulfield, Givings and Reece are seen as outsiders and are removed from the society they inhabit. This might suggest that their true qualities are not easily recognized, and the terms by which the American society of the 1940s and 1950s operates preclude such characters from having a hearing or value. Even if those qualities come at a price in Yates's fiction, that is to say, the apparent harshness or rudeness of their manner, they should be accepted. However, Yates does not allow such sentimentality; the reading has to be tempered with the knowledge that Givings and Reece are unpleasant individuals, and Yates never permits us to think otherwise.

John Givings is not the only character who disrupts the facade of suburban happiness in *Revolutionary Road*. There is one very important character whose behavior appears to straddle the two extremes of self-critical awareness and self-absorbed blindness; adding great depth to the novel, Shep Campbell occupies a moral gray area. Yates creates a figure who has occasional flashes of insight into the sham harmony of suburban living. Although he feels himself to be in love with April Wheeler and is, therefore, just as susceptible to romantic ideals as anyone else, eventually he has the ability to look honestly at his own behavior. Campbell cries over the death of April Wheeler at the end of *Revolutionary Road* but stops when he realizes he is "forcing his sobs."[35] Yates's own voice then emerges strongly to make his point clear: "The whole point of crying was to quit before you cornied it up. The whole point of grief itself was to cut it out while it was still honest, while it still meant something."[36] This is a theme explored throughout his fiction. Occasionally it is given humorous inflection, as when Lucy Davenport mocks Bill Brock's self-absorption: "Have you ever noticed . . . how your sympathy for someone's story . . . tends to evaporate when they get to the part about how long and hard they cried?"[37] Grief, like laughter, can be performed, a fact that Lucy's withering reflection suggests. As we have seen elsewhere,

Yates was fascinated by the way honesty and performance challenged the individual. He was attuned to the fact that the truth of an emotion is easily corrupted by sentimentality, self-interest, or a desire to be seen to do "the right thing," but only very particular characters notice such falsity, and when they do it is never incidental.

The determining characteristics of Yates's low self-monitors set them apart from the group and render them akin to social misfits who critique society but are not accepted by it. Yates, like many writers, felt that this described his position, a feeling that only intensified for him as he struggled to get published. The qualities these low self-monitors show in varying degrees—directness, honesty, and integrity, for instance—are more usually absent in typical Yatesian characters who display fluctuating identity and weak moral backbone. It is easy to speculate as to why Yates's characters are such weak individuals, but as his readers and his critics have observed, he is almost always writing about himself. While he captures his writer/self as a man who stands apart from the crowd in order to observe it, this man is never an attractive figure nor is he successful. A good indication of how he saw himself as a writer and as a man comes in *Young Hearts Crying* in the character of Carl Traynor. Lucy Davenport assesses Traynor's work: "There could never be fifteen books in this uncertain, mistake-making, self-pitying man. . . . He might die early or late, but he would die knowing that except in a single novel he had nothing to say."[38] It is clear to Yates's readers that Traynor is one in a long line of excoriating self-portraits, a failing writer with a poor outlook. In addition, Yates depicts his social self as weak and heavily reliant on alcohol, a man both attractive and flawed in ways that almost always characterize his protagonists.

The reader of a Yatesian tale is carefully maneuvered so that the characters' faults are absorbed along with highly realistic settings and with the trappings of modern existence as exposed as their personalities. In all his work Yates shows how the performative behavior of his protagonists is revealed on many levels. Superficial performances, such as the way his characters dress or decorate and arrange their houses, are overlaid by careful scrutiny of the way they behave, the way they use language, and the way that they often cynically manipulate others. Finally, Yates probes and exposes the deeper emotional performances that they give or struggle to give. Like Erving Goffman, Yates's view of human behavior is determined to a great extent by the understanding that people are almost always performing. Unlike Goffman, Yates does not see this as a precondition of existence, but sees it emerge as a manifestation of people's aspirations and their inclination to romanticize both their lives and their *selves*. In Yates's work, therefore, the reader occasionally meets low self-monitors who appear to be authentically themselves.

Yates had his own performative behavior, which was evident in his style and mannerisms. In his biography of Yates, Blake Bailey makes careful note of the writer's habitual appearance: "Yates seemed to cultivate a lack of sophistication. . . . he always wore the same daily Brooks Brothers uniform: tweed jacket, blue button-down shirt, gray flannel or khaki trousers, desert boots, a rumpled trenchcoat in cold weather, and for special occasions the tailored suit he'd bought in London."[39] Furthermore, Bailey makes the point that Yates's lifelong addiction to cigarettes was part of a bigger pose: smoking for him was "the purest form of adolescent affectation, a way of looking—at last—somewhat masculine and grown up."[40] Bailey sees Yates's smoking habit as a mask or shield behind which the young writer could hide his self-consciousness: "Yates was rarely seen outside the classroom without a butt dangling off his lip, and clearly he looked forward to the day when he'd never have to abstain at all—never have to leave his round-eyed vulnerable face exposed without a smoke screen to squint behind."[41]

Echoes of the behavior Bailey records are unmistakable in Yates's most autobiographical novel, *A Good School*. With comedic effect, Yates describes how protagonist Bill Grove is at great pains to perfect his smoker's performance. That it is a performance is never in any doubt as Yates recalls and lampoons his own youthful folly: "First he had to learn the physical side of it—how to inhale without coughing; how to will his senses to accept drugged dizziness as pleasure rather than incipient nausea. Then came the subtler lessons in aesthetics, aided by the use of the bathroom mirror: learning to handle a cigarette casually, even gesturing with it while talking, as if scarcely aware of having it in his fingers; deciding which part of his lips formed the spot where a cigarette might hang most attractively—front and profile—and how best to squint against the smoke in both of those views."[42] Itemizing the details of Grove's self-conscious attempt to capture a certain look in the mirror highlights a trope evident in much of Yates's fiction: as noted earlier, mirrors, and the images they throw back to the gazer, assert a challenge to fixed notions of reality and fixed notions of selfhood. The reader of any work by Yates will be left to contemplate that challenge.

Richard Yates's characters do not always choose their performances wisely and often find their conception of themselves, and others, undercut by their audience. With Goffman's dramaturgical metaphor in mind, Yates's work reflects the fact that the role of the performer and the role of the audience are inextricably linked; the one sustains, or destroys, the other. It is this fascination with performative behavior that lies behind Yates's frequent use of the movies as a metaphor and as a model for his characters' behavior. The growth of Hollywood and the promise of wealth, status, and fame that were part of this industry seep into his fictional lives and blur the edges between fact and fiction, reality and dream.

Robert Ezra Park suggests how we grow into our performances of selfhood: "In a sense, and in so far as this mask represents the conception we have formed of ourselves—the role we are striving to live up to—the mask is our truer self, the self we would like to be. In the end, our conception of our role becomes second nature and an integral part of our personality. We come into the world as individuals, achieve character, and become persons."[43] How easy he makes it sound. Richard Yates's fictional lives reveal a far more complex progression through life; the performing self often wears an ill-fitting mask and spends his life trying to adjust it, but without the ability to objectify himself, he has no success. Screen idols, and the films that give them a platform, provide Yates's protagonists with clues about how they might behave, about what constitutes relationship or romance, and, most ironically of all, about the nature of authenticity.

5

Influences and Contrasts;
Change and Continuity

6. In the dining room at Babaril in
Mahopac, circa 1958.

In John Barth's novel *The End of the Road*, published a year after *Revolutionary Road*, the reader is immersed immediately in an unrecognizable world, a world without definite contours. While Richard Yates's work attempts to describe the world as he knows it, Barth makes it clear, with his subtle repositioning of the relationship between author, narrator, and reader, that his aim is to challenge or ask questions of his reader rather than to suggest answers. He does this from the start, in a playful manner. The opening sentence of *The End of the Road*, "*In a sense, I am Jacob Horner*,"[1] appears to parody the opening lines of *The Catcher in the Rye* (1951): "If you really want to hear about it, the first thing you'll probably want to know is where I was born"[2] Adopting J. D. Salinger's intimate, truculent tone, but moving into an even more uncertain psychological landscape, Barth's narrative pivots around an exploration of the problematic idea of identity. Even naming itself is difficult as the novel opens with italics, which suggest the provisionality attached to this basic act.

Yates also interrogates and challenges his reader by creating endings that remain open-ended, but Barth goes further and weaves such questioning into every layer of his narrative. Barth's protagonist, Jake, for instance, finds a room to rent and then inverts all the norms of human behavior by trying his best to fail to "qualify" for its rental. Barth is deliberately experimenting with the idea of overturning recognizable performances. He is challenging the idea that one can understand the human psyche by thwarting expectations at every turn:

> It was too perfect and I was skeptical.
> "I guess I should tell you that I practice on the clarinet," I said. This was untrue: I was not musical.[3]

By providing the reader with something of a tabula rasa, Barth can inscribe almost anything onto this character, and he does. Jake is totally unable to make a decision that does not have an equally attractive counterdecision. His first person narrative wars with his irresolution and the rereadings of any given situation for he cannot decide which performance to give. Paralysis of the mind results in immobility, and he becomes inert, directionless, opinionless, silent as a blank space, in short, a nothing. His is a characterless character because, with no ideas about the parameters of his individuality, he cannot make a decision as to how he should project himself. In this novel, the reader is presented with a bizarre series of existential musings on the nature of existence, essence, and choice, none of which are really resolved. Tony Tanner observes that "if there is no one fixed 'reality' then the self can improvise a theoretically endless succession of roles to play *in* the world, just as the author can invent an 'endless succession of names' *for* the world."[4]

Barth, unlike Yates who strove constantly to describe the "real" and the "actual," resolves his character's problems with playful irony. While one doctor has advised Horner that as a cure for his paralysis he should take up the teaching of grammar (denotative of rules and systems), the other encourages him to take up role-playing or Mythotherapy. The doctor describes what he means in the following terms: "Mythotherapy is based on two assumptions: that human existence precedes human essence, if either of the two terms really signifies anything; and that a man is free not only to choose his own essence but to change it at will. Those are both good existentialist premises."[5] As Tanner points out, the doctor is suggesting that "Rather than allowing the self to be defined by the situation it happens to be in. . . . He should become . . . his own mythologizer, and always be ready to adapt his myths and roles to cope with a new situation."[6]

Although Yates would not have upheld this existentialist position, he did explore the insubstantiality of the self and wove it into his portraits. He observed it, however, in a radically different way, as Morris Dickstein suggests: "There could hardly be a writer more different from Barth than Richard Yates. At a time when the realistic aesthetic was waning, or simply migrating from literature into film and television, Yates emerged as one of the last of the scrupulous realists."[7] While Yates's fiction relishes the exposure of affectation, Barth's work suggests we are all always "playing"; notions of performance, therefore, are not so much exposed as observed. Again, through the voice of the doctor, the reader is given some clearer indication of Barth's views, not only on performance but also on writing itself: "all fiction and biography, and most historiography, are a lie. Everyone is necessarily the hero of his own story."[8] He continues, "So in this sense fiction isn't a lie at all, but a true representation of the distortion that everyone makes of life."[9] Yates could never have shared the degree of levity implicit in this view; he believed in the redemptive and instructive power of literature to describe and explain life, life that is as painful as it is real.

Jake's first person narration allows for detached, cynical humor, which gradually takes on a darker and darker aspect as the narrative unfolds. Yates rarely used this form, preferring instead the narrative control afforded by an objective eye, albeit one that moves in and out of mimicking his characters' viewpoints. However, the use of the first person narration was crucial for Barth. Unlike Yates, he was able to weave the sense of the insubstantiality or partiality of characterization into the form and go way beyond what is suggested by Yates's exposé of the performative behavior of his characters. At root, Barth suggests the unstable nature of all truth, a view that has implications for the fiction writer. Again, through the voice of the doctor, and with an apparent flippancy designed to disturb or, at least, challenge his reader, he addresses this issue: "But since no man's life story as a rule is ever one story with a coherent plot, we're always reconceiving just the sort of hero we are, and consequently just the sort of minor roles that other people are supposed to play."[10] It is therefore appropriate that at the end of Barth's novel, wrestling with notions of identity in ways that Yates's characters cannot, Jake wants to go out into the world and *pretend*, if he can, to be a whole person: "In a new town, with new friends, even under a new name—perhaps one could *pretend* enough unity to be a person and live in the world."[11]

It is curious, but entirely consistent with Yates's view of himself as a failure, both socially and as a writer, that if the ill-at-ease, vulnerable young men of

his fiction are all versions of himself, they are not simply presented as figures who are misunderstood but rather as characters who consistently mis-
understand the verbal and nonverbal signals of others. Yates was not alone
in exploring the psychology of failure. F. Scott Fitzgerald in almost all his
fiction, but particularly in his Pat Hobby stories; John O'Hara in his short
stories and novels; John Updike, most notably with Harry Angstrom in the
Rabbit series of novels;[12] and J. D. Salinger in the character of Holden Caulfield, all display an interest in the seductive aspects of failure. These writers
depict protagonists who negotiate the society they inhabit from a weak position. They provide a new version of the man in the wilderness, an isolate
looking in on a society whose notion of success is unavailable to them. Their
work provides a dialectic critiquing advertisements and films that suggest
the ease with which an American middle-class man can hope to acquire a
wife, two cherubic kids, a mortgage, and life in the suburbs; this was the territory that Yates also claimed.

J. D. Salinger marked out some of this territory in *The Catcher in the Rye*.
Published ten years before *Revolutionary Road*, Salinger's novel also critiqued
middle-class performativity, but his explorations are seen through the eyes
of a lone adolescent. Although very different in structure, this was an approach Yates partly adopted in two novels, *A Good School* (1978) and *Cold
Spring Harbor* (1986). In both cases, he avoids the full use of Salinger's first
person narration, taking on its immediacy but, always avoiding the heroic,
resisting its intimacy. In the *Ploughshares* interview, Yates referred to the fact
that "[Salinger's] first two books had an enormous impact on me, as they
did on just about everybody else at the time."[13] That impact is clear to see,
not only in the subject matter but also in the quizzical, humorous tone the
younger writer adopted.

If Yates avoids the creation of heroes, Salinger does not, but Holden Caulfield is a hero with many flaws. Filled with disgust for the world as he finds
it, he is also appalled by himself and the way he too is given to false behavior
and sentimentality. He visits his old history teacher prior to his early departure from school and finds the only way to deal with the man's hectoring
questions is to be as phony as everyone else: "So I shot the bull for a while. I
told him I was a real moron. . . . That kind of stuff. The old bull."[14] He demonstrates as he contradicts himself that his version of events, as well as his
assessment of people, is as unreliable as everyone else's: "I'm the most terrific
liar you ever saw in your life."[15] Nevertheless, the reader is enchanted by this
narrator as much for his sensitivity as for his vulnerability, for his manners
and his willingness to do the right thing: flattering a mother about her dull

son; helping a child put her skate on in the park; giving a charitable donation to two nuns; and giving his sister his time, attention, and love.

Yates's protagonists could never be described as charming the reader in the same way. In his first description of Bill Grove (*A Good School*), for instance, it is to Grove's unkempt appearance and lack of cleanliness that he draws our attention: "The kid was a mess. His tweed suit hung greasy with lack of cleaning, his necktie was a twisted rag, his long fingernails were blue, and he needed a haircut."[16] Rather than attempting to beguile his readers, Yates seeks to shake us out of our comfortable myopia, as if he feels that we have all been brought up sanitized and raised to overlook the unpleasant, even revolting details of human existence. He supplies those details.

Where Bill Grove's and Holden Caulfield's experiences overlap, and where their characterizations ensnare the reader most profoundly, is in their loneliness. The reader is made to contemplate absent parents in both cases. Boarding school may contribute to the situation for the protagonists, but the authors suggest a bigger problem; parental love is constrained by distance but lack of understanding and poor communication create more profound problems. After a lecture from a teacher about his poor work, Grove slopes off to his room: "Alone in his room, Grove sat on the edge of his bed for a while trying to think of nothing—he often did that—."[17] This bleak image is entirely in step with the mood Salinger creates. Caulfield's narrative is punctuated throughout by explicit or implicit references to his loneliness and sense of exclusion: "After he left, I looked out the window for a while, with my coat on and all. I didn't have anything else to do."[18] Both writers make use of the isolation of their protagonists to create observers, individuals who look on from their place of exclusion. Drawing on their own experiences of life as disaffected teenagers, Salinger and Yates create vivid, textured portraits of young men struggling to perform.

John O'Hara is also a natural precursor to Yates. Similarly interested in small-town American communities, hidebound by form and made constantly uneasy by gossip, O'Hara's characters are likewise unstable and self-destructive. Despite Prohibition, they, like Yates's characters, escape through alcohol and infidelity into a version of themselves and of life that ultimately destroys them. O'Hara's first novel, *Appointment in Samarra* (1934), concerns itself with the downward spiral of its main character. Julian English is a college-educated owner of a car dealership. A series of impulsive, illogical acts destroys any vestiges of decorum or status he may have had in the middle-class community of Gibbsville. The man he most despises, his nemesis Harry Reilly, has money, status, and respectability that English both covets and condemns. It is interesting to note that the relationship between these two characters is of a similar order to that described by Yates in *Young Hearts Crying*, where Michael Davenport looks at Tom Nelson with jealous contempt. Both O'Hara and Yates use the device of closely opposed characters to indicate what constitutes success in middle-class, East Coast America as well as to indicate how others view success. While O'Hara's comparisons are quite generalized, Yates provides a more intimate comparison of characters as he highlights the minutiae of performative behavior.

In O'Hara's novel, it is in many respects English's inability to reconcile two contradictory attitudes to the middle-class way of life that leads to his suicide. English cannot abide Reilly's self-glorification and watches him with increasing irritation. Through English's eyes the reader watches and experiences that performance: "Reilly told stories in paragraphs. While he was speaking he would lean forward with an arm on his knee, like a picture you have seen of a cowboy. When he came to the end of the paragraph he would look quickly over his shoulder, as though he expected to be arrested before he finished the story; he would finger his tie and close his mouth tight, and then he would turn back to his audience and go into the next paragraph: 'So Pat said . . .'"[19] Just as Yates's narration of *Young Hearts Crying* has Davenport at its center, and the reader is, therefore, more attuned to his perspective, O'Hara similarly asks us to engage with the battling underdog by keeping English at the center of the narration.

Although an investigation of performance may not be John O'Hara's prime objective in this novel, Harry Reilly's social routine, his presentation of himself as a jocular Irish raconteur, holding the floor and constantly demanding attention, is behind the protagonist's violent action to shut him up. In that respect, Harry Reilly's performative behavior is a narrative springboard from which Julian English jumps. English's subsequent action, throwing a glass full of alcohol and ice into Reilly's face, has a chronotopic function in this text as, time and again, it is referred to by both English and other characters who look back upon it as a pivotal moment. Providing an analysis of the artistic chronotope and its effect on space and the passage of time, Mikhail Bakhtin explained its function: "Time, as it were, thickens, takes on flesh, becomes artistically visible; likewise, space becomes charged and responsive to the movements of time, plot, and history."[20] As if illustrating the "thickening" of time Bakhtin describes, O'Hara removes the narrative pace and energy from the telling of the critical incident the reader never sees. Time is slowed, almost halted, as the reader notices that the band is playing "Something to Remember You By" at the beginning of the incident's narration; the same tune is playing five pages later when normal time is reestablished and English's brave and reckless act is recounted: "The band was playing Something To Remember You By. . . . when Johnny Dibble suddenly appeared, breathless. . . . 'Jeez,' he said, 'Jeezozz H. Kee-rist. You hear about what just happened?'"[21]

That O'Hara does not depict this incident but shows its inception in Julian's thoughts and then reports it, with all attendant drama through the voice of another individual, gives it the greatest possible emphasis for the reader. Indeed, the effect of this incident is drip-fed to the reader so that it is well over a hundred and fifty pages later that we learn of the damage to Harry: "The ice apparently had smacked his cheekbone, and the pouch of flesh under the eye was blue and black and red and swollen."[22] The narrative pulse of this novel is marked out by this one event and given energy by subsequent bleak episodes. It serves to emphasize how far English is sliding out of control, no longer able to abide the form and codes that govern the small-town society of Gibbsville.

O'Hara's narrative technique is one that Yates also adopted. O'Hara shifts seamlessly from the use of a third person narration ("Harry Reilly was telling a dirty story in an Irish brogue . . .")[23] into narration that mimics English's thoughts ("His clothes were good, but he had been born in a tiny coal-mining village, or 'patch,' as these villages were called").[24] The use of "but" here is the subtle indicator that the reader is privy to English's thoughts. It reveals his snobbish irritation at a man who has improved himself socially and financially to a point where he has far exceeded Julian English's power in the community. Like Yates, O'Hara was an acute observer of behavior, as this passage reveals, describing through English's eyes the mannerisms of people held in thrall by Reilly's stories: "It was funny to watch people listening to Harry telling a story. If they took a sip of a drink in the middle of a paragraph, they did it slowly, as though concealing it. And they always knew when to laugh . . . because Reilly signaled the pay-off line by slapping his leg just before it was delivered."[25] The reader is held transfixed by Julian English watching others watching Harry as O'Hara's narrative layering conveys the interwoven performances; this layering technique was later adopted and developed to great effect by Yates. The comparison between O'Hara and Yates is not an original one, for it did not go unnoticed by his contemporaries and was mentioned by Sam Lawrence, Yates's one-time publisher, at his memorial service: "He wrote the best dialogue since John O'Hara, who also lacked the so-called advantages of Harvard and Yale. And like O'Hara he was a master of realism, totally attuned to the nuances of American behavior and speech."[26]

While Yates's stance in exposing Frank Wheeler's pretensions as a frontiersman is unequivocally negative, John O'Hara took a more ambiguous

view of a similarly inauthentic display in his short story "Pardner." The protagonist, Malloy, stops his car at a restaurant for a coffee and a sandwich before continuing his journey back to New York. A "boy who appeared to be
of high-school age"[27] (but who we learn actually owns the restaurant) inflicts
himself upon Malloy and physically occupies Malloy's personal space; questioning Malloy about the smart car he is driving and sitting down at Malloy's table, "the kid" is clearly an irritant. His clothes, Malloy notes, "were
awful";[28] along with his gold jewelry, all carefully itemized, they are sharp,
gaudy, and cheap. Gradually, however, almost imperceptibly, Malloy becomes
less irritated and more amused by the boy's performance as a young, snappy,
wealthy restaurant owner with the attendant bravado and mannerisms: "'The
usual, M'rie,' the kid said. 'You sure you won't have something?'"[29] Before he
knows it, Malloy's reception of the boy shifts from a desire to "slap the kid's
face" to a performance that matches the boy's insufferable bumptiousness.
The reader is in no doubt that Malloy has entered into, and is relishing, a fictional account of his own life. He claims to own a ranch and to have struck
oil. Borrowing the idiom of the hard-living cowboy, he invests his narrative
with the romantic coloring of a clichéd pioneer story: "Sleeping under the
stars. The old chuck wagon comes along about once a week. It's the only life."[30]

What interests me about this story is the way Malloy's performative behavior develops. He sustains a performance of his own artificially realized
"frontiersman's" dream, possibly to amuse himself or to compete with the
kid's big ideas, or possibly because he is just irritated. Nevertheless, there is
also a shade of compassion to his performance; he never laughs in the kid's
face for believing him nor does he embarrass the kid by revealing that he's
duped him. O'Hara suggests a notion of performance-to-protect, to keep
this young man's dreams full of energy and hope, irritating though they may
be to the more mature man. Maybe Malloy sees himself in this young man.
For whatever reasons, there are wonderful descriptions of Malloy relishing his theme and warming to his adopted role; even his wife's name, Sallie
Lou, sounds, with its double construction, as if he's reached into a lexicon of
Southern names to suit his story. The name he chooses for himself, equally
loaded with irony, is Humber Phillips (for the reader, this is only a shade off
Humbug—or even Humbert Humbert[31]—either way, the unreliability of the
narrative is being highlighted). Yates rarely shows his protagonists in such
a compassionate light and only infrequently suggests that performance can
protect (a moment such as Charles Shepard's comments about Gloria Drake
suggests not *all* false performances should be ruthlessly uncovered, for instance). In Yates's work, performance is predominantly exposed and held
up for criticism.

The comparison between Yates's fiction and that of his near contemporary, John Cheever, is often drawn, but their style, narrative voices, and characterizations are markedly different. While the force of Yates's fiction is felt through the reader's immersion in the lives of characters destined to fail and is dependent on a sense of the immediacy and ordinariness of their predicaments, Cheever, in his short stories and novels, remains a detached observer of characters he regards with quizzical interest rather than condemnation. Eccentric figures people his stories and behave in fascinating, odd ways. In "The Swimmer," for instance, a young man, Neddy Merrill, who is presented like a latter-day Gatsby to begin with, and who "might have been compared to a summer's day, particularly the last hours of one,"[32] makes the bizarre decision to swim home, a trip he will undertake via a long list of other people's swimming pools. As the tale unfolds, it becomes clear to the reader that Merrill is undergoing a complete breakdown. Metaphorically speaking, despite his own sense of himself as a pioneer, he is trying to reclaim a lost past. The oddness of the conduct of all those he encounters is as nothing compared to his own bizarre and ever more manic behavior; that initial description with the phrase, "particularly the last hours of one," increasingly haunts the way we perceive this man.

Richard Gray, writing about *The Wapshot Chronicle*, describes Cheever's work as, "an account at once wistful and comic of a wealthy but declining Massachusetts family" and goes on to draw particular attention to his "comic melancholy."[33] It is the comic melancholy that clearly distinguishes Cheever's work from Yates's fiction, since it is arrived at through a detached but humorous tone that Yates never employs. Gray quotes Cheever's perplexed observation that "in this most prosperous, equitable, and accomplished world . . . everyone should seem to be disappointed."[34] The fiction of both writers suggests their interest in the pervasive sense of disappointment that marks the lives they describe, but the tone they adopt is distinct.

Unlike Yates, Cheever frequently addresses his reader directly, drawing attention to the fact that this is a fictional construction, that people behave in odd ways, and that he takes delight in bringing forward the idiosyncratic habits he describes in *The Wapshot Chronicle*: "The house is easy to describe but how to write a summer's day in an old garden? Smell the grass, we say. Smell the trees!"[35] The immediacy of the style is dependent on the energetic, conversational intimacy that foregrounds the writer's task. It is as if Cheever is urging the reader to step closer: "Hear what Aunt Adelaide has to say."[36] Again Cheever addresses readers directly and creates the impression that, puppet-like, his readers and characters can be brought together. By implication, the reader is invited to drop in, eavesdrop, and be amused. In sharp contrast to

Yates's technique of immersion, Cheever's quizzical tone suggests a distance from the sorrows and struggles he describes. The robust, secure voice of the narrator in traditional realist fiction, or the narrator who makes a point of stepping forward as in some of Cheever's work, is replaced in Yates's work by a narrative that imitates a plethora of voices seeking to diminish the role of the omniscient narrator but not quite eradicating him.

While these two authors explore similar territory, literally[37] and metaphorically, their narrative methods are also very distinct. Yates concentrates on recording a particular time and a specific place, honing in on the precise detail and shading of a scene, whereas Cheever generalizes and embraces a wider view. At the beginning of the novel, Cheever creates the means by which the effects of time passing can be experienced when, via a bolting horse, the reader is able to survey the whole town. As Mr. Pincher's horse rushes off, pulling the Women's Society float with Mrs. Wapshot and others aboard, Cheever describes the people, the buildings, and the scenery. This overview of the town (which reads like a swift and intimate historical tour), affords an opportunity to locate and assess change: "Now, past Mrs. Drinkwine's and over the crown of the hill, the west of the village spread out below them—farmland and woods and in the distance Parson's Pond, where Parthenia Brown had drowned herself and where the icehouse, useless now, stood with its ramp sloping down into the blue water."[38] Thus the sweeping eye of the narrative acts like a camera with a wide-angle lens taking in information that no one eye could reasonably have seen. The jauntiness of the telling belies the seriousness of the message; all these places have a history that relates to people and to real lives lived.

In contrast to Yates, therefore, Cheever is interested in charting change and time passing. He is at once mourning the loss of old customs and codes of behavior and, by implication, belittling those who cling to them. In his stories the past is at once nostalgically remembered (worthy of being upheld as a means of recording historical connection and preserving beauty) *and* is dismissed as outmoded, as is suggested by the conduct of adults who cling to its patterns and codes. However, the fact that history has an importance for the present is made abundantly clear. In *The Wapshot Chronicle* it is understood that not to take account of the past, its stories, its quirkiness and attachments, is to live in a cold mechanized present such as is offered by Remsen Park with its anonymous names, Circle K and Circle M. It is a diminished place because it has no history. There the unfriendly faces and the hostile, commercially dominated environment stand in stark contrast to St. Botoloph's where everyone has a clear identity and a role; even the peeping Tom is accommodated and cared for. On the other hand, there are those, like the dominant elderly women, Honora and Justina, who alongside Leander, stubbornly refuse to embrace change and whose implacability provides the novel with much of its comic force. The past haunts the characters and their present actions, suggesting it is not always understood and its lessons not always learned. Helen Rutherford, Leander's daughter by his first wife Clarissa, is the human embodiment of this as she comes to find her father. She turns up filled with bitterness, accusation, and self-righteous anger. The biblical sounding, "I'm your daughter"[39] is followed by "God will be your judge."[40]

Yates's characters are more firmly entrenched in the present of his narratives, looking to the future but rooted, living and often *stuck* in the present. Their nostalgia for the past, if they show it at all, is frequently exposed as being for a past that never existed. Just as Emily Grimes has to correct her sister's view of the past, Frank Wheeler's self-deprecating joke telling involves reminiscences that sound utterly false; historical accuracy does not inform his outlook: "And he began to tell them how he had spent it, or part of it, pinned down by mortar and machine-gun fire in the last week of the war. One small, cold-sober part of his mind knew why he was doing this: it was because humorous talk of the army and the war had more than once turned out to be the final salvation of evenings with the Campbells."[41] Yates's protagonists are people who believe that they, and they alone, can shape their futures based on what is frequently proved to be a rewritten version of their past and misplaced confidence in their own present abilities. Although it is clear to the reader, for instance, that the reason April Wheeler wants to go to Europe is so that she can capture some ephemeral dream and enjoy her now-deceased parents' past happiness, she thinks she wants to go there because of the opportunities it will present to her and Frank. While she is blind to her real needs, what propels her is essentially an "honest," if deluded, sense that she can scrape away the froth of life and by doing so make things right for herself and her family. Her needs, however, remain those of a small emotionally wounded child brought up by an aunt, a child who is still longing for her parents to return from Europe to claim her. This is a time frozen for her in a photograph she shows Frank of when they are first courting: "a yellowed, leather-framed photograph showing both parents, tall and elegantly dressed beside a palm tree, with the inscription *Cannes, 1925*."[42] Even in his characterization of April, therefore, Yates shows people are largely incapable of the kind of self-awareness that will protect them as it informs them. Dreams are compensation for the lives they feel cheat them *and* a spur to affect a change to those lives. Without any basis in reality, those dreams remain unrealizable, out of reach and ephemeral.

Kurt Vonnegut Jr. was both a friend of Yates's and someone whose work

Yates greatly admired. Vonnegut's work was a rare exclusion, therefore, from his dismissal of what was termed *postrealistic fiction*: "The one exception I'd make is Vonnegut, who is often—mistakenly, I think—placed among the 'post-realists.' The difference is that there's real fictional meat in his best work, despite the surface flippancy of his style—real suffering, real passion, real humor."[43] Vonnegut, in his short story "Who Am I This Time?," also takes a play as his central metaphor to pose questions about human behavior and the nature of human interaction that echo Yates's earlier inquiries. The story describes a director's attempt to find actors for his production of *A Streetcar Named Desire*. His leading man is predetermined; there is in their small community a young man who, though shy and awkward in life, can assume the mantle of any character convincingly. He is only confident when he is performing as someone else. Indeed, the premise of Vonnegut's story is that for certain people, there is no self outside performance, a premise similar to John Barth's in *The End of the Road*.

Vonnegut's narrator, the director of the play being described, speaks with a jaunty tone and jocular voice that belies the seriousness of his observations. The reader is informed that he has only previously directed "the installation of combination aluminum storm windows and screens."[44] Where Vonnegut leaves that seriousness unexplored, hovering in the background of a playful narrative, Yates hones it. A Yatesian figure who suffers from acute shyness is shown fumbling and stumbling for words that elude him, and, if found, diminish him, whereas Vonnegut's narrator quips that Harry Nash, his lead actor, "stayed away from all kinds of gatherings because he never could think of anything to say or do without a script."[45] Unlike Yates's work, Vonnegut's story ends with some kind of resolution; the plaintive note sounded by Nash's question, "Who am I this time?"[46] is replaced by a sense that he and his new wife have found a modus vivendi together as she says, "Who are we this time?"[47] The suggestion is that Nash, a clerk in a hardware store, and the leading lady, stunningly beautiful but, by her own admission, "a walking icebox,"[48] can share a life, playing roles that *free* them: "I've been married to Othello, been loved by Faust and been kidnapped by Paris. Wouldn't you say I was the luckiest girl in town?"[49] Performance here is not colored by moral judgment but is a necessary way of finding connection with others, and it enables the characters to develop a role in the community.

In his portraiture, Yates's work rarely shows the compassion of either O'Hara or Vonnegut, though shadows of it emerge implicitly in his depictions of some women. The desire to expose the propensity to be taken in by the inauthentic, shallow, and self-regarding performances of others is Yates's aim throughout all his work. Although his narrative position does not vacillate between empathy and criticism but concentrates on exposing again and again how the characters prop up their own ideas of themselves, characters who are at the same time often attuned and sensitive to the performances of others, the reader is never able to fully dismiss the individuals described. We must recognize the painful truth that the faults of the Wheelers and the Campbells, for instance, are also our own; were they simply social misfits, Yates's first novel would have made very little impact. In his review for the *New Republic*, Jeremy Larner expressed the power of *Revolutionary Road*, pointing up its sociological significance: "To read *Revolutionary Road* is to have forced upon us a fresh sense of our critical modern shortcomings: failure of work, education, community, family, marriage . . . and plain nerve."[50] He was not alone in holding this view. On reading the first full draft of the novel in May 1960, Yates's early publisher, Sam Lawrence, specified the novel's universality in his editorial report: "Frank Wheeler is the prototype of thousands of young Americans who have been in the war, got married too early, began a family by mistake, taken a job which they are indifferent to, and then try to make their lives and marriages work."[51]

With the deftness of a writer who understands exactly how to employ his narrative voice, Yates manages to elicit an empathetic response from his readers so that the tragedy of the characters' lives has maximum impact. If we were able to dismiss these characters as mere types, as Anatole Broyard thinks we might, there would be no tragic force to this book. Broyard, in his essay about Yates's novels in 1984, questions "whether we are being asked to see around, or beyond, the characters to some kind of symbolism—or to take them literally" and goes on to interrogate Yates's position: "Is his perspective metaphysical or entomological?"[52] The implication is that Yates has failed in a duty to the reader because his intentions are not clearly either one or the other. But as Richard Ford intimates, what Broyard suggests is a weakness is in fact one of this novel's greatest strengths: "by allowing two strategies of representing reality to share time, Yates brought to life all the more remarkable a novel; brought us—through art—near enough to life's palpable details that we can recognize our own lives, yet preserved for us a distance from which we can exercise judgment and be relieved that the Wheelers aren't us."[53] The narrative of *Revolutionary Road* skillfully takes us behind these characters and, as it were, into them; the reader stands back from them, as Yates does, and "inhabits" them at one and the same time. It is for this reason that Blake Bailey talks of Yates achieving a kind of double vision: "Yates achieves this kind of double vision—though some would call it inconsistency—with a limited omniscient viewpoint that shifts from character to character, then at apposite moments becomes godlike."[54]

The narrative layering noted in O'Hara's work is a device Yates borrows, but he learns his literary techniques primarily from his heroes, F. Scott Fitzgerald and Ernest Hemingway. Their fiction, and Fitzgerald's in particular, often relies on a doubling of perspective as they examine the social complexities of an earlier age. Malcolm Cowley describes this narrative technique in Fitzgerald's work: "Fitzgerald lived in his great moments, and lived in them again when he reproduced their drama, but he also stood apart from them and coldly reckoned their causes and consequences. That is his doubleness or irony, and it is one of his distinguishing marks as a writer. He took part in the ritual orgies of his time, but he kept a secretly detached position. . . . Always he cultivated a double vision."[55] In *The Great Gatsby* Fitzgerald builds this doubleness into the structure of his novel by filtering the experiences of the text through the narrative eyes of Nick Carraway. We receive everything he sees but do not always experience it in the same way. When Tom Buchanan, for instance, somewhat forcefully asks Nick to admire his landscaped garden, "a sunken Italian garden, a half acre of deep, pungent roses, and a snub-nosed motor-boat that bumped the tide offshore,"[56] Nick, as a character rather than as the narrator, makes no additional comment. This silence on his part is ambiguous since it could mean that he is too inhibited to comment, and at the same time it could suggest his distaste for what he is being shown. For the reader, however, there is no such ambiguity of response; the adjectives, while observant of the garden's impressive grandeur, are dismissive of it in every other way. The reader is struck by its suffocating ugliness and its imposing artificiality and is unable to miss the foreboding references to drowning that emanate from the words "sunken" and "deep."

Similarly, and again at a point early on in the novel when Nick is uncritical and still somewhat overawed by all he sees, he describes Jordan Baker reading aloud from the evening paper to her husband: "the words, murmurous and uninflected, running together in a soothing tone. The lamplight, bright on his boots and dull on the autumn-leaf yellow of her hair, glinted along the paper as she turned a page with a flutter of slender muscles in her arms."[57] Ostensibly a description of connubial harmony, the reader receives it otherwise. The light catching Tom's boots emphasizes the violence that simmers beneath his surface manners. Similarly, Jordan's languid page turning seems to the reader, if not to Nick who makes no observations and seems almost effaced, designed to highlight her slender, feminine, and artfully sexualized arms. She is neither reading for meaning nor to disseminate information but simply for effect. With subtle irony, Fitzgerald conveys the three layers of experience of a moment held: the Buchanans', Nick's, and the reader's. He also conveys so much about the milieu in which the Buchanans and their friends exist, for even though the war has only been over three years, it is now a vague memory and no news is taken seriously. The outside world does not impinge on their self-obsessions, on their little pool of light. Nevertheless, the idle, rich, beautiful young people of the 1920s held an attraction for Fitzgerald as they people all his fiction. He was drawn to them and at the same time highly critical of them. Cowley describes this duality succinctly: "It was as if all his fiction described a big dance to which he had taken . . . the prettiest girl . . . and as if he stood at the same time outside the ballroom, a little Mid-western boy with his nose to the glass, wondering how much the tickets cost and who paid for the music."[58] Nick Carraway's gentle inquiry, and process of self-discovery, personifies the position of that young midwestern boy.

While Yates's ironic stance is less "secretly detached," to borrow Cowley's phrase, and more overtly critical of those who peopled his age, his method of exposure is undoubtedly similar to Fitzgerald's. Yates acknowledges his debt as a writer to Fitzgerald, T. S. Eliot, and Gustave Flaubert in "Some Very Good Masters" and details particularly what he learned about the specifics of his craft from Fitzgerald: "Every line of dialogue in 'Gatsby' serves to reveal more about the speaker than the speaker might care to have revealed. The author never permits his use of dialogue to become merely 'realistic,' with people exchanging flat, information-laden sentences, but contrives time and again to catch all his characters, however subtly, in the very act of giving themselves away."[59] The technique he alludes to goes beyond irony to acknowledge that the way we receive information, the behavior and speech of those around us, is always determined by the "I," be it the "I" of the reader, or author, narrator, or character; meaning is shaped by the interconnection of all these different "I's". Couched in the framework of what is essentially realist fiction, with recognizable settings, linear development of action, and speech that attempts to mimic the shape of natural conversation, Yates does not explore the nature of the "I/eye" in the way of postmodernist writers, such as Jorge Luis Borges, Alain Robbe-Grillet, or John Barth. Nevertheless, his use of narrative layering is a move in a direction they explore more fully. We are constantly reminded that Yates is not interested in the playful or absurd, in the political or the theoretical; an authentic depiction of human experience is at the heart of his creative endeavor.

Writing nearly thirty years before Yates, Nathanael West satirically portrayed a man utterly lost, having discovered for himself the basic insincerity of his "assigned" role. In his novel *Miss Lonelyhearts*, the male protagonist, Miss Lonelyhearts, is seen more often than not as reluctant, immobilized, and unable to function in the society he inhabits: "He stopped reading. Christ was the answer, but, if he did not want to get sick, he had to stay away from the Christ business."[60] The dramatic irony of West's story hinges upon the fact that the reader never learns Miss Lonelyhearts's real name or who he really is; he can only function as an assumed self. The protagonist, having shed his assumed character, has a total collapse and cannot continue without assuming a new role as a devout and incoherent lover of God.

With a characteristically abstracted tone, Miss Lonelyhearts notes that "Man has a tropism for order. Keys in one pocket, change in another. . . . The physical world has a tropism for disorder, entropy."[61] This observation is at the heart of West's second novel. Man is always fighting that tropism to disorder and entropy but finds no meaningful way of doing it. Miss Lonelyhearts is trying to find a "performance," a sustaining belief, and a belief in himself that will support him but finds only corruption, cynicism, and aggression. Even though West writes with apparent levity, interspersing poorly written letters and orgies of violence with the protagonist's contemplative thoughts, the point is a serious indictment of modern life. Miss Lonelyhearts bounds from one scene to another, meeting, even engendering, hostility or, conversely, sentimental dreamers, wherever he goes. Fusing the comic and even absurd scenes of Miss Lonelyhearts's life with a disquisition on the struggle to live meaningfully when there is no apparent depth to anything, and objects have more vitality than humans, West gives this novel its unique power. As Richard Gray notes, West's "is a world stripped of meaning: where there is a play of surfaces and nothing else."[62] Although Yates's work asks questions about how humans behave and posits some rationale for decisions they might make, West, as Gray points out, takes an altogether more abstracted view of society: "West was writing here on the borderline between Modernism and postmodernism: negotiating a move from art as explanation, a source of redemption or redress, to art as a game, a verbal playfield."[63]

Erving Goffman characterized the cynical position that West's protagonist adopted when he wrote about those who believe in their own performance and those who do not. When an individual plays a part he implicitly requests his observers take him seriously; those who look on have to believe he possesses the attributes he appears to possess. But there are those who are not taken in by their own routine and who may be acting for a whole variety of motives: "When the individual has no belief in his own act and no ultimate concern with the beliefs of his audience, we may call him cynical, reserving the term 'sincere' for individuals who believe in the impression fostered by their own performance."[64] It is the understanding that he *is* taken seriously, and the understanding that he advises people about grave situations, that has crippled Miss Lonelyhearts and made him question everything: "He also discovers that his correspondents take him seriously. For the first time in his life, he is forced to examine the values by which he lives. This examination shows him that he is the victim of the joke and not its perpetrator."[65]

West concentrates on existential questioning, mocking the many myths by which humans have found meaning and purpose in life. His protagonist's bleak realization that "Men have always fought their misery with dreams"[66] is at the heart of this story, as is the recognition that those dreams "have been made puerile by the movies, radio and newspapers."[67] As West develops a mode of inquiry that looks at the psychological and social effect of such dreams, Yates's work examines the dreams themselves in all their puerility. Similarly, West skirts over the more prosaic details of the lives he describes, whereas Yates immerses his readers in the minutiae of the day-to-day lives of his characters. While disassociation is a feature of both modernist and postmodernist writing, Yates's work depends on a profound *association* between the reader and the narrative. The reader must feel a deep connection with April's pain, for instance, to feel the full force of the tragic ending and must briefly occupy, or at least feel able to occupy, the Wheelers' social space in order to feel the full force of the intrusive and acerbic comments John Givings makes. The achievement of that level of empathy, balanced by a similar measure of distance, was the essence of Yates's narrative skill.

Inevitably, not everyone shares that view; the most frequent criticism of Yates's work suggests that he was at too great a distance from his characters. In his article "The Lost World of Richard Yates," Stewart O'Nan includes a comment Robert Wilson made in the *Washington Post*: "Yates does not go wrong when his nostalgia flirts with sentimentality . . . problems arise when he moves too far in the other direction, distancing himself from his stories by showing too little sympathy for the characters. . . . When the suburban housewife of *Revolutionary Road* kills herself while trying to abort a child, it is shocking and sad, but without the emotional impact it would have had if she were a character about whom we felt more strongly."[68] The total absence of authorially directed empathy at the most dramatic moment in the text is precisely what gives this novel its power and its strength. Yates resists using the tools of sentimentality and demands that the reader take stock and absorb the experience of other's lives at a realistic distance that, by implication, acknowledges the divide between the fictional and the real.

One should understand that Yates's contribution to the investigation of performative behavior is rooted in his own milieu. He seeks to develop work undertaken by earlier writers but to locate his work, as they do, in the particular environment in which he lived. Edith Wharton and Henry James, for instance, both displayed a similar interest, but their characters were located in the specifics of the American upper classes, those who traveled, those who had connections, and those who had money. With the development of sociological inquiry, the naturalists and realists of the early twentieth century were able to move away from the ballrooms, parlors, and gentlemen's clubs of Wharton's and James's form of realism. As Nancy Bentley suggests, "The professional study of culture was established during just this period in the disciplines of anthropology, sociology, and social psychology."[69] As a result of these new modes of inquiry writers could develop their own methods of investigating human interaction: "it was exactly that social self that had become a new object of scientific interest. Patterns of social habit and convention emerged as 'second nature,' a reality to be stripped away and awaiting its own yet to be discovered causal laws."[70]

For West or Barth, notions of "reality" were inimical; Jake Horner, for instance, highlights the role-playing involved in life as he experiences it. Here, struggling with Joe's inexhaustible questioning, he says he feels satisfied, "at my ability to play a role that struck me as being at once somewhat abhorrent and yet apparently ineluctable. That is, I felt it to be a role, but I wasn't sure that anything else wouldn't also be a role, and I couldn't think of any other possible roles for me anyhow."[71] It is clear that for Barth the writer cannot *investigate* the nature of performance or role-playing but can only play creatively with the roles available; his fiction reflects the sense of life as a game, albeit it a serious and even dangerous one. Yates, on the other hand, takes his characters behind the closed doors of the kitchen and bedroom to describe their most private performances as a way of trying to transcribe the real.

That "reality" is not overtly political, nor does it engage deeply with popular social movements of his time. Jack Kerouac, a direct contemporary whose popular novel *On the Road* was published four years before *Revolutionary Road*, in 1957, was not admired by Yates. Kerouac's meditative style and Beat Generation social politics were anathema to someone who valued the structures and techniques of traditional literature and who, by and large, was conservative in his views. Jealously aware of the popularity of Kerouac's second novel, Yates weaves his scorn for it into a conversation between Lucy and Michael Davenport. After Laura leaves Tonopac to go to California and live the life of a hippie, Lucy calls Michael to tell him: "She wants to bum round with all the other dirty, smelly little vagabonds *on the road*—any road, anywhere."[72]

Looking at the influences that shaped Yates's writing, the links between his work and F. Scott Fitzgerald's are perhaps the strongest. Both authors take time to reflect on dreams of a better life, but it is the writers' own experiences that ensured their work was distinct. Kurt Vonnegut, comparing the two, suggested that Yates "was a more careful writer than Fitzgerald, and one who was even more cunningly observant."[73] He points out that Yates's milieu was not nearly as attractive as F. Scott Fitzgerald's or Ernest Hemingway's: "Unlike them, he did not and could not run away from middle-class life in America. So that is what he wrote about. And, like another outsider, Tennessee Williams, he celebrated the utterly unglamorous gallantry of Americans who had not and could not amount to much."[74] This is to understate the case. Yates's world is one of bars and dingy apartments, of dowdy homes and breaking relationships, ensuring that he focuses on the grim aspects of life with glamour well out of his characters' reach. As Castronovo and Goldleaf express it, "he makes the pursuit of the glimmering prospect a matter of pathetic selves pursuing vanishing horizons."[75]

Similarly exploring the similarities between Fitzgerald's dreamers and Yates's, Richard Russo suggests that since for both writers a world war had just concluded with America victorious, "Everything seemed possible except failure."[76] But he, too, is specific in his description of how their perspectives differ: "Perhaps because they have vivid memories not just of the war but also the Great Depression that preceded it, Yates's dreamers are less audacious, more cautious. They want things as badly as Jimmy Gatz, but they have less in the way of expectation. . . . Dream big and we're expected to fail. . . . Dream small, Yates seems to suggest, and we're expected to succeed. As a result, failure ensures not just disappointment, but humiliation, anguish, and, most dangerous of all, the impulse to dream smaller next time, thereby risking even greater failure."[77] Yates addresses overtly and ironically the connection between his dreamers and those of Fitzgerald in his short story "Saying Goodbye to Sally"; he knew exactly how people who pursued Hollywood glory were perceived. Although Yates invoked images of Hollywood in much of his fiction, this story is particularly apposite to an examination of the power and influence of the film industry in the 1950s and early 1960s. While Fitzgerald's protagonists appeal to the romantic, and their dreams of grandeur, wealth, and the perfect woman intoxicate and excite compassion as they fail, Yates's protagonists are never able to seduce readers. Since the author always takes a critical stance toward those he describes, the reader can never receive them uncritically. That the reader must also recognize something of himself in those "pathetic selves" and those "vanishing horizons" has made the reading of Yates an uncomfortable activity; as the characters have their dreams slowly dismembered, so too does the reader.

Tracing the path of the writers who influenced Yates, one returns time and again to his personal summary of the literary education he had in a hospital in his twenties.[78] It is no surprise that the dominant influences come from Ernest Hemingway and F. Scott Fitzgerald, but the figures of Henry James, Anton Chekhov, Gustave Flaubert, and T. S. Eliot also loom large. In addition, John O'Hara and John Cheever have to be credited as being part of the cultural literary handshake that Richard Ford so eloquently describes.[79]

6

The Writer/Character

7. Yates looking out the door of the
pump house, circa 1958. Courtesy of the
Richard Yates Estate.

In Richard Yates's fiction we see a recurring fascination with the role of the
writer in American suburban society. He is fascinated by the promise of status, independence, and material success as much as he is frustrated by the
writer's inability to deliver any of those things in spite of hard work and commitment to an ideal. For Yates there is no hint of triumphalism, no suggestion that the terms of his artistic endeavor are in any way extraordinary, and
no suggestion that either he or indeed his writer/characters have achieved
anything unusual. He reflects his pessimistic and somewhat misanthropic
perception that people are flawed; not only are his writers not exempt from
these flaws, but also *their* imperfections are the most egregious. However,
the fact remains that in their attempt to shape and order the ravages of life,
and the reality of their *own* lives, writers are gently applauded whether they
can be said to make a difference or not.

Drawing very closely on his own biography, Yates's mid-twentieth-century
characters live for the most part on the East Coast. Like Alice Munro's stories
(although there are many dissimilarities in the way the details of their lives
are used), Yates's work might now be called *autobiographical fiction*. Yates did
not feel there was anything remarkable or difficult about mining and remin-
ing aspects of his own experience or about writing his own character into his
work as long as he didn't slip into sentimentality and nostalgia. Each time

the reader finds narrative overlap in plot, theme, or character trait, there will be subtle shifts that render the event unique. Among the many tropes that align Yates's fictions with his biography is the figure of the writer/character.

Yates's artists and writers are predominantly self-deluded, self-centered individuals who display a mediocre talent at best. In a world where they appear to value so little, they nevertheless nurture that talent and are wholly absorbed by it, usually to the detriment of all other considerations. Consistently, his writers make a stand against postmodernism in a fight *against* frivolity and *for* the serious business of a modern form of social realism. In Yates's fiction, his writers offer the only form of consolation available in the hard process of living. Redemption is not available, but there are fragments of hope and chinks of light, to borrow the central metaphor from his short story "Builders";[1] those fragments are attached to creative endeavor and writing in particular.

In his essay "The Performing Self," Richard Poirier addresses the performance the writer gives as he sets about his task. He describes the writerly act as performative in ways that accord with Yates's style, but while this is described in Poirier's essay in the manner of a revelation, or as an astute criticism, in Yates's work the writer's performance is assumed from the start. Poirier illustrates his ideas about the "performing self" by looking at the work of authors—Robert Frost, Henry James, and Norman Mailer—who witnessed and then transformed in their work real events (though, of course, this was not all they did): "I can't imagine a scene of whatever terror or pathos in which they would not at every step in their account of it be watching and measuring their moment by moment participation. And their participation would be measured by powers of rendition rather then by effots of understanding."[2] Yates does not do this. He may insert himself, as a writer, into his fictions, and in that sense he performs as Poirier describes it in his essay, but he is performing on a fictional stage and not recording events from life. Furthermore, his efforts of understanding are always central to his narrative perspective. The public acts Poirier's writers imaginatively describe do not accord with Yates's themes.

In Poirier's opinion, the writer's public performance has a built-in arrogance and self-satisfaction we would have to look hard to find in Yates's life or work. Poirier's writer makes a self-conscious act of presentation, "spruce, smiling, now a public man, [as he] gives the finished work to the world."[3] To illustrate this, Poirier later talks of the poet Robert Frost being, through his verse, "suddenly transformed into something other than the man we knew at the outset. His voice becomes of no age or place or time celebrating its liberation into myth."[4] Yates, on the other hand, emphasizes not this elevation of himself, or his writer/characters, but their depletion and partial efforts.

Within the home, the whole family suffers in an effort to preserve the artistic ideals of typical Yatesian authors. For the reader, it usually becomes very hard to see why since it is their mediocrity as writers that Yates foregrounds and their flaws as individuals that he dramatizes. Yates's fictions act as both symptom and diagnosis when assessing his problems with writing; with his negative perception of himself to the fore, he presents in fictive terms, with dramatic force, characterizations of writers whose flaws recognizably mimic his own. His dependence on drink and his mental instability, for instance, are characteristic of his protagonists as much as they are features of his own life.

The extent to which Yates's truncated education was a significant contributing factor to his evidently low self-esteem is also given emphasis by angry, scornful male voices in many stories. For instance, it is a recurring feature of John Wilder's breakdowns in *Disturbing the Peace*. In his characterization of Wilder, Yates mocks his own deeply felt resentment. However, not having gone to the right schools, read the right books, or attained the right qualifications were a permanent source of irritation to him. As a result, Yates's creative ability is compromised by his suspicion that his talent may be mediocre and his audience small, and these frustrations are carried over into his depiction of writers. In addition, within his fictions, his attitude to the kind of college education many successful contemporary writers had enjoyed was confused and unresolved; he was suspicious of it and jealous of it at the same time.

Cold Spring Harbor moves obliquely into the realms of a debate about the subject of education. Evan Shepard, encouraged by his young wife-to-be, sets his sights at college in order to study mechanical engineering. However, Rachel's pregnancy arrests their dreams of a better life. Yates makes it clear that Shepard's feckless character is as much to blame for his stalled ambition as the pregnancy that quickly follows this second marriage. By contrast, Shepard's first wife, Mary Donovan, freed from a relationship that by implication diminished her and constrained her, flourishes at college. In this exchange between them—they have become lovers again—two aspects of Yates's attitude to education are made clear:

> "I *like* being single, you see. I like the freedom of it and the way it keeps teaching me new things about myself. I suppose that's an attitude I learned in college."
>
> "Yeah, well, and so what the hell else did you learn in college? How

to read all these fucking books? How to make your bed six inches off the fucking floor?"[5]

Shepard's scorn exposes his view that for women and girls domestic life should supersede intellectual life and that nothing of any practical value within the home can be learned from books. However, Shepard's position is made more complicated by the increasingly contemptuous attitude he shows toward his naive, ill-educated young wife, Rachel Drake; she lacks exactly what Mary Donovan now has.

That Mary and Evan's positions are oppositional and that Evan Shepard's thoughts are contradictory are typical features of this author's attempts to illustrate debates of his time. Marriage and a diminished education were inextricably linked, for men *and* for women. If men were to consider returning to college their wives needed to support them, which ruled out having children. Yates cannot reconcile the irreconcilable, so both positions have dramatic impact. In his view, college education opens doors to an independent life for all students, especially for girls who are constrained by their gender, but it also contributes to the creation of an upper class that looks disdainfully at those who haven't had similar opportunities. In this way Yates exposes the artistic ambition of his fictional writers as he painstakingly appears to dismember his own.

Yates's most caustic social satire is saved for his portraits of writers. As Blake Bailey points out, "Tellingly or not, Yates . . . tended to be hard on characters based on himself."[6] Therefore, his male characters are often struggling writers who wrestle not just with life and art but also with their own fallibility. This is expressed in their mental fragility, a propensity for self-aggrandizing dreams, and their tendency to destroy themselves in a haze of alcohol, cigarettes, and the explosive arguments of failing relationships. While there are exceptions to this "rule" it does, nevertheless, stand as a blueprint for the Yatesian writer, as Maria Russo indicates: "As for writers, they may be the saddest of all Yates' characters, with their refusal ever to admit to failure, their embarrassing secret fantasies of fame and honor, their vain, impotent hopes of being the next Hemingway or Fitzgerald, their bluster about 'moving to Paris to write.'"[7]

Like Hemingway's writer/characters, Yates's figures are particularly vulnerable sexually, but while both writers interrogate ideas about masculinity through the prism of sexual dysfunction, the consideration the two authors give to impotence is quite different. Hemingway explores the effects of sexual incapacity on a man's self-confidence very directly in his characterization of Jake Barnes: "I was pretty well through with the subject. At one time or an other I had probably considered it from most of its various angles, including the one that certain injuries or imperfections are a subject of merriment while remaining quite serious for the person possessing them."[8] With a first person narration, Hemingway is able to indicate the gap that exists between the private and social performance in an understated way. He indicates that the "subject of merriment" among friends is a painful burden Barnes has to shoulder: "It is awfully easy to be hard-boiled about everything in the daytime, but at night it is another thing."[9]

Yates's writer/characters are not all impotent but frequently suffer from some form of erectile dysfunction that saps their confidence socially as well as sexually. As will become evident, they tend not to reflect on this in the manner of Hemingway's figures. They are almost always in denial, externalizing their frustrations and blaming their partners. However, Michael Davenport, reflecting on his poor performance with Mary Fontana, sounds as gently wistful as Jake Barnes: "If he couldn't be a man for her, at least he could be a character."[10] It is always clear in Yates's fiction that for his male writers success is an aphrodisiac. Failure has its own sexual repercussions. That Yates's writers are so often unsuccessful is the reason for the predominance of impotence in their characterizations.

Yates's narratives are all imbued with a deep sense of failure, which Jerome Klinkowitz locates in the pervasive disappointment of his characters: "Both Yates and his craftsmen-characters are sensitive observers and geniuses with language; their worlds, however, yield only disappointment, and persevering in such circumstances pushes the novel of manners to new limits beyond the more accommodating subjects of James, Wharton, and Fitzgerald."[11] It is true that Yates's writer/characters are sensitive, but their sensitivity is almost exclusively toward their own needs. Acutely aware as they are of their own failings, they are rarely sensitive to those around them. Furthermore, Yates shows these characters in the process of *becoming* adept with language; they are not, as Klinkowitz suggests, "geniuses with language" from the beginning. Interested in the developmental process, as is evident in a story such as "Builders," Yates is alert to the sacrifices that need to be made to hone the skills of a true writer in the way that he conceived of the role. However, Klinkowitz is right when he points out that Yates "pushes the novel of manners to new limits." In Yates's hands, the novel has become a finely tuned investigation into how social and cultural manners have become self-centered personal performances learned from popular culture; for Yates, the performances *and* the culture are found wanting.

That Yates's writer/characters are united by the disappointment of their ambitions, however, is not in doubt. The recurring figures of dysfunctional

mothers with an artistic streak, or hapless schoolboys in ill-fitting clothes bewildered by the loss of their fathers through divorce or premature death, are
a testament to Yates's desire to work something out on the page from within
himself first and foremost. He wants to find an aesthetic style and form that
would allow him to accomplish this and to manipulate the reality, the facts,
to suit the story he is telling. An astute chronicler of emotion, Yates creates
scenes, complete with all the attendant ugly or merely prosaic details, that
accurately enhance or reflect the human drama. The description of Frank
Wheeler going to Maureen Grube's apartment provides us with a clear example of such scene setting; by getting the scene right, with the addition of
many visual or sensory details, Yates can then give full attention to the complexities and subtleties of emotion: "Then he was following her hips up a dim
carpeted stairway, and then a door had clicked shut behind him and he was
standing in a room that smelled of vacuum cleaning and breakfast bacon
and perfume, a high, silent room where everything lay richly bathed in yellow light from windows whose blinds of split bamboo had turned the sun
into fine horizontal stripes of tan and gold."[12] The attention to Maureen's hips
propels the narrative focus, as they propel Frank, toward its sexual conclusion, but the details of the smells that linger in her dingy apartment as well
as the yellow light that removes any suggestion of youth, clarity, romance,
or energy ensures the reader understands Frank's conquest is more squalid
than romantic.

In Yates's work, dreams of writing and dreams of escape are often inti-
mately linked with Paris, the idealized romantic city, seen as the favored des-
tination for creative individuals. Clearly, for Yates, Paris is the city where
many of his literary heroes met and developed as writers, so there is a sense
in which the *author's* nostalgia for an earlier time and place is written into
the novel, and it is one of very few details of his fiction that dates it. Thus, in
Revolutionary Road, there may be a touch of self-mockery in Yates's inclusion of Frank Wheeler's wistful suggestion that it would be easier for him
to go to Paris if he were a writer or an artist: "Might make a certain amount
of sense if I had some definite, measurable talent. If I were an artist, say, or
a writer, or a—"[13] And April's response is designed to guide our reading of
this: "Oh, Frank. Can you really think artists and writers are the only people
entitled to live lives of their own?"[14]

Frank's comment is mediated through several different perspectives since
the reader may be aware that this was a romantic dream for Yates himself
and is aware that Frank, whose work was always likely to be "'in the humani-
ties' if not precisely in the arts,"[15] is unlikely to be creative, ever. It is finally

experienced through a growing awareness that Frank has no real interest in going to Europe; this is just another self-interested objection to his wife's plans to reinvigorate their marriage. Morris Dickstein, who writes of *Revolutionary Road* as an antiroad novel, summarizes the layers of perspective and Frank's private aversion to any thoughts of escape: "'Paris' is Frank's road, his dream of escape, but this is a road novel in reverse, with the hero secretly unwilling to go anywhere, except to the next rung of the corporate ladder. For Frank, bohemianism is the pipe dream still cherished by his wife, since it made him the man who first attracted her; she is the keeper of his earlier self, with which he has secretly lost faith . . . he maneuvers his wife into a suburban domesticity that shields him from his own sense of diminished horizons."[16] Those "diminished horizons" are as characteristic of the writer as they are of his protagonists. Yates's own determination to be accepted as a writer reminds us that his frustrations and experiences inform the lives of *all* his writer/characters. His heightened sense of the ridiculous rarely fails to include his own personal ambitions as if he catches himself taking such ambitions too seriously. For that reason, their dreams and delusions are relentlessly lampooned.

One of Yates's first investigations into the role of the writer comes in "Builders," a short story from *Eleven Kinds of Loneliness*—the only one of the collection written after the publication and success of *Revolutionary Road*—and it is unusual on many levels. Not only is it a rare foray into the first person narrative, but it also has a veneer of levity in tone that is absent in most subsequent work.[17] With the protagonist's obsession with Ernest Hemingway in mind, Yates deliberately seeks to emulate the tone of Hemingway's reflective first person narratives so that the narrator speaks in a confessional, casual manner, drawing the reader into his confidence to share his reactions. He chose the first person narrative in order to draw attention to his own progression from dreamer and romantic to a highly reputable writer, a writer who was not averse to showing the hollow pretensions of those around him alongside pretensions and vanities he recognized in himself. Maria Russo draws attention to this: "As hard as he is on writers in general, Yates spares himself least of all. In fact it's in the three stories that most clearly use autobiographical elements that Yates is at his fiercest and most devastating, as if he's entered into a calm fury of anti-heroic truth telling."[18] In that respect the wry manner of this narrative is that of someone looking back at a naive version of his younger self. It is almost as if Yates decides to walk a literary tightrope.[19] He incorporates ideas about the instability of the first person narrator into this story and explores them; the inclusion of incidental details that make up the whole destabilizes any idea of narrative certainty and makes more ambiguous and problematic the effort to glean a message, a clear moral, or any kind of redemption.[20]

It is clear early on that "Builders" is a story as much about self-discovery as it is about writing. Bob Prentice adopts a tone that is gently cynical about his youthful ideals and romanticism: striding out to work each morning, "I was Ernest Hemingway reporting for work at the *Kansas Star*."[21] In a sense his maturity is measured by the degree to which he is able to relinquish his desire to emulate Hemingway and find his own style. Like Yates himself, Prentice, a slow, highly self-critical writer, produces little: "But it was here, of course, under the white stare of that lamp, that the tenuous parallel between Hemingway and me endured its heaviest strain. Because it wasn't any 'Up in Michigan' that came out of my machine; it wasn't any 'Three Day Blow' or 'The Killers'; very often, in fact, it wasn't really anything at all, and even when it was something Joan called 'marvelous,' I knew deep down that it was always, always something bad."[22] The analogy with Hemingway develops through the course of the story until eventually, as he matures and learns more about himself, he states with the whimsical tone of someone looking back at past follies, "With Hemingway safely abandoned, I had moved on to an F. Scott Fitzgerald phase; then, the best of all, I had begun to find what seemed to give every indication of being my own style."[23] He discovers his own style and also the precise value of each chosen word.

Yates was painstaking in his choice of words, agonizing over every last detail, as Blake Bailey describes: "on a good day the most he could write was maybe half a polished page, or just over a hundred words."[24] This is, of course, not unusual; many writers write and rewrite their work over a long period. Yates, however, dramatizes his difficulties as an author in this and other stories. In his later novel, *A Good School*, where Bill Grove is shown developing his skill with words, Yates takes a more extended look at the difficulties a young writer faces. Reflecting on his education, Grove muses over the fact that poor school or good school, he learned to write there: "it taught me the rudiments of my trade. I learned to write by working on the Dorset *Chronicle*, making terrible mistakes in print that hardly anybody ever noticed. Couldn't that be called a lucky apprenticeship?"[25] In the depiction of Prentice's development, Yates provides a description of his own literary awakening; the apprentice, Prentice, has passed through the turmoil of initiation. Thirteen years on, in the present of the narrative, describing the appearance of his twenty-two-year-old self, Prentice calls his hat "a much-handled brown fedora"[26] and goes on, parenthetically, to reflect on his choice of adjective, alerting the reader early on to what he perceives to be his development as a writer as he avoids clichés he would once have used: "('Battered' is the way I would have described it then, and I'm grateful that I know a little more now about honesty in the use of words. It was a handled hat, handled by endless nervous pinchings and shapings and reshapings; it wasn't battered at all)."[27] In the present of the narrative, Prentice demonstrates that he has learned a lot about the precise value of each word; ironically, what he has learned has been taught to him by his dealings with a man he had long wanted to dismiss as a dreamer and a fool.

Bernie Silver is a cab driver who wants to star in a fictionalized version of his ordinary life, a life recorded in "a neat little box of three-by-five-inch file cards. Hundreds of experiences, he told me; all different."[28] For Bob Prentice, a young writer holding down a dull job with *United Press* and bringing in a small income on which he and his wife have to survive, Silver's offer of a way of earning easy money is, in equal measure, ludicrous and exciting, but it is a possible way of fulfilling his own dreams. That he is not a good writer, and that he cannot begin to write like Hemingway, is something he both knows and emphasizes: "I knew deep down that it was always, always something bad."[29] Given the paucity of his earnings and the drabness of his somewhat impoverished life, Prentice is shown as a man with high ideals forced to compromise them in order to accept the promise of wealth that Silver offers him: "how much . . . [he] might expect to salt away when his own fat share of the magazine sales, the book royalties and the movie rights came in?"[30]

With the sardonic tone of a writer who abhors all clichés, Yates depicts Bernie relishing his ornate descriptions of the method he wants Prentice to adopt when writing his stories. The central conceit is that writing a good story is like building a house; it needs foundations, a strong framework, and ultimately there needs to be room for the windows where the light can get in: "Where does the light come in? Because do you see what I mean about the light coming in, Bob? I mean the—the *philosophy* of your story; the *truth* of it; the—."[31] The triteness of this metaphorical allusion to light would jar were it not for the fact that it is entirely appropriate for Bernie Silver with his can-do attitude and easy banter. Using the idiom of a self-made man who believes entirely in his project, Yates creates dialogue with authentic resonance and idiosyncratic inflections to make his character vivid and textured.

In his preface to *The Portrait of a Lady*, Henry James's "house of fiction" metaphor describes the process of a novel's construction and the great care he took to get it right: "That solicitude was to be accordingly expressed in the artful patience with which, as I have said, I piled brick upon brick. The bricks, for the whole counting-over—putting for bricks little touches and inventions and enhancements by the way—affect me in truth as well-nigh innumerable and as ever so scrupulously fitted together and packed-in."[32] Yates parodies James's metaphor in order to show how such "advice," poorly understood and cheaply used, can produce formulaic work lacking any literary merit. It could be argued that Prentice undergoes a form of Jamesian education as he moves to a proper understanding of what James's "house of fiction" really is by the end of the story, a story authentically and idiosyncratically his own.

In writing stories about a cabbie, based (even if not accurately) on a real cabbie, and dominated by Bernie Silver's own ideas about his personality, Yates's author picks up James's notion that "the real thing," in his eponymous tale, is a hindrance to the imagination rather than a spur. In James's novella, his artist had, "an innate preference for the represented subject over the real one: the defect of the real one was so apt to be a lack of representation."[33] James seems to suggest that failing to reproduce an exact copy of something inevitably constricts the imagination. Although James's novella is about painting, like Yates's later work *Young Hearts Crying*, its conclusion acts as a guide to all artistic endeavors. Yates makes use of James's theory in this story as Prentice deviates from the facts of Bernie Silver's life and creates his own fictionalized version. However, his difficulties, and the authorial investigation into what produces good fiction, do not end there.

Prentice worries away at his new task unable to find the right level but unwilling to pull out when so much money has apparently been promised, money that might allow him, like Hemingway, to escape to Paris. However, it is his wife, Joan, who makes the telling criticism that forces him to "lower" his level: "You're *trying* too hard. . . . You're being so insufferably *literary* about it. . . . All you have to do is think of every corny, tear-jerking thing you've ever read or heard. Think of Irving Berlin."[34] So, as if prostituting what talent he has, Prentice, "took that little bastard of a story and . . . built the hell out of it."[35] As he ghost writes more and more stories of Silver's "biography," with ultimately no recourse to the facts of Silver's life, the tales emerge with distasteful ease; describing one as "loathsome,"[36] Prentice draws attention to the fact that has allowed all his youthful principles to slip away. Not only is he not writing from life, or from his own experience, he is also driven entirely by money.

For all the obvious provisional, even negative, aspects of the ending to "Builders," Prentice's narrative voice, while sounding unsure of things and somewhat isolated, belongs to him. It is a voice, after all, that recorded Bernie's story his way. Furthermore, it is the voice of a writer who can acknowledge the role that this small-town cabbie has played in his own life. Prentice sounds genuine and utterly without guile at the end of the story, when, borrowing Silver's metaphor once more, he says, "God knows, Bernie; God knows there certainly ought to be a window around here somewhere, for all of us."[37] Where earlier the metaphor had seemed trite and rather facile, it now has validity in the hands of someone who understands its limitations.

Thus the story we read is less about Bernie Silver, although he is the pivotal center of the tale, and more about a writer who needed to confront his own weaknesses and recognize his limitations before he could succeed at his craft. By the conclusion of the story (which the reader receives as the beginning of Prentice's artistic endeavor), he has found a less stable, more honest version of construction, one that is entirely his own: "I can see that it hasn't been built very well. Its beams and joists, its very walls are somehow out of kilter; its foundation feels weak."[38] The point is that it is *his* construction. He has borrowed Bernie's symbolic idiom but made it individual, not generic; large windows will not illuminate his truths or shed brilliant light on his philosophy: "Maybe the light is just going to have to come in as best it can, through whatever chinks and cracks have been left in the builder's faulty craftsmanship."[39] We are reminded that as in so much of Yates's work the creative impulse is stimulated not by bright light but by half-light, literally and metaphorically, for it is the dimness of half-light that stimulates and excites the imagination.

With this ending Yates brings the reader back to a proper understanding of the Jamesian notion of construction. It is one in which the individuality of the literary "building" counts for far more than its outer perfection. Klinkowitz echoes this suggestion: "One suspects, however, that the experience ghosting for Bernie has taught the narrator his craft—particularly that even ghostwritten stories can't be faked. The art of building depends upon this honesty, even when the projects, such as married life, collapse. . . . Honesty wills itself through in the end, even when offering only a legacy of loneliness and despair."[40] As Bernie Silver has pointed out, there need to be windows, but unlike Bernie, and this is what Prentice comes to understand, they are not alike or all of a size; they cannot be arranged according to some outside agency's decree. They are arranged according to the need of the individual artist: "The house of fiction has in short not one window, but a million—a number of possible windows not to be reckoned, rather; every one of which has been pierced, or is still pierceable, in its vast front, by the need of the individual vision and by the pressure of the individual will."[41] The repetition of the word "individual" makes clear where Henry James's emphasis falls, and this is developed as he goes on to describe the "unique instrument" of the observer at the windows: "they are . . . as nothing without the posted presence of the watcher—without, in other words, the consciousness of the artist."[42] The consciousness of the artist is the critical aspect of a sound literary construction, a construction that might be quirky but will definitely be original.

Yates does not allow the reader to forget that the price of Prentice's awakening has been unequivocally high. All of the old certainties, the dreams and cocksure swagger of a would-be Hemingway, and the undoubted snobbery of an arrogant young man who thought he was better because he was clever, have gone. His wife, Joan, a rather shadowy figure in the background of the story, and the one with the practical sense, has also departed, taking with her their daughter. Prentice has lost his job with the *United Press* but has ended up as a writer for an industrial public relations office where he seems as clueless as he was with the *United Press*. In the "now" of the reflective narrative, he is alone. He records that he is in a figurative darkness: "And where are the windows? Where does the light come in?"[43] But for Yates it would seem that this is a positive place to be, without preconceptions and without the arrogance and snobbery of his youthful self.

A year after the publication of *Eleven Kinds of Loneliness*, Yates echoed the creative moral of his earlier story while praising the work of the writers he chose for *Stories for the Sixties*: "None of [the stories] betrays the uncomfortable sound of an author trying to speak in a voice not his own."[44] In all his fiction he pursued the search for his own voice just as Prentice had. Justly proud of "Builders," Yates told his good friends DeWitt Henry and Geoffrey Clark why: "But then, after all that work, I thought I'd try a direct autobiographical blowout, and see if I could make decent fiction out of that. So as a sort of experimental warm-up I wrote the story called 'Builders,' which was almost pure personal history, with a protagonist named Robert Prentice who was clearly and nakedly myself. And I think that story did work, because it *was* formed. It was objectified. Somehow, and maybe it was just luck, I managed to avoid both of the two terrible traps that lie in the path of autobiographical fiction—self-pity and self-aggrandizement."[45]

In *Young Hearts Crying*, his sixth and penultimate published work, Yates explores the role of creativity in postwar America as young writers and painters jostle with one another and negotiate the demands of their often-overinflated egos, trying to find an outlet for their talents without undermining their ideals. He dramatizes his view of the role of the artist in the broadest sense, eliding his opinions of the work of fine artists with his view of writing. Perhaps he does this in an effort to put some critical distance between himself and his characterizations and between himself and his predicament as a writer, and, perhaps because, by the mid-twentieth century, the commercial success of abstract expressionists such as Willem de Kooning, Jackson Pollock, Arshile Gorky, and Mark Rothko was more apparent than similar commercial success in the literary world. It might also have been that he felt it was easier to capture succinctly the chaos he felt was at the center of such movements in visual terms rather than in literary ones, easier to describe and make vivid an artistic movement over a literary one. In positioning Michael Davenport (writer) alongside Tom Nelson (painter), Yates reveals his nervous appreciation of the success of postmodern art; highlighting its success, he also draws attention to its apparent frivolity. Moreover, in contrast to the way the reader engages with his writers, whether we admire them or not, Yates ensures the reader remains aloof from his artist figures and observes them and their work with some detachment.

On first meeting the painter Tom Nelson, Davenport's interior narrative reveals his thoughts (which seem very much like *hopes*) that Nelson is probably carrying drawings for spare parts or tools and that he's probably about to "spend hours tracking [them] down in the warehouses of some dismal place like Long Island City."[46] He discovers, to his horror—and a horror that highlights his own insecurities before it highlights Nelson's commercial success— that Nelson is actually taking his pictures rolled up with a rubber band to the "'Modern"; he, unlike Davenport, is known and a recognized, respected figure: "The rubber band came off, the mottled roll of papers was unfurled and then gently rolled the opposite way to help them lie flat, and six bright watercolor pictures were laid out for the man's inspection—almost, it seemed, for the delectation of the world of art itself."[47]

Having discovered that Nelson is a painter, Davenport immediately creates a comforting mental image of Nelson's probable line of work in a way that does not threaten his own artistic insecurities: "Perhaps, then, he was limited to the art departments of advertising agencies, or perhaps, since 'watercolors' did suggest pleasant little scenes of boats moored in their harbors . . . he might be limited to the kind of stifling gift shops where pictures like that were displayed for sale along with expensive ashtrays."[48] Repetition and stress on the word "limited" convey Davenport's acute desire to consign this man to a place "below" him, not in terms of class but in terms of artistic endeavor. He is aghast and not a little jealous when he discovers how successful Nelson is, but what really irks him is how that success is achieved. Both bewildered and horrified by Nelson's casual approach to his art, Davenport is absolutely uncomprehending about his method as he explains to his wife Lucy: "You know what he paints his pictures *on*? Shelf-paper. . . . Said he'd started using it years ago because it's cheap, then he decided he 'likes the way it takes the paint.' And he does it all on his fucking kitchen floor."[49]

However, Davenport's incredulous tone at what he describes as Nelson's "kind of scratchy, blurry pen-and-ink drawing with a water-color wash,"[50] is hard to interpret; is he admiring or contemptuous, or an undecided mixture of the two? In conjunction with the process he describes above, Yates, through Davenport, produces an image of the artist at work that sounds like a parody of Jackson Pollock's working method:

> Having the canvas on the floor I feel nearer, more a part of the painting. This way I can walk around it, work from all four sides and be in the painting, similar to the Indian sand painters of the West.
>
> Sometimes I use a brush but often prefer using a stick. Sometimes I pour the paint straight out of the can. I like to use a dripping fluid paint. I also use sand, broken glass, pebbles, string, nails, or other foreign matter.[51]

The success and popularity of postmodernism, whether literary or artistic, was by implication a criticism of Yates's preferred style, and more irritating still, the slick ease with which it emerged appeared, to him, to be distasteful. It is in stark contrast to the painstaking labor of Yates's own, and his writer/characters', artistic method. Thus the tone of Davenport's voice is as important as what he says. There is what reads like a sneer as he quotes Nelson's casual approval of shelf paper as a surface. It reveals not only exasperation but also incomprehension, feelings that Yates labors with some enjoyment: "Says he keeps a big flat surface of galvanized tin there, to make the right kind of surface; then he lays a soaking-wet piece of shelf-paper on it, gets down on his haunches and goes to work."[52]

Nelson's casual attitude, his apparent modesty, and his undoubted success act as a goad to the older, struggling writer who recounts to his wife Nelson's description of his working method. Imitating Nelson's voice and inflections, Davenport explains to her that a painting takes perhaps, "twenty minutes if I'm lucky . . . Then about twice a month I go through 'em and throw a lot of 'em out—maybe a quarter or a third—and whatever's left are the ones I bring into town. The Modern always wants first pick."[53] While the imitation reveals that Davenport can dismiss him from a rational standpoint, it also highlights his envy. Nelson is in the middle of renovating a large house in Putnam County with apparent effortlessness and, much to Davenport's irritation, "borrows" the appearance of different military personnel by simply buying hip bomber jackets. He wears them because he likes them and not because he is trying to make a statement; to the less frivolous and less secure Davenport, his behavior is anathema: "He's just standing there calm as hell in his damn zipped-up tanker's jacket, looking like he couldn't care less."[54]

It might be a surprise to find ourselves shoulder to shoulder with Davenport for a moment, given his often bitter, cynical reading of people, but Yates allows no other response as he guides the reader's distaste for what he perceives to be the superficial vacuities of modern art, vacuities embodied in the gushing young woman who greets Nelson as he arrives at the Museum of Modern Art: "'Oh, Thomas Nelson,' she said, 'Now I know it's going to be a good day.'"[55] His is not art produced from hours of grueling suffering in the garret of creativity, a clichéd "ideal" that is observable in the portraits of all Yates's writers. This is art that has apparently been "put together" sometime between breakfast and supper. The implication is that it is about as skillful as putting up wallpaper and it is, of course, ironic that this artist's work is so sought after.

Nelson is happily married, confident, charming, charismatic, upwardly mobile, and modest; there is nothing destructive or self-destructive about the way in which he lives his life. In his characterization of Nelson, Yates places him as a powerful counterpoint to his struggling writer. Davenport, with very little visible success, an increasingly turbulent marriage, erratic self-confidence, and struggling to perform artistically and eventually sexually, may have laudable aims, but his lack of money and recognition render him far less productive and positive an individual. While he personally suffers for his art, he makes everyone else suffer too. Yates refuses to sentimentalize or romanticize the dilemma of the artist and is at pains to undercut his writers' sense of their own superiority. His depiction of the writer is very similar to the portrait Norman Podhoretz so starkly paints when he talks about young writers who "regarded themselves, without exception . . . as superior to their jobs":[56] "the truth is that they would have despised virtually any job, having been educated to believe that the only vocation worth pursuing was the vocation of Art or something similarly 'pure,' similarly free of the taint of commerce and of the bourgeois spirit."[57]

It is as if through the medium of art Yates is mocking his own inability to understand, or place any value on, "modern" writing. He can see that the playful, postmodernist approach to the text is both successful and welcomed by the literary world, but *he* feels its shallowness and its lack of authenticity; its ambition to repel or shock, rather than to draw the reader in, seems to suggest that to him it should be condemned. Superficiality is the obvious criticism of Nelson's kind of work, and this would appear to be Davenport's, and Yates's, own position, yet it is a criticism that sounds resentful and somewhat hollow when "the world," as represented by the "Modern," not only accepts it but also delights in it. As he highlights contradictory positions about marriage and education, Yates also dramatizes and explores this dichotomy about artistic endeavor; he seems to share Davenport's resentment *and* to criticize or expose it.

For the reader, much of what the artists in this novel say makes good sense. Another painter, Paul Maitland, for instance, makes this inarguable point: "But if a picture's any good it's self-sufficient; it needs no text. Otherwise, all you're getting is something clever, something ephemeral, something of the moment."[58] Attention is drawn to the fact that Yates has a habit of moving his opinions between characters, thus testing his arguments and ensuring their validity. The reader becomes aware, for instance, that narrative empathy flits back and forth between Lucy Davenport and her husband, though more often resting with Lucy. In this way Yates also reinforces the fact that there are no simple solutions to his inquiries; even within the mind of a single character opinions fluctuate and are debated. The striking ambiguity implicit in Davenport's distaste for his artist/friends and the way they live their lives is one such gray area. On the one hand, Yates is mocking his own position as a writer of realist fiction by highlighting the success of artists who have started to develop new styles with some success, and this is wealth and recognition for which Davenport longs. On the other hand, in Davenport's attitude to the artists he comes across, Yates fleshes out something of his own disquiet at the tendency toward either a false adoption of an artistic lifestyle, a highly self-conscious bohemia, as portrayed by the character of Paul Maitland, or the production of what appears to be a highly commercialized product, depicted by Tom Nelson's work.

It is noticeable that all the painters in *Young Hearts Crying* are part of a more modern, commercial, accepting and less idealistic world than their failing literary counterparts; they have adjusted and adapted to their times. Whether Yates was horrified by them and their art or not, he emphasizes the success of these artists, and that emphasis is something the reader cannot ignore. This method of obfuscation helps to give the impression that Yates is depicting widely held beliefs. Furthermore, it would seem that Yates wants the reader to notice Nelson's ability to remain detached from his work, in contrast, of course, to Davenport. As a corollary, Nelson's ability to edit his pictures ruthlessly has to be read as part of his wider ability to control his life rather than be controlled by it. Nelson, in particular, plays at being an artist, taking on the performance and appearance of one, playing the role flippantly, cheerfully, and with the relish of someone who has worked out the rules of a game, rules that Davenport cannot begin to decipher.

As with all Yates's writer/characters, Michael Davenport, the Harvard-

educated writer at the heart of the novel, takes himself and his literary pretensions very seriously. Through him Yates depicts many of the different ways
in which a writer with high ideals is vulnerable as he struggles to maintain
an authentic version of himself in the face of anxieties about class, money,
relationships, and artistic style. However, his standards for himself and for
others, as well as for his art, are very quickly questioned and eroded. Within
the first few lines of the novel, Yates writes: "He didn't have much patience
with myths or legends of any kind . . . what he wanted, always, was to get
down to the real story."[59] But the "real story" does not always present itself
in a way that suits Davenport's expectations, and his resistance to myths and
legends is very short-lived. Despite his determination to resist posturing and
sentimentality, Davenport fails every test. Yates's use of that warning note,
"at first," alerts the reader that this is a battle he will lose; we are engaged
not with *whether* he'll lose but with *how* he'll lose. It is no surprise to the
reader, therefore, that "after a year or two he began to relent a little. Most of
the courses *were* stimulating; most of the books *were* the kind he had always
wanted to read."[60] Against his best efforts, he is constantly caught up in the
mythologizing and has to extract himself, bruised, confused, and resentful.

Furthermore, when Davenport's second wife fails to praise his manuscript
as much as he would have liked her to, Davenport deeply resents her honesty. The mimetic narrative draws attention to the way he blames *her*, rather
than facing the truth of his work's weakness: "It might have seemed only fair
of her to come through with some show of excitement, even if she'd had to
fake it."[61] This is a measure of how far he has traveled from his youthful ideals and is indicative of the rhetorical flourishes and self-deluded arguments
of a typical Yatesian dreamer. While Davenport might wish his wife had had
the compassion to "fake it," the reader alone assesses the degree of compromise with truth that this would have entailed. Davenport has no such perspective over his own desires and demands. This is not helped by the fact that
everyone around him seems to live quite happily with the myths and legends
that Davenport sees as indicative of entrapment. In this way, not only Davenport but also society at large is implicated in Yates's criticism.

Every aspect of Davenport's character trips and falls at the hurdles his
principles have erected. Even the description of how he falls in love is touched
with Yates's wry satirical tone, drawing attention to the fact that ideals are
expendable and are particularly expendable when confronted with a pretty
girl handing out flattery: "Then one spring afternoon in his junior year—all
bitterness gone, all cynicism drowned—he wholly succumbed to the myth
and the legend of the lovely Radcliffe girl who could come along at any mo-

ment and change your life."[62] Bitterness and cynicism would appear to have been necessary armor against the shallow dishonesties of the world as Yates depicts it.

Often understandably referred to as a writer of dark tales, Yates uses a wry, witty voice that amuses even at some of the bleakest moments of his narratives, and nowhere more than when he is sending up the characters who most obviously dramatize his own position in life. With that in mind, the debate played out in his work between the traditionalists and the postmodernists is often comical and is usually at the expense of writers who take themselves and their craft too seriously; it is clear in the depiction of Davenport's attitude toward Tom Nelson that he puts his own pretensions under rigorous scrutiny. In a similar vein, in *The Easter Parade* Yates explores his ideas about teaching and writing. Emily Grimes's current boyfriend, Jack Flanders, returns home one evening, and, like Davenport, he vents his spleen in mimicry of his nemesis: "Try to understand. I'm what the kids call 'traditional.' I like Keats and Yeats and Hopkins and—shit, you know what I like. And Krueger's what they call 'experimental'—he's thrown everything overboard. His favorite critical adjective is 'audacious.' Some kid'll get stoned on pot and scribble out the first thing that comes into his head, and Krueger'll say 'Mm, that's a very audacious line.' His students are all alike, the snottiest, most irresponsible kids in town. They think the way to be a poet is to wear funny clothes and write sideways on the page. Krueger's published three books, got another one coming out this year, and he's in all the fucking magazines all the fucking time."[63] Like Davenport railing against Nelson's manner and technique, Flanders begins by being angry with Krueger's methods, but jealousy toward his success is the emotion the reader receives most forcibly: "and baby here's the kicker—here's the punchline: the cocksucker is nine years younger than me."[64] The reader may have some sympathy with Flanders's anger at the commercialization of culture (and Yates guides that sympathy with subtlety), but the reader can only be distanced by both his and Davenport's lack of dignity, their lack of "audaciousness," their childishness and the personal attacks they each make. Aware that these were his own preoccupations and his own weaknesses, Yates is quietly mocking himself every time. He makes his readers well aware that teachers such as Krueger and artists such as Nelson are the ones who are successful and admired.

In this way Yates commits to paper a dramatization of his jealousy and mistrust of new artistic movements emerging in the 1950s and 1960s. These trends toward a loose experimental style were trends he knew to be highly successful. Tony Tanner, taking a theoretical overview of American fiction from the 1950s to the 1970s, places a great deal of emphasis on the dilemma for the American writer when looking for new ways to express himself without losing his coherence, on the one hand, or being constrained, on the other: "It is my contention that many recent American writers are unusually aware of this quite fundamental and inescapable paradox: that to exist, a book, a vision, a system, like a person, has to have an outline—there can be no identity without contour. But contours signify arrest, they involve restraint and the acceptance of limits."[65] Davenport is seized by this paradox, and in *Young Hearts Crying* Yates gives the dichotomy dramatic emphasis.

Even though Davenport is often an unlikeable character, behaves badly, and has a whole host of weaknesses that are clearly defined, Yates will not allow his readers the comfort of total dismissal. The reader may well admire Davenport's principles, for they shun shallow artifacts and determine that he will not live off his wife's inherited three or four million dollars. Indeed, it is impossible not to admire his dogged determination to find his own literary voice: "He had established a working alcove in one corner of the attic of their Larchmont house—it wasn't much, but it was private. . . . On most nights he worked in the attic until he ached with fatigue, but there were other times when he couldn't get his brains together, when he would sit there in a paralysis of inattention, smoking cigarettes and despising himself until he went back downstairs to bed."[66] Using the interplay between mixtures of idioms, Yates makes Davenport's failings resonate with a sense of human vulnerability with which the reader can engage. With one idiom Yates suggests in the vernacular what Davenport might have said, "it wasn't much, but it was private." With the other, adding poetic depth, Yates suggests what he might have thought, "there were . . . times when he couldn't get his brains together when he would sit there in a paralysis of inattention, smoking cigarettes and despising himself."

Yates's writers have a very particular love of their workspace, even if that space is cramped and inadequate. The spaces are carefully mapped and, by implication, fiercely protected. At this point in the novel, Davenport's space is a corner of an attic. Later in the same novel it is "the pump shed, where the kerosene stove left a fine coating of soot on his hands and face and clothes."[67] The struggle Davenport is experiencing with his writing seems in some way to be compounded, if not caused by, the filthy conditions in which he is trying to work. Indeed, Yates seems to suggest, with the emphasis he places on it, that the worst aspect of Davenport's material poverty is that the room he calls his own affords no creative sanctuary.

The need for working conditions that are conducive to thought highlights a problem for the writer of any era and is something that Yates was acutely aware of: there is always a need to make money. Writing and commerce are presented with some ambivalence, for how does the writer stay true to artistic ideals while at the same time earn enough money to support himself and his family? His fiction is populated with writers who strive to fulfill the former ambition but fail to fulfill the latter. Indeed, in his life, this was a balancing act that Yates never successfully mastered. In refusing to compromise his literary ideals, he remained if not impoverished very far from financial good health. With his friend Kurt Vonnegut Jr., he attempted to address the issue of the writer's pride conjoined with the difficulty of finding work that could sustain them. In the late 1960s they were invited to give a lecture on "The Writer and the Free Enterprise System." Vonnegut described this "very unpopular lecture" with characteristic humor: "We would talk about all the hack jobs writers could take in case they found themselves starving to death. . . . Dick and I found out you can almost always get work if you can write complete sentences."[68] Blake Bailey emphasizes the predicament Yates was in when he highlights his early struggle to produce a novel. Having attempted a novel that did not work he went back to short stories: "the level of his work was now consistently excellent, but if anything less saleable than ever."[69] So, although Yates was keen to attack the would-be writer for an excess of pride when it came to earning money, he was continually subject to the same feelings of degradation he lampooned.

The ambivalence Yates felt is a deeply embedded preoccupation in American literature. Arnold Gingrich alludes to it when writing about Fitzgerald's work: "Despite the fact that, as Fitzgerald himself had said, he had become so interested in the Pat Hobby stories that he felt a great deal was going into them, they were for a long time dismissed as being 'done to pay the grocer.' . . . But to counterbalance that consideration, the thing to remember is that Scott Fitzgerald wrote for his living all the twenty years of his working life."[70] Like Fitzgerald and Hemingway, Yates had to write for money urgently needed. This is, of course, quite unlike the highly self-conscious role of the writer as a member of the social and intellectual elite, as evidenced in the works of great modernists like Eliot, Pound, Joyce, and Yeats. Moreover, with the changing face of society in the 1960s and 1970s, and the expense incurred by the breakup of marriages and the raising of children, it was a far more urgent preoccupation than that which inspired Henry James's notion of a "living wage."[71] Therefore, Yates tries to marry in his fiction what he was less successful in uniting in his life; writing is at once an art *and* a trade, an expression of high, literary ideas and ideals and a means of making money.

In *Revolutionary Road*, Yates depicts a man who writes without placing any value on, or displaying any commitment to, the written word. Frank

Wheeler, who works in sales promotion for Knox Business Machines, has no interest in either the words he uses or the product he is paid to write about. He struggles to make sense of a document that looks "as if it had been typed in a foreign language,"[72] and he lets a brochure out into the market that he knows is substandard: "Frank had known at the time that it was a mess—its densely printed pages defied simple logic, as well as readership, and its illustrations were only sporadically relevant to its text—but he'd let it go anyway."[73] Wheeler has no feeling for his work and no connection with the words he glibly recites into his voice recorder: "Fingering through the papers from the central file with his free hand, lifting a sentence here and a paragraph there, he continued to recite into the Dictaphone."[74] It is not so much *what* he is writing that is interesting and is held up for scrutiny as his mood and manner; the master of evasion, he places most of his in-tray in a drawer, but it is to his easy self-assurance and the lack of any value that he places on words that Yates draws attention. This was, of course, the antithesis of Yates's own style. With irony the reader cannot miss, and relishing the clichéd phrases that constitute office talk, Yates paints the scene as Wheeler's boss heaps praise on his slick endeavors: "Frank, this is a crackerjack. They're just tickled to death in Toledo."[75] Frank Wheeler may not be a writer of fiction but his position as a writer is very relevant to how he is received. One of the subtler ways in which Yates steers judgment of him is by portraying a man who squanders words (among other things) for money and immediate gratification; there is, therefore, a strong sense of moral disapproval in the way Wheeler leads his life.

In contrast to the many harshly judged writer/characters in Yates's fiction, there are occasionally writers who are treated with a gentler hand. In *The Easter Parade*, Sarah and Emily Grimes both try their hand at writing, but without success. In Sarah's case her attempts are thwarted by the restrictions of her marriage and the loss of any self-respect consequent on that marriage. This provides Yates with the means to investigate the role of women and the diminution of their identity in marriages dominated and controlled by men. Sarah, who says "I love to write"[76] and tells her sister and Jack Flanders that she is writing a kind of historical novel about their ancestors, is clearly able. She impresses her audience to the degree that on returning home with Emily, Jack says, "she *does* write well; I wasn't just saying that."[77]

During this visit and when talking about, or reciting from, her work, Sarah's character is given more depth and fluency than at any other time in the novel. This underscores how writing features in her life both as an ambition and as something to which she commits time and energy; it literally puts life into her and briefly offers her a means of escape. Thus it is all the more

disturbing to Emily that with such commitment to the idea so clearly demonstrated during their visit, Sarah's subsequent letter dismisses her novel: "I
have shelved *George Fall* because it turned out that I couldn't proceed very
far without doing research in Montana. Can you imagine me ever getting
to Montana?"[78] The reader, and by implication Emily, reads this as another
indictment of Tony, Sarah's bullying husband. He has demonstrated his lack
of interest in her work; his patronizing smile had "seemed to say that if this
sort of thing gave the little woman pleasure, well and good."[79] It seems clear,
even if unstated, that he has prevented her pursuing her dream. Her claim,
in the same letter, that "I am still writing, though, planning a series of humorous sketches about family life"[80] has no conviction behind it for Emily or
the reader, not least because her life appears so utterly miserable. The truth
is that Yates, for all his oddly misogynistic "turns," is promoting the idea of
greater freedom within relationships for women, whether wives and mothers or not. Perhaps the question to ask is whether he is promoting that freedom for all women or simply for women who are also writers.

Emily makes many attempts to write as a way of escaping from her evident loneliness and as a way of trying to bring some shape to her otherwise disordered existence. A pattern develops whereby in her writing she
tries to reflect on, and make productive, the experiences she has undergone.
Klinkowitz notes this pattern as "a peculiar rhythm in her life: a brief experience followed by an attempt to express it in writing."[81] The reader is told,
for instance, "In the space of two years she had two abortions";[82] her method
of dealing with the physical and emotional trauma is to reject psychiatry
as too expensive and "might not be worth the effort"[83] and to turn to writing about the experience instead. She has to acknowledge though that what
she has written does not read well: "For several evenings and most of one
weekend she worked on the abortion article, but in the end she stowed it in
a cardboard box that she called 'my files,' and put the typewriter away."[84] Just
in case the reader is too empathetic at this point, and dragged too far into
a perspective that is unalterably Emily's, Yates concludes the episode with
typical levity as he broadens the reader's perspective again: "She would need
the table for parties."[85]

Termination—literally, of pregnancy and metaphorically, of life—is a motif
that recurs.[86] Emily's attempts to write about her experiences of abortion are
treated with a degree of flippancy as a means by which Yates can illustrate
how vulnerable and naive she is; romantic notions about relationships get in
the way of practicalities and responsibility. However, there is a more serious
side to episodes in her life that hover not far below the surface. Yates tackles
the issue of abortion here in a more complex way than in *Revolutionary Road*,

where it is included as a consequence of the difficulties encountered in a relationship but not given ideological emphasis. While Emily's abortions remain "episodes" among many in the narrative of her life, Yates does convey the harsh truth about what abortion is and points out, through Emily's writing, a degree of hypocrisy in the way America views it: "It is painful, dangerous, 'immoral' and illegal, yet every year more than _____ million women get abortions in America."[87] However understated it may be, by including the issue of termination, Yates ensures that it sits as an uncomfortable corollary to the sexual freedoms his characters enjoy, and as Yates presents the issue, it is the women alone who carry this burden. This does suggest an element of awareness and understanding of a woman's position by Yates, although that sensitivity to a woman's right to choose remains in odd contrast to his, to my mind, evident disgust at women's exploration of their sexuality.

Later in *The Easter Parade*, Emily, romantically involved with the poet Jack Flanders, tries to write again. She tries to appropriate some space "as far as possible across the room from him"[88] and can only begin "when the housework was done."[89] Yates makes it clear that Jack, with his oversized ego, dominates the house; thus he controls and diminishes her and her writing. When she suggests that he might like to use "the *little* room for working,"[90] he replies in terms that ensure that both she and the reader take note of his patronizing and proprietorial attitude: "No. I like to be able to look up and see you. Moving in and out of the kitchen, hauling the vacuum cleaner, whatever the hell you're doing. Lets me know you're really here."[91] Of course, while it highlights his insecurity, what it also does is remind him that Emily is at his disposal and is there to look after him. When Emily finally does get to her typewriter he questions her, "Writing a letter?"[92] He cannot conceal the fact that her activity threatens him. By suggesting that she is writing a letter he can restore his own mental equilibrium as he swats away any seriousness attached to her task. Time and again, Yates draws attention to a competitive streak in couples that mirrors the debate about gender roles in the late 1960s and 1970s; competition extends here to writing as an activity, as a means of earning status and money. Emily, however, is determined in her ambition and settles down to her magazine article: "The idea had been simmering in her mind for days."[93] It is clear, however, that the demands of life with Jack, together with her own flagging confidence, make it impossible for her to continue.

Only when Jack visits his children and Emily is alone does she discover how much he physically and emotionally cramps her. Thus the issue of space becomes even more important as she rediscovers herself: "She had been exclusively concerned with Jack for so long that it was oddly refreshing to sit down with this letter and remember who she was."[94] Months later, and after traveling with Jack to Europe, Emily resurrects her manuscript, but decides "the essential point of the article was a lie: she *hadn't* discovered the Middle West, any more than she had discovered Europe."[95] This has the ring of Yates's own voice railing against writing not "*felt*."[96] Emily's last effort at writing, and writing using the details of her own life's collapse, carries with it a central irony; her writing about unemployment fails *because* she is unemployed and female and has neither the focus nor the force to gain any perspective on her position.

There is a tightrope to be walked, in Yates's view, between writing that is not from lived experience and writing that is too close to the author's life so that there is not enough distance to "form" the work. Yates observes a central dichotomy for women of the era. Without men in her life, Emily lacks energy and self-worth. Drinking heavily and now alone, the description of her rotting article reads like a metaphor for her prematurely disintegrating life: "That was as far as Emily's article went. It had been rolled into her typewriter for weeks; now the paper was curled and sun-bleached and gathering dust."[97] Klinkowitz also assesses her failure to write specifically in terms of her gender: "As she noted when failing to write about her earlier subjects, Emily had not really experienced anything at all. Here Yates's strategy in choosing a female protagonist becomes especially clear. As a woman in the male-dominated society of these previous decades, she has found it hard to express herself in any form except that of passivity."[98]

Yates's particular kind of hard-hitting, antiromantic, sparse prose places him firmly alongside other writers such as John O'Hara, John Cheever, Norman Mailer, John Updike, and Raymond Carver; however, they were all more successful than he was in his lifetime. These writers draw attention to the fictional construction of the American Dream as it is played out both in relationships and in the home, but they all offered some form of redemption that it is hard to discover in Yates's work. Yates tentatively offers the *possibility* of redeeming hope in creative endeavor, and perhaps too in a fulfilled relationship, but both are always provisional and usually compromised in his fictions. Refusing to play the elegiac card other writers such as Cheever employed, Yates presents writer/characters that are obdurate in their pursuit of truth but never commercially successful. Furthermore, harmonious, long-term, relationships are almost entirely absent because Yates's characters appear unable to protect their partners from themselves; there is always the inexorable sense that the ego of one will destroy the dreams of the other.

Yates provides many portraits of writers and artists in his fiction and addresses notions of creativity from many angles, but what is striking is how similar his characters are. Many episodes and characterizations recur in his stories, reworked and renamed but familiar nevertheless. Poirier, when writing about Norman Mailer's autobiographical inclinations, suggests a problem for the writer that might also be Yates's: "He wants to make himself an 'art work' which will provide the protective and illuminating context for all the other works he will produce. But the habits thus engendered can and do lead to something like over-self-production."[99] As noted in the previous chapter (and confirmed by even the briefest glance at Blake Bailey's biography), Yates's material is highly autobiographical, and this is most obvious when it comes to his portrayal of writers, but whether this is to be judged as "over-self-production" or as adding depth to his inquiries is something only the reader can decide. Even though, as Yates says himself, writing about writers is a risky business and an unappealing thing to do, for the most part his portraits act as a telling commentary on life for a particular kind of writer in postwar America. He steers clear of romanticizing them, and at best they are only ever mediocre in their achievements and recognition, but that they resonate as individuals is not in doubt as their frustrations and oversized egos loom out of the page.

Set against Richard Poirier's description of writers, "each of them is of an extreme if different kind of arrogance,"[100] Yates's self-consciousness, lack of confidence, and his intellectual and social anxiety make an opposing portrait of the writer making his offering. His fictions show that he was well aware of the performative nature of his task, but somewhat paradoxically he has none of the arrogance to brandish his work as if it is merely part of that performance. By this I mean Yates's work was part of himself to such a degree that he, at the end point, the point of publication, no longer saw the book he had produced and handed over to the world as just a performative act: it had meaning, relevance, and was worth something.

Like Yates himself, his writers struggle to produce work that is "felt," not clever or intellectual but keenly observed and true to the life they lead. That this means they are poor husbands; critical, competitive friends and hopeless fathers; dependent on alcohol, prescription drugs, cigarettes, and flattery is too bad; it is the only portrait Yates knew. Lee Siegel says of Yates's style, "At times he writes less like an artist than like a witness" and says his prose "suggests a profound humility before life's inscrutable sadness."[101] But behind that "sadness" and the deep pessimism that pervades his work, his writers battle on, against the odds. They remain multiple self-portraits of a man who knew no other way to make sense of his world.

7

Realism, Form, and Technique

8. Yates on a bench in Fahnestock State Park, New York, circa 1961 or 1962. Courtesy of Grace Schulman.

It is well documented that by the early 1960s, the literati—the scholars and editors of literature—regarded realist fiction as passé. Sharon Monteith describes a sense of the shift away from realism when she examines "the turn in the literary tide": "The emphasis on individual awakening and rebellion is part of the reason that realist fiction delineating 'social norms' is felt to recede in the 1960s, despite Richard Yates and John Cheever, and perhaps because their characters are chronic dreamers who worry less about social revolution or the spirit of reform than about being tortured by conformity and deadened by suburbia, concerns that animated the Cold War fifties."[1] Monteith goes on to make the point that "narratives about the 1950s began to feel 'historical' very quickly unless they weighed in with 'sixties' issues"[2] and typifies the change in direction for fiction as "a movement [that] coalesced around writers for whom alienation became absurdist disaffection."[3] In the light of her comments, Richard Yates had given himself a steep hill to climb if his work was to be recognized and applauded.

Stewart O'Nan, writing about the weak reception of Yates's second novel, *A Special Providence*, emphasizes this issue of timing in ways that chime with Monteith's encapsulations of the 1960s literary landscape: "All in all, [the book was] a success, except that in the past few years American writing, like the rest of the culture, had changed drastically. The metafictionalists were in, as were fantasy and sci-fi, and mad satire. Donald Barthelme's surrealistic fictions ran nearly monthly in the New Yorker [*sic*]. Compared to the experimentalists, Yates's traditional approach seemed a throwback, easily ignored."[4]

Writing about writers is one means of challenging the limitations of traditional realist fiction while at the same time valorizing it. Yates does this with the full knowledge that it is a very difficult, and in some senses unappealing, thing to do: "Writers who write about writers can easily bring on the worst kind of literary miscarriage; everybody knows that."[5] He describes with some relish one of his first writer/characters (a relish detectable under his surface apology) and suggests that writers are often very difficult people: "I can guarantee that he won't get away with being the only Sensitive Person among the characters, but we're going to be stuck with him right along and you'd better count on his being as awkward and obtrusive as writers nearly always are, in fiction or in life."[6] His intention, as his tongue-in-cheek tone suggests in this short story, is to demystify the hallowed ground the writer traditionally occupies. He wanted to present a realistic, gritty, and three-dimensional account of what kind of life writers of the mid-twentieth century, writers such as he was, actually led.

A slow, painstaking author, Yates was always dissatisfied with the early drafts of his work, and the process of revision was time consuming and expensive for him. He explained the need for meticulous corrections and revisions in the *Ploughshares* interview: "Most of my first drafts read like soap opera. I have to go over and over a scene before I get deep enough into it to bring it off. I think I'd be a slick, superficial writer if I didn't revise all the time."[7]

However, Yates knew that he could never change and write with a speed and confidence that he saw in the work of others. In a letter to DeWitt Henry, Yates suggested that the time it took to write a book bore no relation to its worth: "Maybe it takes you and *me* a long time to write our books, but it took Fitzgerald exactly ten months to write *Gatsby*, and Wallant less than a year to write *The Pawnbroker*. Working time, in other words, has nothing whatever to do with quality."[8] In the light of the comment that follows, this seems disingenuous.

Thinking back to a time following the publication of his first novel and first book of short stories, Yates's highly self-critical nature and his frustration with his own writing methods is revealed: "What happened after those two books was my own fault, nobody else's. If I'd followed them up with an-

9. The second page of an early draft of *Revolutionary Road*.
Courtesy of the Howard Gotlieb Archival Center for Research
at Boston University.

other good novel a few years later, and then another a few years after that,
and so on, I might very well have begun to build the kind of reputation some
successful writers enjoy. Instead I tinkered and brooded and fussed for more
than seven years over the book that finally became *A Special Providence*, and
it was a failure in my own judgment as well as that of almost everyone else,
and it was generally ignored. . . . I can't honestly claim my stuff has been neglected; it's probably received just about the degree of attention it deserves.
I simply haven't published enough to expect more—not yet, anyway."[9] Sev-
enteen years later, in an interview with the *Los Angeles Times*, he reflected
on a particular difficulty as he summed up his life's work: "I'm one of these
writers who has the misfortune to write his best book first."[10] While in my
view this is an accurate assessment of his achievement, it does not do jus-

tice to his many other fine pieces of work since Yates, aware of their muted critical reception, implicitly devalues them. His short stories, in particular, display an economy of style and depth of understanding of human behavior that should not be overlooked.

In addition to his own work, Yates was a teacher of writing, though he always queried whether this was a subject that could be taught.[11] As Blake Bailey documents, Yates taught creative writing for many years, initially at the New School for Social Research in New York and later at Columbia, at the Iowa Writers' Workshop, at Boston University, at the University of Southern California, and finally at the University of Alabama. By considering some of the advice he gave his students, it is possible to glean what he valued in writing. At Yates's memorial service DeWitt Henry talked of Yates's style of teaching: "I hear his vigilant hectoring always, for genuine clarity, genuine feeling, the right word, the exact English sentence, the eloquent detail, the rigorous dramatization of a story. Don't evade, don't cheat."[12] The author Elizabeth Cox recalls similar advice in a recent article about meeting Yates: "'What does your character *really* say, here, in this moment?' Yates asked me again and again. And I had to answer right away, at our lunch table or wherever we were. He didn't let any insincere or dishonest remark go unchallenged. 'Why did the character enter the room at this particular moment? What was he doing just before he entered?' Knowing Yates was an exhilarating exercise in straight talk. Never had I been with someone who spoke so directly and expected such reciprocal honesty, and it changed me. As a writer, I learned to want only what was true in every moment."[13]

As an editor, Yates was equally eloquent. Writing at the end of his introduction to a collection of short stories, Yates gives us an indication of how he values the search for authenticity in writing: "each writer has accomplished what he set out to do, and that what he set out to do was neither false nor trivial."[14] The lack of expansive praise mirrors the quiet tones of the stories he has chosen; to his mind, they illustrate a series of unobtrusive and unromantic truths. In his own work, and in order to approximate the "reality" he is describing, Yates employs a patchwork of voices and perspectives to enrich and enliven the scene depicted and to come closer to the truth of all experience. In that respect, Yates looks *back* at literary figures like H. G. Wells, who calls for the novel "to be a discursive thing; it is not a single interest, but a woven tapestry of interests,"[15] and *forward* to a time when "reality" is approximated by the interplay of many voices, often unidentified, and often clashing within a text. By generally steering clear of the autobiographical *I*, Yates seems to want to bury himself as author in an omniscient narration or in an imitation of a variety of voices.

Yates wrote determinedly within what was perceived as an outmoded realist tradition. Like the great traditional realists his work emulates, he felt it was both possible and laudable to *try* and capture a sense of reality on the page. While "reality" itself may elude all writers, not all writers, and particularly not all realist writers, acknowledge this fact; Yates does. He was acutely aware that the act of writing is an act of editing and refining; fiction emerges through the prism of the writer's experiences and through his idiosyncratic use of language as well as through the form and structure of his story. Yates realized, therefore, that a faithful transcription of "reality" was impossible, that "reality" could only be approximated, but it was still, to his mind, the only goal worth pursuing. He was appreciative of the complexities and required compromises of such an aim and admitted to molding the reality he described. However, in his final interview, Yates made it clear that the term *realist* and the idea of classification were abhorrent to him: "All fiction is filled with technique," he complained. "It's ridiculous to suggest one technique is any more realistic than any other."[16]

In my reading of Yates's fiction, it is revealing and useful to compare him to those writers he regarded highly and to situate him within writerly debates. He greatly admired many of the well-respected realist novelists of the late nineteenth and early twentieth century, notably Gustave Flaubert and Anton Chekhov, but also F. Scott Fitzgerald and Ernest Hemingway. He particularly admired Flaubert for his perfectionism, his labored search for the mot juste, and for the moral complexity of his writing. The degree to which Yates only ever writes about himself is something he recognizes with Flaubertian ease and an acknowledged debt to his literary forefather:

> I'd written a good many careful, objective stories over a good many years—stories in which there may always have been an autobiographical element in one sense or another, but in which none of the characters was ever wholly myself. Then I wrote *Revolutionary Road* the same way: There's plenty of myself in that book—every character *in* the book was partially based on myself, or on some aspect of myself, or on people I knew or composites of people I knew, but each of them was very carefully put through a kind of fictional prism, so that in the finished book I like to think the reader can't really find the author anywhere—or, to put the same thing another way—he can find the author everywhere. I've always admired Flaubert's great line: "The writer's relation to his work must be like that of God to the Universe: omnipresent and invisible"—and I was trying to live up to that ideal.[17]

And Yates is right when he indicates that in his first novel he manages to disguise his biography and to dilute his perspective across many characters. April Wheeler is, at moments, identifiable as a mouthpiece for the author, but Yates equally speaks through Frank Wheeler and Shep Campbell as well as through John Givings and Michael Wheeler.

Yates's characterizations all depend on his association with the characters' experiences so that the fictional prism obscures his presence but not his voice. Echoing Flaubert, Yates asserts with some force his autobiographical claims for *The Easter Parade* when he tells Susan Braudy that it "was . . . actually . . . well . . . is . . . my autobiography, sweetheart. Emily fucking Grimes is me."[18] With no villains who could easily be held responsible for the failings of the communities he describes, Yates implicates everyone. Indeed, this was exactly his intention and was what he loved most about his favorite novel, *Madame Bovary*: "Nobody and everybody is to blame in that book, as Emma perceives when she writes her suicide note to Charles, and as even Charles is able to understand when he tells Rodolphe that he holds nothing against him. There are no villains in that book, any more than there are in what I guess is my second all-time favorite novel, *The Great Gatsby*."[19] Like Flaubert, Yates was interested in provincial life, in the dreams and aspirations of his characters, and in the grimness of lives that were so vastly different from the dreams that propelled them. Both these writers sought to avoid simplistic resolutions to the vast array of complex problems that accompany the human condition.

Yates's debt to Chekhov is clear, not least in the sense that Chekhov, here writing about *Ivanov*, also avoids a neat arrangement of character and morals: "I wanted to be original—there is not a single villain or angel in my play. . . . I have not found anyone guilty, nor have I acquitted anyone."[20] *The Seagull* alone throws up many areas of thematic similarity between Yates and this Russian writer: they are equally fascinated and troubled by the role of the writer in society and by the form their writing should take; they present a bleak, constricted view of society in general and of love in particular; and they both explore the battle to find truth in communication. Chekhov and Yates begin their first play and first novel respectively with a theatrical performance; acting itself is an objective correlative to the drama that unfolds. It is no surprise to the audience or reader that these dramatic scenes end badly. Treplieff's suicide and the disastrous attempt at a self-inflicted abortion (which leads to April's death) confirm what the reader or audience has suspected since the start of both narratives: everything will slide toward disintegration.

In act one of *The Seagull*, the stage is set with great precision; everyone and everything has been held up for the right moment as they wait for the moon to rise for the play to begin. This is, of course, both highly romantic and ridiculous. Together with Treplieff's excited comment that the stage is "Just like a real theatre!"[21] the theater audience has a heightened sense of the unreality of the situation: "The curtain rises. A vista opens across the lake. The moon hangs low above the horizon and is reflected in the water. NINA, dressed in white, is seen seated on a great rock."[22] This is perfection in theatrical terms; nature provides both scenery and lighting, but this also adds to the impression that Treplieff, the writer, is dangerously blurring fiction and reality. Chekhov challenges notions of reality and unreality immediately and suggests divisions in the perspectives people have on the world even as he evokes questions about the stability of his principal figure. At the same time, his questions about the function and form of literature are placed in the central frame of his work. I suggest that Yates mirrors this pattern with his use of the play at the beginning of *Revolutionary Road*.

Treplieff's play, with its heightened, poetic language, suggests his inclination toward modernism and experimentation; as he explains to his uncle, "we must have [the theater] under a new form."[23] Set against the characterizations of Treplieff, the dramatist, and his mother, the actress, and their positions with regard to form, is that of the writer, Trigorin. Famous, successful, and driven, he seems, like Treplieff, to act as one of several Chekhovian voices in the drama. Although his success sets him apart from a Yatesian figure, his personality—dark, brooding, manic, selfish and self-absorbed, greedily plundering all his conversations and experiences for inspiration—is remarkably similar to Yates's writer/characters. Indeed, that was how Yates saw himself. But it is the mania of Treplieff's writing, the isolation it enforces and the adulation it demands, that is echoed more closely in the portraits of characters in *Young Hearts Crying*, "Builders," and *Disturbing the Peace*.

When Robert Prentice, at the end of "Builders," explains that the form of his work cannot be predetermined by rules and frameworks laid down by others but must adhere only to his own imaginative output, he sounds very much like Chekhov's writer, Treplieff: "The conviction is gradually forcing itself upon me that good literature is not a question of forms new or old, but of ideas that must pour freely from the author's heart, without his bothering his head about any forms whatsoever."[24] Treplieff's self-destructive character and daring approach, his inability to compromise, and his desire to break with old forms[25] leads him further into a creative wilderness than Trigorin's socially acceptable work ever does. Chekhov, like Yates later, suggests that the creative process comes only at the expense of personal happiness.[26] As they explore the passions of their protagonists, both writers indicate a strong link between the creative spirit and the mental instability that Chekhov describes: "Violent obsessions sometimes lay hold of a man: he may, for instance, think day and night of nothing but the moon. I have such a moon. Day and night I am held in the grip of one besetting thought, to write, write, write! Hardly have I finished one book than something urges me to write another, and then a third, and then a fourth—I write ceaselessly."[27] The closest Yates comes to emulating this creative mania in his fiction occurs in *Young Hearts Crying* and his portrait of Michael Davenport. In his own life, however, he appeared to emulate it more consistently. As his biographer notes: "For Yates there was no more resting between books (if he could help it) . . . the only rewarding escape was writing . . . his life in Boston was almost entirely built around his work; whenever he deviated from his narrow routine, disaster had a way of pouncing."[28]

As a writer who excels most obviously in the writing of dialogue—especially of dialogue that often obfuscates and avoids communication—and utterances that highlight the distinction between the thought and the word articulated, Yates greatly appreciated F. Scott Fitzgerald's work. He describes the effect Fitzgerald's fiction had on him in his twenties: "But F. Scott Fitzgerald's 'The Great Gatsby' turned out to be the most nourishing novel I read."[29] He goes on to indicate what aspects of Fitzgerald's style he tries to emulate: "You can figure out the important part of it almost at once: Every line of dialogue in *Gatsby* serves to reveal more about the speaker than the speaker might care to have revealed. The author never permits his use of dialogue to become merely 'realistic,' with people exchanging flat, information-laden sentences, but contrives time and again to catch all his characters, however subtly, in the very act of giving themselves away."[30] Beyond similarities of style, Yates and Fitzgerald share an interest in a particular kind of American Dream and a sense of romantic longing in their protagonists. While Fitzgerald wrote about the playgrounds of the rich from his own observations and experiences, such romance acts as a silent counterpoint to the grim relationships of Yates's middle-class dreamers in fictions that were also embedded in his own milieu. It is as if Yates's dramas would have no resonance without the dilemmas and romances of Fitzgerald's stories for Fitzgerald's narratives hint at a dark underbelly to life that Yates then goes on to explore more fully.

Yates and F. Scott Fitzgerald are also united as writers threatened by mental instability. Their mental illnesses are not incidental to their craft but are frequently, in different ways, the dramatic center of their work. Fitzgerald places the experience of mental disorder at a distance from his reader using a third person narrator in, for example, *Tender Is the Night*. Although the novel explores the complexity of Dick Diver's mental and physical disintegration, together with Nicole's fragility, and has their toxic relationship at its heart, the activity of the text is filtered for the reader. We read about what is happening but feel ourselves to be at a distance. That distance is heightened by the narrator and by the sense that, for the majority of Fitzgerald's readers, this is not the world they inhabit; this is a refined world of wealthy, cultured, well-traveled people. The sanatorium treating Nicole, for example, is an exclusive place of great comfort and specialized care, described by one of its doctors as "a rich person's clinic."[31] Unavailable to the majority, it is expensive, secluded, orderly, and pristine. Yates's approach is very different.

In *Disturbing the Peace*, Yates immerses himself and his readers in the grim details of mental and physical disintegration so that the reader witnesses and experiences the writer's collapse in every sense of the term. Unlike Nicole Diver, John Wilder, incarcerated in Bellevue over the Labor Day weekend, has to negotiate the full horror of a state institution. The feeling of entrapment is only one aspect of an experience that Yates is clear demeans humans. The props with which this man feels better about life are reduced to a base level: "If he could eat, if he could drink this coffee and find a cigarette and a telephone, there might still be a chance of the world's coming back to normal."[32] Wilder is diminished in a vast institution that offers no sanctuary save for "a little ell facing the locked front door," but it is also a place "where rational things were most likely to happen."[33] Yates invokes the idea of normality and rationality as a way of conveying the alienation of his protagonist in an environment that accommodates neither concept. The body itself seems to exist at a distance from the mind as it flinches and squirms without apparent permission: "One hand leaped to his wet brow and clung there. . . . The hand fell back to his thigh, but he knew he was squirming because he heard his chair creak."[34] Without personal pronouns to bind the man with the hand, Yates creates a powerful sense of Wilder's disorientation and metaphorical dismemberment.

Since there is little room for rational thought or discussion that doesn't threaten the new inmate in Bellevue, Yates concentrates on foregrounding its physicality and focuses our attention on the smells, sounds, and discomfort Wilder experiences: "He felt warm grit under his feet until he stepped on something slick; then he saw that the black floor ahead was scattered with gobs of phlegm."[35] For Wilder no less than the reader, since we receive our impressions through his eyes, the feeling of confinement is intense: "there was nothing to see but air shafts and windowless walls."[36] At this stage in the novel, Wilder is not manic. He is there because the effects of sleeplessness and frequent alcoholic binges have left him mentally and physically exhausted. In that respect his impressions of Bellevue are conveyed in a clear, if appalled, manner. During his time in Vermont with Pamela, however, Wilder has a complete breakdown, a manic episode that leaves him bewildered, exhausted, and with even lower self-esteem than before.

As a result of Yates's desire to convey the full force of a mental breakdown, the collapse in logic, the heightened terror and the fear about what is actually happening is woven into the narrative. In addition to the disjointed language of a man in the full throws of manic disorder, Yates uses a range of literary devices in order to convey the impression that Wilder's mental state is sliding out of control. One small visual detail is his use of the recurring symbol of a tree. At the beginning of this major breakdown, Wilder is described leaving the rehearsal (ironically ruminating on his ability "to find order in chaos"[37]) until "he stopped and steadied himself with his arm around the trunk of a tree."[38] Earlier, at the lake with his wife, Janice, Wilder clings "with one arm tight around the trunk of a tall rustling tree in the silence of the yard"[39] to ward off the nightmarish vision of himself attacking her. The tree suggests healthy, organic, stable growth, rooted and, if not permanent, long lasting; the strength of the symbol, therefore, is in the way it highlights, by contrast, Wilder's instability. To accentuate the sense of Wilder's dislocation at Bellevue, the narrative is dialogue-based, punctuated by rapid-fire questions and answers, with language that Wilder, and the reader, struggles to follow: "Hey, save me, buddy, okay?"[40] The exchanges between inmates and between the inmates and Charlie, the nurse, are disconcertingly aggressive so that Wilder's already fragile mental health is constantly assaulted until he too adopts the language of the ward: "You're an arrogant, insolent, overbearing son of a bitch, Spivack. You're a prick."[41]

As a way of indicating that, once again, his protagonist is becoming manic, Yates creates the impression that Wilder's perception is distorted. Overloaded with alcohol, befuddled by lack of sleep, and on a cocktail of drugs, in Wilder's hyperreality simple objects become enlarged and threatening: "He looked fixedly at his portion [of steak] and knew that if only he could cut into it and eat it some balance might be restored to the evening, some act of self-rescue might be performed, but the sight of it was nauseating. So was the sight of his huge baked potato, its own bulk overwhelmed by a gout of sour cream and chives, and so was the glistening amplitude of his salad."[42] To a lesser degree, Yates extends the use of this device through Wilder's saner moments so that the reader has the sense that he is never fully in control. Objects exert a power and have an authority that is absent in Wilder's perception of humans. The string beans that Janice is snapping, the stool she is sitting on, and the tennis shoes she is wearing, for instance, are all irritants that fuel his rage.[43]

In his attempt to project an unvarnished version of his protagonists, Yates runs the risk of alienating reader empathy and perhaps even, at times, reader interest. In most of his fiction, this is confined to specific episodes, and usually it is in their drunken rages that his characters are most alienating. In this novel, it is a dominant feature of the narrative. Wilder, often drunk and often aggressive, does little to elicit our compassion. The tone and texture of Wilder's idiom is set at the beginning of the novel with a phone call to his wife: "There was a girl in Chicago, little PR girl for one of the distilleries. I screwed her five times in the Palmer House. Whaddya think of that?"[44] Yates is so averse to sentimentality creeping into his characterizations that he deliberately confounds any expectation the reader might have that they will identify with his protagonists in a linear and accumulative way. In most of his fiction, reader empathy is skillfully maneuvered between characters since, despite their weaknesses, Yates wants their humanity to resonate. At times the reader recognizes the truth of what Frank Wheeler says, for instance; at others, April's words hold the reader's attention. In *Disturbing the Peace* though, Yates challenges his reader to appreciate the grim truth of mental collapse for all its unpleasant details and as a result deliberately thwarts the reader's expectation to feel empathetic. Not all readers accept this challenge. However, as we see later with Emily Grimes, the process of distancing the reader, as he strives for ambiguity in characterization, can be far more subtly achieved.

Learning from Fitzgerald, Yates draws attention to the fragility of language in dialogue that often misses its mark; this was not solely the preserve of the postmodernists. Tony Tanner, writing about Herman Melville, Nathaniel Hawthorne, and Edgar Allan Poe, makes the point very clearly:

> My point is that American writers seem from the first to have felt how tenuous, arbitrary, and even illusory, are the verbal constructs which men call descriptions of reality. . . . This has meant that, while American writers have established an authentically realistic (at times documentary) literary tradition, there has also been from the start in American literature an intermittent sense of the futility of pretending that the putative exactitude of words can ever measure up to the actual mystery of things.[45]

Alluding to a similar idea, Yates states that the first draft of *Revolutionary Road* was, "very thin, very sentimental" and focuses on the kind of dialogue he had given his protagonists:

> they talked very earnestly together even when they were quarreling. . . . It took me a long time to figure out what a mistake that was—that the

best way to handle it was to have them nearly always miss each other's points, to have them talk around and through and *at* each other.
There's a great deal of dialogue between them in the finished book,
both when they're affectionate and when they're fighting, but there's
almost no communication.[46]

This lack of communication among a barrage of words, in contrast to his
expressive use of silence, brings Yates intuitively close to Bakhtinian notions
of the dialogic nature of experience:

Language—like the living concrete environment in which the consciousness of the verbal artist lives—is never unitary. It is unitary only
as an abstract grammatical system of normative forms, taken in isolation from the concrete, ideological conceptualizations that fill it, and
in isolation from the uninterrupted process of historical becoming that
is a characteristic of all living language.[47]

Almost any conversation written by Yates could be used to illustrate the
point Bakhtin makes since all his work draws attention to the voices battling
within a text. As Jerome Klinkowitz notes in the conclusion to his study of
American manners, the dialogic nature of the three writers' texts—those of
Richard Yates, Dan Wakefield and Thomas McGuane—is what gives them
richness and authenticity:

Each author has mastered an individual style which speaks in its own
voice, yet all three show great sensitivity to the wide range of other
voices within their fiction. Perhaps because each has written for the
screen and heard how unique lines can sound when spoken by talented
actors, their fiction cherishes the subtle nuances of individual speech.[48]

Yates fully explores the subtleties of voice, interior and exterior, as he examines in many different ways the gap between the word articulated and
the thought or intention behind that word. In a review of Gina Berriault's
fiction, Yates's comments clearly illustrate what he valued most in writing:

She renders their speech with a fine and subtle ear for the shy or strident inaccuracies, for the bewilderment of missed points and for the
dim, sad rhythms of clichés; but when she takes us into the silences of
their minds, their thoughts and feelings come out in prose as graceful,
as venturesome and precise as she can make it.[49]

Yates draws attention to the way in which thoughts are often betrayed by words and actions. April Wheeler's reflective interior thoughts at the end of *Revolutionary Road*, for instance, exemplify how people slip into an inherently false mode of communication, borrowing from the idiom of film or magazine romances. Her thoughts suggest it is almost easier to adopt an insincere voice than to find one's own:

> And all because, in a sentimentally lonely time long ago, she had found it easy and agreeable to believe whatever this one particular boy felt like saying, and to repay him for that pleasure by telling easy, agreeable lies of her own, until each was saying what the other most wanted to hear—until he was saying "I love you" and she was saying "Really, I mean it; you're the most interesting person I've ever met."[50]

The repeated, ironic, use of "easy" indicates that the falsity may, as here, have arisen without any malicious design or desire to cheat truth. The effortlessness with which such insincere performances are given indicates that this behavior is both prevalent and encouraged.

What Yates suggests is that even if the intention to adopt a false role was not there to begin with, it emerges in the end as one after another characters' relationships collapse under the strain of communication that misses its mark. The implication of Yates's observations is not that language is inadequate or unclear, in the way much postmodern fiction suggests it might be, but that language is used dishonestly as part of an ongoing performance. When characters such as April Wheeler or Emily Grimes wake up to the realization that so much around them is artificial, that all their relationships are built on shifting sands, and that they themselves are implicated because they have adopted a language not their own, the result is catastrophic. Since their experiences closely mirror Yates's, their catastrophes are, in a very real sense, his own.

As noted, Yates's work depends on a deep sense of association between the reader and the characters described; their language and their evasions have to be recognizable and recognizably inadequate to the enormous task of honest self-expression. The whimsical and intellectually challenging style of, for instance, Donald Barthelme, could never be replicated or even admired by Yates. Barthelme's stories are not written from life, in the realists' understanding of that term, but are written from an interest in form and ideas and are designed to destabilize the reader. His short story "Me and Miss Mandible" is dependent not, as in Yates's work, on the reader's recognition of a situation but rather on the reader's shock and sense of defamiliarization: "Miss Mandible wants to make love to me but she hesitates because I am officially a child."[51] The situation, and the jaunty tone in which that situation is described, clashes in a way that complements the dual perspectives of adult and child. Seen by everyone as an innocent youngster, the narrator assures us he has been married, has been in the army, and has worked for an insurance company. We have no way of knowing whether the narrator is dreaming, is psychologically impaired, or is commenting on the adult perception of childhood.

Within the disquieting framework of his story, Barthelme fuses both comic detail and profound observation so that the reader must make of it what he will. The man/child, looking about him at the school where he is being (re) educated, draws attention to the lies by which we live, but he does this with a cool detachment that belies the seriousness of the comment: "But I say, looking about me in this incubator of future citizens, that signs are signs, and that some of them are lies. This is the great discovery of my time here."[52] Although the school itself (which may be read as a metaphorical representation of all the institutions we put our faith in throughout our lives), and the rhetoric it relies upon, emphasizes notions of correctness and rightness, the narrator suggests such confidence is misplaced: "Who points out that arrangements sometimes slip, that errors are made, that signs are misread? '*They have confidence in their ability to take the right steps and to obtain correct answers.*' I take the right steps, obtain correct answers, and my wife leaves me for another man."[53] This short story demonstrates Barthelme's commitment to the notion of art as artifact, as Richard Gray expresses it, and shows how he pursues this by drawing attention to the distance between the writer and his work, "to the displacement of the work from the world."[54] Yates, on the other hand, all but eradicates that gap as writer/character and character/observer blur the lines between the creator of a work of art and the lives that work of art sets out to encapsulate.

The erasure of a *clear* picture of the novelist writing his story is, therefore, ironically, the result of radically different approaches to writing. One approach involves a total immersion in the details and experiences of the novelist's life, producing fiction that is a reliving and reshaping of that life. This fiction is designed to provoke an enhanced empathy with the experiences of the novelist while not actually foregrounding his person; the writer/characters act as a filter through which the novelist's experiences are further explored. Life in biography and life in art produce literature that is *felt*. If this is not to degenerate into a soup of sentimentality the novelist has to be as self-critical as he is critical of his characters since very often they are versions of himself. While, to my mind, Yates masters this art, he did not convince many of his contemporary critics who felt the characters to be thoroughly unlikeable, so harshly did Yates scrutinize them: "The Wheelers are young, pathetic, trapped, half educated, and without humor—meaningless characters leading meaningless lives—and Mr. Yates's attempts to lend drama to their predicament, through an unconvincing introduction of madness and violence into the story, serves only to emphasize the flimsy nature of his work."[55]

Another approach (though by no means the *only* other approach), and one many of the postmodernists adopted, involves an apparent denial of any authorial objectivity by the creation of a hyperreality that does not seek to replicate anything and smiles at eccentric parallels between this hyperreality and the ordinariness of life as the "invisible" author experiences it. The contrast between the style of many of the postmodernists and Yates's fictive technique shows the different intentions of such novelists. But overlaps occurred that Yates neither saw nor, with his distaste for postmodernism, wanted to see. He shaped his fiction around events he had witnessed or experienced—the divorce of his parents, incarceration in a mental hospital, alcoholism—while others approached their fiction with very different aims.

John Barth's, Donald Barthelme's, and Jorge Luis Borges's stories evidence an authorial voice that seeks to encourage a displacement between the world as the author knows it and the world as the author creates it. Thus the narrator of "Tlon, Uqbar, Orbis Tertius" can assert with conviction, "I owe the discovery of Uqbar to the conjunction of a mirror and an encyclopedia."[56] Borges is "playing" with notions of authorial certainty; he deliberately confounds the reader's expectations to raise questions about narrative authority he felt to be trusted too often. Thus within the context of this story the narrator/character describes the discussion he has with his dinner companion, Bioy Casares: "we had lost all track of time in a vast debate over the way one might go about composing a first-person novel whose narrator would omit or distort things and engage in all sorts of contradictions, so that a few of the book's readers—a *very* few—might divine the horrifying or banal truth."[57] The discussion he alludes to, albeit in a fictional context, indicates exactly the kind of preoccupation that informed Borges's narrative style and the layered form of his work. That Casares, the Argentine novelist, actually existed and was a longtime friend of Borges's (and that this may well have referred to an actual conversation they had) adds to the sense that real life and fictional life will always overlap and inform the perspectives of both. Borges plays with this notion, with the phrase "a *very* few" drawing attention to his elitist preoccupation. Yates, on the other hand, adopts an approach that is devoid of such playfulness; his work, fully accepting of the conventions of realism (in this respect) and the conjugal link between author and protagonist suggests a serious attempt to blur the edges of any such overlap. Furthermore, Yates's fiction does not require a specialized readership. With ordinary men instead of heroes, and with dreams of acceptance and competence replacing heroic desires, his fictions are designed to have a broad appeal.

Borges foregrounds the *I* so blatantly and emphatically that one comes to mistrust it as a signifier of any real human shape. It becomes a disembodied voice commenting on the fiction, and the layers of fiction, it narrates. The *I* is, therefore, frequently the focal point of a narrative in his *Fictions*. Thrust to the fore, though undelineated among many narrative voices, it challenges the reader to interpret the interplay between voices and the layers of meaning they indicate. There is a sense of delight in the fictive landscape the *I* surveys in Borges's work, and within much postmodern fiction the role of the *I*/eye is fully interrogated. For Yates, however, there is no sense of such wry fictive muscle flexing. Looking across the body of his work at the recurring ideas, issues, characterizations, and themes, the author's presence and biography is suggested all the more strongly; "felt" experience is authenticated by the links between his life and that of his protagonists. Furthermore, his use of the first person singular, although only rarely employed, draws directly on his own experiences in an almost confessional way.

Essentially a traditionalist, not just in style but also in manner, Yates also rejected the literary claims and ethos of the New Journalists who were increasingly popular through the 1960s. Tom Wolfe could describe his first foray[58] into this type of writing in terms that were anathema to Yates: "It's hard to say what it was like. It was a garage sale, that piece . . . vignettes, odds and ends of scholarship, bits of memoir, short bursts of sociology, apostrophes, epithets, moans, cackles, anything that came into my head, much of it thrown together in a rough and awkward way. That was its virtue. It showed me the possibility of there being something 'new' in journalism."[59] It is exactly the sense of a "garage sale" that Yates deplored in this kind of writing, though he did not dismiss all the New Journalists' work. Joan Didion, at least, escaped his censure.[60]

Unlike Yates, Wolfe revels in the disjointedness and the patchwork effect of his writing, emphasizing its chaos, as Richard Gray suggests: "[most of Wolfe's essays] are notable for . . . their wit, bravura and high-octane prose: a baroque pop style that offers a sardonic reflection of, and comment on, their subjects. Wolfe is . . . intent on making sly fun of the shiny surfaces and strutting heroes of his culture."[61] Yates found no room for either chaos or bravura in his work, as Stewart O'Nan suggests: "There's nothing fussy or pretentious about his style. If anything, his work could be called simple or traditional, conventional, free of the metafictionalists' or even the modernists' tricks."[62] The trickery may be missing, but this is, to my mind, a slightly misleading statement since Yates does incorporate some of the "mannerism" of the metafictionalists into his realist framework but without drawing any attention to them. In Yates's view, autobiographically led stories were stories that needed the shaping power of imagination to form them. Yates might have included the odds and ends of human life in one sense (the fantasies that usually remained hidden, the wife beating not generally alluded to, the social jealousies inspired by apparently insignificant trivia), but he brought these aspects of life to the fore with fine and subtle art. There is never any sense that Yates is accurately describing, recording, or reenacting real events as a primary determinant of his fiction. Real events are used but only as far as they illustrate naturally the dimensions of his fictive characters.

Even if Yates was not interested in documentary or reportage as a style for his fiction, it is fair to assume that he would have agreed with Tom Wolfe's opinions about the history of fiction: "Realism is not merely another literary approach or attitude. The introduction of detailed realism into English literature in the eighteenth century was like the introduction of electricity into machine technology. . . . And for anyone, in fiction or in nonfiction, to try to improve literary technique by abandoning social realism would be like an engineer trying to improve upon machine technology by abandoning electricity."[63] However, Wolfe's claim that the New Journalists had irrevocably changed the face of the novel, when they had, in fact, primarily changed the face of journalism, seemed premature and ignorant of the fact that the novel depended on both realism and artistry, as Georg Lukács made clear: "all writing must contain a certain degree of realism . . . realism is not one style among others, it is the basis of literature; all styles (even those seemingly most opposed to realism) originate in it or are significantly related to it."[64] The arguments Wolfe put forward were designed to provoke debate among those who dismissed realism: "By giving up the devices of realism— such as realistic dialogue, status detail and point of view—the Neo-Fabulist becomes like the engineer who decides to give up electricity because it has 'been done.'"[65] The New Journalists were, however, also up against the determined social realists such as Yates. These were writers who found that they wanted to continue, but modernize, a nineteenth-century tradition. What Wolfe failed to realize in his polemic is that by using the tools of the novelist he too was shaping and distorting "reality." While Yates knew that, Wolfe is less inclined to make this admission.

Liberal minded though he thought he was, Yates seems to have hated the liberties the New Journalists were taking in the name of "realism." His antipathy toward a broad acceptance of "all" writing is given humorous and dramatic force in an argument between Lucy and Michael Davenport in *Young*

Hearts Crying as Lucy defends the writers who achieve best-seller-list status. Davenport dismisses her suggestion that their success is accomplished by writing "what a great many people want, or need"[66] as utterly naive. It is hard not to read his response as a very thinly disguised version of Yates's own view: "Oh, come on, Lucy, you know better than that. It's never been a question of what people 'want' or 'need'—it's a question of what they're willing to put *up* with. It's the same rotten little commercial principle that determines what we get in the movies and on television. It's the manipulation of public taste by virtue of the lowest common denominator."[67] While there is undoubtedly truth, from a Yatesian perspective, in Davenport's position, it offers solace to a writer who is not successful commercially and who struggles to produce serious literature, a writer such as Davenport, or Yates himself. The success of others goes hand in hand, therefore, with the comforting thought that they have "sold out."

In the *Ploughshares* interview Yates drew attention to his antipathy to the direction writing had taken by 1972: "I've tried and tried, but I just can't stomach most of what's now being called 'The post-realistic fiction.' I can't read John Barth with anything but irritation. I can't read Donald Barthelme at all. I can read hardly any of the many other new 'post-realists,' whatever their ever-increasingly famous names may be. I know it's all very fashionable stuff and I know it provides an endless supply of witty little intellectual puzzles and puns and fun and games for graduate students to play with, but it's emotionally empty. It isn't *felt*."[68] Yates's letters are peppered with the colorful language of a man who abhorred all "isms" and did not mince his words about any subject. In a letter to DeWitt Henry (July 24, 1972), Yates embellishes his published criticisms:

> I wanted very much to mount an all-out attack on the whole fucking "Post-realistic School," and I think I brought it off rather nicely in a short space. I didn't mention one of the most loathsome of that breed— Robert Coover—by name, because I know the little sonovabitch personally, and a good many people know I know him, and it might have read like a vindictive personal vendetta, the sort of thing I've always despised in "literary" essays. Nor did I mention Robert Scholes by name, though we both know he is chiefly responsible for the current fashion of "post-realism" (I think he even coined that phrase)—and there again the reason was personal. I've known him for many years too, spent many evenings in his house, etc., and though I never liked him much I was always very fond of his wife—and she died very recently of cancer (see how infernally complicated these things can be?).[69]

Castronovo and Goldleaf sum up the critical difference between Yates and many of the experimentalists when they point out that while Yates, "specializes in describing Americans ground down by the quiet, relentless demands of fitting into the affordable house and the office cubicle," some of his contemporaries who occupied critical attention at the time, "chose not to chronicle such inconspicuous defeats, favoring shock, sexual revelation, apocalypse, stylistic experiment, and rage as their hallmarks."[70] This assessment is rather too neat; there is plenty of shock and sexual revelation in Yates's work.

In one of Yates's later novels, *A Good School*, one of the characters argues in favor of mimesis, and as so often happens the reader may peer behind him and see Yates: "I want people to *feel*," Haskell told him. "I want people to experience *life*."[71] For Haskell, as for Yates, writing was a serious business and carried with it responsibilities to be honest and faithful to experience. It is the playfulness and ironic distance incurred by whimsical ironic narratives, the "witty intellectual puzzles and puns and fun and games" that Yates felt created fiction at odds with experience. All his working life he strove to have a story accepted for publication in the *New Yorker* magazine; it was a measure of acceptance by the literary world for Yates and he looked on jealously at those who had "made it." Blake Bailey provides us with a colorful picture of his frustration and desire: "'All I want is a story in the goddamned *New Yorker*!' he'd rage when discussing the ups and downs of his career; also he'd started referring to staple writers for the magazine with an almost reflexive opprobrium—particularly 'John fucking Cheever' and 'John fucking Updike.'"[72] The fact that his work wasn't widely accepted in his lifetime was a constant reminder to Yates that he had chosen an unfashionable course. Bailey discloses that following his final rejection by the *New Yorker*, "Yates was very, *very* disappointed. It was the end of one of his fondest dreams."[73] Ironically, and it is a measure of how the tide has turned for Yates, the *New Yorker* finally published one of his stories—"The Canal"—on January 15, 2001. "The Canal" is included in *The Collected Stories of Richard Yates*.

It is also germane to the student of Yates to ask how his work sits alongside that of the naturalists such as Theodore Dreiser, Sherwood Anderson, and Sinclair Lewis. These writers believed that people are victims of circumstance, powerless to act against social and environmental forces that constrain them. Lee Siegel, for instance, makes the point that "Strangely, you won't ever hear Yates mentioned in connection with the American naturalists."[74] Although Anderson's writer in *Winesburg, Ohio*—a collection of interrelated short stories—is almost the only character for whom there is any hope in a bleak and lonely town, Yates's novelists are lesser mortals with ill-defined talent. Anderson suggests that despite the environment and the many dysfunctional relationships that surround George Willard, he occupies an elevated position, both physically, since his office looks over the main street, and psychologically; people come to him for advice, to vent their spleen, or to court his sympathy. The portrait of George adheres to the modernist belief in the redemptive possibilities of art, but it is only a suggestion of such a position and is not developed beyond George's "escape."

The story cycle ends with George leaving the confines of this town; while others remain locked in their lonely worlds, watching from windows, George acts. In spite of that, he is, among other things, emotionally underdeveloped and is no match for the more detailed portraits that Yates produces. However, the advice Kate Swift gives to her former pupil, as she encourages him with his writing, sounds very Yatesian in its determination to get beneath surface manners and superficial characterization: "You will have to know life," she declared. . . . "You must not become a mere peddler of words. The thing to learn is to know what people are thinking about, not what they say."[75]

There are interesting similarities between Sinclair Lewis's novel *Main Street* and Yates's first novel. Lewis adopts an equivocal tone about the world he conjures up in *Main Street* and his protagonist's response to it. Like Yates, forty years later, his protagonist is a woman fighting against drowning in a backwater where small town gossip and prejudice infect her every ambition. The reader is in no doubt that Carol Kennicott is naive and foolhardy in her singular attempts to take on the traditions of a small, midwestern town but is encouraged to empathize with her since, while he mocks her zeal and passion, Lewis balances this with careful emphasis on the enervating atmosphere of Gopher Prairie: "It was not only the unsparing unapologetic ugliness and the rigid straightness which overwhelmed her. It was the planlessness, the flimsy temporariness of the buildings, their faded unpleasant colors."[76] However, Yates's portrait of April Wheeler, suffocating slowly in suburbia and wishing to go to Paris and support her family, or of Emily Grimes drunkenly careering through a series of one-night stands, encourages no such romantic empathy in the reader. The reader may feel it, and many readers do, but Yates, unlike Lewis, does not demand or encourage it.

Whether identified as naturalist or realist, both Lewis and Yates ensure that the boundaries of their protagonists' ambition are in direct relation to the terms of their confinement. Carol Kennicott wants a voice that is heard and status that she has earned herself rather than as her husband's wife. The idea that Carol and Mrs. Dr. Kennicott are two distinct personalities warring to be made whole is made explicit when, having leaped around in the slush and snow, she sees that she is being spied on: "She stopped, walked on sedately, changed from the girl Carol into Mrs. Dr. Kennicott."[77] Her trip to the seat of power in Washington is an appropriate place for her to try and resolve this dichotomy. Indeed, the reader is made aware that "She felt that she was no longer one-half of a marriage but the whole of a human being."[78] April Wheeler dreams of a Parisian life in order, like Carol, to become whole. In her mind, it would be a place where she could work and her husband could write, for Paris is emblematic of artistic and social freedoms she cannot find in suburbia. Her vision of Paris is appropriate in illustrating Yates's depiction of this actress manqué, though it undoubtedly dates the novel in a specific way. Paris was the center of artistic longing for artists of a previous generation, and while Yates identified with such longing, just as he identified with Hemingway and Fitzgerald, his contemporary readership may not have been so willing to accept this particular dream.

Lewis and Yates may both examine the role of women in society and investigate what it is to be American in the twentieth century with a high immigrant population and rising personal ambition, but their approach is highly distinct. In *Main Street* and *Young Hearts Crying*, we meet women who are pushing against the social strictures that seek to tame them, but with sixty-four years between publication dates, different questions arise for the authors. While Lucy Davenport's ambition is centered on finding a role for herself within her marriage, and then as a single woman, Carol's ambition is vast as she seeks to understand and be understood in Gopher Prairie. Lewis is unequivocal in his use of this town as representative of hundreds of other similar frontier settlements that have settled into a gray mediocrity by the late nineteenth and early twentieth centuries, and his characters are similarly both specific and generic: "The universal similarity—that is the physical expression of the philosophy of dull safety. Nine-tenths of the American towns are so alike that it is the completest boredom to wander from one to another."[79] If Yates adopts a similar position to Lewis in relation to the story he tells, he is far subtler about his dual perspective. Lewis uses his characters to make specific points about the political and social landscape and attacks a narrow-minded understanding of what it is to be American. He presents sweeping observations about the growth of America and Americanization, a world standardized and pure that dulls down all communities and all aspirations to the same colorless, shapeless format: "Sure of itself, it bullies other civilizations, as a traveling salesman in a brown derby conquers the wisdom of China and tacks advertisements of cigarettes over arches for centuries dedicate [*sic*] to the sayings of Confucius."[80] Yates, on the other hand, makes his reader work harder and avoids sounding overtly didactic.

Lionel Trilling makes the point that "Sinclair Lewis is shrewd, but no one . . . can believe that he does more than a limited job of social understanding."[81]

This could not be said of Yates's finely honed characterizations, steeped as they are in an understanding of modern psychology and sociological thought. The weakness of Lewis's novel is in his attempt to make the reader believe that with new self-knowledge and a measure of freedom, Carol willingly returns to her former home and husband. This exemplifies a very distinct approach to endings between the novelists. Yates finds very little resolution in his dramas and is prepared for the sake of authenticity to push his characters toward their downfall. Lewis's work, on the other hand, as Richard Gray suggests, depends on an outcome that always indicates a compromise with truth: "So the pattern that characterizes all Lewis's satires of American provincialism is established: the impulse to escape the restrictions of class or routine leads to flight, but the flight meets with only partial success and is followed by a necessary compromise with convention. In the end the critique is muted, not least because the last word is given to Will Kennicott who, for all his stolidity, is portrayed as honest, hard-working, kindly and thrifty."[82]

Ultimately Carol returns to Gopher Prairie accepting of its ways, relieved of some of her ambitions and with a limited freedom within her marriage that has been hard won. There is no such romantic tendency in any of Yates's novels. As Morris Dickstein observes, for Yates, and his artistic ambition, there was no compromise available: "From Salinger and Ellison to Yates, the best writers of the fifties identified with the outsider, not with a dominant culture they found hollow and oppressive. They saw rebellion, neurosis, and madness as forms of lucidity, and portrayed adjustment and sanity as symptoms of deadly compromise."[83] As if to clarify the point, Michael Davenport (*Young Hearts Crying*) bemoans the fact that the literary world has fought shy of the truth of life for the American proletariat: "'Look, I'll give you Dreiser and Frank Norris and those guys,' he would explain, 'and I'll even give you the early Steinbeck, but for the most part there hasn't *been* a proletarian literature in America. We're scared shitless of facing the truth, that's what it amounts to.'"[84]

Even though Yates and more experimental writers had very different approaches to their craft, there were areas of overlap. While Yates made it clear that he regarded labels and categories as limiting and reductive, he might well have agreed, for instance, with Walker Percy's assessment of the modern novelist: "And since the novelist deals first and last with individuals . . . it is the novelist's responsibility to be chary of categories and rather to focus upon the mystery, the paradox, the *openness* of an individual human existence."[85] Percy was interested in the role and development of the postmodern writer, with the stress on *openness*, while Yates's interest and emphasis lay on the term *individual*. However, Percy's and Yates's views do show an alignment; individual experience is at the heart of both methods of inquiry. Percy isolates the problem for the novelist's protagonist; he is a man whose only problem is "to keep from blowing his brains out."[86] In Yates's fiction the authorial interest seems centered on the *process* toward that position of self-annihilation, on how, to use Percy's phrase, that protagonist "has very nearly come to the end of the line."[87] Thus while Percy's concerns, and the concerns of most of the postmodernists, are overtly epistemological and philosophical, Yates's lie in the more prosaic arena of human interaction and the interplay of everyday exchange. As the postmodernists highlight and even relish the bizarre in life, Yates is drawn to the mundane so that epistemological concerns are not flaunted but linger in the background of his narratives. Even if Yates harks back to an earlier time in his construction of the novel, in his ideas he prefigures many of Percy's thoughts. His novels attempt to disturb rather than confirm, but within the recognized frameworks of realist fiction. While the perceptions of the role of the writer are similar for Percy and Yates, therefore, the focus of inquiry was very different. Conversely, while the perceptions of the role of the writer are different for Wolfe and Yates, the focus of inquiry, the desire, for instance, to replicate the imprecision of speech, was very similar.

It is true, of course, that there are as many different forms of *postmodernist literature* as there are of *realist literature*; both terms are insecure and are regularly challenged. For Yates there was a truth that could be uncovered, even if the means by which he would pursue this truth could only provide a partial uncovering of the reality he perceived. However, Yates was not interested in striving to find truth, in Truman Capote's pursuit of the concept as a journalistic recreation of *actual* events,[88] nor in Wolfe's kind of journalistic eavesdropping, but was after a truth that in descriptions of events and in reenactment of dialogue could, like Hemingway's fiction, stimulate recognition in the reader's mind.

For Yates, as for Hemingway, literature and the art of writing had great value. This valorization of the written word is made explicit by Hemingway, in a work such as *The Sun Also Rises*, where Jake reads Turgenieff and reflects upon his reading: "I would remember it somewhere, and afterwards it would seem as though it had really happened to me. I would always have it. That was another good thing you paid for and then had."[89] Books do contribute something; they provide a clear and immediate literary experience and become part of life. These precepts are implicit in all of Yates's fiction. Although never seen musing on books that they themselves have read, Yates's writers struggle to produce something worthwhile and lasting, thus the value of literature permeates all their portraits. In a sense, this valorizing of the written word is another veiled attack on the way in which film is designed for easy and immediate consumption and echoes J. D. Salinger's perspective. In his imagined utopian retreat, Holden Caulfield suggests how his brother could come and visit, but only if he came in order to write stories: "but he couldn't write any movies in my cabin, only stories and books."[90]

Richard Yates may have never attempted an aesthetic for the novel, but he was categorical about what he did *not* want. As we have seen, he could not abide the playfulness imbued in work that essentially stemmed from the idea of art as artifact, an attitude toward which Castronovo and Goldleaf draw our attention: "Postrealist fiction, *to his mind*, tended to ignore emotional problems in favor of intellectual puzzles; postrealist writers saw themselves not as chroniclers of the contemporary scene but as 'fictionists,' technical innovators in a long literary tradition, on which their work commented and to which it often alluded. . . . Their subject was primarily their work, and it concerned fiction and ideas instead of people and their lives."[91] Although this provides a comprehensive dismissal of postrealist fiction and suggests no areas of overlap where a realist writer might, for instance, be interested in ideas about writing as well as about people, it does echo the kind of sweeping expostulations Yates himself made. He explored the possibilities of the modern, realist form self-consciously and deliberately. However, utterly confounded as he was by what he saw to be the pretentious and hollow literary move toward experimentation in both the form and style of many of his contemporaries' work, he did not dismiss the debate about style but dramatized it within his fiction. By swiftly glossing over Yates's comments about postrealist fiction and by omitting a consideration of this aspect of Yates's work, Castronovo and Goldleaf overlook its importance. The frequent portraits of writers and artists who contemplate their own methods of creative inquiry in apparent isolation (and in opposition to what appears to be a general trend in a different direction) provide a clear indication of the seriousness with which Yates observed the literary fashion of his time.

In Yates's mid-twentieth-century landscape the comfortable certainties and beliefs of previous centuries are no longer present. Not disputing the necessity for a moral sense in a work of art, Yates examined it in ways that were different from those of earlier writers. He wrote from a perspective that challenged established beliefs and conventions but found very little to replace them. Furthermore, he relished moral ambiguity; it forced readers to engage with the complexity of the issues at hand, and it prevented easy, sentimental resolution.

With the emphasis on Christianity, religious beliefs were particularly scrutinized in his fiction. An indictment of any religious form of consolation is to be found at the end of *A Good School* when the protagonist, Bill Grove, meets up with a former school friend. Bucky Ward has returned from the war full of affectations, false bravado, and his own explanation as to why he was saved: "'Why me? Out of all those others, why me? Oh, I'll never be sure, I suppose, but I think I know. I think it's Christianity. I think it's Jesus.' And so he had resolved to become a man of the cloth. I haven't seen or heard from him in thirty years."[92] Perhaps emulating Hemingway's use of omission for dramatic effect, Yates keeps Grove silent. Since Grove seems to represent aspects of Yates himself in this novel, framed as it is by a first person narrative, the unspoken dismissal of the self-deluding Ward strongly indicates Yates's position. It would seem that this is how Yates views belief; it sidesteps realities that are too uncomfortable to bear. Moreover, although underplayed here, the move toward silence is a refuge Yatesian figures often seek; words, he suggests, are not always an efficient way of communicating. April Wheeler, for instance, is at her most expressive when she remains silent and obdurate in the face of Frank's tirades, and Howard Givings, turning off his hearing aid at the end of *Revolutionary Road*, becomes most expressive as he lapses into "a welcome, thunderous sea of silence."[93]

The ending of *The Easter Parade* throws further light on Yates's views of Christianity. Emily Grimes, now a lonely alcoholic, finally agrees to enter her nephew Peter's home after hurling a tirade of abuse at him. The aptly named Peter is an Episcopalian minister. His lifestyle, kindly forbearance, and generosity of spirit in the face of his aunt's verbal attack on him might well be read as a form of redemption at the end of this novel. However, I read this as Yates posing a fundamental question about the role of Christianity in modern life. He does not condemn it outright, recognizing that for some, such as Peter, it offers solace. However, he does suggest that the comfort it offers sidesteps uncomfortable truths that a character like Emily wants addressed. Among critics and readers of Yates, this ending has been much debated, and, I think, the ambiguity has been overstated. Lee Siegel characterizes this debate in an article for *Harper's Magazine*: "Peter's invitation to enter yet another family romance could be read—indeed, almost demands to be read—as the bitterest of ironies. But since he seems happily married, with his family intact, perhaps Emily does stand, if unsteadily, at the threshold of redemption. Yet is it the redemption of religious grace or the promise of 'alert' psychoanalytic 'understanding' that offers no love or sympathy? Are those the jingling keys to heaven's gate (as Peter's name suggests), or are they the coins of selfishness and greed? It hardly seems to matter. The expectation of grace in a world without God and mere psychiatric understanding in a world without grace are like two sides of an obscene joke. That is Yates's zero-degree ethos."[94] I find the equivocation of Siegel's reading unconvincing. Yates has prepared the ground for this moment from the very beginning of the novel.

In the course of her life Emily cannot accept any facile answers to anything; she is characterized as always challenging the easy comfort others take from a romanticized or sentimental reading of a situation. For example, as a child she corrects her sister about their father's job, always insisting on facing things head on: "Emily, though, was a stickler for accuracy, and as soon as the boy was out of earshot she reminded her sister of the facts. 'He's only a copy-desk man,' she said."[95] Peter is a contrasting figure to Emily in terms of his belief in addition to his stable domestic life. Although it is true that he is not seen as a diminished figure, he is *felt* to be one. The price for finding consolation in Christianity is apparently ignoring (or failing to see) the reality of what is going on in his parents' home. As a woman of nearly fifty,[96] Emily hasn't quite given up insistently digging for truths, such as when she probes Peter for information about her sister he cannot supply:

> "Well, it's the *fall* I want to hear about. How did she fall? How was she hurt?"
>
> "I wasn't there, Aunt Emmy."
>
> "Christ, what a cop-out. You weren't there. And you never even asked?"[97]

It is not just that Peter cannot supply the answers that Emily wants, he hasn't even thought about asking the questions.

Happiness has always eluded Emily, and this glimpse into Peter's "perfect" life is too much for her. Peter, ever attentive and forgiving, gently calms her down and offers, essentially, to share what he has with his elderly aunt: "'All right,' he said quietly. 'All right, Aunt Emmy. Now. Would you like to come on in and meet the family?'"[98] The novel ends on this gentle, very ordinary note of Christian forgiveness and the suggestion of inclusion. A broken woman, Emily has no choice but to "[go] on in and meet the family." She has nowhere else she can go. The narrative tone is particularly important here. Built into this apparently familial scene there is a sense that in acquiescing, in entering Peter's family home and accepting it as her own, Emily will be capitulating to the pretense that is offered by both the idealized fiction of the modern American suburban family and, furthermore, by Christianity. Emily Grimes is no hero and has neither the strength nor the means to reject her nephew's offer.

Walker Percy, writing a year before this novel and referring to the postmodern hero, suggests he has "forgotten his bad memories and conquered his present ills and . . . finds himself in the victorious secular city."[99] Yates's implicit rejection of Christian redemption, a solution that middle America has long held dear, is, therefore, very much of its time. While one can undoubtedly argue that Peter is seen as a welcoming savior *and* the naive peddler of untruths, to my mind Yates is clearer than such a reading suggests. He has drawn Emily's uncompromising character very carefully. That Peter is a priest just adds to the sense that his happiness, from the subtle perspective of Yates's narrative, is synthetic.

It is never a surprise to the reader of a Yates story that the characters lack courage, nor is it a surprise that Yates's fascination with endings dominates all his narratives. Time and again the protagonists are balanced on a precipice through the negative prism of collapse or failure. Social, emotional, and often psychological disintegration is the starting point for so many of his stories, and his novels in particular. Nowhere is this clearer than with the first sentence of *The Easter Parade*: "Neither of the Grimes sisters would have a happy life, and looking back it always seemed that the trouble began with their parents' divorce."[100] From the outset, a "happy" resolution to the story of the Grimes sisters' lives is not going to happen; what concerns Yates, and therefore the reader, is how they deal with that unhappiness. Attention is drawn to the fact that Yates is interested not in the plot but in the process, not in the outcome but in the inexorable drive toward that outcome. In the same vein, the beginning of *Disturbing the Peace* mirrors this pattern with the uncompromising pairing of "everything" and "wrong": "Everything began to go wrong for Janice Wilder in the late summer of 1960."[101] Like Fitzgerald before him, Yates asserts his "endings" as a point of departure for his stories.[102]

Although this pattern of inverted beginnings and endings is apparent in much of his fiction, it is most starkly drawn in Yates's novels. In *Revolutionary Road*, for instance, the "final dying sounds"[103] of the Laurel Players' dress rehearsal deliberately and ironically has all the sonorous downbeat inflection of the final act of a tragic play; this particular metaphor is completed with the novel's ending when Mr. Givings, turning off his hearing aid, hears only "a thunderous sea of silence."[104] A gentler version of the same anticlimactic opening is apparent in Yates's short stories; a problem is identified but not explained. The beginning of "The B.A.R. Man" uses this method: "Until he got his name on the police blotter, and in the papers, nobody had ever thought much about John Fallon."[105] The reader then has to wait sixteen pages to know how or why he is arrested; warned as to the route this story will take, we have to be attentive to find out the "why" and "how" of the detail.

Yates's strength as a writer is in engaging his readers straightaway and then holding their attention by weaving in and out of different points of view. Each story is thus given pace and fluency since the narrator's authority is diluted by the presence of characters that appear to speak directly to the reader. Looking again at "The B.A.R. Man," the following sentences illustrate the complexity and yet fluency of Yates's ability to convey points of view as the perspective shifts between characters: "The trouble might never have happened if his wife had not insisted, that particular Friday, on breaking his routine: *there was a Gregory Peck picture in its final showing that night, and she saw no reason why he couldn't do without his prize fight for once in his life.* She told him this on Friday morning, and it was the first of many things that went wrong with his day."[106] The narrator leads the reader to a point, a colon in fact, where Rose's voice is detectable through the use of her idiom. Just as the reader is absorbing the shift in view, Yates pulls the reader back to the narrative voice that mirror's Fallon's perspective. The issue, therefore, of how and why John Fallon is arrested is given dramatic energy by the method Yates chooses for the telling; again, it is the process that is highlighted rather than the "plot."

In Yates's fiction the personal predicament for the protagonist is generally the first thing that he addresses, and he makes it clear that the idea of a resolution, a romantic and comforting ending, or, indeed, a tragic resolution,[107] is anathema to his form of realism. Very occasionally Yates's stories proffer a very gentle glimmer of hope, but that hope, as in *The Easter Parade*, is so often steeped in ambiguity. As illustrated by the stories discussed in this chapter, Yates displays his aversion to overtly fictionalized, final endings just as he does to starkly drawn good guys and bad guys. Moving close to the postmodern technique whereby a novel's end is merely a continuation, with further, wider, questions posed, Yates's endings offer no tidy fictional packages. Writing about postmodern fiction, Alain Robbe-Grillet could be describing the end of a Yates novel: "For the function of art is never to illustrate a truth—or even a question—known beforehand, but to give birth to questions (and also perhaps, at the appointed time, to answers) not previously formulated."[108] Again, "The B.A.R. Man" provides an example of this inclination to extend the questions beyond the confines of the story. A story that has ostensibly been *about* Fallon and his insecurities has raised questions about something much wider and more disturbing, in this instance, McCarthyism. While some kind of resolution to the story is offered, however superficially, the reader is quickly aware that two political issues, at least, have been thrown up without comment. One is of course the damage done by McCarthy and his supporters, damage felt particularly keenly by artists, writers, and anyone who appeared to challenge the government. The other is the notion of how returning servicemen were reintegrated into the society they left behind when they went to war. Yates resists commenting directly about either of these political and social issues, but he leaves them hovering in the background of his story. However, toward the end, nearer the surface of his drama, he asks the reader to work out the connections between Fallon's behavior and his frustrations, between Fallon as a person and Fallon within his social milieu.

Yates's attitude toward the inclusion of contemporary political and social problems in his fiction is well illustrated by "The B.A.R. Man"; he touches on them but only insofar as they have a bearing on his characters and their relationships, and it is usually with his endings that such wider issues connect with the individual characters. In that respect, and like Fitzgerald, what begins as a concern for and about an individual becomes a concern for and about modern American society. This is not achieved in the heavy-handed manner of naturalists such as Theodore Dreiser and Sinclair Lewis but is a subtler process of inquiry. Like a camera pulling back from the face of one character to encompass the whole group, Yates's endings pose questions that go beyond the confines of the individuals. Just as the ending of *Revolutionary Road* might leave the reader considering issues that encompass loneliness, abortion, and suburbia, the ending of *The Easter Parade* raises questions about the role religion plays in a modern society while at the same time highlighting the fate of unmarried women. One gets the sense that Yates is attempting to mirror the way political events, or social dilemmas with a political dimension (and one thinks of April Wheeler's or Emily Grimes's abortions in this context) impinge on the lives of ordinary men and women; they are felt and debated only insofar as they affect the individual.

Yates manipulates small elements of his fictions to direct his reader's attention in very specific ways. The narratives frequently oscillate between a heightened unreality—captured using the clichéd idiom of sentimental film and the artifice of magazine poses, for instance—and a bluntly asserted reality that in its deliberate ugliness undercuts any form of sentiment. It is those blunt assertions the reader is left pondering. In *The Easter Parade*, for instance, Sarah Grimes, having just met the dashing Tony Wilson, is described as "sleepwalking back into the apartment, allowing herself to be late for work."[109] Her walk, imitative of the lead actress in a romantic film, is swiftly countered by the description of her mother's entrance: "Pookie came into the living room, her eyes wide and her uncertain lips glistening with breakfast bacon grease."[110] Similarly, at the wedding that follows, Pookie Grimes is described dancing with her daughter's new father-in-law: "she batted her eyelids and sank . . . dreamily into his arms."[111] By contrast, and from Geoffrey Wilson's perspective, "she clung to him like a slug."[112] In this novel, the Grimes sisters are differentiated by these two positions: Sarah is the romantic whose behavior and speech always resonate with the contrived sentiment of film and Emily is the pragmatist who asks questions, stands apart and, with the reader, stares in bewilderment at an uglier reality.

Nonetheless, the way in which we receive Emily is more complicated than this binary opposition makes it sound. Yates manipulates the reader's empathy for her in a complex, potentially risky, manner. To begin with the unfairness of her life as a young child, together with her obvious distance from her mother, makes it easy to applaud her straightforward, no-nonsense approach to all things, especially in view of her mother's and sister's frivolity. Then Emily begins to behave in a questionable manner; she gets drunk, she sleeps around, and she has several abortions. However, it is not until Emily denies her sister sanctuary that the reader's empathy for her is really challenged. Acting purely out of self-interest and greatly threatened by Sarah's neediness, Emily is shown in a deeply unattractive light. Nevertheless, and unlike his characterization of John Wilder, Yates manages to sustain reader interest, if not wholehearted reader empathy, by making the reader identify with her very human mistakes.

The characters who challenge Emily's behavior are not figures with whom the reader can easily identify. Howard Dunninger, her lover, is a man who is still in love with his wife and we sense will leave Emily at any moment. He is clearly unimpressed by Emily's response to Sarah's call for help and voices his criticism: "What do you *want* from her? You want her opening her heart to you every five minutes? . . . When she *does* that, you say you 'don't want her dragging down your life.'"[113] The reader may recognize the truth of what he says, but, without any real empathy toward Howard, it doesn't resonate as deeply as it might. When Emily sees Tony Wilson (now Sarah's husband and a man we know has beaten her up on many occasions) standing red-eyed at the graveside, she assumes he's faking his pain and has been rubbing his knuckles into his eyes. But Yates reiterates the detail of his red eyes at other moments by the graveside and at the wake: his eyes are "red and swollen,"[114] they are "inflamed,"[115] and finally they are "still swollen."[116] With these details, Yates asks the reader to stand back from Emily's quick dismissal of Wilson's grief and her easy assumptions that he didn't love the woman he also abused. Love, as Yates knew, and as he describes it, takes many forms, and most of them do not accord with the cinematic version.

Emily is shown to be judgmental and intransigent, but Yates sustains our interest in her by giving her faults that given the particular circumstances are easy to understand. As a way of avoiding simplistic characterizations, Yates frequently looks for the right moment to add ambiguities and inconsistencies in behavior to create depth and a sense of human texture. He spells this out in *Disturbing the Peace* when John Wilder questions the way the central character is developing in the film script: "The way it stands now we all believe Ralph's story. . . . But what if we played it so nobody'd be quite sure whether to believe it or not? I don't want to make Ralph a liar—nothing that blatant—but I want him to be a very complicated, troubled kid. . . . I guess what I'm after is a little whaddyacallit, a little ambiguity in the scene."[117] The characterization of Emily depends on such thought-provoking ambiguities since Yates intends to make his reader work. As Wilder expresses it, "I want the audience to sort of read between the lines here."[118]

Making his approximations, with his own version of realism, separating himself deliberately from fashionable innovative techniques and settling for his own idiosyncratic methods and form, Yates perfected his style. Ironically, given his generally critical tone toward social realism, this is precisely what Ronald Sukenick is calling for: "There is no such thing as fiction. Instead there is a continuing fictive discourse which continually redefines itself. There is certainly no such thing as THE novel. Instead there are as many novels as there are authentic novelists, and . . . every form should be idiosyncratic."[119] He goes on, rather grudgingly, to accord a limited place in contemporary fiction to the realist novel: "There is no contemporary Novel. The contemporary situation is rather that different kinds of novels may serve different purposes. The authority of the realistic/naturalistic mode is too deeply embedded in our tradition to lose its utility for fiction. There are persuasive reasons today for writing fiction in the realistic forms, even though such writing in no way represents 'the state of the art.' Realism, for example, can be useful during the emergence of a minority or oppressed culture into increased consciousness. It can provide a means for the presentation and evaluation of the data important to the life of a cultural group when it most needs to hold the mirror up to itself and its surrounding milieu."[120] Yates *was* writing about a specific culture and social group in a way that no one else was doing in quite the same way. The overlaps in terms of subject matter with, among others, John Cheever, John O'Hara, and Raymond Carver, do not detract from the fact that Yates's "mirror" uniquely reflects what life in America was like for the suburban, aspirational, middle classes behind the closed doors of their homes and offices. By carefully describing their surroundings, he dramatizes their alienation; by immersing us in their dialogue, he immerses us in their lives.

8

The 1950s and Gender Roles

10. (Left to right) Richard, Sharon, and
Sheila, taken in the South of France,
circa 1952. Courtesy of the Richard Yates
Estate.

As is evident from all Richard Yates's work, his writing is never overtly political or polemical, but it makes fascinating reading as it reflects the turmoil
and contradictions about gender roles and relationships that were evident
at the time he came of age. Yates lived through a period of enormous political and social upheaval; the mid-twentieth century saw American troops
fight in the Second World War as well as in Korea and Vietnam. Civil rights,
and the movement to create an equal and just society in the United States,
ensured that huge changes were occurring domestically as well as abroad.
However, none of these landmark historical events take center stage in Yates's
work. With the exception of the Second World War, which is a crucial and
dominant aspect of his second novel, *A Special Providence*, they are referred
to but are generally not of principal significance in his narratives. It is his

formative years, the 1950s, that Yates scrutinizes most closely, with his own development dramatically examined and reexamined through his fiction.

His writing displays a prescient awareness of gender politics, but, as with his political commentary, his expression of this consciousness is fused into his broader narratives. Therefore, while Yates should be seen as a commentator on, or an observer of, the way gender roles were shifting in the postwar era, his considerations are never primarily driven by ideological matters but are the result of the way patterns of change impinged on his own life. In that respect, his considerations about the role of women are apparently contradictory. On the one hand, homemaking and motherhood is seen to be unsatisfying, and on the other, women who find themselves outside a partnership and outside domestic fulfillment are seen to be lonely and self-destructive. However, in his early work, up to and including the publication of *Eleven Kinds of Loneliness* in 1962, Yates's depiction of the struggles men, and more particularly women, encounter, both within and outside the home, quietly prefigures some of the concerns the second wave of feminism adopted. In order to understand how Richard Yates viewed relationships, marriage, and the different roles and expectations for men and women in the 1950s and early 1960s, it is also important to consider how other commentators, including social historians and sociologists, viewed that period.

Through the course of his narratives, Yates writes against the grain of the idealized nuclear family America promoted following the Second World War. Norman Podhoretz explains the basic reason for the promulgation of an idealized version of America as a reaction against prewar liberalism and points toward the shift from "rights" to "responsibilities": "With an eye on the liberal emphasis on the rights of man, revisionism pointed to the correlative duties and responsibilities of man."[1] While many writers concentrate on the implications of this ideal in terms of class and race, recent sociological and historical commentaries often focus on what this meant for the family. As Warren Susman points out, "Every major institution in the United States promoted the home, togetherness, and the family. One sign of this was the family focus that proliferated in advertising: 'family-size carton, family room, family car, family film, family restaurant, family vacation.'"[2] Similarly, Elaine Tyler May suggests the importance—symbolic, practical, and emotional—of the home and the family at the start of the Cold War: "It needed heavy protection against the intrusions of forces outside itself. The self-contained home held out the promise of security in an insecure world. It also offered a vision of abundance and fulfillment. As the Cold War began, young postwar Americans were homeward bound."[3]

In much of his fiction, Yates displays an intuitive sense of the power and representational force of the home but he also suggests that our state of mind and the state of our relationships may determine how we view that home. The first sight we have of the Wheelers' new home in *Revolutionary Road* is confused by Mrs. Givings's and April's differing perspectives—deliberately so, since it highlights April's uncertainty about her life and this move to the suburbs. The house is described as "a sweet little house . . . [with] a sweet little setting,"[4] by Mrs. Givings, the agent. However, April's assessment challenges this ideal image: It looks "*small and wooden*, riding high on its *naked concrete foundation*, its outsized central window staring like *a big black mirror*."[5] Extending the idea of the home as a metaphor for relationship, Elaine Showalter's work provides an explicitly feminist interpretation since the home, where women were "destined to find fulfillment," "came to symbolize the female body."[6] "The woman was the wife of the house, wedded to it, bound to it. Caring for it was like the obsessive cleansing, purification, and care of her own female body."[7] More radical than Yates, Showalter articulates the idea that the home is a metaphor for the female body with "signs of sexuality and procreation."[8] For Yates the house is a metaphor for a relationship that is not gender specific. He writes against notions of security and abundance, depicting the home instead as a locus of friction, incomprehension, and division. Looking behind the facade of suburban conformity and metropolitan plenitude, Yates reveals something of the loneliness and anxiety, both economic and social, that characterized his own life.

Although not alone in doing this, Yates was ahead of his time, drawing attention to issues, particularly in respect to gender roles, that did not become part of mainstream thinking until after the publication of Betty Friedan's *The Feminine Mystique* in 1963. In his later work, work still predominantly set in the late 1950s and early 1960s, Yates went on to develop his investigation into how women inhabit a proscribed space in life and how men struggle to understand their changing roles. The interest and excitement Friedan's work caused eclipsed other writers' investigations into the territory she marked out as her own. Not only did Yates's early work precede her, but also his later work depends on the same careful scrutiny of female roles that were limited and inhibited by men. Works such as *Young Hearts Crying* (1984) and *Cold Spring Harbor* (1986) appeared after the second wave of feminism, but in terms of Yates's oeuvre, they are a continuum of the explorations he began in the 1950s.

Although Yates continued writing until his death in 1992, he rarely strayed outside the specific time frame of the mid-1950s to 1963. *The Easter Parade* (1976), his fourth novel, which does stretch that rather narrow time line, suggests his increasing awareness of the difficulties of life for women. His story centers on the struggles of his female protagonist, Emily Grimes, and her older sister Sarah. As I have indicated in chapter 6, both sisters try to become writers and for different reasons fail in this ambition. Their frustrated attempt to write is just one of the ways Yates uses to indicate how men, threatened by female ambition, hold back the women they live with. Showalter also alludes to this when, echoing Virginia Woolf and Charlotte Perkins Gilman,[9] she indicates in her chapter on the 1950s that "women writers tended to be isolated in their rooms, homes, and marriages."[10] At the same time, Yates also weaves domestic violence into this novel, suggesting an understanding of the vulnerability of women *within* marriage. Furthermore, his inclusion of abortion in several works, notably *Revolutionary Road* and *The Easter Parade*, suggests attentiveness to, and sensitivity toward, the wider political debate about the rights of women.

By highlighting the issues he does, and by placing them in narratives set earlier, Yates's work reinforces a contemporary revisionist view that sees the 1950s, not the 1960s, as the time when women's rights became a new part of the sociopolitical agenda. However, I do not, and could not, argue that Yates was a protofeminist; he was not. There is a real split between Yates's *intellectual* appreciation of how life is peculiarly difficult for women within marriages that constrain or diminish them and his *emotional* distaste for anything that smacks of a political move to address those issues. Blake Bailey draws some attention to Yates's feelings on the subject when, in the early 1970s, Yates's second wife, Martha, was thinking of leaving him: "Largely to spare his feelings, she'd spoken in rather vague terms about wanting to 'find herself,' and Yates concluded that she'd become a 'womens'-libbing bitch' as he sometimes put it. He couldn't speak calmly on the subject; partly, perhaps, because his mother's 'independence' had caused him so much grief, Yates's hatred for all 'feminist horseshit' bordered on the pathological."[11] Set against his work, the contradictoriness of his attitude toward women and their roles is evident. His observations about gender roles in his fictions only make sense if one understands that his views were not driven by ideological concerns. In a letter to Geoffrey Clark he states his views and dismisses criticism of those views in the same breath: "The disorders of the 60's did seem to be harder on girls than on men—and I don't care if that's an oversimplification or not."[12] Noticing how constrained they were, Yates felt women should be able to work and have a life independent of the home, but feeling the effects of this in *his own* life, he felt they should still put the concerns and needs of their husbands first; to do less was to earn his contempt.

Despite showing much interest in the plight of the "diminished female" characters in his fictions, Yates's scorn is heaped on feminists and postmodernists alike, and it is with some relish that he fuses the two in *The Easter Parade*. The magazine article Emily begins writing about being "on the dole" is never finished, but in its incomplete version ends with this stark explanation for her predicament: "I am a woman, and I am no longer young."[13] Radical feminists who took every opportunity to see their gender and aging as explanations for the loss of their jobs, his writing suggests, may be overlooking the fact that they are, for instance, drinking too much and have become inept. He appears to throw down the gauntlet to contemporary feminist views in this late part of the novel and does so using a mocking narrative tone.

Emily is invited to a party, a grim affair with no single men, but the hosts tell her about Trudy, their neighbor, who gives masturbation classes to lonely women: "Sort of the ultimate in radical feminism. Who needs men?,"[14] the host dryly observes. Emily goes along with others to see Trudy's studio and finds herself looking at "what looked like a sculptured sunburst of many podlike aluminum shapes,"[15] cast, Trudy explains, from her students' vaginas. "There were no more parties,"[16] Yates writes. As Bailey points out, this "elliptical leap . . . nicely summarizes his attitude toward radical feminism."[17] Trudy's view that masturbation is a viable alternative to sex with a man is made to sound as absurd as her studio looks since the podlike aluminum sculptures of vaginas make a mockery of feminist artistry.

On a more personal level, the ending of parties for Emily is indicative of her slide toward isolation; she gives up writing because "She would need the table for parties,"[18] and now the parties themselves are shelved. An essentially conservative writer, Yates abhorred radicalism of any kind; women independent of men was something Yates was both contemptuous of and feared. He expressed similar contempt toward homosexuality with equally contradictory results. Despite highlighting the homophobia prevalent in the 1950s in a story such as "A Clinical Romance," or in his depiction of artists in *Young Hearts Crying*, Yates was homophobic. In an interview with Yates's daughters, Monica Yates recalled his horrified reaction when she suggested that she might join the army: "Everyone in the army is lesbians! You can't go in the army, baby."[19] Although this comment was doubtless meant to be funny, Yates's fictions reveal a deep unease about homosexuals.

What is clear from much of the social history and sociology about the 1950s and early 1960s is that where gender roles were concerned, the period was a time of great confusion for both women and men. Susan J. Douglas, a baby boomer, looks back at the period as the beginning of an ongoing continuum of contradictory messages about female selfhood: "To explain this schizophrenia, we must reject the notion that popular culture for girls and women didn't matter, or that it consisted only of retrograde images. American women today are a bundle of contradictions because much of the media imagery we grew up with was itself filled with mixed messages about what women should and should not do, what women could and could not be. This was true in the 1960s, and it is true today. The media, of course, urged us to be pliant, cute, sexually available, thin, blond, poreless, wrinkle-free, and deferential to men. But it is easy to forget that the media also suggested we could be rebellious, tough, enterprising, and shrewd."[20] The sense of confusion outlined here is reproduced in Yates's work with women often seeking something more than just marriage and motherhood. They suffer in bewildered silence as they experience their personal sense of fulfillment declining, in ways and for reasons they often do not understand, just as their material circumstances are improving. While their husbands or boyfriends have jobs and provide for them, most of Yates's female protagonists struggle to find meaningful employment and a satisfactory sense of self-worth.

The confusion about gender roles that they experience is still apparent today, as Douglas suggests, and is, to my mind, one of the reasons Yates's fictions resonate with a contemporary readership. Douglas draws particular attention to the role of the mass media in bolstering and confirming contradictions about gender roles at the heart of American postwar society: "Along with our parents, the mass media raised us, socialized us, entertained us, comforted us, deceived us, disciplined us, told us what we could do and told us what we couldn't. And they played a key role in turning each of us into not one woman but many women. . . . This has been one of the mass media's most important legacies for female consciousness: the erosion of anything resembling a unified self."[21] Investigating such disunity throughout his fictions, Yates examines how women like April Wheeler struggle to be good wives and mothers in a suburban environment that promises so much but fails to engage them.

In her attempt to persuade Frank to move to Europe, April explains her behavior the previous evening with the Campbells: "I *was* bored. That's part of what I'm trying to say. I don't think I've ever been more bored and depressed and fed up in my life than last night."[22] She wants not only a change of environment but a job and status as well: "The point is you won't be getting any kind of a job, because I will. Don't laugh—listen a minute."[23] With Frank's implied derision, Yates conveys the popular view of such a radical change; it was unthinkable that a woman should consider supporting her family without, as a consequence, emasculating her man. Arguing against Frank's view that her proposal is unrealistic, the repetitions of April's counterargument indicate how passionate she is about her plan to escape: "I happen to think *this* is unrealistic. I think it's unrealistic for a man with a fine mind to go on working like a dog year after year at a job he can't stand, coming home to a house he can't stand in a place he can't stand either, to a wife who's equally unable to stand the same things, living among a bunch of frightened little—my God, Frank, I don't have to tell you what's wrong with this environment—"[24] Yates, mindful that the demands placed on women are even more confusing than those placed on men, ensures that April's approach is cunning and intelligent. Her persuasive argument is carefully nuanced toward Frank's needs and lack of fulfillment rather than toward her own desire to work and experience a different kind of life. Her method may be artful but the reader does not, at this stage, feel that this is merely a cynical ploy on her part; April has maintained her belief that Frank is "the most interesting person I've ever met."[25] It seems she genuinely wants to give him the opportunity to explore his potential. Shouldering the blame for the fact that they settled down with a child neither really wanted but that she saw as her responsibility for conceiving, she blames herself for the fact that they have bought into the "great sentimental lie of the suburbs."[26]

April's argument for going to Paris is predicated on her fierce belief in Frank. She believes that her high opinion of him and her confidence in the kind of man he could become is universally shared: "But if you mean who ever said you were exceptional, if you mean who ever said you had a first-rate, original mind—well my God, Frank, the answer is everybody."[27] The irony of this is impressed on the reader as Yates explores Frank's idiomatic thoughts, which reveal his weakness and vanity: "'Had Bill Croft really said that?'"[28] He cannot win the argument without demolishing April's high opinion of who he is and of who she has married, but this is not within his capabilities. Thus the "note of honest doubt"[29] he thinks he may have heard in her voice is immediately countered by his acquiescence: "Okay, let's say I was a promising kid."[30] Developing his swagger, "his voice had taken on a resonance that made it every bit as theatrical as hers. It was the voice of a hero."[31] Far from condemning Frank for this inability to put his wife straight, Yates offers up his fallibility as a man to a reader who may very well recognize that with such small dishonesties all marriages are weakened. With these apparently trivial indicators of human, and particularly male, posturing, Yates critiques notions of heroism in their contemporary form. Through several of his male protagonists, he suggests that the mid-twentieth-century "hero" is a pastiche of Hollywood lead actors and billboard icons. The hero has all the substantiality of a man in an advertising campaign, and the reader is invited to watch him flounder as, posing and preening, he checks his image in mirrors and adjusts his voice just as he adjusts his hair.

In his search for authenticity and truth in men and women, Yates had much in common with Ernest Hemingway, but their methods were quite distinct. Often using first person narratives whose protagonists are seen to reflect upon their own behavior, Hemingway makes the search for the authentic explicit. In his characterization of Jake Barnes in *The Sun Also Rises* (1926), for instance, he produces two different kinds of authentic heroes to consider: Romero, the bullfighter, is the Hemingway hero in action, while Jake, the writer, is the champion of words. Yates, on the other hand, shuns the whole idea of heroism in his search to find truth and honesty among unremarkable, middle-class people. He observes how the ordinary man will borrow slivers of heroic fabric to coat his otherwise average behavior. As we see above, Frank's voice alters as he sees potential in himself and in the moment. Borrowing the language of sociological investigation again, Yates's characters are high self-monitors but, ironically, do not display much self-knowledge or objectivity about their behavior. Yates uses moments such as the one just referred to, with Frank preening and posturing, to indicate the gap that exists between how his protagonist wants to be seen and how he *is* seen. Usually it is the reader who does the real "seeing," rather than the other characters.

April typifies the gap his female characters have to negotiate. That gap is, Yates suggests, a difference encouraged by a society that asks its women to take second place to their male partners and to place a greater value on their needs and their ideas of themselves. Although loneliness, dissatisfaction, and resentment characterize April's life, domestically imprisoned as she feels herself to be in their neat little home, the reader is aware that the real danger for April comes from the construction of Frank she has made in her mind. At this stage in the novel, the reader sees that Frank has to face "the graceless, suffering creature whose existence he tried every day of his life to deny,"[32] but has not yet seen April confront the reality of the man she is trying to put on a pedestal. As she learns to face the truth of who Frank is, and, therefore, the truth about the shifting sands of their marriage, Yates suggests with her tragic end that the reality she stumbles upon is too much to bear.

Yates's women are unsure of how to navigate between the old restrictive traditions they have rejected, but which have left their mark, and new freedoms that promise so much but, if grasped, would leave them isolated, misjudged, or ensnared by freedoms too complex to negotiate. In *The Easter Parade*, Yates examines how Emily Grimes attempts to live independently without relying on a man; she finds out about life and herself by exploring her sexual and social freedoms. But when these freedoms result in two abortions, the second pregnancy by a man she can't even name, Yates implicitly encourages some distance between the reader and the protagonist. This is gently compounded by a more detailed description of Emily after a drink-fueled night waking up "naked in bed with a strange man, in a strange place, with no memory of the night before."[33] Rather than merely suggesting moral condemnation of Emily's behavior (as suggested in the previous chapter, such condemnation is much more obvious later in her self-interested treatment of her sister Sarah), Yates's writing shows how society has failed Emily. His work implies that her drinking and unsuccessful relationships, both personal and at work, are partly the result of the unequal pressure men and women have to cope with in order to live independently. Yates's purpose is to draw attention to the many contradictions that postwar women had to negotiate and always struggled to understand.

In all his fiction, Yates places emphasis on such contradictions. His story "Evening on the Côte d'Azur" explores the predicament of freedom within marriage for a bored, frustrated, and, as it transpires, naive American housewife whose husband is away at sea. She cannot make up her mind whether to agree to her girlfriend's suggestion that they spend an evening out together. Knowing it sounds like an innocent enough suggestion, and wanting to have fun with her friend, she also senses that they will be pushing aside accepted codes of behavior: "'Ah, I dunno,' Betty said. 'Look, I don't want to sound like a prude or anything, Marylou, but I got three kids and I got a lot of responsibilities. I'd feel kind of funny going out like that.'"[34] The only way this ordinary, unworldly woman can interpret the sexual liaison with a sailor that ensues is as the beginning of an affair. The sailor, however, similarly ordinary but, as a man and a naval officer often away from home, is long practiced in the art of such dalliances and deceptions. He has all the control as he makes clear when he scoffs at the junior cadet questioning him: "Oh, Jesus Christ, Junior. When're you gonna grow up? Whaddya think—I told her my real name?"[35]

Yates suggests that postwar men were no less bemused by changing social codes conflicting with traditional expectations as, time and again, the reader meets male characters who fail in their domestic relationships, are unhappy or bored at work, and, crucially, who find the sexual appetite of the women they encounter threatening. His books negotiate a crisis in masculinity characteristic of the 1950s and early 1960s and act as both symptom and diagnosis. Susan Douglas suggests that girls and women received mixed messages about how they were supposed to behave,[36] and suggests that this also had implications for young men: "The legacy of the 1950s was that no 'nice' girl ever, ever, went all the way before marriage, and no nice woman ever really liked sex."[37] While Yates more often highlights the falsity of this view with regard to women and their sexual inclinations, he also draws attention to the way in which it ensnares men.

In "A Clinical Romance" one of the subtle indicators of Lynch's naïveté and lack of social intelligence comes in a conversation with a fellow TB sufferer about his new girlfriend: "He had not taken her 'all the way,' however. 'I could have,' he said. 'I could have twenty different times, we were so close to it—I'm not saying that to brag or anything, I just mean I could have very easily—but I didn't, and I think that was one of the things she liked about me at first.'"[38] That Costello, his nemesis, not only steals the girl but also is clearly having sex with her from the beginning of their relationship demonstrates two things: it confirms Lynch is out of step with changing social mores, and it draws attention to the confusing messages men were receiving about sex and relationships at a time before the sexual revolution of the 1960s brought such uncertainty out into the open. Since they have been brought up to think women, or "nice girls," lack sexual desire, when experience challenges these views, many men in Yates's fiction are not just threatened but emasculated.

Yates was not writing against marriage in *The Easter Parade* any more than he was in *Revolutionary Road*. He believed in the institution and wanted only to draw attention to the way it had been corrupted. He was furious, for instance, with the way Atlantic–Little, Brown packaged his first novel and in particular the inclusion on the front cover of Alfred Kazin's comment: "This novel locates the American tragedy squarely on the field of marriage." Kazin's comment was taken out of context, he claimed, and, by using it as they did, Atlantic–Little, Brown would put many people off reading the book: "After all, who but a maniac or a God damn fool would sit down and write a novel attacking marriage? And who'd want to *read* such a novel?"[39] His aim, here, as elsewhere, is to highlight the false expectations that are heaped on marriage by romantic ideals propagated everywhere in magazines, advertising, films, and television. The pressure of these combined forces makes not only marriage but also early marriage the route to an "independent" life every young woman should take in the 1950s. In addition to these idealizations, I would suggest that Yates's old-fashioned views about women direct his thoughts. He isn't writing against marriage but is writing to show how the promotion of female sexual demands and the access to abortion is, in his view, attacking marriage from within. In effect a fundamentally conservative man, his argument is nuanced against modern lifestyles and modern social politics.

In the late 1950s and early 1960s, pregnancy melodramas played their part in broadening the spectrum of how girls and women were viewed and judged. Films such as *A Summer Place* (1959)[40] with Sandra Dee and *Love with the Proper Stranger* (1963)[41] with Natalie Wood provided women with alternative role models. As Susan Douglas suggests, such films also urged the viewer to absorb the ambivalence of gender identity: "The big-breasted, out-of-control sluts on one end of the continuum and the tight-lipped ice maidens on the other served as monoliths to be rejected, while the ones in the middle, caught in the crosscurrents of discourses about 'good' and 'bad' girls, were the ones meant to be recognized as authentic by teenage girls. In other words, young girls were socialized as viewers to identify with ambivalence itself."[42] Similarly, in Yates's fictions, the reader is not asked to identify with the paragon of virtue perpetuating a myth about the limitations of female sexual desire, nor, on the other hand, asked to celebrate the new, libidinous, sexual freedoms. Yates's women are all between these two extremes, whether, like Rachel Drake, struggling to shake off the legacy of an upbringing that has promoted innocence, and particularly sexual ignorance, as a virtue, or, as with Emily Grimes, fully grasping the needs of her sexual and independent self. However, the balance he strives to achieve is lost in the regular use of strident male voices with voyeuristic inclinations.

Yates only knew about failure and, artistically and emotionally speaking, was only interested in the fractures that appear, the complexities that divide, and the constraints that diminish the experience of marriage.[43] In the *Ploughshares* interview he makes this clear: "I guess I'm not very interested in successful people. I guess I'm more interested in failures."[44] His own experience of marriage drew him inexorably to examine the near impossible task of making it work. As a way of illustrating this, at the end of *Revolutionary Road* Yates describes Shep Campbell, a man found to be solid, dependable, and kind, shaken to the core by April's death. He finds himself agreeing with his wife's comment that the experience has brought them closer together, but, as his interior thoughts indicate, the terms of that "working marriage" are bleak and compromised: "Looking at her now in the lamplight, this small, rumpled, foolish woman, he knew he had told the truth. Because God damn it, she was alive, wasn't she?"[45] Even in his affirmations Yates's voice remains negative.

In the short story "The Best of Everything," Yates confronts the idealization of marriage directly. He explores the private misery of a young girl who feels less excited about what she will gain in marriage and seems more aware of the independence she will lose. She knows she ought to be caught up in the enthusiasm her friends and colleagues share for her impending nuptials, but their delight merely highlights a pressure on her to conform. Yates exemplifies how society's perception of marriage, particularly in the 1950s, is uniformly unquestioning. However, with Grace's evident bewilderment, he illustrates how it restricts the individual to voice her concerns. Emphasizing the public excitement, Yates indicates how it threatens to engulf Grace as she is "pummeled . . . with old times and good wishes" and "her head rang with the words and the corners of her mouth ached from smiling."[46] With the verbs he chooses, Yates draws attention to the fact that Grace feels assaulted and vulnerable. Amid the noise, excitement, and expectation, Yates directs attention to her disaffected interior voice and isolation: "With an effort of will Grace resumed the guileless, open smile of a bride."[47] The devastating implications of this line are left to drift and to disturb the reader quietly, for with one image Yates indicates the level of performance that will be necessary for the rest of Grace's life. Called up by Ralph, her fiancé, a boorish man buoyed up with the exhilaration of the moment as it focuses on him, Grace can hardly respond: "She tried to sound excited, but it wasn't easy."[48] Yates pieces together a portrait of two people utterly unsuited to a life together, and it is clear that the success of their marriage will be predicated upon the kind of submissive, compliant behavior from Grace that Yates's story depicts.

Most commentators retrospectively link the increased incidence of early marriage, and the consequent population explosion, to the years of uncertainty and hardship during World War II. Additionally, Brett Harvey points out that the war, and the relevant freedoms it made available to women, created a fear about women's growing autonomy and their emergent sexuality: "What if women's sexuality couldn't be curbed? What if not enough of them were willing to return home and start creating the nuclear families that would in turn create the demand for goods that the nation's prosperity depended on?"[49] Marriage and child rearing were a way to control women and reestablish the norms that American society felt matched its growing prosperity and status after 1945. The possibilities for education and economic independence that seemed to be offered to young postwar women went hand in hand with a societal pressure to miss out on these opportunities in favor of fulfilling their duty as women. Wini Breines's work highlights this apparently contradictory development: "For young, white, middle-class women, the 1950s were a time when liberating possibilities were masked by restrictive norms; they grew up and came of age in a time when new lives beckoned while prohibitions against exploring them multiplied."[50] This conundrum is one Yates dramatizes throughout his fiction. While men, Yates's work suggests, are also the victims of such pressures and the glamorous falsehoods that accompany them, he indicates it is women such as Rachel Drake who carry their burden. Poorly educated, dependent on men for their self-esteem, constrained by a weight of social and moral strictures, and steered by society toward one end that is supposed to fulfill all their needs, marriage and consequent child rearing, women's lives are compromised at every turn.

Following the publication of *The Feminine Mystique* (1963), Betty Friedan's views on the need for white, middle-class, and educated women to return to work in order to be fulfilled were seen as the main thrust of a newly emergent discussion about how men and women should lead their lives and how they should view, help, and sustain each other. Yates, in his early work, anticipates some of her concerns, drawing attention to notions of marital disharmony, to women seemingly trapped by gender stereotypes as much as by dominant husbands and lovers. There was, his work indicates, no room in 1950s America for the fourth dimension[51] that Friedan later called for, where women could have an identity outside the home through work: it is an idea his fiction often interrogates.[52] While the inception of the debate about a woman's role is normally ascribed to the work of Betty Friedan, contemporary sociologists and cultural historians repeatedly challenge this view of the historical roots of feminism. Among others, Jessica Weiss is forthright in her criticism: "Friedan oversimplified middle-class women's predicament in the 1950s, overstated the all-consuming quality of the domestic ethos of the decade, and hid the vast diversity of women's experiences behind the full skirts of the bored middle-class homemaker."[53]

Weiss also suggests that dialogue about gender roles and the division of labor within the home has consistently been wrongly attributed to the effect of Friedan's book. It was not, she argues, the baby boomers who argued on college campuses and in bars and kitchens about how to lead more fulfilling lives; it was their mothers who faced this dialectic in the early 1950s, well before Friedan published *The Feminine Mystique*. Women were already juggling their domestic responsibilities with full- or part-time jobs a decade before Friedan's book appeared. Weiss goes further than pointing out a historical inaccuracy when she accuses Friedan of ignoring the evidence of such change: "Yet, Friedan was no revolutionary. Indeed, her views echoed a significant strain of positive opinion about women and work that developed in the 1950s and that she ignored in her research. . . . Often viewed as the keepers of tradition, women who gave birth to the baby boom fostered changes, undermining the traditions that they are credited with maintaining."[54] Thus Weiss's work suggests that by the time Friedan's work was published, "change was already afoot"[55] a "full decade before Friedan published her incisive survey of women's magazines, writers countenanced work for married women and mothers, suggesting that domesticity was not enough for many American women."[56] Sharon Monteith also makes the point that Freidan's book "was rather . . . conservative in many ways," since the disquiet among women and girls she explores "is more representative of the 1950s when she began work on her book than the 1960s when she published it."[57] Women in the 1950s were not discussing *whether* to go back to work but were exploring ways to effect this change while also maintaining their roles as wives and mothers.

Richard Fried's work concurs with these views. He acknowledges the im-

portance of Betty Friedan's work against "a sort of inchoate crusade by magazine editors, academics, and the therapeutic professions to exalt domesticity
and to devalue autonomous achievement by women in any other sphere."[58]
However, he puts it in a different context and adds some statistical weight
to Weiss's and Monteith's arguments: "despite the image of women immured
in the ranch house, many of them lived at least part of their lives outside
that cloister. The number of female workers climbed steadily in these years.
That was especially true of married women, 30 percent of whom worked outside the home by 1960. Such rates may not be equated with an upsurge of
feminism, but neither do they suggest placid domesticity."[59] Adding necessary depth to this perspective, Susan J. Douglas isolates not only the reality
of women's pay but also what kind of jobs they were engaged in, suggesting
that only low-paid, service jobs were available to them: "Their median income was only 60 percent of what men made."[60] However, acknowledging
the dangers of a monolithic view of the 1950s, Martin Halliwell challenges
the interpretation that these retrospective views have placed on the era. He
suggests that too sweeping a picture of cultural change characterizes how it
is now seen: "Recent historians have challenged the theory that women were
simply victims of the decade, but widespread college engagements and falling
marriage ages were sure signs that motherhood and housework had become
sanctified."[61]

Yates's work should be seen as part of the challenge to the perspective that
held Friedan responsible for new and radical ways of seeing womanhood. By
frequently addressing the limiting nature of women's domestic roles, their
boredom, and their confusion about what was expected of them in contra-
distinction to what they wanted, Yates's early fictions accurately reflect the
awareness of a debate not yet formalized. In his later fiction, work still set
predominantly in the 1950s but written after 1962, he goes on to develop
this perspective. It is clear that a woman's understanding of her role was at a
turning point in the 1950s. Questions about how women led their lives were
already simmering beneath the surface of life in America, and this is precisely
the picture that emerges from reading Yates's fiction. Yates depicts a world in
which men and women do battle, aware that, while the society they live in
offers material comfort in the form of suburban communities and promotes
conformity through marriage and child rearing, it is not enough. He wants
to address the fundamental anxieties and failings of communication that existed between men and women that were, in part, a result of women's dissatisfaction with the conditions of their lives. His fictions accurately register
Fried's description of this era: "We sense 'the fifties' as a unique era that we
think we know and often recall fondly. In fact the decade was more complex

than the era we may wish to remember or imagine, a fidgety mix of anxiety and relaxation, sloth and achievement, complacency and self-criticism."[62]

Yates would have avoided all claims to being an accurate chronicler of the times. However, in a life notable for the absence of men in it, the women he grew up with, and later lived with, add interesting depth and texture to his understanding of this "other" gender and to the era he investigates. Although not interested in women's rights, Yates's mother brought up her two children in an unconventional manner. She was determined to see herself as a sculptor, and despite only a modicum of artistic talent, shackled her children's lives to the fulfillment of this ambition. His sister, Ruth, a smart young woman with a talent for writing, was, as Blake Bailey suggests, "hard to pigeonhole."[63] That she was quick, creative, and had some ambition would not have escaped the notice of her younger brother. Fictionalized by him as Sarah Grimes in *The Easter Parade*, Ruth made a poor marriage to a Laurence Olivier look-alike[64] and, like Sarah, died young, an alcoholic, lonely woman who, while devoted to her sons, had never been able to fully make use of her creative talents.

Yates's first wife, Sheila Bryant, was an intelligent, determined woman who became the instigator of much that he was to learn about women pushing against the accepted norms of traditional female behavior. When they married in 1948, Sheila was twenty and Yates twenty-two. Throughout their marriage, Sheila was not keen on the idea of having children and was desperate to get a job and do something challenging with her life. Both before and after the birth of their two daughters, this was a source of tension between them, and when they finally divorced in 1959, Sheila began training as a teacher. This job was to sustain her for the rest of her working life. Yates's fictional representations of these women are an interesting indicator of his struggle with early signs of questioning gender roles. What his fiction does not do, however, is suggest that women were, in any organized fashion, becoming articulate about their situation.

Yates's female characters appear to fall into two categories: young women struggling to communicate with the men in their lives, women we generally sympathize with, and older women, mothers, who restrict their sons and daughters, unequivocally damaging them in the process. April Wheeler, a young woman closely modeled on Sheila Bryant,[65] is sympathetically treated as far as her domestic loneliness and lack of intellectual fulfillment is concerned. At the beginning of her quest to persuade Frank that moving to Paris would be a good idea, she rails against the suburban conformity that has become their life, and specifically against the people they live among: "Well, how *did* everything get so awful then? . . . How did we ever get *into* this strange little dream world of the Donaldsons and the Cramers and the Wingates—

oh yes, and the Campbells, too, because another thing I figured out today is that both those Campbells are a big, big, big, colossal waste of time."[66] The reader has some sympathy with this view having just read about the previous evening's vapid conversation and Frank's outburst against their self-indulgent society: "'I mean talk about decadence,' he declared, 'how decadent can a society get? Look at it this way. This country's probably the psychiatric, psychoanalytic capital of the world.'"[67] Even as the reader cheers Frank's diatribe against the infantilizing nature of suburban living, the perspective shifts with April's evaluation of it. Not only was it an evening that left April with "a stare of pitying boredom in her eyes,"[68] as she later says, "We're just like the people you're talking about! We *are* the people you're talking about!"[69] Although Yates, as we have seen elsewhere and throughout, avoids making one character easier to identify with than another, it is ultimately April who holds the reader's sympathy longest in this novel and April's predicament that is most fully explored.[70]

Similarly, in "The Best of Everything," Yates directs his reader's sympathies to his female protagonist, Grace.[71] While Grace, as we have seen, is directed by those around her, and propelled toward a romantic and idealized view of what is about to happen, Ralph is seen as nervous, unwilling, and far happier with "the lads"; it is the lads who move him to tears, the lads who touch him with their surprise party and their wonderful gift. His first loyalties are to his best friend, Eddie, and, not for the first time in a Yates story, suggest an element of homoeroticism the story leaves unexplored: "Eddie was his best friend" and "Half the fun of every date—even more than half—had been telling Eddie about it afterwards."[72] Such phrases suggest not just Ralph's closeness to Eddie but his dependence on him, a closeness, dependence, and comfort that may be read in opposition to his aloof attitude toward his future bride. Slowing his narrative to describe with great precision the moment when Eddie gives Ralph his wedding present, Yates draws quiet attention to the intensity of feeling that exists between these two men: "Then the crowd cleaved in half, and Eddie made his way slowly down the middle. His eyes gleamed in a smile of love, and from his bashful hand hung the suitcase."[73] Yates's description, reading like a parody of a bridal march, emphasizes the disparity between his bride and his best friend. But it is not just Ralph against whom we read Grace; her friend and roommate's snobbery forms another dialectic in this tale as Martha mimics and parodies Ralph's speech: "'Isn't he funny?' Martha had said after their first date. 'He says "terlet." I didn't know people really said "terlet."'"[74] His cultural background is also ridiculed: "Oh, and all those friends of his, his Eddie and his Marty and his George with their mean, ratty little clerks' lives and their mean, ratty little . . ."[75] The reader, while not empathetic toward the brutish Ralph, nevertheless feels Grace's discomfort at her roommate's snobbery.

Yates captures the discrepancies between a male and female experience of marriage and courtship and underlies the fear for both genders about the step into the unknown that they are about to take, but it is to the isolate and disempowered that we are drawn. Grace greets Ralph at the door in the expensive negligee she has bought for their honeymoon. She is unaware of the surprise party Eddie has thrown for Ralph, a party Ralph is desperate to return to. He enters her apartment barely even noticing her provocative garb, seductive tone, or the promise of some unencumbered premarital sex that they imply: "'Hi, baby.' He brushed past her and walked inside. 'Guess I'm late, huh? You in bed?'"[76] His quick-fire snappy dialogue is beautifully contrasted with her languid movements as, mimicking the seduction techniques of Hollywood starlets, "She closed the door and leaned against it with both hands holding the doorknob at the small of her back, the way heroines close doors in the movies."[77] Directed by Grace, Ralph finally comments on her negligee, but his response is characteristically vulgar and further emphasizes the lack of any emotional investment in their partnership: "'Nice' he said, feeling the flimsy material between thumb and index finger, like a merchant. 'Very nice. Wudga pay fa this, honey?'"[78] Yates is keen to suggest that both men and women are imprisoned by the language and behavior available to them. Ralph's cocksure swagger and dismissive attitude suggests a parody of masculinity.

Yates condemns narrow definitions of masculine behavior, and the groups of men that promote such behavior, in a manner that seems similar to J. D. Salinger's views. Holden Caulfield's descriptions of school life sum up the restricted nature of accepted male interests: "It's full of phonies, and all you do is study so that you can learn enough to be smart enough to be able to buy a goddam Cadillac some day, and you have to keep making believe you give a damn if the football team loses, and all you do is talk about girls and liquor and sex all day, and everybody sticks together in these dirty little goddam cliques."[79] While Salinger's narrator rails against the idea of such male posturing, Yates, through Ralph, demonstrates it in action. Just as Grace borrows her stance from seductive film stars, Ralph borrows his from the macho gangster movies of the time; he knows no other way to signal his masculinity.

In this story, Yates draws attention not just to the societal pressure to marry but also, like Hemingway, to the lack of understanding between the sexes. He highlights the fears and disappointments marriage will bring as so much is given up for the promise of so little. The impending marriage is imagined with ominous finality; doom laden, it indicates not the beginning of some shared adventure but the end of all that they love. As Ralph imagines it, "after today, like so many other pleasures, it would all be left behind."[80] For Grace it is her work that will go; for Ralph, his lads' nights and his friendship with Eddie. One has the impression of two people being forced together despite their fears and reluctance and despite the enormity of the gap between them. Love and marriage, as in Hemingway's work, is astringent and destructive. Using very different settings, but with an equally antiromantic approach, the gulf between men and women absorbs the attention of both writers. In "The Snows of Kilimanjaro," for instance, Harry reflects upon his own expedient behavior and the fact that he is with this woman because she is rich and because his life force is spent: "It was not her fault that when he went to her he was already over. How could a woman know that you meant nothing that you said; that you spoke only from habit and to be comfortable? After he no longer meant what he said, his lies were more successful with women than when he had told them the truth."[81] It is their ability to be reflective and self-critical, in the way that Harry is, that sets Hemingway's protagonists apart from Yates's central figures: neither Grace nor Ralph can be articulate about their own feelings or motives.

In *The Easter Parade* Yates probes more deeply what marriage might entail for young women but balances his inquiry with an equally unforgiving look at what happens to those who do not marry. While he presents Emily Grimes's struggle to live meaningfully outside marriage, he depicts her sister striving to live a life of significance within a marriage that restricts and threatens her. Listening to her sister's description of how she and her future husband, Tony, hook arms when they drink, Emily's sardonic narrative comment makes clear both her pity and the shades of her jealousy: "Everything about Sarah's romance with Tony was almost too nice to be borne."[82] Deftly inserting an appropriately nuanced objective correlative, the couple in an Easter parade photograph, Yates is able to comment indirectly on Sarah's marriage: "The camera had caught Sarah and Tony smiling at each other like the very soul of romance in the April sunshine, with massed trees and a high corner of the Plaza hotel just visible behind them."[83] Emily's mother and sister send her to get multiple copies of the newspaper in which the photograph appears: "And whether she was annoyed or not as she left the house, Emily knew how important it was to have as many copies as possible. It was a picture that could be mounted and framed and treasured forever."[84] The mimetic narrative draws attention to Emily's thoughts and lays gentle stress on "could," emphasizing the practicality of the task at hand at the same time as highlighting its conditionality. The implication is clear: the photograph *could* be "mounted and framed and treasured forever" by a person willing to mount and frame and treasure an image of happiness, or, in more cynical terms, to use and believe in a celluloid, idealized moment of romantic pantomime. With such subtleties of language, Yates conveys to the reader Emily's despair and her conviction that the photograph will become an iconic image. The picture acts as a metaphor for Sarah's inability to face the truth and is poignantly observed by Emily after her sister's funeral, "hanging awry, as if from the impact of some heavy blow that had shuddered the wall."[85] Since Sarah has died after a fall, and her husband is suspected of pushing her, the photograph remains a powerful indicator of the dishonesty surrounding this marriage. Where marriage is concerned, there is some inevitability in the fact that Yates always directs our attention toward separation rather than union.

9

Parents and Sex

11. Vincent Matthew Yates, Richard's father. Date and photographer unknown. Courtesy of the Richard Yates Estate.

12. Ruth "Dookie" Yates, Richard's mother. Date and photographer unknown. Courtesy of the Richard Yates Estate.

In contrast to the largely sympathetic treatment Yates gives his younger women, the mothers of his fiction are treated harshly. Esther Grimes, or Pookie, in *The Easter Parade*, Alice Prentice in *A Special Providence*, and Gloria Drake in *Cold Spring Harbor* provide three of many examples in Yates's fiction of maternal failure and the consequent familial dysfunction that accompanies it. The author displays little empathy toward their socially ambitious paths through life, their alcoholism, and in Alice's case, her desire to work. In all three novels, Yates interrogates the nature of home and how, as a construct, it can be so easily polluted by the unreasonable, often self-centered, demands of the mother who is at its core. No mother is more demanding, isolated, and pathetic than Alice Prentice in *A Special Providence*.

One of the reasons *A Special Providence* is perhaps Yates's least successful and least admired work is that he remains too close to the characters he describes, a fact he acknowledged with characteristic ease and insightful self-criticism: "I suspect that's why *A Special Providence* is a weak book—one of the reasons, anyway. It's not properly formed; I never did achieve enough fictional distance on the character of Robert Prentice."[1] Reworking the main character of his 1962 short story, "Builders," a protagonist Yates acknowledged as "clearly and nakedly myself,"[2] Robert Prentice's wartime experiences and the difficulties he has trying to free himself from his cloying and dependent mother form the central drama of the story. Yates was clearly trying to continue the "autobiographical blowout"[3] he'd begun with "Builders." However, I suggest that the weakness of the novel is not only Yates's lack of distance from Robert Prentice but is also in his portrayal of Robert's mother, Alice Prentice.

Even if Yates felt that with "Builders" he'd "managed to avoid . . . self-pity and self-aggrandizement,"[4] it seems that both traps awaited him in his second novel, and not just in the portrait of the protagonist. Alice is a prototype for all of Yates's mother figures, the closest he comes to creating a portrait of his own mother, Dookie. In that respect, driven by both love and contempt for Dookie, Yates diminishes and caricatures her.[5] Blake Bailey also highlights the fact that Yates is far more openly critical of his maternal characters than he is of other figures of his fiction: "Yates's compassion for human weakness, for the flaws that make failure so inevitable, is everywhere in his work—with the occasional exception of certain characters based on his mother, which range from the rounded and essentially forgivable Alice Prentice in *A Special Providence* to Dickensian grotesques."[6] Nevertheless, I take issue with Bailey's exception to this claim when he suggests that Alice is "rounded and essentially forgiveable."[7] For me, Alice Prentice *is* the "Dickensian grotesque"[8] that Bailey sees more clearly drawn in Yates's other novels. The reader cannot fail to see the poignancy of Alice's predicament as a single woman, impoverished and self-deluding in her social ambitions. However, the reader does not achieve the same level of empathy with her that Yates engineers in some of his other portraits of mothers, although *any* compassion the reader has for his mother figures is always highly circumscribed.

In the long prologue to *A Special Providence*, Yates describes Robert Prentice's leave from the army in 1944. Deciding to spend the time with his mother, he makes the journey from the camp in Virginia to New York. Prentice is alarmed to find his mother living in penury and near squalor but continuing to borrow money and drinking heavily. Using the metaphor of the movies (a metaphor that he overworks in this novel), Yates indicates how Prentice makes life more palatable by seeing "himself as the hero of some inspiring movie about the struggles of the poor."[9] The problem for him is "that his

mother refused to play her role": "He kept hoping to come home and find
her acting the way he thought she ought to act: a humble widow, gratefully
cooking meat and potatoes for her tired son, sitting down with a sewing basket
as soon as she'd washed the dishes, darning his socks in the lamplight and
perhaps looking up to inquire, shyly, if he wouldn't like to call up some girl."[10]
Yates draws attention to Prentice's traditionally inflected understanding of appropriate male and female roles as he visualizes the adoring, attentive mother,
dutifully taking care of all the housework and dancing attendance on a son
who has been out to earn a living to support them both. However, the ideal
that Robert Prentice imagines is one that blurs marital and filial devotion.
Prentice, like Yates who created him, suffers from having to be both son and
spouse to a woman who needs a man to support her, literally and figuratively;
this confusion is reflected in his imagined dream homecoming. By ascribing
to Prentice this particular version of what an idealized return would entail,
Yates indicates a basic problem in the nature of their relationship, a problem,
he suggests throughout the text, that seals their fate.

With Prentice's imagining, Yates sets up a model of maternal care and de-
molishes it as a possibility as he then describes her subsequent behavior. He
captures the growing distance between the protagonist and his mother, a distance compounded and exaggerated by her emotional response. Following
an argument about money that Alice is not able to win, she has the first of
several tantrums: "And she burst into tears. As if shot, she then clutched her
left breast and collapsed full length on the floor, splitting an armpit seam of
the dress."[11] Ridiculous in its extravagance and grotesque and immature in
its attempt to manipulate, Alice's behavior alienates her son and the reader.

The representation of domineering mothers, and of mothers who control
and exert power over their sons, occurs time and again in Yates's fictions with
the intertextual resonances indicating how deeply he felt the failings of his
own mother. Shades of inappropriate maternal behavior are hard to miss, as
is indicated by one particular image in *A Special Providence*:[12] a woman uses
her male child as a life model for her sculpture. The naked child is made to
endure discomfort and shame as the mother invades her child's privacy and
undermines his dignity. He is belittled when his young friends peer into the
barn where his mother has her studio. Although Alice is described as seeing
"Bobby round-eyed with humiliation, hunched over with both hands hiding
his genitals,"[13] she barely registers his mortified state and insists he continue
posing. Both the reader and the boy looking back experience this as a form
of cold-hearted selfishness and insensitivity, coming as it does after he has
been observed by "three or four pairs of eyes peering in through an inch-
wide crack in the wallboards."[14] According to Bailey, "Dookie's favorite model

for her faunlets, often posed in the nude, was the small, obliging Richard."[15] There is something deeply poignant about Yates's rendition of this idiosyncratic event in *A Special Providence* that one almost does not need the confirming detail from Bailey that the event mirrored exactly his own experience.

In Yates's work, motherly love is complicated by the fact that his maternal figures are weak-willed and selfish. Furthermore, he draws significant attention to the manner in which their requirement for love and physical comfort is transformed into something ugly and perverse as they seek that comfort from their sons. These are the shadows cast by loneliness and the urgency of their need. In "Oh, Joseph, I'm So Tired," Yates writes about another cash-strapped woman who thinks she can make it as a sculptor. She lives beyond her means with her two small children, propelled by thoughts of future success and social acceptance among the wealthy and influential. Through no fault of their own, but simply as a result of their youth and dependence, the young boy and girl are trapped by the dreams and whims of their unrealistic, desperate mother. They are lonely and bewildered by her erratic, selfish behavior but have no choice but to follow where she leads. This is especially true of the boy, who narrates the tale as an adult. In the present of the narrative his blunt assertion dispels any illusions about her abilities: "She wasn't a very good sculptor."[16]

With echoes of the narrative structure of "Jody Rolled the Bones," the dual time frame is critical to how the reader understands the complexities of the child/mother relationship. As an adult, the son adopts a compassionate, wistful tone, but as a child, it is the fact that he is utterly dependent and at her mercy that Yates foregrounds. This is nowhere more apparent than when he is woken in the night as she climbs, drunk, into his bed: "She'd had too much to drink and wanted to lie down, but instead of going to her own room she got into bed with me. 'Oh,' she said. 'Oh, my boy. Oh, my boy.' It was a narrow cot and there was no way to make room for her; then suddenly she retched, bolted to her feet, and ran for the bathroom, where I heard her vomiting. And when I moved over into the part of the bed she had occupied my face recoiled quickly, but not quite in time, from the slick mouthful of puke she had left on her side of the pillow."[17] Yates relishes the visceral description of the "slick" "puke" as much as he enjoys suggesting an echo of female orgasm in this woman's motherly moans; beyond that, he conveys disgust.

The implication of this parody is that the mother is so "lost" through loneliness, disappointment, and drink that she regards sleeping with her son as normal, failing to recognize his "private space" and blind to his suffering as she invades it. The scene has particular resonance in Yates's oeuvre since it is a reworking of an incident in the earlier fiction, *A Special Providence*.[18] Having argued with her sister and brother-in-law (with whom she and her son are staying), Alice gets into bed with the teenage Bobby: "He was so warm, and the bed so soft, that she started to cry again as she pressed against him. He woke up and stiffened in her arms."[19] It seems appropriate, therefore, that Bobby Prentice's brutal severance of his relationship with his mother at the end of Yates's second novel should carry veiled suggestions of the cold ending to a misjudged affair: "He said he was out of the Army now, and feeling well, and that he would write again soon. He wished her luck."[20]

With no father or husband, the lines between filial and spousal devotion are confused and distorted in *A Special Providence* and "Oh, Joseph, I'm So Tired." Both homes are dominated by the neediness and immaturity of the two mothers, and that gives rise not only to the sons being overburdened emotionally but also to inappropriate, quasi-sexual behavior. Yates draws attention to the fact that it is the needs of the mother, not those of the child, that take precedence over all else. Seen with such clarity, the default position of the law courts to award custody of children to the mother appears to be both negligent and sentimental. It would seem that Yates felt this very strongly, not as a father (though there is no doubt that he hated being separated from his daughters), but as a son who rarely saw his father and was left in the care of a mother he felt couldn't even take care of herself.

Ultimately, the only way Robert Prentice can survive and find his independence is to terminate all relationship with his mother. However, whatever else these quirky, dysfunctional mother figures are, they are brave and have at some level to be commended for their optimism. In this respect, "Oh, Joseph, I'm So Tired" is more successful than the earlier work. Yates conveys a depth to the character of Helen that he does not achieve with the relentlessly selfish portrait of Alice Prentice. The narrator, her son, puts himself in her position as he imagines her journey home after she has failed to impress President Roosevelt with her sculpture of his head: "There would be no photographs or interviews or feature articles, no thrilling moments of newsreel coverage; strangers would never know of how she'd come from a small Ohio town, or of how she'd nurtured her talent through the brave, difficult, one-woman journey that had brought her to the attention of the world. It wasn't fair."[21] The reader is forced to contemplate her "brave, difficult, one-woman journey" through the compassionate guidance of the narrator's voice. Therefore, despite the terrible facts of her meeting with Roosevelt and the subsequent lunch, Helen managed "to make it sound like a success."[22] This forces the reader to acknowledge a truth that Yates felt deeply: human tragedy can be very banal.

The repetitions that occur across Yates's work make it easy to presume that there was an oedipal element to Yates's relationship with his mother. This interpretation would clearly have embarrassed him as an adult; it is likely, therefore, that he tried to make sense of the relationship at a distance, that is to say, in his fictions. Because Yates draws so heavily on his own biography, there is a danger that connections are made, and then assumed to be fact, between the fictional dilemmas he describes and the complexities of his own life and upbringing. The Yatesian scholar must steer a path between being overzealous in making connections between Yates's life and that of his characters and being too reticent to make such links when they would broaden understanding of Yates's worldview and, in this instance, his complex and contradictory views about women. He was a writer who plundered his own experience but was not necessarily faithful to its details. However, in his repetitions Yates makes such connections more certain, so that rather than seeming unfair or unwise to speculate about the dark side of his relationship with his mother, the student of Yates feels compelled toward such considerations. For instance, it might have been the case that Dookie Yates strayed, when drunk, into inappropriate behavior with her son. Moreover, in a psychoanalytic reading of his work, it is hard not to see a correlation between his highly critical portraits of mothers and his warped perspective of female sexuality in general.

To balance the argument that links Yates's life too closely with that of his characters, it is also important to note that Yates is *not* writing memoir. In addition, his interrogation of dominant, demanding mothers reflects a concern of his time; such mothers provided powerful images in much literature of the 1940s and 1950s: "In numerous popular and scholarly books and articles, mothers were blamed for inadequate children. In fact, the discussion was about sons, not children, because it was sons about whom commentators, influenced by Freud and certainly by sexism, worried. Much of the popular literature, like *Generation of Vipers* by Philip Wylie, who coined the term 'momism,' was explicitly misogynist ("momism" refers to a social phenomenon of widespread mother domination where the matriarchy is an informal power structure sustained by sentimentalism). Thus, ironically, the most idealized figure of the period, the mother, became a scapegoat."[23] Addressing concerns about motherly protectiveness, Wini Breines asserts that "It was argued that mothers were tying their sons to their apron strings, making babies of them, even castrating them, by being overprotective."[24] In light of these comments, Yates's portraits of mothers in general and Alice Prentice in particular seem both personally *and* culturally inflected.

Breines also makes the point that is at the heart of the confusion about gender roles and sexuality in Yates's work when she details the link between strong mothers and weak sons: "The deep anxiety about masculinity after the Second World War was closely linked with fears of female strength."[25] Dominant mothers, she suggests, threatened not just their sons' health and well-being, social and sexual, but threatened the strength of the country: "The fear that mothers would incapacitate children was really a fear that they would emasculate their sons, create dependent and weak men whose masculinity was in doubt, and spoil their (and their nation's) chances of success."[26] Elaine Tyler May pursues a similar argument when she describes the fine line that women had to tread: "Mothers who neglected their children bred criminals; mothers who overindulged their sons turned them into passive, weak, and effeminite [sic] 'perverts.'"[27]

It is clear that Yates is highly attuned to the effect on sons of bad mothering, but the daughters of his fiction have their own obstacles to overcome. He is well aware that when it came to advice about relationships, and specifically advice about sex, parents in postwar America too often shirked their duties. Keeping teenagers of either gender in ignorance of the "facts of life" was something that Yates deplored. In *Cold Spring Harbor*, Gloria Drake avoids talking to her daughter about sex since "nice people didn't find it necessary to discuss things like that."[28] But she goes further than this when she catches Rachel looking at a magazine article about "sexual relations before marriage."[29] She removes the magazine and throws it away. Yates makes it clear that Gloria's careless mothering, which includes not telling her daughter about menstruation, can only partly be put down to the general prudery of the time since the narrative voice is unequivocal in its condemnation of her: "this attitude . . . seemed always to come from carelessness, or laziness, rather than from any kind of principle."[30]

To avoid such truths, as Gloria Drake is inclined to do, in favor of a sentimental and romantic view of life is to avoid reality, and it is her daughter who bears the consequences. Rachel's vulnerability as an ignorant and dependent young woman is more than implied by the phrase that is consequent on this ignorance: "Rachel began to suspect that Evan Shepard could do anything he wanted with her."[31] Young women such as Rachel were steered toward marriage; within marriage the unruly passions of sexual attraction could be managed and contained: "In the face of Kinsey's evidence, efforts to achieve sexual repression gave way to new strategies for sexual containment. Marriage was considered to be the appropriate container for the unwieldy American libido."[32] It is, therefore, deeply ironic that even Gloria Drake, who has kept her daughter ignorant and has stage-managed Rachel's romantic outlook, has cause to regret that her daughter is marrying so young and marrying out of choice a young man who "looked bland":[33] "And only after making those assumptions about Evan was Gloria able to identify the unsatisfactory thing she had sensed in all of this. Wouldn't it be a pity, really, for a girl to get married just for the sex of it?"[34]

The dysfunctionality of Yates's female-dominated homes has to be seen in conjunction with the absent fathers of his fiction. True to his experiences as a child, fathers are distant figures. They play only minor roles in the dramas the author depicts, but their absence is critical. In the war sections of *A Special Providence*, Yates places special emphasis on the effect of the absent father by drawing attention to Prentice's dependence on an older soldier, Quint. He comes to rely on Quint, and it begins to irk the older man who rebukes him harshly: "'I'm through. I've had it. I'm through being your goddam—' he hesitated over the final word, and when he brought it out it seemed calculated to be the cruellest word he could have chosen: '—your God damn father.'"[35] In *Cold Spring Harbor*, Curtis Drake is a remote figure, kept at a distance from his children by his ex-wife. Rachel Drake has to negotiate "Her mother's ungoverned displays of emotion [which] were frightful"[36] in order to travel to her own wedding with him. However, when Curtis Drake is around he brings a calm authority and perspective to the situation. Similarly, Sarah and Emily Grimes have no paternal buffer at home against which they can withstand the daily vicissitudes of their social-climbing mother.

Through the character of Walter Grimes, Yates critiques ideas about heroism in relation to fatherhood. As with all children, the girls want to see their father as a hero but have to accept his honest admission that he is "only a copy-desk man"[37] whose desk is "On the rim."[38] Emily is determined to look honestly at things, no matter how much she wants Walter to be heroic; indeed, Yates makes it her central characteristic from early in the novel. Even once Sarah and Emily are older, their parents' divorce and the consequent loss of time with their father are felt keenly as they exchange stories of the past that move them both. The girls privately guard their own memories of their father, and Yates makes it clear how the capacity for hurt still exists. Sarah, for instance, reveals she was not, as a child, visiting an orthodontist, as claimed, but was going instead to Manhattan to spend time with Walter: "And even now, at thirty-six, Emily was jealous."[39]

In *A Good School*, Yates portrays the complexities of a filial relationship for a boy brought up primarily by his mother when he describes a visit to the boarding school that the protagonist's father makes. Bill Grove is unable to articulate the word "Dad," suggestive as it is of a relationship they simply did not have: "He remembered having no trouble with the more childish 'Daddy,' years ago, but 'Dad' eluded his tongue."[40] To overcome the problem, he calls his father "nothing at all."[41] Poignantly emphasizing the distance between them, Yates ensures that the absent father has no name. It is, therefore, a self-conscious performance at the end of his father's brief visit that enables Bill to attempt to close the gap: "'Thanks for coming out, Dad.' It sounded almost as natural as he'd meant it to."[42] Honest in his depiction of the gap that widens between fathers and sons when they live apart and scarcely know each other, Yates rigorously avoids sentimentality.

Yates creates a similar tension in his short story "Lament for a Tenor," and in many ways this story reads like a rehearsal for the issues that arise in *A Good School*. As with so much of Yates's fiction, the first sentence announces the problem to be faced: "Jack Warren's parents had been separated as long as he could remember, and he realized, whenever he stopped to think about it, that he hardly knew his father at all."[43] The kindly father remains a distant figure, unknown and unknowable to his gauche son. Thus when hearing at school of his father's sudden death, Jack cannot cry: "the truth was simply that his father's death had left him cold, and he knew it. He also knew he would have to do something about it; he couldn't possibly go home this way."[44] He is determined to behave in the correct way but "a vague sense of finality was all he could evoke—not grief, not even a suggestion of tears."[45] As with Bill Grove's filial performance at the end of his father's visit, Jack finds that he too is acting when tears finally come: "and Jack knew he wasn't crying for his father at all, but for himself—a boy bereaved."[46]

Shep Campbell's self-critical restraint at the end of *Revolutionary Road* reminds the reader of Ralph Waldo Emerson's thoughts about grief: "People grieve and bemoan themselves, but it is not half so bad with them as they say. There are moods in which we court suffering, in the hope that here, at least, we shall find reality, sharp peaks and edges of truth. But it turns out to be scene-painting and counterfeit. The only thing grief has taught me, is to know how shallow it is."[47] Yates alludes to such "scene-painting and counter-feit" in his characterization of Campbell. Similarly, when he describes how Emily Grimes arrests her tears after her father's funeral, Yates hones in on the way Emily catches herself behaving with a lack of authenticity: "But she stopped crying abruptly when she realized that even that was a lie: these tears, as always before in her life, were wholly for herself."[48] By contrast, her sister Sarah has made a final dash back to the pew because, "it was required that her bowed face crumple and her shoulders shake one final time."[49] The performance of "correct" behavior is not the same *as* correct behavior, and Yates, like Emerson, never allows the two to be confused.

For the most part, Yates concentrates on the grief and longing for the child whose family is ripped apart by divorce, but in the short story "Oh, Joseph, I'm So Tired" he also captures the agony of separation, suggesting both the child's *and* the father's perspective. It is a moment captured only fleetingly, but it haunts the story of two children living with a mother whose sense of reality is always questionable. The children have been out with their father for the day and the time comes when they have to say goodbye. Yates's description uses all the senses to suggest the physicality, tenderness, and warmth of their father: "And those hugs of his, the climax of his visitation rights, were unforgettable. One at a time we would be swept up and pressed hard into the smells of linen and whiskey and tobacco; the warm rasp of his jaw would graze one cheek and there would be a quick moist kiss near the ear; then he'd let us go."[50] Following their embrace, Edith races after her father, thinking he has forgotten to give them the stamps he talked about earlier, and shouts at him: "He stopped and turned around, and that was when we saw he was crying. He tried to hide it—he put his face nearly into his armpit as if that might help him search his inside pocket—but there is no way to disguise the awful bloat and pucker of a face in tears."[51] Never able to lose sight of the integrity of the character whose emotions he is evoking, Yates's narrator, the boy as an adult, reflects on their childish awkwardness and ineptitude: "It would be good to report that we stayed and talked to him—that we hugged him again—but we were too embarrassed for that. We took the stamps and ran home without looking back."[52]

Read from a twenty-first-century perspective, we may judge that what Yates was highlighting about children and their parents was unremarkable; in the context of the 1960s, however, we have to view it differently. He makes strong connections that we would now take for granted between childhood traumas, specifically divorce, and adult unhappiness, neediness, and addiction. Able to draw heavily on his own experience (he was not even three years old when his parents divorced, and he went on to divorce the mothers of his own daughters), Yates avoids moral judgments but places divorce and marital discord at the center of almost all his fictional tales. It was a fact, so he suggests, of twentieth-century life, and its effects ran deep; as a consequence, the children he writes about are often bewildered, lonely observers. The Wheeler children who excitedly try to "help" their father build the garden path have no idea why he suddenly turns on them. They are not to know that he is rehearsing in his mind not only the details of the argument he had with their mother the night before but also all that has gone wrong in their marriage. The children become the outlet for his anger and he snaps. He grabs Michael and hits him violently. Their fearful response is powerfully evoked: "Michael found his need to cry so sudden and so deep" and "Jennifer watched him, round-eyed, and . . . [then] her own face began to twitch and crumple and she was crying too."[53] For all that they have wanted to be with their father, he remains a volatile figure whose moods they do not understand, and they seek refuge with their mother.

Facing his own responsibilities and failings as a parent, Yates was ever mindful of the effect of his divorce from Sheila on their two daughters, and he hated making them suffer the consequences of those failings; he knew, however, that they did suffer. Bailey describes one of his visits to New York to see his two daughters: "eight-year-old Monica was upset over the brevity of his visit, and acted moody and unresponsive."[54] Undoubtedly a deeply caring father (one who strove to be "a father worthy of the name"[55]), the only way Yates could cope with his own, as well as his children's, pain was to use it to inform the emotional complexity of his fictional portraits. In *The Easter Parade*, Yates delicately suggests an uncomfortable correlation between trauma as a child and emotional development as an adult. He creates an objective correlative of Emily's fist that resurfaces throughout the novel; the image of Emily "biting her wet fist"[56] as she looks at her injured sister vividly suggests her distress. This image is developed later in the story as a small indicator of the anxiety and powerlessness she feels throughout her life.[57] It acts as a way of reminding the reader that Emily is a child who needs protecting, and even as a woman she remains emotionally needy and underdeveloped.

In his last published work, *Cold Spring Harbor*, Yates returns to childhood and traces the path of his protagonist, Phil Drake, to mid-adolescence. This young boy's viewpoint makes it clear that almost all the adults he comes into contact with are severely lacking in common sense, are deeply unimaginative, are dependent on alcohol-fueled dreams, and are fundamentally unsuited to caring for children. Again, Yates indicates it is the children who carry the load of the parents' failures. In 1981, critic Robert Towers suggested that it was "as if Yates were under some enchantment that compelled him to keep circling the same half-acre of pain."[58] He might have had in mind Yates's propensity to recreate aspects of his childhood in so many stories. In this novel, there is, for instance, the familiar figure of a social-climbing, pathetically weak and dependent mother. More to the point, the portrait of the son, Phil, develops that of Bill Grove in *A Good School*. Phil Drake is an angry, disaffected young man. He is at a loss as to how to occupy his time with no real friends and no sense that though loved he is never understood or nurtured. Sent away to a school his absent father cannot afford, he is left to his own devices when he returns home. He is aware of the fact that he fits in nowhere, certainly not at home, for that is a place dominated by his boozed-up mother and an older sister happy to pursue the kind of dream of a life she finds in her magazines.

The interrogation of mothers and fathers in Yates's work is very closely linked to his investigation of the concept of home. In step with his own experience, his characters never live very long in any one place, and as suggested earlier, where they do live is deemed homely only if the relationships fostered there are stable and nurtured. Yates critiques the notion of home in much of his fiction, quietly suggesting that the instability and insecurity of his adult characters can be traced in part to the impoverishment of their childhood experiences. The sense of their deprivation is not primarily a result of their transitory existence, although they do indeed move about with alarming regularity between New York basement flats and Westchester suburbs; nor is it predominantly caused by the material poverty typical of all his depictions of childhood. It is more usually the result of their lack of close relationships with the adults in whose care they live, as is the case with Emily Grimes and Phil Drake. We understand that April Wheeler's insecurities as an adult are a logical extension of her lonely childhood, during which she was all but abandoned by the parents she loved and brought up by a series of aunts. Yet, in spite of that, she still idolizes them: "The only real fun I ever had was when one of my parents came for a visit. They were the ones I loved."[59] Furthermore, the images of home projected across a nation advertising a new suburban ideal are, Yates suggests, implicitly perpetuating a myth. Frank Wheeler's attack on suburban conformity has some political resonance here: "It's as if everybody'd made this tacit agreement to live in a state of total self-deception. The hell with reality! Let's have a whole bunch of cute little winding roads and cute little houses painted white and pink and baby blue; let's all be good consumers and have a lot of Togetherness and bring our children up in a bath of sentimentality."[60] Focusing his attack on the deceptions behind the projected images of the home, Frank might as well be spitting, "Let's all play at being Blanche DuBois."[61]

In Yates's families and homes emotions whirl chaotically and destructively for all the characters concerned. Further to my discussion of how home is represented in his fiction in the previous chapter, I want to draw attention to the fact that Yates sketches the physical details of domestic space sparsely, and these details are usually grim. Far more interested in conveying the interplay of emotions than the details of the soft furnishings, Yates takes us into the minds of those who inhabit each home. A large proportion of *Revolutionary Road*, for instance, takes place in the Wheelers' home, but only at rare moments of heightened tension or excitement does Yates linger over the physical details of place: when the young couple are first looking around the house, when the Givings family are first invited in for drinks, and when the final breakfast scene takes place.

In *A Special Providence*, returning to New York on leave, Robert Prentice mulls over what the term *home* means or does not mean to him; it is presented as a series of negatives with the only affirmation coming from a formal document: "He had spent most of his life in New York, or near it, but no section or street of it had ever felt like his neighborhood: he had never lived in one house for more than a year. The address now shown on his service record as his home was a walk-up apartment in the West Fifties, on a dark block beyond Eighth Avenue, and as he made his way there he tried to conjure a sense of homecoming among the blown newspapers and the flickering bar signs."[62] The reality of home for those without money or a stable family life, Yates suggests time and again, is dirty, grimy, and smelly: "Wherever they lived he seemed always to be the only new boy and the only poor boy, the only boy whose home smelled of mildew and cat droppings and plastilene, with statuary instead of a car in its garage; the only boy who didn't have a father."[63] The repetition of "the only . . . the only" adds the dramatic coloring needed to convey Prentice's sense of being different and an outsider. In *Cold Spring Harbor*, the details of Gloria Drake's home, "which smelled of cat droppings and cosmetics and recent cooking,"[64] provide a comparable assault on the senses and ensure that the reader identifies more closely with her unexpected visitors, Charles and Evan Shepard.

The slovenly behavior of the maternal characters at the heart of the dwellings Yates describes, their lack of cleanliness and good manners, for instance, provides a further indictment of the Yatesian concept of home. In *The Easter Parade*, Yates itemizes every visual detail of Pookie's sloppy behavior, for it was with such indignities his own mother offended and alienated him. The reader shares Emily Grimes's horrified gaze as, silently, she watches her mother read a magazine; the description of her mother's grotesque habits is so slow and detailed it is almost as if Yates is recalling patterns of behavior that scarred him. In our understanding of Emily, they are a useful rider to the impression we are building of her as an outsider, a person different and set apart: "Pookie would slowly, absently wipe her thumb against her moist lower lip and then wipe the thumb against the lower right-hand corner of each page, for easier turning; it left the corners of all the pages wrinkled and faintly smeared with lipstick. And tonight she had eaten fudge, which meant there would be traces of fudge as well as lipstick on the pages. Emily found she couldn't watch the process without grinding her teeth."[65] The "misdemeanors" Pookie is committing are minor but are felt to be deeply offensive by a writer whose own home was infected by similar behavior.

Within Yates's fiction, it is clear that mothers, however slovenly in their own habits, are primarily responsible for steering their daughters away from the temptation of premarital sex toward marriages shrouded in romantic, sentimental myths. In postwar America, sex within marriage was encouraged alongside early marriage since this would inevitably lead to children and the rebuilding and strengthening of the nation. Men and women, as Wini Breines explains, were urged to learn about each other's sexual needs, as long as such learning took place in a marital bed: "Marital sex and simultaneous orgasm were promoted as ways to stabilize the family, and attention to marital sex in marriage and sex manuals thrived. Experts prescribed sex in marriage; the effusive encouragement of marital sex contrasted sharply with the obsessive warnings about premarital sex and threatening admonitions to girls and women to remain virgins."[66] However, Breines also goes on to argue that "sexual ignorance was common. All the ingredients for self-consciousness and tension were present."[67] It is the gap between the promoted ideal and the lives that were lived that interests Yates. Perhaps, in his later fiction, he is exploiting the knowledge Kinsey provided that premarital sex was rife and that marriage was anything but the ideal it was set up to be. In addition, as suggested earlier, Yates appears to feel that marriage is threatened by the sexual liberation of women. However, the most likely explanation for Yates's somewhat cynical view of marriage is that it simply reflects his own experience and observations. His exploration of sex and marriage is undertaken from the perspective that a strong and healthy marriage is a laudable ideal, but despite all the advertisements and government promotions to the contrary, it is a very difficult thing to achieve.

There is no indication, even in works written in the late 1960s or early 1970s, that Yates celebrates new sexual freedoms available to everyone. Mired in the complexities of his own sexual awakening in the two previous decades, Yates writes to emphasize sex as an activity fraught with insecurity and competition, a power game that draws attention to the divide between men and women rather than to their union. This is ironically alluded to in *The Easter Parade* when Andrew Crawford, again unable to maintain an erection despite a year of treatment, refers to their failed coupling as, "A technical knockout" and calls Emily "the winner and still champion."[68] Almost all the young men of Yates's fiction fear sexual performance and are particularly wary of the expectations of their female partners. In *A Good School*, Larry Gaines's teenage anxieties are typically Yatesian as he expresses feelings of intimidation his girlfriend Edith's obvious desire causes: "But all the way out across the quadrangle, with his arm around her, he had to fight a rising sense of panic. He was a virgin. His plan, all along, had been to lose it with some nameless girl in Algiers, or wherever the Merchant Marine might take him—he had even thought he might contrive to develop a wide range of sexual techniques before coming home to Edith—but that excellent idea was closed to him now because she was crowding him; she wanted it; she wouldn't settle for anything less."[69] The plan he had in his head was just that, a plan, immediately unrealizable and fanciful, and Yates focuses on his rising panic and her apparent demands with the final insistent clauses. Sex, therefore, is always presented as a struggle, problematic, fraught with confusion, and heavily inscribed with a sense of selfishness and failure.

In Yates's fiction, women are portrayed as having a normal sexual appetite, at least to begin with. Emily Grimes, for instance, loses her virginity to a passing soldier in a park, and in the description of their coupling Yates subtly suggests *his* selfishness and *her* unfulfilled needs: "She expected pain but there wasn't time to brace herself before it was there . . . and with it there began an insistent pleasure, building to what gave every promise of ecstasy before it dwindled and died. He slipped out of her, sank on one knee into the grass beside her leg and rolled away, breathing hard."[70] The narrative focus is on Emily's disappointment, on the words "dwindled and died." However, the notion that Yates is in any sense writing from a perspective that prefigures feminism is disrupted in an extraordinary way by vicious outbursts from men who, later in the novel, attack Emily, her body and her sexuality. The fact that crudely graphic, almost violent, outbursts occur across several novels suggests that the perspective is one countenanced by the author at some level. The balanced initial impression of his female characters is disturbed by the creeping suspicion that Yates's women are voracious; they are seen to be sexually demanding in a way that appears to disrupt the balance of their relationships.

A character such as Emily Grimes is as free to explore sexual relationships as any of the male characters she meets, yet built into this story is an implicit condemnation of the number of her sexual partners. This paradox is never fully resolved in Yates's work and occurs despite his apparently rational understanding and acceptance of a more liberal, rounded perception of women. Yates's narratives zigzag between showing empathy for women's needs for sexual fulfillment and barely concealed aggression and dislike. In the context of *The Easter Parade*, it is as if Yates wants to find a counterbalance to the initial impression he has created of Emily as a modern, sensitive, articulate, sexually active, and essentially likeable young woman whose needs are not understood by the men she encounters. He wants to present her wounded, diminished, and battered, but the means he chooses for doing this raise questions about his perspective of women in general and of sex in particular. Perhaps women who act on their desires are only, or are especially, seen as avaricious to a man who cannot perform. However, one also has to note the rigidity of the moral framework that hampered women's sexual activity in the 1950s; good women were supposed to be passive, inert, and compliant.

In her unsatisfactory relationship with Andrew Crawford, Emily is subjected to a tirade of abuse about her sexual desire *and* about her body. Crawford's anxieties about his weak sexual performance drive him to seek refuge in jealous and crude assaults as, without any basis in fact, he hypothesizes about Emily masturbating with thoughts of her brother-in-law, Tony Wilson, in her mind. Haunted by his inability to please her, Crawford goes on the offensive:

> "I'll bet you masturbated over him. Didn't you? Oh, I'll bet you tickled your little nipples until they came up hard, and then you—"
> "Stop it, Andrew."
> "—and then you went to work on your clitoris—picturing him all the time, imagining what he'd say and how he'd feel and what he'd do to you—and then you spread your legs and shoved a couple of fingers up your—"
> "I want you to *stop* this, Andrew."[71]

His graphic language, and the degree of disgust behind it, culminates with a final repetitious bombardment: "Do you want to know something, Emily? I hate your body. Oh, I suppose I love it too, at least God knows I try to, but at the same time I hate it. I hate what it put me through last year—what it's putting me through now. I hate your sensitive little tits. I hate your ass and your hips, the way they move and turn; I hate your thighs, the way they open up. I hate your waist and your belly and your great hairy mound and your clitoris and your whole slippery cunt."[72] This passage is disquieting not for the thoughts it reveals but because of the violent passion and energy behind them. Yates makes scant attempt to suggest how warped a perspective this is and leaves this reader bewildered by its graphic force.

Yates seems to relish references to female sexual desire and practices as much as references to female genitalia presented through the prism of male anger and peep-show distaste. It is hard not to see such writing at times as an unusually cheap device to shock. *The Easter Parade*, with its many female characters, affords the opportunity for some gratuitous, semipornographic images such as the "anatomically perfect drawing of a woman reclining naked with her legs apart, fondling one breast with one hand and applying an electric vibrator to her crotch with the other."[73] In the context of the story being told, Trudy's "life-sized renderings of open vaginas . . . all with intricately different kinds of outer and inner labia"[74] represent a direct challenge to Emily's (and, as I have suggested, the author's) apparently old-fashioned view of art and sexuality: they alienate and isolate her. On another level, they may alienate and isolate the reader since the graphic detail appears excessive and prolonged. Yates's imagery appears to distort the female body as he highlights women's vaginas, and, more specifically, focuses on fingers (or vibrators) inserted into vaginas; it is very explicit, very exact, very "anatomically perfect," as if Yates himself rests his gaze there and cannot look away. It is impossible to ignore the suggestion that the narrative voice resents the fact that women's fingers can perform a function that the flaccid penises of Yates's frequently impotent men cannot.

The difficulty with these descriptions is that they go beyond the purposes of the narrative, mockery or no mockery; they seem superfluous and at variance with Yates's usual control and the general subtlety of his descriptions. In *Cold Spring Harbor*, for instance, an incidental character, Ralph, the chauffeur, accosts the two teenage friends Flash and Phil Drake. For no apparent reason he makes salacious, sexual remarks about Flash masturbating and then criticizes the maid, Amy: "'Well, Amy's kind of a good kid,' Ralph confided as he put the hose back to work on the sudsy, dripping limousine. 'Or at least she *coulda* been a good kid; it may be too late now for any man to straighten her out. Know what her trouble is?' And he turned his smile on both the boys, who were dumbly waiting for the answer. 'She finger-fucks herself too much. Simple as that.'"[75] Not even the ironic and humorous metaphor of the hose can take the vitriol out of this outburst. With echoes of Andrew Crawford's verbal attacks on Emily, this passage adds nothing to the narrative except to act as some kind of a warning to the boys that women are unhealthily sexually self-absorbed. For the reader, it raises a different kind of question, not about the character but about the author who has given him such graphic language for no obvious purpose. The author's own attitudes toward sex have seeped through with disquieting results.

Yates's "voices" spit out sexual images with explosive distaste; the overriding impression, whether the sex is onanistic or partnered, is one of revulsion toward female sexuality, and the recurring element of voyeurism in his narrative position is hard to ignore. In *Cold Spring Harbor*, Mary Donovan is described masturbating in her bedroom as she fantasies about Evan Shepard. The narrative perspective, with its graphic detail, *seems* voyeuristic even if there is no obvious spying male character. However, Yates's purpose is to indicate her sexual desire: "She would pretend that her own hands were those of Evan Shepard, and she'd allow them to roam and fondle various parts of herself, taking their time, having their way with her, until the sweet tension was almost unbearable; then at last she'd achieve the spasm and the helpless little cry that meant she could probably fall asleep."[76] While images of women masturbating provide a method of confronting women's sexual desire, the impression is distorted since we receive Yates's use of such images through the prism of male fantasy. Her hands, described in ways that highlight their disassociation from Mary, seem animated by the impulse of the narrative toward such fantasy, a narrative that never loses the sense that it is created and driven by Yates's male perspective and voyeuristic eye.

The gaze of men and boys seems almost equally fascinated *and* disgusted in these instances of peeping Tom behavior. A young boy in one of Yates's short stories, for instance, tells his friend that he could see up the friend's sister's skirt: "I could see the crack, and the hair."[77] This boy's angle of vision and his evident interest combined with distaste typify Yates's attitude to women's bodies and sexuality. Similarly, in *Disturbing the Peace*, Spivack's outburst about his sister's sexual habits is voyeuristic in its imagining, violent in both tone and imagery, and, I suggest, is of questionable value to the narrative: "She lets that slippery bastard fuck her every night. He works the old cock up in there and shoves it around till she screams."[78] Spivack's outburst is as much in character as all John Givings's less-sexualized attacks, since both are institutionalized mental patients and their behavior lies outside what is perceived as normal, but it still interrupts the control Yates usually displays. If Yates is holding such individuals up for criticism, he only partly succeeds mainly because the outbursts of these men are so poorly integrated into the sequence of events. Reliant on mimetic narratives throughout his fictions, Yates's technique is suddenly weakened as these strident male voices disrupt the rhythm of the story being told and sex appears to be confused with male fantasies of sex.

Men who are inclined to see female sexual desire through the lens of pornographic film or magazine images have always formed part of the shifting equation of human understanding of sex and gender roles. Again in *Disturbing the Peace*, George Taylor's boastful account of infidelity with his "sweet little package of trouble,"[79] Sandy, is a composite of male fantasies. He is "fifty-six and burly"[80] and Sandy is "a laughing, full-breasted girl"[81] with a voracious sexual appetite who is forthcoming about her willingness to satisfy him: "I want to blow you while you're doing eighty miles an hour on the Jersey Turnpike."[82] By deliberately plundering typical male fantasies of casual and forbidden sexual encounters, Yates amusingly draws attention to this man's smugness and arrogance. However, while many of his male characters share this idiom, and this acts as a way of drawing attention to the way men viewed women as playthings and objects, Yates draws scant attention to men holding a healthier outlook.

Yates may be striving to capture the voices and thoughts of men who felt threatened by the articulation of female sexual rights (voices still commonly heard in the 1950s and 1960s before they were educated to think otherwise), but the unbalanced and repeated appearance of outbursts attacking women and their sexuality suggests a problem of authorial perspective. It is not women who exclude men in Yates's fiction; it is men who exclude women and then, like Andrew Crawford, appear to punish them for their desire and their independence. Writing about Yates's early sexual experiences when he was in the army, Blake Bailey makes the point that "to some extent sex would always be a problematic business."[83] This does not of itself prove very much. It would not have been uncommon for young men brought up in the 1930s and 1940s to be both uninformed and squeamish about sex. However, it is hard not to surmise that Yates's narrative perspective becomes enmeshed with persistently intruding anxieties about his own sexual performance for, as Bailey points out, "Like his characters Andrew Crawford, Michael Davenport, and Bill Grove, he proved to be almost totally impotent."[84] This is the work of a man who fears women's sexuality because he does not fully understand it and because he fears what it will reveal about him. Crudely put, female sexual desire becomes threatening to a man who cannot perform every time. In writing repeatedly, and with some aggression, about women whose desire seems voracious, together with men who cannot satisfy that desire, Yates the man appears to be more in control than Yates the novelist.

The presence of homosexual love—much less accepted in the 1950s and '60s—casts a shadow over many of Yates's male characters and their relationships with women and acts as a further attempt by Yates to question the truth of the genial image of the pure, middle-class, heterosexual family that, as Breines points out, was promoted everywhere: "Home, especially in the suburbs, meant a white, heterosexual, nuclear family-based society."[85] In Cold War America homosexuality was seen as perverted and as damaging as murder or rape. Moreover, it was seen as a threat to the emergent American nation: "Homosexuality was incorporated into the demonology of the McCarthy era by linking communism with immoral and antimasculine behavior."[86]

Andrew Crawford's verbal attacks and wounding remarks about Emily's body are indicative of the pain for both sexes if the complexities of gender and sexual identity remain unacknowledged. In America of the 1950s, open discussion about sexual identity was uncommon, and Yates's depictions reflect exactly the confused and fearful spirit of the times. Elaine Tyler May, for instance, talks about the fact that "the postwar years brought a wave of officially sponsored homophobia."[87] The man whose behavior could be classified as antimasculine is caught in a net; either he is homosexual and terrified of admitting it to himself and others and so he attempts unsuccessfully to imitate the behavior of a heterosexual man—to my mind this describes Crawford—or, like Yates perhaps, the man struggles to "be male" in a way that society will recognize.

A psychoanalytic reading of Yates's writing in this sphere might suggest that the degree of anger and the violence of several of his male characters' language as they reflect unfavorably on their own performance reveal self-loathing in the writer that is impossible to ignore. Blake Bailey draws little attention to this facet of his work but does say that Yates "disliked the way he looked"[88] and "fixed on his round eyes and plump lips as physiognomic signs of weakness; more to the point, he thought they made him look feminine, 'bubbly,' and he had a lifelong horror of being perceived as homosexual."[89] He worried about both his appearance and, even if in a jokey manner, his inclinations. In Susan Braudy's speech at Yates's memorial service she recalls him saying (with reference to how much of his own character is in *The Easter Parade*), "I'm not saying I'm a cross-dressing creep, or a damn homo . . . or well . . . maybe I am."[90] As a writer, he was particularly sensitive to the assumption that he might be homosexual in ways that are best indicated by Tom Nelson's observations in *Young Hearts Crying*: "Point is, you see, a lot of those characters think 'artist' equals 'fag,' and I guess you can't blame them."[91] It is clear that in all Yates's work he interrogates the idea, and ideal, of masculinity; society's notion of what it is to be male seems limited and never sits easily with his male protagonists.

Despite his fears about his own sexuality and despite his open dislike of homosexuals, Yates's fiction challenges the bigoted views of the era. He captures a contemporary view of homosexuals in a conversation between the male inmates of a tuberculosis ward in one of his collected stories, "A Clinical Romance":

> "But it was a funny thing, to look at him you'd never think he was any different from you and me." . . .
>
> "Sure," Costello said. "That's the way a lot of them are. Look and act just like anybody else."
>
> "That's the kind you want to look out for," Lynch said. "I hate them sneaky bastards." . . .
>
> "No reason to hate 'em," Costello said, shrugging.
>
> "Oh, no?" Lynch glared at him. He looked tough sitting there, his pajama top open across his chest, a tiny religious medallion swinging on its damp silver chain among the hairs. "Well, I do. I hate their guts, every one of 'em."[92]

Fear of homosexuals is increased due to the fact that they "look and act" just like everybody else. Homophobics argued that this allows homosexuals to threaten the nation in a similar, subversive way to the silent communists creeping over the borders. Yates makes it clear that limited ideas about masculinity are also being challenged in this story, as evidenced by the figure of the aptly named Lynch; his hairy chest and religious medallion are not incidental to how the reader receives this exchange. It is as if his masculine strength and religious sensitivity are justifications for his bigotry. The accepted opinion of the time was that homosexuality was caused by "momism." Both were feared and derided in ways that Yates embraces, not least because his mother, with her stifling dependence and careless neglect, had created her own version of momism.

Although it seems wrong to lay the author's life alongside that of his characters, in works that draw so heavily on biography it is impossible not to draw such inferences, so that what Bailey terms Yates's "frank, utterly unapologetic homophobia"[93] seems entirely in keeping with male characters who are desperate to hide either their homosexual inclinations or who struggle with the fact that they are not sufficiently "male." The protagonist of *A Good School*, for instance, is alarmed when he hears about his teacher's comment that he has "psychological problems." Grove's interior thoughts explain why: "'Mental attitude' might be an acceptable term, but any word beginning with 'psych' had come to frighten him. All such words spoke of darkness beyond hope. . . . And the worst thing about them, according to what little he'd been able to read of Sigmund Freud, was that they had their roots in sexual anxiety."[94] Taken alongside Yates's own, as well as his characters', avowed hatred of all things psychiatric or psychological,[95] something of a new craze (as he saw it) in 1950s America, it is hard not to read Yates's fiction as an attempt to hide the very thing it reveals.

The character of Lars Ericson in *The Easter Parade* is interesting in this context; with him Yates endeavors to challenge further his own preconceptions about sexual identity and create a "figure of the times," a man who would seem modern and be an appropriate representative of the way sexuality was discussed in the 1970s. Ericson has no sexual "problem" and remains the best lover Emily ever had, since Yates makes it clear that, with his virile "manhood," Emily experiences prolonged orgasms: "It grew from him like the sturdy limb of a tree; it prodded and thrusted and plunged in her; it drove her slowly and steadily into a long-sustained delirium for which the only possible expression was a scream; it left her weak and panting and feeling like a woman, waiting for more."[96] But nothing is ever without complication in Emily's life. She is devastated and bewildered when Ericson ends the relationship with the casual information that, "I happen to be bisexual, you see."[97] With Emily's naïveté in the face of this information ("You mean homosexual?"[98]), Yates brings to the fore what he knew to be his own sexually conservative views.

The greatest "norm" against which Yates was writing was what he saw as the predictable fiction of happy couples living harmonious lives in elegant homes with beautifully turned-out, well-behaved children. For Yates, this was a fiction propagated by Hollywood, magazines, the advertising industry, and political rhetoric. Not one of these elements accorded with his own experience, either as a child growing up in the 1930s and 1940s or as a parent and husband in the 1950s and 1960s, as Jerome Klinkowitz makes clear: "[Yates] drew his fiction not just from the world around him but from his sometimes painful experience in it. Although his writing encompasses society in its largest forms, his perspective is almost always from its smallest unit, the family. And because the family is inevitably torn by divorce, the sightline is deliberately askew."[99] The "painful experience" that Klinkowitz notes gave rise to Yates's careful, painstaking, dismembering of dreams that he felt ensnared his characters, since, in Yates's world, hopefulness was a trap.

Indicating the narrow, domestic focus of postwar Americans, in the face of global and national catastrophes, Wini Breines's retrospective analysis concentrates on America's unbounded optimism. She describes the positive outlook they were encouraged to adopt, an outlook that avoids any suggestion of disharmony, whether it be marital or political: "Backyard barbecues, family television watching, and soda fountains tell of easy times. In spite of the Holocaust, atom bomb, and McCarthyism, Americans, it appears, felt secure and content. For them, Auschwitz and Hiroshima did not presage the end of Western culture's claim to superiority. Americans' concerns focused instead on their personal fortunes. This was a family time that took for granted the democracy, prosperity, and invincibility that allowed many to relish the good life they could now afford."[100] Breines's view is compelling in its account of the comfort and security Americans embraced. With the emphasis on protection, she acknowledges how a policy of containment grew out of a fear of communism: "Literal and figurative boundaries were important in the fifties, a period in which distinctions between 'them' (foreigners and deviants) and 'us' flourished. The borders of the United States became a central metaphor in the fears of invasion by communists."[101] This was a past that was traumatic for Americans and a past that propelled them toward an eager espousal of normalcy. The experiences of the Depression era, followed quickly by the Second World War, created a sense of urgency about embracing the calm, or apparent calm, that succeeded the 1930s and 1940s. There was, in this time of Cold War tension, a feeling of disquiet that needed to be numbed, a disquiet that W. H. Auden described as belonging to the "age of anxiety."[102]

Rather than numbing societal unease with his fiction, Yates wants to confront and analyze it, to probe its raw places and let questions, rather than pat answers, emerge. In eviscerating dreams of wealth and social mobility, his starting place is always his own family. While all writers borrow from their own experience of life as they shape their fiction, Yates does it more nakedly than most. His fictions emerge from a patchwork of personal incidents and observation of those around him. That his writing about sex asks more questions than it answers is not a weakness, but that the writer reiterates the same questions and never appears to find any resolutions for his sexual inquiries may well be. Yates's view of women and their sexuality seems distorted or askew, as Klinkowitz terms it, since, like several boys of his fiction, he peeps up their skirts. He gives the impression of being like Phil Drake, one of his many alter egos, furtively spying through a parted curtain, watching his sister and her husband making love: "Oh, Jesus, it was the loveliest and most terrible thing he'd ever seen; it was the source of the world; and his shame was so immediate that he let the fabric slip back into place after only a second or two."[103]

What Yates would like his reader to be clear about is that when it comes to understanding the opposite sex and relationships in general, there is no such thing as distortion, for that implies a norm or an ideal that this author would like to suggest does not exist. However, this balanced opinion is disrupted by Yates's loss of narrative control when writing specifically about women and sex. He appears to lose the equilibrium that would normally encourage the reader to see a partial view as inevitable and even judicious; instead, Yates becomes like a writer with two voices. The dominant voice is intelligent and empathetic toward women but always rigorous and never sentimental; the other voice is angry, salacious, and voyeuristic. This latter view is limited, furtive, often distorted, and is weakened by the perspective of a viewer not capable of fully taking part in the act itself. Similarly, the narrative control and broad-minded vision Yates would like to think he has in this realm is disturbed by socially and sexually conservative views that trickle out through the writing. The recurrence of impotent men, masturbating women, and the sense we often get that the male protagonists are beleaguered by female desire are evidence enough that Yates did not have much to say that was rounded or positive about sex.

10

America in the Postwar Years

13. Portrait of Richard taken in the early/mid-1970s in New York. It was among the papers salvaged from the fire in Yates's New York apartment in 1976, hence the water stains.

Richard Yates's published works span the period between 1961 and 1986. His writing life began in his teenage years and continued until his death in 1992. Nevertheless, he is very much a writer of the fifties, where the term *fifties* is expanded to include the early part of the subsequent decade. His work is predominantly (though not exclusively) set in a relatively small time frame, 1955–63, and reveals much about this critical postwar period. America wanted its self-confidence reflected and enhanced in its literature. If not that, it wanted the style of its new fiction to be revolutionary and innovative, for this was the way that America, newly raised to the position of the world's greatest superpower, felt it should face itself and the world. As noted, Yates's fiction harked back to the realist fiction of a former era. Neither the subject matter of his work nor the technique he chose suited the general forward-looking thrust of the time. As a result, the ways in which he extended the realist form were seemingly underappreciated or overlooked.

A strong underlying current in all of Yates's work is the need to scrutinize postwar optimism and replace it with a balanced view of how society validates or alienates the individual. While Yates chose fiction as his medium, C. Wright Mills's work of social history investigated similar issues on a broader scale. Writing in 1959, Mills is hard-hitting in his assessment of the precariousness of the political situation in postwar America and Europe. He sees the way forward as dependent on the "sociological imagination," which he describes as empowering and privileging the individual in a new way: "[it] enables its possessor to understand the larger historical scene in terms of its meaning for the inner life and the external career of a variety of individuals."[1] He argues: "The sociological imagination enables us to grasp history and biography and the relations between the two within society. That is its task and its promise."[2] This is precisely the arena into which Yates steps. Concentrating on domestic lives and individual failings, Yates fuses a sense of the history of the era with the intimate details of relationship and family and is unequivocal in his suggestion that American optimism is not only misplaced but also damaging. His fictions accurately reveal the apparent comfort and the deep, troubling anxiety that underpin any sense of security.

The postwar era was complex in terms of social and political upheaval. Richard Fried sheds some light on why this was the case: "The historian must therefore note the irony that the two major currents of the era—the mobilization of the Cold War and the emergence of an economy of abundance—had divergent and paradoxical effects on those who sought change and on those who wanted to halt it. These two historical currents sometimes encouraged one side, sometimes the other—which is why this decade is in retrospect so perplexing, so difficult to categorize."[3] In the 1960s, Norman Podhoretz, discussing the attacks a new generation of postwar writers made on the liberal attitudes of the 1930s and 1940s, suggests that "America had grown to a position of great responsibility, and the attitudes of Americans must be made commensurate with the country's new status."[4] The notion that America should promote an ideal version of itself had many implications for its citizens—political, social, and cultural. Vance Packard asserts that postwar America had a desire to see itself as egalitarian and classless, even if, in Packard's view, that was not the reality: "The rank-and-file citizens of the nation have generally accepted this view of progress toward equality because it fits with what we would like to believe about ourselves. It coincides with the American Creed and the American Dream, and is deeply imbedded in our folklore."[5]

Fried's retrospective study of the 1950s echoes Packard's observation about the stratification of American postwar society: "Society was not as classless as champions of affluence claimed."[6] By weaving his perceptions about class into his fiction, Yates did not endear himself to a readership that, as Lionel Trilling also points out in 1950, consistently avoids the issue: "It would seem that Americans have a kind of resistance to looking closely at society. They appear to believe that to touch accurately on the matter of class, to take full note of snobbery, is somehow to demean themselves. . . . Americans will not deny that we have classes and snobbery, but they seem to hold it to be indelicate to take precise cognizance of these phenomena."[7] Americans wanted to believe they had moved on from the ways of their European forefathers and all that such a change suggested in terms of class and opportunity; such ideas inevitably fed into accepted wisdom about culture and literature in particular.

Yates's penchant for the grim, lonely, and fractured aspects of human relationships, the bleak and isolated face of both suburban and metropolitan community living, creates an unwelcome commentary on the newly invigorated American Dream of prosperity and materialism. Unlike the British understanding of the term *upper class* (which historically referred more to birthright than to money, though this has changed and is still changing), to be upper class in American society is predominantly based on material wealth. Nevertheless, wealth that has been in a family over several generations is still seen as superior and indicative of greater social clout than any graces new money might confer. Yates's work, like that of the social historians referred to, indicates a class consciousness that is attuned to the middle classes struggling to make ends meet in a postwar world. Where Yates's perspective is unique is the emphasis he places on the gray areas between the haves and the have nots. He highlights the fact that seismic shifts have occurred in the class system since the war and suggests the confusion that ensues for those brought up with a framework that no longer exists. *Young Hearts Crying* has Michael Davenport's sense of bewilderment about class at its heart.

On the one hand, Davenport can relax into an appreciation of his girlfriend's parents' home, appraising it with an artist's intellectual eye: "[he] let his gaze follow the lofty ceiling line of one bright wall until it met at right angles with another, far away, that opened onto other and still other rooms in the shadows of the afternoon. This was a place suggesting the timeless repose that only several generations' worth of success could provide. This was class."[8] Yates's description of the rooms receding into the distance from Davenport's vantage point figuratively refer to the generations of Blaine money, unknowable and in "the shadows" to someone without such an inheritance. Davenport is at ease because he is not involved with the Blaine family beyond dating their daughter. However, "a shy announcement that would greatly complicate everything between them"[9] occurs shortly after he and Lucy marry. Unwittingly, he has married a woman who has three or four million dollars to her name; because he is now emotionally connected to this money, these are dollars that he thinks threaten to undermine his masculinity. What the reader realizes quite quickly is that from the moment he is told about her money, that emasculation begins. He becomes an aggressive inverted snob, a man who feels embittered and disempowered.

Michael Davenport's interior thoughts chart his new understanding that it is no longer valid to make assumptions based on birth and money. Paul Maitland might have gone to Amherst for reasons other than family wealth; he now questions the historic assumption that Amherst was "an expensive school for society boys and intellectual lightweights."[10] The stereotypes upon which he's relied to give him clues about how to behave "were said to have broken down since the war."[11] Davenport's awareness that he cannot pigeonhole Maitland is intrinsically linked to his inability to deal with the fact that he doesn't know how to place himself. He is a writer but one who can only link the romantic but clichéd adjective "struggling" to his name if he denies the fact that he is married to a millionaire.

The confusion about money and class in this novel is something that resonates with Yates. Preoccupations about money and class dominated the postwar world he lived in and remind him of the personal discomfort he suffered since he was always a poor boy in ill-fitting clothes at an expensive private school. His fiction suggests that he feels the newly invigorated sense of social and material aspiration is damaging American lives; he writes to expose this in all his work. However, Yates's attack on status symbols is very particular and is predominantly located in the domestic lives of his protagonists. His aim is to question the sentimentalized and fictionalized notion of family in 1950s America.

Somewhat paradoxically, it is the very ordinariness of Yates's characters—individuals leading diminished lives in drab surroundings—and the uncomfortable intimacy of his dialogue-based fiction that makes Yates's work stand out. With the plight of the ordinary man an increasingly common feature of postwar writing, Yates could be said (in this respect) to be in step with the times as he textures sad, unfulfilled lives very convincingly. His insight into the quiet longings of his vulnerable characters enables Yates to question and undercut the insidious, false notions the advertising and Hollywood industries were propagating. These are falsehoods that, he suggests, humans inexorably live by.

John O'Hara, John Cheever, Sloan Wilson, and John Updike all display a similar interest in the growth of suburban materialism and the loneliness and narrowness of the middle-class lives they depict. What is unique about Yates is his determination to take his investigations a step further. Avoiding sentimentality and neatly woven endings that reassure rather than challenge, he reveals the existence of a dark underbelly in the lives of his dreamers, prevaricators, egoists, and performers. It is one thing to avoid creating heroes and to expose the characters' propensity to put people on a pedestal only to watch them fall off; it is quite another to challenge the reader's need for a similar panacea. The reader is often made aware of the timelessness of Yates's observations as the questions his fiction pose remain worth asking today.

Yates's interest in writing about the ordinary men and women of the American middle classes was inextricably linked to the environments they inhabited. These were the monotonous, faceless, inorganically constructed arcadias of the suburbs and the run-down, unglamorous areas of Manhattan. In the 1950s, intellectuals who saw the city as an arena for creativity scorned the suburbs, but suburban development can no longer be so easily reviled. More than half the population of the United States lives in suburbia, and suburban environments have changed the face of social politics. The suburbs allow millions of Americans to live comfortably in houses they own within relatively easy reach of the cities in which they work. However, Yates was keen to expose the false dreams that those promoting suburban living encouraged. The reality was that suburbia acted like a narcotic on an individual's sense of independence. Blake Bailey is at pains to explain this: "Amid the affluence of postwar America, the temptation was particularly keen to accept the easy rewards of suburban comfort, an undemanding job, and to fill the emptiness that followed with dreams of potential greatness or adventure. But to pursue such dreams in fact—as Yates well knew—required a resilient sense of autonomy. . . . And in a society where one's status depends almost entirely on the nice house and 'good' job, one must possess a formidable sense of self-worth . . . to risk failure by leaving the beaten path."[12] This is indeed the struggle that Yates dramatizes in his characterization of Frank and April Wheeler, as well as many other of his protagonists.

In his historical analysis of urban and suburban growth, James Howard Kunstler makes it clear that the end of World War II signaled a change in the way housing was envisaged and planned. A pattern of development began alongside the rapid growth of industry: "America redirected its economic energies to what it barely had begun before war broke out: the Great Enterprise of emptying the old cities and building a substitute of far-flung auto suburbs."[13] In *The Easter Parade*, Yates picks up on this change, not as a massive indictment but with a tone of regret about the alteration to the physical landscape: "Great Hedges is long gone. He sold it to a developer," and "The fields on either side of the road gave way to dense masses of houses, and to shopping centers with acres of parked cars."[14] Kunstler describes this new, bleak version of autonomy and of the American Dream very starkly; while what was desired might have been a cottage on a sacred piece of earth, to borrow Kunstler's phrasing, what developers such as William Levitt built was, "less a dream than a cruel parody. The place where the dream house stood—a subdivision of many other identical dream houses—was neither the country nor the city. It was noplace. If anything, it combined the worst social elements of the city and the country and none of its best elements . . . except for some totemic trees and shrubs, nature had been obliterated by the relentless blocks full of houses."[15] Kunstler's work concentrates on the practical and aesthetic diminution of these new dream communities, whereas Yates is attentive to showing the effects of that diminution on the lives of the people who inhabit them. Their ideas converge, however, with the understanding that community is not something one can just buy, build, or invent.

That these constructed communities failed the people who lived there by offering few civic amenities was one obvious problem. Another was the fact that their focus was elsewhere as they looked back at the city they clung to; they existed to service the working population of great cities such as New York and Chicago. This meant the inhabitants were dislocated in a way that Yates's characters always are. The colorless suburban homes he describes create a sense of longing, and not *be*longing. However, this has to be qualified by the understanding that loneliness also characterizes Yates's urban environments. Modern living in *all* its forms is critiqued and found wanting by this writer.

Yates subtly expresses anxiety about how American suburbia appears to be assaulting the life of the individual, and the individual seems to be desperate to conform, in the manner in which he describes the Wheelers' attempts to visualize themselves in the house they are shown. Using the idioms of his characters, Yates suggests that they will have to twist and wrench their possessions, and thus, he suggests, themselves, to fit into this environment: "Their sofa could go here and their big table there . . . a sparse, skillful arrangement of furniture would counteract the prim suburban look of this too-symmetrical living room. On the other hand, the very symmetry of the place was undeniably appealing—the fact that all its corners made right angles, that each of its floorboards lay straight and true, that its doors hung in perfect balance and closed without scraping in efficient clicks. . . . The gathering disorder of their lives might still be sorted out and made to fit these rooms, among these trees; and what if it did take time? Who could be frightened in as wide and bright, as clean and quiet a house as this?"[16] The narrative voice

mimics first one voice, then the other, as April and Frank rehearse the possibilities for this house. With his subtly inflected description, Yates makes it
clear that their exploration of the place is colored by their immediate concerns *and* their deep-rooted anxieties, as a word such as "prim" is negated
by "appealing." The reader is left in no doubt that the house, with its "symmetry," is seen by the Wheelers as a necessary antidote to the disorder of
their lives. However, as his description develops, Yates encourages the reader
to see that it is an environment that becomes increasingly sterile with every
graphic phrase, and it is the reader who cannot escape, as the Wheelers do at
this point, from the notion that the marriage is unstable. By introducing the
notion of fear in the abstract, Yates suggests it as a concrete idea. The clean
suburban house, with its manicured garden, is an ideal of egalitarian living,
an ideal that is born out of Hollywood images of picket fences and neat gar-
dens. In Yates's version of it, it is infected and carries with it false promises
and subtle suggestions of a gothic house of horrors.

Exploring dreams of upward mobility, Yates traces the path from gray
cityscapes to suburban greenery in many stories, but if the suburban life appears to offer a new start and an injection of hope, there is always disenchant-
ment awaiting his characters; relationships still wilt and dreams never flower
for long. Richard Ford suggests that Yates's depiction of suburbia would have
appeared to have been an attack on such environments at the time of the novel's publication: "In 1961, *Revolutionary Road* must have seemed an especially
corrosive indictment of the postwar suburban 'solution,' and of the hopeful
souls who left the city in search of some acceptable balance between rough
rural essentials and urban opportunity and buzz."[17] Ford indicates that the
suburbs of Yates's first novel were "monotonous, anesthetized buffer zones"
that manage "to trivialize and contaminate"[18] any ideal of suburbia. They fare
no better in Yates's penultimate novel from 1984 when Lucy and Michael
Davenport move to Larchmont. The commuters who appear to "take pride
in their very conformity" walking "in clusters"[19] to the station, as Davenport
observes them, are implicitly infected by the atmosphere of their suburban
lives. Pat Nelson fails to find anyone "who wasn't just sort of all Larchmont,
inside and out."[20]

In order to explore Yates's view of suburbia and suburban living, *Revolutionary Road* needs close critical attention. In answer to the comment that
with this novel he "lambasted the suburbs," Yates's reply is interesting in its
denial: "I didn't mean to. The book was widely read as an anti-suburban novel,
and that disappointed me. The Wheelers may have thought the suburbs were
to blame for all their problems, but I meant it to be implicit in the text that
that was *their* delusion, *their* problem, not mine."[21] While the suburbs in a

Yatesian tale neatly reflect and echo the vacuity of the relationships he so deftly describes, it would be wrong, Yates suggests, to see the paucity of the environments as some kind of excuse for the characters' behavior. Many readers appear to find this hard to believe of *Revolutionary Road*. Yates may have thought he was not blaming the suburbs for the tragedy that unfolds, but it has to be noted that he is not entirely successful if he meant to exonerate them. The personal struggles of all the central characters—April's, Frank's, Mr. and Mrs. Givings's, the Campbells', and John's—all seem nurtured by the environment they inhabit. The "anesthetized buffer zones" that Ford refers to impress their depleted energies on the reader with great force.

Like so many of his characters, Yates was dismissive of the constructed, tidy, and, by implication, stifling atmosphere of the suburban town, even if he was loath to admit it. In *Young Hearts Crying*, Davenport is relieved that it is dark when he shows his guests around Larchmont: "all its glaring, oppressive tidiness was softened and made gentle in the dark."[22] He wants to be taken seriously and does not enjoy Bill Brock's mockery when he scoffs, "You're like a couple of young marrieds in the movies—or in *Good Housekeeping*!"[23] Beyond the sense of Davenport's class-conscious shame, Yates makes one of many sardonic comments about the status symbols of the time. It is the accumulation of such sideswipes at cinematic and magazine versions of reality in Yates's fiction that afford the reader a sense of their prevailing and damaging influence.

In the manner of Anton Chekhov or Gustave Flaubert, Yates uses the setting, and the suburban landscape in particular, as an indicator of his characters' emotional or psychological state; the environment is very much part of a Yatesian story. As with Michael Davenport's daily journey in the later novel, Frank Wheeler's commute is described in terms that mean his boredom and lack of individuality are mirrored in the depiction of the other commuters who are diminished in Kafkaesque terms by Wheeler's and Yates's gaze: "How small and neat and comically serious the other men looked, with their gray-flecked crew cuts and their button-down collars and their brisk little hurrying feet! There were endless desperate swarms of them, hurrying through the station and the streets, and an hour from now they would all be still. The waiting mid-town office buildings would swallow them up and contain them, so that to stand in one tower looking out across the canyon to another would be to inspect a great silent insectarium displaying hundreds of tiny pink men in white shirts, forever shifting papers and frowning into telephones, acting out their passionate little dumb show under the supreme indifference of the rolling spring clouds."[24] While Wheeler distances himself from the other commuters, observing their comic seriousness, the reader is left in no doubt that he is very much part of the suburban pack.

As Yates writes in *Revolutionary Road*, these suburban places were not built to "accommodate a tragedy," and tragedy, as all of Yates's work emphasizes, is inexorably part of life: "The Revolutionary Hill Estates had not been designed to accommodate a tragedy. Even at night, as if on purpose, the development held no looming shadows and no gaunt silhouettes. It was invincibly cheerful, a toyland of white and pastel houses whose bright, uncurtained windows winked blandly through a dappling of green and yellow leaves. Proud floodlights were trained on some of the lawns, on some of the neat front doors and on the hips of some of the berthed, ice-cream colored automobiles."[25] The symbols of suburban affluence are vividly presented by Yates's floodlights, "neat front doors" and "ice-cream colored automobiles"; the very name "The Revolutionary Hill Estates" is as constructed as the "toyland" it represents. But beyond the serious nature of his exposition, Yates's specificity is humorous: his floodlights are "proud" and the lights are angled to catch the gleaming "hips" of the cars. His satirical portrait of these new "invincibly cheerful" arcadias, for that is what he creates, may have been too much to bear for Yates's contemporary readers.

April Wheeler's empty, lonely life and her tragic end add further weight to the impression that *Revolutionary Road* is an attack on suburbia. However, Yates is subtle in his approach. Rather than directly criticizing this new landscape, Yates weaves elliptical observations into his descriptions of characters and landscape, both exterior and interior. At the very beginning of this novel, Yates sets up a metaphorical description of suburban charmlessness and conformity as he describes the Laurel Players leaving their play rehearsal: "The Players . . . would see a landscape in which only a few very old, weathered houses seemed to belong; it made their own homes look as weightless and impermanent, as foolishly misplaced as a great many bright new toys that had been left outdoors overnight and rained on."[26] The few "weathered" houses that are left appear threatened by the "impermanent" new buildings springing up around them. Just as he gently criticizes suburban behavior dependent on cinematic mannerisms and movie sentiments in the rehearsal itself, Yates subtly criticizes this new suburban environment.

As suggested, Yates is not entirely successful in exonerating suburbia since his criticisms of the suburban dream stand out. In *Revolutionary Road* he places emphasis he did not intend on the suburban setting; it is given concentrated focus and is used as the natural landscape for his depleted individuals. However, while this novel is undeniably his greatest work, it is too often seen in isolation. In his other works, Yates is equally aware of the hardships of city life; we see this in *The Easter Parade*, for example: "In 1940 they moved back to the city, and the place Pookie found for them was no ordinary apartment: it was a once-grand, shabby old 'floor through' on the south side of Washington Square with big windows facing the park. . . . The kitchen and bathroom fixtures were rusty antiques. . . . It was on the ground floor, which meant that passengers on the double-decked Fifth Avenue buses could peer into it."[27] An exposé of city life for individuals with little money and few connections is no less evident in his other novels and short stories. In *Disturbing the Peace*, for instance, John Wilder and Pamela Hendricks rent an apartment that seems "as impersonal and transient as a motel suite,"[28] and lest we think that this is simply the result of their straitened circumstances, the whole city is damned in the following description: "Beverly Hills looked suitably rich, but the houses . . . were too close together. The Hollywood Hills were prettier and some of them commanded nice views, but the canyons led too quickly into the enormous suburban waste of the San Fernando Valley."[29] The great city of Los Angeles, home to Hollywood and the place where dreams come true, immediately looks very disappointing.

While Yates finds little to recommend community living in 1950s America, whether it is suburban or metropolitan, Sloan Wilson depicts the growth of suburbia as a necessary development toward greater economic prosperity and egalitarian opportunity for those who have been unable to afford homes and land within the commuter belt around New York. His novel *The Man in the Gray Flannel Suit*, set in 1953, published in 1955, and made into a film in 1956, provides a far more palatable, populist view of American life, and American family life, than anything Yates ever wrote. Even though the territory Wilson and Yates cover is similar—both novelists deal with middle-class, postwar marriages in which individuals struggle to find meaning and purpose in suburban Connecticut—their standpoint is radically different. Yates examines these aspects of life with a satirical eye, whereas Wilson's work is shaped by optimism, a sense of Christian redemption, and deeply felt conservative values. Wilson's work serves as a possible example of the kind of "mature" literature that Norman Podhoretz refers to as he bemoans the sanitized lives he read about in the 1950s: "It is a literature of an unearned maturity, a maturity almost wholly divorced from experience, an expression, really, of the fear of experience—a maturity that has become a means of protecting one's neat little existence from the disruptive incursions of experience."[30] Whichever novelists Podhoretz has in mind, Yates's fiction provides a clear refutation of this claim.

In *The Man in the Gray Flannel Suit*, the growth of suburbia is debated as the proposal to build a new school in South Bay, Connecticut, excites passions that run high on both sides: with a new school will come new housing. The reader is left in no doubt where moderation and reasonable argument lie as Mr. Parkington speaks with the nervous, paranoid tones of someone who will reject change at any cost, however reasonable: "This new school will send taxes up. That will drive the owners of big estates out. If the big estates are broken up, housing projects will come in. Housing projects bring more children than they do money."[31] Short, punchy sentences indicate how he envisions a total collapse of the old, established way of life. Every full stop attempts to negate any argument against such seamless logic. However, Tom and Betsy Rath, who admit to having a financial interest in the town's housing development, will not be silenced by his arguments.

Tom Rath's contention is that change cannot be held back, an argument designed to appeal to a nation already in the midst of enormous economic development: "I was born in South Bay too, and I like the town the way it is. As a matter of fact, I liked even better the way it used to be, didn't you? It was prettier before the houses went up on the golf course. What I'm trying to say is, the town *is* changing, and we can't take a vote to stop change. If the Zoning Board lets me start a housing project, I'll do everything possible to keep it from being unsightly, or a financial drain on the town, but I don't promise to keep my grandmother's house and land unchanged. That's impossible."[32] Wilson gives Rath the voice of reason, a voice committed to ideas of change and improvement and to the morally acceptable idea of development for the sake of future generations. In addition, as Tom Rath's affair with an Italian woman is revealed, Wilson makes honesty and forgiveness the crucial element of any viable future for this family. There is at the core of this populist novel a romantic and deeply Christian notion about how relationships develop and survive; indeed, the novel's success at the time of its publication was dependent on this.

Yates's perspective on suburban conformity is very different. Observing and itemizing his characters' tendency to romanticize the details of their ordinary lives, Yates repeatedly suggests that this tendency is as dangerous as lying. This was not incidental but utterly deliberate and deeply felt; he wanted to undercut what he saw as "a general lust for conformity"[33] in postwar America. Therefore, with *Revolutionary Road*, Yates produced what he hoped was "an indictment of American life in the nineteen-fifties."[34] He wanted to look at areas of suburban life that were often neglected or glossed over, and he knew he had no panaceas to offer. Just as he was keen to reflect in his work his observations about new challenges to female social roles, but was not a feminist, so he was highly aware of the stratification of society without being a socialist.

As has always been the case, the artist critiques contemporary views of society and throws up questions that undercut comfortable, and comforting, notions of national excellence and superiority. Although not overtly political, Yates was not apolitical. His emphasis is first and foremost on the complexity of the human relationships that stand at the forefront of his fictions rather than on the political context from which his dramas spring. His work displays a sharp awareness of gender and racial politics, for instance, but, as with all his political commentary, it is fused with his broader narratives. Racial tension does not feature as strongly as one might suppose it would, bearing in mind that Yates's first three publications emerged at the time of the civil rights movement. However, occasionally, in works such as "A Really Good Jazz Piano," and *Disturbing the Peace*, Yates attempts to dramatize the kind of dangerous prejudice common among the white middle class.

Of all the black figures in his work, his characterization in *Disturbing the Peace* of Charlie, the kind, patient, black nurse in charge of the Men's Violence Ward at Bellevue stands out and appears to be a direct challenge to preconceptions about race. However, this challenge goes further than placing Charlie on the moral high ground. At the end of the novel, with Wilder hallucinating (so the reader is not entirely sure whether what follows actually happens), two other black nurses behave in radically different ways to the irreproachable figure of Charlie. Randolph and Henry, taunting and jeering at their vulnerable patient, help encourage the reader to broaden his perspective and deepen his understanding of racial prejudice and the tensions it excites. Henry satirizes comfortable Democratic views with sarcasm: "and you believe in Civil Rights . . . and you admire Dr. King and you thought it was Just Awful about Emmett Till, but that's not what I mean. . . . Deep down you wish we'd all go away. You think our lips are too thick and our noses are too flat and you shudder at the thought of our kinky hair."[35] However unpleasant these two characters are, Yates makes it clear that the energy behind their jibes and taunts is fueled by white prejudice: "Oh, you don't mind us too much when we speak Perfect English, like your old friend Charlie at Bellevue, isn't that right?"[36] Yates suggests that black people not only ridicule liberal whites who think they understand the nature of racial oppression, but also ridicule black people, like Charlie, who mimic the mannerisms of white people in order to succeed and be accepted. Yates depicts the problem but can offer no solution.

Yates was not a campaigner by nature, nor was he a southerner with personal experience of the horrors of segregation. Unlike his friend William Styron, for instance, whose narratives are frequently set in the South and have racial tension at their center, Yates had not been brought up with the daily awareness of the terrible, violent, and haunting divisions created by unequal laws and bigoted opinions. As a white, middle-class man from the East Coast, Yates's work concentrates instead on a degree of alienation and disorientation within the white, aspirational, suburbanized society. While not ignoring the issue of racial inequality, his primary aim is to be true to what he has experienced. Within the overtly privileged white society, he locates a pervasive sense of disaffection, a mistrust of other people (and people who are "other"), and an inability to cross the divide between different cultures.

Every aspect of Yates's life was an attempt to resist romanticism and to pursue the truth of experience as he knew it. Relationships, work, culture, aspirations, and homes are all scrutinized in this vein. While the families Yates portrays often conform superficially to the nuclear family unit of American ideals, he undercuts any such sentimentalized version of that portrayal by drawing attention, constantly, to the cracks not far below the surface. The Wheelers in *Revolutionary Road*, for instance, bear a striking resemblance to Joseph Kahl's ironic portrait of the American family: "It is promulgated through the newspapers and magazines and movies, which build up a picture of the way of life of the 'typical' or 'average' American that is supposed to be the gift of God and the constitution to all loyal citizens. This pattern, which we can label 'living well,' begins with a single-family house of some six or seven rooms on a small but neat plot of suburban land. In it live a mature but perpetually youthful couple with their two (recently, three) small children. They own their home and maintain it by hobby labor with garden tools and paint brushes."[37] Since the Wheelers attempt to live exactly like Kahl's portrait of domestic harmony, Yates, through the course of the novel, draws attention to the vast gap that exists between seeing this as an ideal and the grim and lonely reality of such a lifestyle. Yates's other fictional families don't even come close to this model of marital and familial togetherness. In all his writing he shows the impossibility of achieving such a romanticized and idealized vision of life, since for his struggling families such happiness is out of reach.

Defiantly unsentimental, Yates appears to offer no redemption for his characters' dilemmas and tragedies, and David Castronovo and Steven Goldleaf provide their own explanation for this: "The child of a broken home—and a lifelong observer of dislocations and disorders—he told stories about psychologically and socially stifled people living in an atmosphere of *official optimism*."[38] In other ways, too, Yates writes against the prevailing mood and conservatism of the time. In *The Easter Parade* Yates's awareness of contemporary gender politics is made evident in his portrayal of the central protagonist, Emily Grimes, and her sister, Sarah. However, his appreciation of the awareness of the role of women, and the issues that arise from his awareness, is not heavily underscored in the way it would be in an overtly feminist text. This arises partly from the fact that feminist politics were not part of mainstream thinking during Yates's early career as a writer and partly because Yates disliked any critical stance that smacked of being an "ism."

Throughout his life he maintained a fairly consistent position regarding women and work, suggesting that the women in his texts had an unequal struggle to cope with yet offering no solutions to the problems he identifies. To complicate the picture, Yates often portrays liberated women in ways that suggest their cold-heartedness, as we see in "A Natural Girl," for instance. This story begins with the following sentence: "In the spring of her sophomore year, when she was twenty, Susan Andrews told her father very calmly that she didn't love him anymore."[39] The tension this declaration of independence causes forms the emotional crux of the story. Yates intimates that the liberation of women comes at the expense of viable, mutually interdependent relationships with men.

Yates chose his own way to reflect life in 1950s and 1960s America. His perspective, with its contradictions as well as its observations, enriches our understanding of that time. There is now renewed interest in that time and, with the economic crisis apparent at the end of this century's first decade, there are curious echoes of the postwar era. Maria Russo, writing about Yates's reissued short stories in 2001, concurs with this view: "These stringent, ruthlessly straightforward (yet never, thank God, 'minimalist') stories are set mostly in the late '40s and '50s, yet they're perfect reading for right now, when we're just starting to reacquaint ourselves with economic downturn and widespread economic anxiety, when our political discourse is insipid and our mass culture seems more vacuous than ever."[40] The present fascination with the mid-twentieth century, the time in which the baby-boom generation emerged and, in the early twenty-first century, reached their middle age, is not restricted to literature. In Britain, the television series *The Hour*[41] had something of a cult following, and films such as *A Single Man*[42] and *An Education*[43] attest to a curiosity about the postwar era on both sides of the Atlantic. Furthermore, the enormous popularity of the American television series *Mad Men* is evidence of a growing attention to the world Yates wrote about time and time again.[44] It depicts Madison Avenue advertising executives chain-smoking their way through every bourbon-filled meeting, and male-dominated offices where women, in tight skirts and put-it-out-there bras,[45] take dictation and regular pats on the bottom. That Matthew Weiner, producer, writer, and occasional director of *Mad Men*, gave his actors a copy of *Revolutionary Road* to read before they started filming the first season is a story I cannot verify, but it has the feel of truth about it. If you want to know about the work/life balance in the early 1960s, who else would you read?

Conclusion

14. Yates speaking to students at Emerson College, Boston, in the early 1980s. The photo, which was taken by Karen Couture, was uncovered by DeWitt Henry and is reprinted courtesy of Emerson College.

It has now been a few years since the film *Revolutionary Road*[1] was released, and the attention it brought anew to Richard Yates's work has understandably waned. However, his fiction is no longer languishing in second-hand bookshops, unread or admired by only a distant few. The film brought so much attention to his fiction that there have been several reprints of all his published works in the last few years. Universities have finally placed Yates on their syllabuses and people across America and Europe no longer ask, "Richard who?" or "Is that Y-E-A-T-S?" However, and despite Blake Bailey's masterful biography, to date there has been no extended critical appraisal of his fiction. This book is an attempt in that direction. I have endeavored to let Yates's voice do the talking. Using a detailed analysis of many passages from a range of his novels and short stories, I have investigated his technique and some of the important issues his work brings to the fore.

Bleak? Yes. Yates's stories resonate with the sensibilities of a man who found much in the human condition that disturbed and alienated him. But Yates was also a deeply compassionate writer, attuned to the difficulties of life in the 1950s and 1960s for men and women. He creates characters who, although flawed and failing, are not condemned. As Richard Price expresses it in his introduction to the new Everyman edition of Yates's work, "Yates pities his characters but has no choice but to doom them."[2] With humor that often suggests that their weaknesses are also his, Yates exposes pretension and arrogance in the day-to-day interactions of husbands and wives, office workers, and neighborhood friends, and the one thing we can be sure about is that these relationships will always collapse. But Yates's writing is so understated that the reader scarcely realizes how, or even when, the collapse happened. As Price suggests, the tone of Yates's very particular voice is perfectly in tune with his characterizations: "In part, the beauty and the genius of his voice lies in how its gently inexorable tone so eerily mirrors the muffled helplessness of the characters themselves."[3]

It is apparent from the work of many social historians looking back at the late 1950s that there was an inconsistency between America's egalitarian ideals and the fact that social stratification was still very much part of postwar society. Exploring this inconsistency was Richard Yates's project; dispelling the growing myth of American exceptionalism was the wider task. There was disparity between what was *actually* happening and what people wanted to *say* was happening, as Vance Packard suggested: "The discrepancy arises partly as a result of a generalized desire on the part of United States adults—particularly businessmen—to support the American Dream. Also it arises from the widespread assumption that the recent general rise in available spending money in this country is making everybody equal. Class, in fact, has several faces and income is just one of them."[4] Political rhetoric that suggested that class distinctions had been all but eradicated was, historians indicate, blinkered and idealistic. In the immediate aftermath of the war, the United States of America was a newly ascendant nation. With its rapidly increasing industrial output, and with a workforce swelled by returning GIs, it was investing in its future. Postwar building projects and the growth of suburbia fed into a general desire to be upwardly mobile and to ignore the facts that social stratification was an uncomfortable corollary to this wealth-based mobility.

The growth of the advertising industry was part of the general thrust forward and socially upward: "The prize darlings of the advertisers, however, are the families who move about a great deal . . . people who move frequently undergo a tremendous 'upgrading urge.' With each move a family makes, it tries to get a better house and more of the 'extras.' . . . If they move into an area where quite a number of the neighbors have clothes driers, they feel they must have one, too, and quickly."[5] Describing an American middle class hungry for its share of the promised future, David Krasner puts the development of social mobility in the context of the war just won: "the late 1940s and 1950s enjoyed unprecedented prosperity. . . . Upward mobility was a fact of economic life, and returning soldiers demanded their share of the American Dream."[6]

Physically and socially, mobile middle-class Americans needed to underpin the power of their newfound status and were easy targets for the men of Madison Avenue. As James Howard Kunstler explains, "In America of the 1950s there was little interest in fixing up old things. America had just won a big war and its citizens felt entitled to new things."[7] It is precisely this kind of allegiance to material goods, and the status they bestowed, that Richard Yates wrote to expose. With every one of his works, he challenges the idea that the new, the material, and the overtly successful should be celebrated, either politically or socially. The growth of the advertising industry, with an emphasis on surfaces and "things," was linked to the entrenchment of social stratification, as Packard describes: "The vigorous merchandising of goods as status symbols by advertisers is playing a major role in intensifying status consciousness."[8]

Specializing in fiction that takes as its central thrust failed or failing relationships and misplaced dreams, Yates explores his characters' dependence on the acquisition of material goods and implicitly comments on their insistent tendency to romanticize the details of their lives. For the emphasis it places on the surface of things, this insistence, he makes clear, is tantamount to lying. Wini Breines, in her retrospective account of the era, takes note of this tendency in more emphatic terms: "In American society, the mass consumption of the goods that advertising sells teaches that style and exteriors, appearances, count for a good deal. . . . Owning the correct products, approximating the 'in' style, is the means through which people build identity, belong, and create status; they represent themselves through consumption. Surfaces determine one's fate. . . . Image is the most important element in social life."[9]

As more middle-class people moved to suburban, landscaped homes, the appraisal and envy of one's neighbors' material wealth and status was an inevitable outcome. This material competitiveness has to be seen as a negative force, Vance Packard suggests, as it fed everyone's insecurities: "When any of us moves into a new neighborhood—and 33,000,000 Americans now do this every year—we are quickly and critically appraised by our new neighbors and business acquaintances before being accepted or rejected for their group. We, in turn, are appraising them and in many cases attempt not to commit what some regard as the horrid error of getting in with the wrong crowd."[10] It is these insecurities that Yates dramatizes. Often glossing over the acquisition of large material goods, such as the smarter house or faster car, Yates focuses instead on the small details that give people's aspirations away: the flimsy negligee, the sharp suit, the garden sprinkler, cocktail shaker, or sofa that indicate to the world their self-improvement and social mobility. It is equally clear that those, such as Gloria Drake, Alice Prentice, or Pookie Grimes, who lack such material goods are socially impoverished.

As noted in the final chapter, this postwar era was a time when the seeds were sown for the black power movement that led to civil rights and racial integration in 1960s America. From this form of civil disobedience, the feminist revolution, the gay rights and antiwar movements were made possible. Changing attitudes about race and gender have been well documented, but retrospective studies of the era occasionally suggest a coherence that Yates's work strongly indicates was lacking. The 1950s and early 1960s was a time of confusion and uncertainty, and it is this gray area of adjustment that Yates explores and brings to life. There was a strong sense of dissatisfaction with established patterns of behavior but no clear idea—or too many competing ideas—as to what should replace them. In advance of the hippie generation by a number of years, for instance, individuals aware of a dystopian reality had little idea what form their utopia might take.

Without any coherent vision of what might be possible for men and women, Yates, nevertheless, suggests that the space women occupy is limited by men who diminish them. The problem for Yates, particularly in respect to gender politics, is that he was very much *of* his time. He does not always achieve enough distance from his own experience to give a balanced view of the situation he explores; illustrating how men repressed women is not the same as valuing or championing women. Yates does not vociferously defend any of the new rights of the 1960s, of women, of black people, or of homosexuals, even if largely sympathetic to these newly vocal groups. His fiction seeks to demonstrate in ways that may have diminished his readership that such changes were more complex than the liberal idealists of his time might care to acknowledge. His opinions are not supportive of the radical left; nor do they wholeheartedly lurch toward the conservative right. Brought up in an age of continued black suppression, of homophobia and entrenched sexism, it was not possible, his fiction suggests, for men and women to "flick a switch" and become instantly cleansed of the bigoted views of previous generations. While the people of his fiction are undoubtedly exposed for their outmoded and divisive way of thinking, the radical social change they are asked to embrace remains anathema to them, and to him.

Yates is determined to strip away the facade that the white, middle-class American used to hide behind. If this entails destroying some long-held belief in a dream of possibility and potential that is essentially meritocratic, then so be it. Yates is prepared to take that dream and study it under a microscope, however uncomfortable that might make his readers feel. Now, over twenty years since Yates's death, with a black president of the United States enjoying a second term in office and with gay marriage being widely debated if not routinely accepted, it is hard to register that it wasn't always thus. Much has changed in two decades, and has changed because many people, like Yates, wrote to expose the iniquities of a so-called free society. But Yates, avoiding the declamatory manner of many of the artists (the writers, painters, sculptors, and musicians) of the 1960s and 1970s, had his own unique, rather quiet, way of addressing the issues as he saw them. One aspect of his writing, as he dismembers the dream of a truly democratic society, is the way in which he always implicates himself; as a dreamer and as a bigot, he never lets himself off the hook.

Yates indicates how people of both genders take refuge in self-aggrandizing fantasies and demonstrates how the aspirations of his characters are not only indicative of a human tendency to mythologize and exaggerate but also represent something far more dangerous. It is the refusal to see things as they are that implicitly prevents them from ever living fulfilled lives. David Castronovo and Steven Goldleaf describe Yates as taking "the fiction writer's path": "his evaluation of American faults does not indict General Motors or local government, but instead provides clear examples of how individuals passively let commerce and the neighbors swallow up their lives."[11] They remind the reader that Yates is less interested in the politicization of his perceptions about Americans in the mid-twentieth century and more interested in the dramatization of those observations: "Yates's narrative voice pulls back from the declamatory style, leaving the speeches to his characters and to critics of the era."[12]

Although he wrote at a time of profound social change, Yates negotiates the complexity of those changes only in ways that accord with the human dramas he explores. He does not scrutinize the class system, but he demonstrates social snobbery and material competitiveness at work. He does not use his fiction to campaign for women's rights, but he constantly challenges the idea that all was running smoothly between the sexes in the workplace and within the American home. In addition, Yates's writing demonstrates the existence of negative attitudes to other races and homosexuals without at any time proselytizing for change. His purpose was not to campaign but to illustrate, not to fabricate but to depict, and within all his fiction he never lets his mind wander from the uncomfortable facts of life as he led it and life as he witnessed it.

As Yates's work emerged slowly through the 1960s and 1970s, critics took issue with his very autobiographical fiction. The often-repeated tropes and recurring characters were undoubtedly a barrier to the promotion of his work and an irritation to some of his readers. His use of his life in his work adds to the peculiar kind of vulnerability this writer must have felt when his work was scrutinized on publication and so often rejected. Castronovo and Goldleaf see the strengths and weaknesses in the autobiographical streak in his work: "Driven by the desire to expose types and states of mind rather than former acquaintances, Yates . . . is often quite literal in his use of details from life; yet his tendency to go over the ground of his parents' divorce and his unhappy childhood is more obsessional than denunciatory: he tells exemplary facts of his time rather than intimate secrets. . . . Yates is interested in arranging patterns of dishonesty in his time."[13] It is this idea of "arranging patterns of dishonesty," as he searches for authenticity in his characters, and one suspects, therefore, his life, that I find particularly interesting in Yates's work. Theo Tait, like Castronovo and Goldleaf, suggests in his review of *The Collected Stories* that there are benefits and weaknesses in this use of biography: "This autobiographical strain accounts both for the visceral immediacy of Yates's writing, and for some of its limitations. . . . But when Yates's stories are encountered en masse . . . the uniformity of experience begins to chafe, and his limited repertoire of stylistic gestures becomes apparent."[14] It is undeniable that the repetition of characters and their behavior can "chafe," but it is equally true that repetition provokes deeper engagement with the author's vision of life in the mid-twentieth century—the cultural lie of optimism he seeks to expose—and with his own life and difficulties.

While the success of *Revolutionary Road*, and its status as Yates's finest work, suggests he achieves what he set out to achieve in terms of a fictional prism, some of his subsequent work resists that prism and nakedly remains a form of autobiography—I am thinking particularly here of *A Special Providence* and *Disturbing the Peace*. It is somewhat ironic therefore that Yates's criticism of Thomas Wolfe initially sounds so uncompromising: "He never achieved any detachment, any distance on himself."[15] These might well have been the terms of his own perceived failings as a writer. Ever alert to his faults, however, Yates modifies his view of autobiographical fiction: "It's just that I think it's a very, very tricky thing to undertake, that's all, and you have to be one hell of an artist to bring it off. To *form* it."[16] The last story he wrote for *Eleven Kinds of Loneliness*, "Builders," is, in a sense, proof to him that he could "bring it off." Many writers claim that Yates's elegant prose and sparse dialogue inspired them (writers such as Richard Ford and Richard Russo, to name but two), but his work has been equally influential on the fictional use of autobiography, as is evident in the work of contemporary writers such as Alice Munro and Nick Hornby.

Autobiographically based or not, and aware too that Yates was usually hardest on himself, it would be wrong to dismiss Yates's fictions as being only ever focused on himself. In this respect I cannot agree with Martin Napar-steck's comments that "He was, as a writer, not an observer of other people. He always looked inward."[17] In my view, Yates was an extraordinary observer of other people, of their peculiar habits, small tics, and idiosyncratic manner-isms, their aspirations, performative behavior, and dialogue. It might well be the case that Yates related everything he saw back to his own experiences, to filter them and make sense of them, and that he saw his own weaknesses in those of other people. However, it would be entirely wrong and a profound misreading of his work not to notice the acuteness of his observing eye and the way he acts as a witness. Moreover, his extraordinary facility in captur-ing the richness and inflections, as well as the limits and hiding places, of human dialogue should not be overlooked. Without an ability to look be-yond himself and his own preoccupations his work would have very little resonance for any reader. For the most part, he is masterful in this as he quietly buries his own voice in his mimetic narratives. However, troubled, contradictory, and probably revealing more than he meant to in relation to his feelings about sexuality, and women's sexuality in particular, Yates, as we have seen, was not always successful in his ambitions; like all artists he had his Achilles' heel. Less evident in his first two published volumes, the barely concealed aggression toward women exploring their sexuality in works such as *The Easter Parade* and *Disturbing the Peace* alerts us to an element of his way of thinking that he never resolved and, to my knowledge, about which he was never questioned. Nevertheless, these are only elements among an impressive whole.

In the literature of the 1950s and 1960s, traditional, realist fiction was unpopular and seen as outdated: new, unconventional forms of writing were celebrated and widely discussed. Yates, therefore—and of course, he was not

the only one to do this—maintained and transformed the mimetic traditions of the nineteenth-century novel at a time when art as imitation was
generally discredited. He firmly maintained his belief in the novel's potential to reflect and illuminate. His apparent inclination to look backward may,
however, have cost Yates a contemporary readership. Blinded by his inclination to employ the form of the late nineteenth- and early twentieth-century
novel, the readers of his time overlooked the very modern ways in which he
extended that form. Ronald Sukenick, arguing against the "comforting illusions"[18] of social realist fiction makes the following point: "Form is itself a
metaphor and that of fiction is perhaps the most inclusive for our society.
The form of the traditional novel is a metaphor for a society that no longer
exists. Mario Praz has described the detective story as a bourgeois fairy tale,
but one could apply the description as well to the novel of social realism. Its
present function is to sustain a series of comforting illusions."[19]

Ronald Sukenick expressed this view in 1974 but I suggest, in opposition
to his opinion, that Yates demonstrates time and again that the realist novel
had, and always will have, a role to play in commenting on contemporary reality, on social structures, on the role of the writer, and on the ever-changing
face of marriage and relationship. Furthermore, there are no "comforting illusions" in his work. With his ambiguous, even unresolved, endings, his narrative shaped and driven by dialogue with only a sparing use of the omniscient
narrator, and with his use of autobiographical detail, it could be argued that
he helped to modernize the realist novel and, to an extent, helped to narrow
the gap between the metafictionalists and the traditionalists. By implication,
Yates asks the reader to consider that the novelist of social realism can avoid
the kind of reassurances Sukenick describes. He suggests it is possible to use
its form to disrupt in ways with which Sukenick (who argued that "there is
an absolute and necessary conflict between art and the status quo"[20]) would
have agreed. However, Sukenick makes the assumption that all novels of social realism are essentialist, pursuing the same monolithic path. Surely it can
be argued that the enduring popularity of the "realistic" novel is *because* it
has changed, developed, and thrown away many, if not all, of the "comforting illusions" of the nineteenth-century version of itself?

Patently, all novels of social realism are *not* the same any more than novels
described as postmodern mirror each other in style, form, or purpose. John
Updike, Ernest Hemingway, Gustave Flaubert, Henry James, Philip Roth,
Edith Wharton, and thousands of others might all be described as writers
of realist fiction, but the methods they use are distinct in every case. Yates
does not depart from established literary norms as much as the experimentalists of his time, but he acknowledges the insubstantiality of fact, the par-

tial nature of any perspective, and the provisional nature of artistic endeavor within his version of the realist novel. Richard Ford emphasizes that *Revolutionary Road* defies any easy taxonomy: "Realism, naturalism, social satire—the standard critical bracketry—all go begging before this splendid book. *Revolutionary Road* is simply *Revolutionary Road* and to invoke it enacts a sort of cultural-literary secret handshake among its devotees."[21] Like Ford, I am cautious about using the word *realist*, bearing in mind that all "ism's," "ist's" and literary classifications were abhorrent to Yates. Thus, throughout I have used the terms hesitatingly, sparingly, and knowing that they are only useful in a very specific series of contexts.

Contrary to what critics of social realism suggest is possible, therefore, Yates finds elasticity in the realist form that gives his work enduring resonance. In many novels he incorporates a critique of this literary form, weighing up its strengths and weaknesses, and, as we have seen in *The Easter Parade*, pitting it against more fluid, "audacious" forms.[22] When it is suggested that a novel such as Steinbeck's *The Grapes of Wrath* confronts the reality of poverty, one of the boys in *A Good School* expostulates that even this is a neatly packaged form of realism: "That's an evasion of reality too, don't you see? When everything's tied up in a neat little dramatic package, you can forget it the minute you walk out of the theater."[23] For Yates, the avoidance of sentimentality is a prerequisite for good fiction, whatever the form, and 'neat little dramatic package[s]' are always to be avoided. Yates, like the naturalists, portrays Americans struggling to stay alive in a society that seems indifferent to them, but his characters' efforts seem far more unrelenting and more domestically focused. Although the pessimistic tone that characterizes naturalists' work is a notable feature of Yates's fiction, their work occupies a different kind of landscape and a different kind of emotional territory. Normally associated with a bleak and rather violent outlook, their fiction has within it a suggestion of hope, a romantic tendency, which Yates rarely shows. The moral ambiguity of his work makes it far harder to lay the blame for the collapse of marriages, jobs, and families at the feet of some political or social agent.

Yates's reliance on the exactitude of language was directly born out of his passion for the masters of realistic fiction, especially Flaubert, Fitzgerald, and Hemingway. But few of the notable authors of the mid-twentieth century onward shared the belief in the certainty of language as a means to recreate or transpose reality onto the page. That Yates's characters use language in ways to enhance their performances—and in that sense, corrupt the truth available to them through language—is what he seeks to expose through his writing. Furthermore, his choice of words for his characters goes hand-in-hand with an equally specific choice of gesture; truth is uncovered as mannerisms strengthen or undercut what is said. For the postmodernists, it was the surface of things that shaped their creative work with little or no sense that there was anything beneath the surface to uncover. As Alain Robbe-Grillet expresses it: "While essentialist conceptions of man were facing their doom, and the idea of 'condition' henceforth replacing that of 'nature,' the *surface* of things has stopped being the mask of the heart for us, a sentiment which served as a prelude to all the 'beyonds' of metaphysics."[24] Robbe-Grillet suggests that there are no depths to uncover and no masks to remove; surface is all.

Yates investigated the superficialities of human interaction and vividly brought to life performative behavior at every level of society. One can see that he remained at a great distance from sharing views such as Robbe-Grillet's even though these were ideas that informed, or described, the work of so many novelists of the twentieth century. Just as he critiqued social realism within his work, Yates never missed an opportunity to disparage the postmodernists whose work irritated him so deeply. While novelists such as John Barth, Donald Barthelme, and Vladimir Nabokov played with notions of performance, masks, and role-playing in ways that emphasized the insubstantialities and uncertainties of character, of communication and of relationship, Yates's work was firmly rooted in the notion that there was a truth to be uncovered and that, with exactitude of language, he could reach that truth and unmask artificiality. Equally, this adherence to truth distanced him from the work of the New Journalists who blurred the edges between reportage and fiction and who relished the opportunities this gave them.

Yates had chosen to write in a way that avoided slick passages of extraneous detail, flights of fancy, and fantastical or philosophical passages that deviated from the task at hand. The task, as he saw it, was to transcribe onto the page what he had observed about the complexity of human relationships and the experience of being an American man living in a postwar society where so much was promised and, in his view, so little achieved. In many ways, he was writing against a very particular critical view of American literature of the 1950s, such as that expressed by Norman Podhoretz in 1957. Podhoretz felt that postwar literature was mature but did not reflect the texture and grime of experience: "The world is seen at a distant remove, commented on quietly and wisely, never struggled with or confronted full in the face."[25] Podhoretz becomes more graphic as he reinforces this point: "It is a literature written by Olympians who got to the top of the mountain not by inching their way up the slippery faces of rocks and arriving bruised and torn and bloody, but who were safely deposited there by helicopter and who know nothing about mountains except that the air on the peaks is rarefied."[26]

Yates's work acts as a direct refutation to this charge since he is able to produce character after weary character, struggling, torn, and bloodied, and very
much stuck on the side of that metaphorical mountain.

By rigorously presenting such an antiromantic domestic landscape with
few redeeming features to lighten the tone, Yates may have added to the reasons that he had a limited readership. The critic and novelist Carolyn See,
who reviewed two of Yates's books, summed up the negative response his
work often provoked: "He's not going to get the recognition he truly deserves
because to read Yates is as painful as getting all your teeth filled down to the
gum with no anesthetic."[27] If an anesthetic is what you need, avoid Yates. Despite his obvious talent as a short story writer, Yates's work held only a limited appeal for contemporary magazines. Evidently the *New Yorker* felt his
stories were too cryptic, the morals unclear, the subject matters too bleak,
the political positions too weakly stated, and the endings unresolved and
ambiguous; his were realistic stories that did not obey the conventions of
realism. Quoting Roger Angell's rejection note with evident dismay, Blake
Bailey summarizes the position of the *New Yorker*: "Though Yates was skillful, readable, confident, accomplished and whatever else, his vision of life
was *repulsive*. Thus spake *The New Yorker*."[28]

Writers have always described failure, and Yates's contemporaries were
no exception to this, but Yates relishes and savors that failure. His narrative
focus is not on whether his characters could succeed but is always on the
terms of their disappointment, which is measured out in every aspect of their
lives. If readers of the time found Yates's work too bleak and too critical of
a society that was looking forward with optimism, they missed the fact that
Yates was almost always hardest on himself.[29] While he looks in depth at societal deceptions and the affectations of those who will, insistently, believe in
the falsehoods of egoism, his writer/characters always come off worst. These
are the multiple self-portraits of a man who wouldn't look away from his
own weaknesses and appeared to find something almost seductive in what
Elizabeth Venant, in an article about him, calls his "sense of the sad."[30] Again,
this tendency may have alienated his early readers. Yates's daughter Sharon
has her own theory about why the novels sold so poorly during her father's
lifetime: "The hardness of my father's books has to do with the fact that there
aren't people who are transformed in them. . . . That's a very un-American
idea, that you're not transformed through your suffering. You don't arise and
overcome and change. People can't re-make themselves; they are what they
are and their problems and their sufferings and their lives grow from that,
really."[31] And asked in the same interview what her father might have made
of his newly found acclaim, Sharon is unsure: "Good news as much as bad

news could get him all worked up and cause him to fall apart. He'd drink too much, he'd forget to take his medication and the next thing you'd know he'd be in an altercation with a policeman in the street."[32]

Notwithstanding the limited success Yates enjoyed in his lifetime, therefore, there were, and are, many who mourn the lack of attention his work has received. Dan DeLuca, writing in 2001, reflects on Yates's literary status in a newspaper article: "The word on Richard Yates is that he's a late, great giant who was grossly under appreciated in his lifetime and shamefully forgotten since his death in 1992. A writer's writer who came of age during World War II, Yates is a chronological link between F. Scott Fitzgerald and Raymond Carver in the all-too-realistic literature of collapsing American dreams."[33] It is the tone of reflection and regret that one notes in this extract from DeLuca's article, and similar observations were made by other reviewers of Yates's republished work at the turn of this century. A comparable lament comes from Salman Rushdie (a new reader of Yates's work in 2008), who underlines the impact Yates's work had on him in an interview: "I've just finished his book *Revolutionary Road* and I'm now reading *Easter Parade*, and I'm feeling kind of foolish not to have read this wonderful writer before. . . . Nobody writes about bad marriages better than this guy."[34]

Richard Ford, in his introduction to the latest edition of *Revolutionary Road*, suggests the importance of this novel in unequivocal terms: "If we finally see the Wheelers and their social set as strange remote 'fifties types' with their smoky Paris reveries, their gooey business pontifications, their no-fuss sexual dalliances, their memories of youth and a just war fast receding, we should still, I would plead, let this novel have its way with us. . . . *Revolutionary Road* looks straight at us with a knowing and admonitory eye, and invites us to pay attention, have a care, take heed, and live life as if it mattered what we do, inasmuch as to do less risks it all."[35] Yates, as I have demonstrated, does look us in the eye at the same time as he observes a wider malaise at the heart of American society. Lee Siegel's 2001 review of *Revolutionary Road* expresses the singular force of Yates's work and reemphasizes for us the influence he had as a writer on those who came after him: "And he is an acknowledged influence on the style and sensibility of an entire line of writers—from Raymond Carver through Ann Beattie, Andre Dubus, Tobias Wolff, Richard Russo, Richard Ford, and Jayne Anne Phillips—who consider themselves to have been fathered by Hemingway and, as it were, brought up by Yates. These writers have long and eloquently regretted the latter's lapsed reputation."[36]

The strength of the voices of those writers who, Siegel suggests, were "brought up by Yates," and who are now regarded very highly by American publishers, editors, and reviewers, must in part account for the current resurgence of interest in his work. As noted, Sam Mendes's film has also created a sudden wide appreciation of *Revolutionary Road*.[37] More generally, there is now a renewed interest in the 1950s and 1960s as the current generation of editors, writers, publishers, and readers looks back at the time from which they came. As the huge success of the TV series *Mad Men* demonstrates, this resurgence of interest in the era is not confined to the page.[38] For Americans particularly, though not exclusively, Yates's work has a part to play in an understanding of that era: "Yates is not only a fine writer, but his fiction represents an important aspect of the American experience: the confusion of the postwar boom. No one portrays the Age of Anxiety as well or as deeply as Yates, or the logical fallout of American individualism, the impossibly high hopes of the '40s and '50s curdling, turning bitter. And like his idols Hemingway and Fitzgerald—especially Fitzgerald—Yates lived a life that provides a mirror for the work, an easy handle for a public that likes personalities more than books."[39] However, although much is made of Yates as a writer both of and about the 1950s and 1960s, and rightly so, his voice, and the observations it carries—what it leaves out, as well as what is included—is timeless.

These details notwithstanding, it is hard to pinpoint Yates's exact views in his fiction, for he splits his perspective over many characters. By his own admission, he is Emily Grimes in *The Easter Parade*, as well as, at times, Andrew Crawford. In *Young Hearts Crying*, his voice emerges in the characterizations of both Michael and Lucy Davenport. And in *Revolutionary Road*, April Wheeler seems to think as Yates in her passionate search for truth and her desire to pull her family out of the "toyland" of their lives. April is his interior self, struggling, and scrabbling to do something more than buy into the false hopes offered by their suburban living. Frank, on the other hand, is also Yates, as his exterior self, a young determined man, arguing against the impracticalities of his wife's dreams; he is Yates working at Remington Rand, commuting into the city from suburbia. He is Yates's father the corporate man, supporting two young children and finding his wife incomprehensible in her desire for both a bohemian kind of Left-Bank dream and a world where women have strength enough, and power enough, to support their family. Yates is also John Givings the psychotic purveyor of unpalatable truths, and he is the small boy, Michael, dependent on his sister's care, constantly bewildered by the adult world and witness to the terrible arguments that determine the terms of his parents' separation. On all its different levels, this is autobiography and the split self. Tony Tanner draws attention to what he refers to as "The problematical and ambiguous relationship of the self to patterns of all kinds—social, psychological, linguistic—[that] is an obsession among recent American writers."[40] Although the modernist preoccupation with new forms of writing reflected this "obsession," in Tanner's words, an attempt "to find a *stylistic* freedom which is not simply a meaningless incoherence,"[41] Yates, and many others, took a different course. Yates concentrated instead on examining the insecurity and instability of the age not through linguistic and lexical innovations but through incisive and unsparing characterization and dialogue within a traditional form.

The question as to why Yates's work was, if not unread, largely unrecognized and unacknowledged in his lifetime, remains answered in only a provisional way. While novelists have long dealt with central figures who earn their own downfall, Yates's protagonists never have any hope of *not* doing that. The reader always knows that they will fail. In addition to this, and in ways that make this writer stand out, Yates never enables the reader to like his central figures. They are always diminished people who, objectively speaking, the reader would prefer to dismiss, but Yates's skill is in not allowing the reader to do that. Yates's readership remains absorbed by writing that is precise, with tales that are fluently told, so that it is impossible to look away. The uncomfortable truth is that while his characters may be unlikeable, the reader always identifies with them, not despite, but because of, their failings.

Eccentric to a degree, almost always poor, often alone, and devoted to the art of writing, Yates was not an easy man to deal with as his wives, daughters, girlfriends, publishers, agents, and friends made clear to Blake Bailey. He had a mission to write and allowed nothing to get in his way. In an article in *The Observer*, Nick Fraser describes the dark comedy of Richard Yates's final years: "In his last, illness-wracked years, Yates required a portable oxygen tank. He drove an old car around the university campus streets of Tuscaloosa, Alabama, puffing cigarettes and inhaling oxygen, to the horror of passengers."[42] This was his performance; until he died he was constantly perfecting that role, the disgruntled writer/smoker/drinker to the end. His life had been devoted to writing that disturbed the easy affirmations of life in general and of the postwar era in particular. It was his fate that the era didn't claim him and celebrate him.

Afterword

Monica Yates

I've never doubted my father's work. My first real reading of *Revolutionary Road* came when I was twenty. It took my breath away. As Kurt Vonnegut Jr. put it years later, eulogizing Richard Yates and addressing his entire life's output, "I did not find even one paragraph which, if it were read to you today, would not wow you with its power, intelligence, and clarity." Those remarkable paragraphs formed scenes, chapters, themes, observations—a perfect novel—that wowed me even more. I was lucky enough to turn right from that reading into a long close friendship with my father.

At the time of his death he was living in Alabama in a one-bedroom bungalow on a cul-de-sac of ten more identical ones. "Talk about the end of the line," he said of that lane in Tuscaloosa. "These little shitboxes ought to be named 'No Hope.' 'Washed Up.' 'Tough Luck.'" He grunted in the disgusted way that made me laugh. "Gonna die in Dixie."

When I visited him he was wheeling himself over the gray linoleum in a desk chair, followed by a tumbleweed of snarled oxygen tubing nearly as big as he was, now so stooped and curled inward by the struggle to breathe or gain purchase over one of his coughs. "I keep turning up the damn tanks but I don't seem to be getting any," he told me. We sat talking as I worked through the tangles in the tubing. "That can't make much of a difference," he kept saying. "I don't think that's the problem."

But it was. When the tubing was all stretched out the gauge leaped to 10. Dad hooked on his cannula and took a puff—what constituted a deep breath for him by then. "That's almost too much. Wow."

Although it was an improvement I knew he would lapse when I left. He would not be careful of his oxygen supply. He would forget that it mattered.

Anyway, the story goes that one night when he was living in that bungalow, he "got smashed" (as his daughter who so loved him sober, I wish this hadn't had to be a part of it). He sat on the side of the saggy daybed with its inadequate sheets and blankets, the paperback edition of *Revolutionary Road* with its much-hated cover in his hand, and read the magnificent first chapter aloud to himself, his resonant baritone growl now a broken instrument whose tone kept failing and dropping to a whisper. In a phone call, he told his friend Bob Lacy that he was "crying like a baby . . . Tears running down my cheeks." As Blake Bailey put it: "if he felt sorry for himself at all it was [only because] he'd never write again—but such a mood was touched with a kind of exaltation when he considered the transcendence of his life's work."

Once when I was bemoaning the state of "my life," Dad said, "For God's sake. 'My life,' 'my life.' That's magazine talk. Who cares about your life?" He knew it didn't matter. His scrimpy sixty-six years on this earth versus Philip Roth's wealth and adulation, going strong into his eighties. Both dead in the end. He didn't know how to get comfortable in life, so what?

He knew for certain *Revolutionary Road* was a better book than most, and one of the ones that would live. Future artists would feel accompanied by him as he had felt accompanied by Flaubert, Fitzgerald, Chekhov. Future generations of ordinary people would feel accompanied as well. Scholars were going to study him.

Hard as it is for those of us in comfortable lives to grasp, it was much, much more than enough. Who cares about your life?

I like to think it was Sam Mendes's adaptation he saw scrolling in his mind's eye as he read his own words aloud that night; the music, the colors, the careful script, the pitch perfect performances . . . someday there would be the right director, the right cast, and it would be exactly as he dreamed.

I hope he knew all kinds of lovely, consoling things: that there'd be generations of readers like my friend Ginny: "when deeply unhappy, I've always read your father, who articulates situations equally dismal, but with wit and symmetry—bleak, bleak, bleak, but perfect and funny. Works like a charm." There'd be young men like the agent Richard Morris at Janklow & Nesbitt Associates, a product of DeWitt Henry's program at Emerson College, who told me he (and "plenty of others like me") considered Dad his "literary father." That there'd be a Kristoffer Tabori (the actor whose readings of *The Easter Parade* and *A Good School* for Audible are an example of the kind of artist-to-artist conversation his work will provoke for as long as literature lives).

There'd be James Woods at the *New Yorker*, delivering an analysis of *Revolutionary Road* that would have had him shouting yes! yes! at every precisely considered point, as Dad finally got his due from the goddamned *New Yorker* magazine. There'd be a twenty-one-year-old who'd set up a website in his honor, and a Facebook page. There'd be bloggers arguing about which book was the best. There'd be an Andrew Wylie to take over the agent's reins from the loyal yet "sleepy" Ned Leavitt and oversee the publication of all his books in forty countries. He'd find a fan base in Russia. *Eleven Kinds of Loneliness* would become something of a best seller in China. Maybe, just maybe, he *knew*.

It was John Wilder crying "there's greatness in me!" and experiencing glory in the Vermont countryside, but it wasn't John Wilder, and it wasn't Yates himself in manic psychosis. It was real. This time there would be no awakening in a urine-smelling cell; there would be death, though, and he was "so tired" he was ready for that.

Shortly after the daybed epiphany Dad got a will, because—"The books aren't worth two cents now, but there may be something for you girls later on." The resulting document is a basic boilerplate about possessions he never had, but the Alabama lawyer added paragraphs assigning the rights to the works to his three "girls," with me as the executor. The idea that he was leaving us something almost cheered him.

He didn't talk to me about the kind of decisions I might need to make. For years after his death there wasn't much to it beyond throwing the occasional $27.50 royalty check in the kitchen drawer, being happy for the Boston-based uptick in interest spearheaded by Stewart O'Nan. One night Blake Bailey called. He was just a guy, albeit an uncanny listener, who hadn't done anything yet. We talked for a while. I told him, "I don't think there's much of a story there, but go ahead." His "Are you kidding? I can't wait to get to the typewriter!" led to the miraculous biography *A Tragic Honesty*.

Kate Charlton-Jones approached me much further down the road, past the Leo/Kate/Kathy/Mendes movie announcement (a piece of serendipity with which I as executor had nothing to do). She was studying American literature, with a concentration in Richard Yates, at a British university.

While the London *Times* has always seemed to me as anti-Yates as America's NPR and the William Shawn/Roger Angell *New Yorker* ever was, after all it was the BBC that got the movie made and I knew Dad was always pleased by any serious attention from his beloved England.

Fingers crossed, as Kate would say.

Well, what do you know? Out of her research has been born a book, *Dismembering the American Dream*, which brings a whole new level of rigor and depth to the nascent field of Yatesian scholarship.

I'm tempted to quote swaths of Kate's excellent prose, so eloquently does she say what needs to be said—from her introduction, for instance: "To read

Yates's tales of disordered lives is to uncover not misery (though the lives he describes are sad and profoundly lonely), but an insightful, enriching, and often-humorous understanding of human weakness and vulnerability."

And this: "Often seen sidestepping challenges and failing at every kind of domestic or social hurdle, the protagonists limp off into a murky distance at the end of a typical Yatesian tale."

Her chapter on Yates and Hollywood is worth the price of admission. "Yates makes his condemnation of that culture silently clear as he juxtaposes the moth-eaten chair and all the grime and grease of their existence with [his characters'] determined insistence that lives like theirs can mirror Hollywood" . . . "a cocktail of social expectations and a simulation of film behavior."

I tend not to give Dad his due as a novelist of ideas. Throughout her book, but most comprehensively in her chapters on 1950s America and Theories of Selfhood, Kate shows how theorists Erving Goffman, Ian Burkitt, George Herbert Mead, and others wrestled with the questions that were at the core of what he was doing. It's gratifying to see the moods and issues that preoccupied my father identified and studied in other contexts by guys who got a lot more respect from the academy than he ever did.

In her examination of Yates as a stylist, Kate lays out the mechanics that make his writing so exhilarating and examines the prose. She shows us how "[Yates] seamlessly shifts from a third person narrative stance to mimicry of general conversation before arriving at the particular speech enacted" (chapter 1).

I never tire of this stuff, and her explication of his technique is as good as any I've seen. At her most professorial, she strikes me as that thrilling lecturer a student never forgets. The erudition to back up the enthusiasm is simply there, because she's naturally a scholar, and part of her nuanced response to the world is to investigate all the avenues of context. Like Blake, Kate is on target about Yates's feelings for women versus his distaste for the feminist movement, his meticulous perception versus his own confusion on the domestic front. She is able to accept his "I wish I had a girl who'd make Brussels sprouts for me" (a line that reportedly shocked a Tuscaloosa grad student) at its wistful face value, his limiting vision of what women would or should achieve as a generality of his realist wisdom. I did find her to be tone deaf on the subject of his sexuality; scenes from *Easter Parade* that struck her as voyeuristic, misogynistic, bordering on pornographic, to my reading are merely tender, albeit a creepy kind of "Dad" tenderness. Admittedly, there are unsavory aspects. An awful lot of experience with impotence. Had no use for the camp aesthetic, and saw homosexuality as a disappointing fate. Mother problems, a victim of sexual prep school bullying, not good with tools or cars or remotely athletic. Felt he'd been a flop as a soldier. It's a thorny thicket, though one lined more with failure at masculine roles than with repressed sexual desire for men. All in all I'd say Kate nailed it. Plenty of erudition in there for the tenure track to sink its teeth into!

Dismembering the American Dream is strong and true and deeply felt. Kate is one of the future readers Dad knew were coming that night on the daybed in Tuscaloosa. He would have been honored by her careful attention.

Notes

Introduction

1. Richard Yates, "Some Very Good Masters," *New York Times Book Review*, April 19, 1981, 3.

2. *Revolutionary Road*, directed by Sam Mendes; featuring Kate Winslet, Leonardo DiCaprio, and Kathy Bates (DreamWorks SKG in association with BBC Films, released December 2008 [USA] January 2009 [UK]).

3. Blake Bailey, *A Tragic Honesty: The Life and Works of Richard Yates* (London: Methuen, 2004, first published 2003), 359.

4. Nick Fraser, "Rebirth of a Dark Genius," *The Observer*, February 17, 2008, http://www.theguardian.com/books/2008/feb/17/biography.fiction, accessed February 20, 2008.

5. Tennessee Williams, Kurt Vonnegut Jr., Joan Didion, and Andre Dubus are just some of the people who publicly praised Yates's work.

6. Vance Bourjaily in Bailey, *A Tragic Honesty*, 126.

7. Unnamed *Harper's* editor to Monica McCall, ibid.

8. Dan DeLuca, "The Collected Stories of Richard Yates," Knight Ridder/Tribune News Service, June 13, 2001, http://www.highbeam.com/doc/1G1-75512763.html, accessed September 20, 2013.

9. David Castronovo and Steven Goldleaf, *Richard Yates*, Twayne's United States Authors (New York: Twayne Publishers, 1996), 7.

10. Review of *Revolutionary Road*, *The New Yorker*, April 1, 1961, http://www.richardyates.org/bib_rrnyorker.html, accessed September 20, 2013.

11. Kurt Vonnegut in Bailey, *A Tragic Honesty*, 295.

12. Richard Russo, introduction to *The Collected Stories of Richard Yates* (London: Methuen, 2004, first published 2001), xviii.

13. Richard Yates in DeWitt Henry and Geoffrey Clark, "An Interview with Richard Yates," *Ploughshares* 1, no. 3 (1972): 76.

14. Richard Yates, *Young Hearts Crying* (London: Methuen, 1986, first published 1984), 208.

15. F. Scott Fitzgerald, *The Great Gatsby* (London: Penguin, 1950, first published 1926), 188.

16. Salinger's first novel, *The Catcher in the Rye* (1951), is devoted to exposing inauthenticity, performative behavior, and social codes and undoubtedly helped shape Yates's views on these subjects.

17. Bailey, *A Tragic Honesty*, 114.

18. Yates in Henry and Clark, "An Interview with Richard Yates," 67.

19. In his novel *A Long Way Down*, one of Nick Hornby's suicidal protagonists explains, "Earlier that week . . . I'd finished *Revolutionary Road* by Richard Yates, which is a totally awesome novel. I was going to jump with a copy—not only because it would have been kinda cool, and would've added a little mystique to my death, but because it might have been a good way of getting more people to read it." (Nick Hornby, *A Long Way Down* [London: Penguin, 2006, first published 2005], 22.)

20. Richard Ford, introduction to *Revolutionary Road* (London: Methuen, 2001), xiii.

21. Benjamin Lytal, "Reconsiderations: Richard Yates's 'Revolutionary Road,'" *New York Sun*, July 2, 2008, http://www.nysun.com/arts/reconsiderations-richard-yatess -revolutionary-road/81093/, accessed August 9, 2008.

22. Morris Dickstein, "Fiction and Society, 1940–1970," in *The Cambridge History of American Literature*, vol. 7, ed. Sacvan Bercovitch (Cambridge: Cambridge University Press, 1999).

23. Richard Yates, *Revolutionary Road*, introduction by Richard Ford (London: Methuen, 2001).

24. Richard Yates, *The Collected Stories of Richard Yates*, introduction by Richard Russo (London: Methuen, 2004).

25. *Richard Yates: Revolutionary Road, The Easter Parade, and Eleven Kinds of Loneliness*, introduction by Richard Price (New York: Everyman's Library, Alfred A. Knopf, 2009).

26. Martin Naparsteck, *Richard Yates Up Close: The Writer and His Works* (Jefferson, NC: McFarland, 2012).

Chapter 1

1. Richard Yates, *Revolutionary Road*, introduction by Richard Ford (London: Methuen, 2001, first published 1961), 3.

2. Ibid.

3. Erving Goffman, *The Presentation of Self in Everyday Life* (London: Penguin, 1959), 28.

4. J. D. Salinger, *The Catcher in the Rye* (London: Penguin, 1994, first published 1951), 114.

5. Yates, *Revolutionary Road*, 6.

6. Ibid.

7. Blake Bailey, *A Tragic Honesty: The Life and Work of Richard Yates* (London: Methuen, 2004, first published 2003), 230.

8. Yates, *Revolutionary Road*, 7.

9. Ibid.

10. Ibid.

11. Ibid.

12. Ibid.

13. Ibid., 13.

14. Ibid.

15. I am reminded of Nina's words toward the end of *The Seagull*, when she describes the paralyzing sense of her own inadequacy on the stage: "I never knew what to do with my hands, and I could not walk properly or control my voice. You cannot imagine the state of mind of one who knows as he goes through a play how terribly badly he is acting." Anton Chekhov, "The Seagull," trans. Marian Fell, in *Six Famous Plays* (London: Gerald Duckworth, 1958), 98.

16. Yates, *Revolutionary Road*, 13.

17. Ibid.

18. Ibid.

19. Jerome Klinkowitz, *The New American Novel of Manners: The Fiction of Richard Yates, Dan Wakefield, and Thomas McGuane* (Athens: University of Georgia Press, 1986), 21.

20. Richard Yates's novel was published on December 31, 1961, and Edward Albee's play was first performed on October 13, 1962.

21. Goffman, *The Presentation of Self in Everyday Life*, 15.

22. Yates, *Revolutionary Road*, 27.

23. Ibid., 304.

24. Ibid., 296.

25. Ibid., 15.

26. Ibid.

27. Ibid., 28.

28. Ibid., 14.

29. Ibid., 218.

30. Lionel Trilling, *The Liberal Imagination: Essays on Literature and Society* (London: Penguin Books in association with Secker and Warburg, a Peregrine Book, 1970, first published 1950), 212.

31. Leon Samson, "Americanism as Surrogate Socialism," in *Failure of a Dream? Essays in the History of American Socialism*, ed. John H. M. Laslett and Seymour Martin Lipset (Garden City, NY: Anchor Press/Doubleday, 1974), 430.

32. Richard Yates, *Young Hearts Crying* (London: Methuen, 1986, first published 1984), 82.

33. Ibid., 3.

34. Ibid., 4.

35. Goffman, *The Presentation of Self in Everyday Life*, 56.

36. Yates, *Revolutionary Road*, 18.

37. Ibid.

38. Ibid.

39. Richard Yates, *Cold Spring Harbor* (London: Methuen, 2005, first published 1986), 100.

40. T. S. Eliot coined this phrase; he felt that in order to express emotion in art, there needs to be an object, or series of objects, that can act as an indicator of a particular emotion; the object becomes an objective correlative because it calls forth a specific emotional response in the reader. T. S. Eliot, "Hamlet and His Problems," in *The Sacred Wood: Essays on Poetry and Criticism* (London: Methuen, 1920).

41. Richard Yates, "Some Very Good Masters," *New York Times Book Review*, April 19, 1981, 3.

42. Yates, *Revolutionary Road*, 45.

43. Ibid.

44. Ibid.

45. Ibid.

46. Ibid.

47. Ibid., 296.

48. Ibid.

49. Ibid.

50. Ibid., 290.

51. Ibid.

52. Ibid., 292.

53. Ibid., 296.

54. William James, *Selected Writings of William James* (London: Everyman, 1995), 208.

55. Yates, *Revolutionary Road*, 299.

56. Tennessee Williams wired a blurb two days before publication: "Here is more than fine writing; here is what, added to fine writing, makes a book come immediately, intensely, and brilliantly alive. If more is needed to make a masterpiece in modern American fiction, I am sure I don't know what it is." Tennessee Williams in Bailey, *A Tragic Honesty*, 227.

57. Yates, *Young Hearts Crying*, 205.

58. Orville Prescott in Bailey, *A Tragic Honesty*, 228.

Chapter 2

1. Blake Bailey, *A Tragic Honesty: The Life and Work of Richard Yates* (London: Methuen, 2004, first published 2003), 23.

2. Richard Yates, "Some Very Good Masters," *New York Times Book Review*, April 19, 1981, 3.

3. Richard Yates, *Disturbing the Peace* (London: Methuen, 2007, first published 1975), 9.

4. Ibid., 79.

5. Yates, "Some Very Good Masters," 3.

6. J. D. Salinger, *The Catcher in the Rye* (London: Penguin, 1994, first published 1951), 72.

7. Ian Scott, *American Politics in Hollywood Film* (Edinburgh: Edinburgh University Press, 2000), 9.

8. Ibid.

9. *The Wizard of Oz*, directed by Victor Fleming; featuring Judy Garland (MGM, 1939).

10. *Gone with the Wind*, directed by Victor Fleming and George Cukor; featuring Clark Gable, Vivien Leigh, Leslie Howard, and Olivia de Havilland (Selznick International Pictures, 1939).

11. By the 1950s, this inclination toward liberalism was seen in a much more threatening light as fears about the rise of communism intensified.

12. Mark Wheeler, *Hollywood: Politics and Society* (London: British Film Institute, 2006), 52.

13. Ibid., 54.

14. Ibid., 93.

15. Ibid.

16. *Mr. Deeds Goes to Town*, directed by Frank Capra; featuring Gary Cooper and Jean Arthur (Columbia, 1936).

17. *It's a Wonderful Life*, directed by Frank Capra; featuring James Stewart and Donna Reed (Liberty, RKO, 1946).

18. By the 1950s, this move toward the production of films with a carefully packaged sentiment had broken down; edgier films glamorizing the social outcast and risk taker were extremely popular. Films such as *Rebel without a Cause* (1955), *The Wild One* (1953), or *On the Waterfront* (1954) were designed to attract a younger, hipper audience.

19. I am thinking of Douglas Sirk's films here and, in particular, *All That Heaven Allows*. Even as Sirk's film provides a familiar diet of romance and sentiment, it nevertheless manages to take a hard look at class snobbery and the role of women within middle-class America. *All That Heaven Allows*, directed by Douglas Sirk; featuring Jane Wyman and Rock Hudson (Universal International Pictures, 1955).

20. Yates, "Some Very Good Masters," 3.

21. Ronald Sukenick, *In Form: Digressions on the Act of Fiction* (Carbondale: Southern Illinois University Press, 1985), 86.

22. The collection was published in 1962; this story was written nearly ten years earlier in 1953.

23. Yates, "A Glutton for Punishment," in *Eleven Kinds of Loneliness* (London: Methuen, 2006, first published 1962), 71.

24. Ibid.

25. Ibid.

26. Ibid., 73.

27. Ibid., 88.

28. F. Scott Fitzgerald, *The Price Was High*, vols. 1 and 2 (London: Picador, 1981, first published 1979).

29. Bailey, *A Tragic Honesty*, 152.

30. Richard Yates in DeWitt Henry and Geoffrey Clark, "An Interview with Richard Yates," *Ploughshares* 1, no. 3 (1972): 69.

31. Yates, "A Glutton for Punishment," 88.

32. Ibid., 86.

33. Ibid., 81.

34. Jerome Klinkowitz, *The New American Novel of Manners: The Fiction of Richard Yates, Dan Wakefield, and Thomas McGuane* (Athens: University of Georgia Press, 1986), 27.

35. Yates, "A Glutton for Punishment," 76.

36. Ibid., 76.

37. Ibid., 77.

38. James Howard Kunstler, *The Geography of Nowhere: The Rise and Decline of America's Man-Made Landscape* (New York: Simon and Schuster, 1993), 105.

39. Richard Yates, *Cold Spring Harbor* (London: Methuen, 2005, first published 1986), 27.

40. Ibid., 55.

41. Susan J. Douglas, *Where the Girls Are: Growing Up Female with the Mass Media* (London: Penguin, 1994).

42. Yates, *Cold Spring Harbor*, 86.

43. Yates, "A Glutton for Punishment," 74.

44. Ibid.

45. Ibid., 85.

46. Ibid., 78.

47. Richard Yates, *Revolutionary Road* (London: Methuen, 2001, first published 1961), 5.

48. Yates, *Disturbing the Peace*, 186.

49. Brian Neve, *Film and Politics in America: A Social Tradition* (New York: Routledge, 1992), 2.

50. Richard Yates, *The Easter Parade* (London: Methuen, 2004, first published 1976), 13.

51. Ibid.

52. Ibid., 18.

53. Ibid., 23.

54. Ibid., 21.

55. Bailey, *A Tragic Honesty*, 257. Bailey charts each flicker of interest as the likelihood of the project seems strong at first and then fades.

56. Yates in Bailey, *A Tragic Honesty*, 266.

57. George Bluestone, introduction to William Styron's *Lie Down in Darkness*, a screenplay by Richard Yates (Cambridge, MA: Watertown Ploughshares Books,

1985), 7. It is worth noting that Yates wrote very painstakingly when producing his own fiction but unusually fast when he was not dealing with his own material.

58. Natalie Wood had been due to play the part of Peyton opposite Henry Fonda in the role of her father, Milton Loftis.

59. Bailey, *A Tragic Honesty*, 270.

60. Ibid., 269.

61. Bailey quotes an account by Yates of a meeting with the Hollywood producer Al Ruddy. Mimicking the idiom of "The Industry," and of Ruddy in particular, Yates brings to life in his letter to his friends the Schulmans (July 11, 1965) the whole self-aggrandizing ethos of this particular world: "let's take a property like *Revolutionary Road*. Let's take the ending. Is that a problem? Why hell, let's face it, of course it's a problem. Nine guys out of ten in This Town would cop-out on a problem like that—but wait. Listen. Do I know what *he's* gonna do?" Yates in Bailey, *A Tragic Honesty*, 347.

62. The failure to turn the *Lie Down in Darkness* screenplay into a film is reproduced in *Young Hearts Crying* (223) as a throwaway incidental detail. It occurs when the writer Carl Traynor tells Lucy Davenport what he has been up to since they last met.

63. Richard Yates, "Saying Goodbye to Sally," in *Liars in Love* (New York: Delacorte Press/Seymour Lawrence, 1981), 214. Interestingly, the phrase "writing the screenplay for one of the very few contemporary novels he admired" occurs again in one of his drafts of his unpublished work, *Uncertain Times*. The Richard Yates Collection, Howard Gotlieb Archival Research Center at Boston University, Massachusetts. While it is almost certain that had he lived to complete this novel, Yates would have edited out this overlap, it suggests that there were experiences in his life that haunted him and that he would rework creatively many times; this experience was clearly one of them.

64. Yates, "Saying Goodbye to Sally," 215.

65. Ibid., 216. Bailey's description of Yates's house in Hollywood, when he was working on the screenplay, as a "damp mildewy hovel" also suggests the very high degree of overlap that existed between the experiences of the writer and his protagonist. Bailey, *A Tragic Honesty*, 270.

66. Yates, "Saying Goodbye to Sally," 219.

67. Ibid.

68. Ibid., 232.

69. Ibid., 236.

70. Ibid., 238.

71. Ibid., 219.

72. Ibid., 225.

73. Ibid., 238.

74. Ibid., 270.

75. Ibid.

76. Ibid., 272.

77. There is some playful intertextuality here between "Saying Goodbye to Sally" and F. Scott Fitzgerald's unfinished novel, *The Last Tycoon*. Sally Baldwin's friend and housemate, Jill, has a live-in lover named Woody Starr, a painter on black velvet of ridiculous, trashy caricatures, pictures designed to please tourists; he signs his pictures "Starr of Hollywood." We are immediately alerted to Fitzgerald's similar "star" pun as he too names one of his characters Monroe Stahr. In terms of success and status, Yates's Starr is Fitzgerald's Stahr's polar opposite. However, Yates elevates Woody Starr morally above the other characters, as he is the only person who takes any interest in, or shows any care of, the young boy, Kicker. That he becomes a victim of Jill Jarvis's heartless prank, with his hands getting stuck to a tub of roses, further distinguishes him for the reader.

78. Yates, *Disturbing the Peace*, 187.

79. Ibid., 189.

80. Ibid., 191.

81. Ibid., 192.

82. Ibid.

83. Ibid., 194.

84. Ibid., 195.

85. Ibid., 196.

86. Norman Podhoretz, *Doings and Undoings: The Fifties and After in American Writing* (London: Rupert Hart-Davis, 1965), 47.

87. Yates in Henry and Clark, "An Interview with Richard Yates," 71.

88. Richard Yates in DeWitt Henry and Geoffrey Clark, unedited interview for *Ploughshares*. The Richard Yates Collection, Howard Gotlieb Archival Research Center at Boston University, Massachusetts.

89. *Revolutionary Road*, directed by Sam Mendes; featuring Kate Winslet, Leonardo DiCaprio, and Kathy Bates (BBC Films in association with DreamWorks SKG, released December 2008 (USA), January 2009 (UK).

90. Monica Yates, *Here's Hoping*, written for richardyates.org, March 29, 2008, http://www.richardyates.org/bib_shapiro.html, accessed April 20, 2008.

91. Stewart O'Nan, "The Lost World of Richard Yates: How the Great Writer of the Age of Anxiety Disappeared from Print," *Boston Review* (October/November 1999), http://bostonreview.net/BR24.5/onan.html, accessed September 10, 2007.

92. Blake Bailey, "*Revolutionary Road*—the Movie," *Slate*, June 26, 2007, http://www.slate.com/articles/news_and_politics/summer_movies/2007/06/revolutionary_roadthe_movie.html, accessed April 3, 2009.

93. Salinger, *The Catcher in the Rye*, 94.

94. Yates in Bailey, *A Tragic Honesty*, 345.

Chapter 3

1. Ian Burkitt, *Social Selves: Theories of the Social Formation of Personality* (London: Sage Publications, 1991), 3.

2. Ibid., 29.

3. Ibid., 37.

4. Ibid., 48.

5. David Castronovo and Steven Goldleaf, *Richard Yates*, Twayne's United States Authors (New York: Twayne Publishers, 1996), 15.

6. Erving Goffman, *The Presentation of Self in Everyday Life* (New York: Anchor Books, 1959), 2.

7. Ibid.

8. Lionel Trilling, *The Liberal Imagination: Essays on Literature and Society* (London: Penguin Books in association with Secker and Warburg, a Peregrine Book, 1970, first published 1950), 213.

9. Jerome Klinkowitz, *The New American Novel of Manners: The Fiction of Richard Yates, Dan Wakefield, and Thomas McGuane* (Athens: University of Georgia Press, 1986), 8.

10. Richard Yates, *Revolutionary Road* (London: Methuen, 2001, first published 1961), 137.

11. Ibid.

12. Ibid.

13. Ibid., 139.

14. Ibid.

15. Many works can be consulted about this aspect of language as a social construction. Perhaps the most important are Mikhail Bakhtin's "Discourse in the Novel," in *The Dialogic Imagination*, ed. Michael Holquist, trans. Caryl Emerson and Michael Holquist (Austin: University of Texas Press, 1981); P. N. Medvedev and M. M. Bakhtin, *The Formal Method in Literary Scholarship: A Critical Introduction to Sociological Poetics*, trans. Albert J. Wehrle (Baltimore: Johns Hopkins University Press, 1978); and V. N. Voloshinov, *Marxism and the Philosophy of Language*, trans. Ladislav Matejka and I. R. Titunik (New York: Seminar Press, 1973).

16. Martin Halliwell, *American Culture in the 1950s* (Edinburgh: Edinburgh University Press, 2007), 10.

17. Yates, *Revolutionary Road*, 23.

18. Frank Wheeler is supposed to be a writer. He produces advertising copy to support his family until he is free to write fiction.

19. David Milch quoted in Blake Bailey, *A Tragic Honesty: The Life and Works of Richard Yates* (London: Methuen, 2004, first published 2003), 239.

20. Richard Yates, *The Easter Parade* (London: Methuen, 2004, first published 1976), 49.

21. Goffman, *The Presentation of Self in Everyday Life*, 24.

22. Castronovo and Goldleaf, *Richard Yates*, 6.

23. Yates, *Revolutionary Road*, 258.

24. Klinkowitz, *The New American Novel of Manners*, 157.

25. Richard Yates, *Young Hearts Crying* (London: Methuen, 1986, first published 1984), 50.

26. Ibid., 87.

27. Norman Podhoretz, writing about the 1950s, referred to it as "this Age of Sociology." Norman Podhoretz, *Doings and Undoings: The Fifties and After in American Writing* (London: Rupert Hart-Davis, 1965), 144.

28. William James, *Selected Writings of William James* (London: Everyman, 1995), 207.

29. Clearly, from the end of the nineteenth century the work of Sigmund Freud (1856–1939) had an enormous influence on the way notions of the self were understood. This was particularly true of his work on the repressed self and the unconscious.

30. Mark Snyder, *Public Appearances, Private Realities: The Psychology of Self-Monitoring* (New York: W. H. Freeman, 1987), 47.

31. Ibid., 48.

32. Ibid., 50.

33. Castronovo and Goldleaf, *Richard Yates*, 17.

34. Burkitt, *Social Selves*, 59.

35. It was the postmodernists who reflected the lack of moral coloring that Castronovo and Goldleaf wrongly attribute to Yates. I will look at this aspect of the postmodern novel in my examination of the work of Nathanael West and John Barth.

36. Richard Yates, *Cold Spring Harbor* (London: Methuen, 2005, first published 1986), 21.

37. Ibid.

38. Ibid., 30.

39. Richard Yates, "Doctor Jack-o'-Lantern," in *Eleven Kinds of Loneliness* (London: Methuen, 2006, first published 1962), 1.

40. Ibid.

41. Ibid., 3.

42. Ibid., 7.

43. Ibid., 9.

44. Ibid., 10.

45. Ibid., 15.

46. Ibid., 18.

47. Richard Yates, "A Compassionate Leave," in *Liars in Love* (New York: Delacorte Press/Seymour Lawrence, 1981).

48. Ibid., 162.

49. Ibid., 165.

50. Ibid.

51. Ibid.

52. Ibid.

53. Ibid., 171.

54. Ibid., 172.

55. Ibid.

56. Ibid., 145.

57. Ibid., 146.
58. Ibid., 173.
59. Ibid.

Chapter 4

1. Mark Snyder, *Public Appearances, Private Realities: The Psychology of Self-Monitoring* (New York: W. H. Freeman, 1987). As noted, Snyder uses the term "self-monitor" as a way of indicating the ability to observe, regulate, and control the behavior of the self.

2. Richard Yates, *Revolutionary Road* (London: Methuen, 2001, first published 1961), 184.

3. Ibid.

4. Ibid.

5. Ibid.

6. Ibid., 284.

7. Ibid., 185.

8. Ibid.

9. Ibid., 186.

10. Morris Dickstein "Fiction and Society, 1940–1970," in *The Cambridge History of American Literature*, vol. 7, ed. Sacvan Bercovitch (Cambridge: Cambridge University Press, 1999), 220.

11. Yates, *Revolutionary Road*, 185.

12. Ibid., 282.

13. Ibid., 285.

14. Ibid.

15. Ibid., 287.

16. Erving Goffman, *The Presentation of Self in Everyday Life* (London: Penguin, 1959), 141.

17. David Castronovo and Steven Goldleaf, *Richard Yates*, Twayne's United States Authors (New York: Twayne Publishers, 1996), 46.

18. Richard Yates, "Some Very Good Masters," *New York Times Book Review*, April 19, 1981, 21.

19. Richard Yates in DeWitt Henry and Geoffrey Clark, "An Interview with Richard Yates," *Ploughshares* 1, no. 3 (1972): 69.

20. Dickstein, "Fiction and Society, 1940–1970," 220.

21. Richard Yates, "Jody Rolled the Bones," in *Eleven Kinds of Loneliness* (London: Methuen, 2006, first published 1962), 38.

22. Ibid., 44 (my italics).

23. Ibid., 46 (my italics).

24. Ibid., 54.

25. Ibid.

26. Ibid., 55.

27. Ibid.

28. Ibid., 56.

29. Richard Russo, introduction to *The Collected Stories of Richard Yates* (London: Methuen, 2004), xiii.

30. Yates, "Jody Rolled the Bones," 38.

31. Ibid., 39.

32. Ibid.

33. Ibid.

34. Ibid.

35. Yates, *Revolutionary Road*, 331.

36. Ibid., 332.

37. Richard Yates, *Young Hearts Crying* (London: Methuen, 1986, first published 1984), 42.

38. Ibid., 240.

39. Blake Bailey, *A Tragic Honesty: The Life and Work of Richard Yates* (London: Methuen, 2004, first published 2003), 251.

40. Ibid., 63.

41. Ibid., 64.

42. Richard Yates, *A Good School* (London: Methuen, 2006, first published 1978), 89.

43. Robert Ezra Park, *Race and Culture* (Glencoe, IL: Free Press, 1950), 250.

Chapter 5

1. John Barth, *The End of the Road* (New York: Secker and Warburg, 1981, first published 1962), 5.

2. J. D. Salinger, *The Catcher in the Rye* (London: Penguin, 1994, first published 1951), 1.

3. Barth, *The End of the Road*, 12.

4. Tony Tanner, *City of Words: American Fiction, 1950–1970* (New York: Harper and Row, 1971), 230.

5. Barth, *The End of the Road*, 86.

6. Tanner, *City of Words*, 238.

7. Morris Dickstein, "Fiction and Society, 1940–1970," in *The Cambridge History of American Literature*, vol. 7, ed. Sacvan Bercovitch (Cambridge: Cambridge University Press, 1999), 217. While Dickstein explores the differences between these two writers he unites them as both inventing "a kind of anti-road novel . . . [offering] a counterstatement to the kind of self-liberation celebrated by Kerouac" (ibid., 210).

8. Barth, *The End of the Road*, 87.

9. Ibid.

10. Ibid.

11. Ibid., 179.

12. John Updike, *Rabbit Run* (1960), *Rabbit Redux* (1971), *Rabbit Is Rich* (1981), *Rabbit at Rest* (1990).

13. Richard Yates in DeWitt Henry and Geoffrey Clark, "An Interview with Richard Yates," *Ploughshares* 1, no. 3 (1972), 76.

14. Salinger, *The Catcher in the Rye*, 11.

15. Ibid., 14.

16. Richard Yates, *A Good School* (London: Methuen, 2006, first published 1978), 16.

17. Ibid., 21.

18. Salinger, *The Catcher in the Rye*, 55.

19. John O'Hara, *Appointment in Samarra* (New York: Vintage Books, 2003, first published 1934), 11.

20. Mikhail Bakhtin, "Forms of Time and of the Chronotope in the Novel," in *The Dialogic Imagination*, ed. Michael Holquist, trans. Caryl Emerson and Michael Holquist (Austin: University of Texas Press, 1981), 84.

21. O'Hara, *Appointment in Samarra*, 15.

22. Ibid., 171.

23. Ibid., 10.

24. Ibid., 11.

25. Ibid.

26. Seymour Lawrence, "Requiem for Richard Yates," in *Richard Yates: An American Writer, Tributes in Memoriam*, ed. Seymour Lawrence (New York: Seymour Lawrence, 1993), 61.

27. John O'Hara, "Pardner," *Selected Short Stories of John O'Hara* (New York: Modern Library, 2003, first published 1994), 29.

28. Ibid., 30.

29. Ibid., 31.

30. Ibid., 32.

31. Vladimir Nabokov, *Lolita* (London: Penguin, 1980, first published 1955).

32. John Cheever, "The Swimmer," *Collected Stories* (London: Vintage, 1990), 776.

33. Richard Gray, *A History of American Literature* (Oxford: Blackwell Publishing, 2004), 605.

34. Cheever in Gray, *A History of American Literature*.

35. John Cheever, *The Wapshot Chronicle* (Alexandria, VA: Time-Life Books, 1965, first published 1954), 36.

36. Ibid., 37.

37. Blake Bailey footnotes the point that in the 1950s, Cheever rented the same house that Yates's family had lived in on the Beechwood estate in Scarborough-on-Hudson: "The Beechwood estate is located near a street named Revolutionary Road" (Blake Bailey, *Cheever: A Life* [New York: Alfred A. Knopf, 2009], 177).

38. Cheever, *The Wapshot Chronicle*, 21.

39. Ibid., 201.

40. Ibid., 202.

41. Richard Yates, *Revolutionary Road* (London: Methuen, 2001, first published 1961), 67.

42. Ibid., 39.

43. Yates in Henry and Clark, "An Interview with Richard Yates," 76.

44. Kurt Vonnegut, "Who Am I This Time?," *Welcome to the Monkey House* (London: Vintage, 1994, first published 1968), 14.

45. Ibid., 15.

46. Ibid., 16.

47. Ibid., 26.

48. Ibid., 20.

49. Ibid., 26.

50. Jeremy Larner in Bailey, *A Tragic Honesty*, 229.

51. Sam Lawrence in ibid., 204.

52. Anatole Broyard in Richard Ford's introduction to *Revolutionary Road* (London: Methuen, 2001, first published 1961), xix.

53. Ford, introduction to *Revolutionary Road*, xx.

54. Bailey, *A Tragic Honesty*, 233.

55. Malcolm Cowley, *A Second Flowering: Works and Days of the Lost Generation* (London: Andre Deutsch, 1973), 31.

56. F. Scott Fitzgerald, *The Great Gatsby* (London: Penguin, 1950, first published 1926), 14.

57. Ibid., 24.

58. Cowley, *A Second Flowering*, 31.

59. Richard Yates, "Some Very Good Masters," *New York Times Book Review*, April 19, 1981, 3.

60. Nathanael West, *Miss Lonelyhearts* and *The Day of the Locust* (Toronto: A New Directions Paperbook, George J. McLeod, 1962, first published 1933), 3.

61. West, *Miss Lonelyhearts*, 30.

62. Gray, *A History of American Literature*, 551.

63. Ibid.

64. Erving Goffman, *The Presentation of Self in Everyday Life* (London: Penguin, 1959), 18.

65. West, *Miss Lonelyhearts*, 32.

66. Ibid., 39.

67. Ibid.

68. Stewart O'Nan, "The Lost World of Richard Yates: How the Great Writer of the Age of Anxiety Disappeared from Print," *Boston Review* (October/November 1999), http://bostonreview.net/BR24.5/onan.html, accessed September 10, 2007.

69. Nancy Bentley, "Wharton and the Science of Manners," in *The Cambridge Companion to Edith Wharton*, ed. Millicent Bell (Cambridge: Cambridge University Press, 1995), 50.

70. Ibid.

71. Barth, *The End of the Road*, 114.

72. Richard Yates, *Young Hearts Crying* (London: Methuen, 1986, first published 1984), 350 (my italics).

73. Kurt Vonnegut in Seymour Lawrence, "Requiem for Richard Yates," 14.

74. Ibid.

75. David Castronovo and Steven Goldleaf, *Richard Yates*, Twayne's United States Authors (New York: Twayne Publishers, 1996), 7.

76. Richard Russo, introduction to *The Collected Stories of Richard Yates*, xi.

77. Ibid.

78. Yates, "Some Very Good Masters," 3.

79. Richard Ford, introduction to *Revolutionary Road*, xiv.

Chapter 6

1. Richard Yates, "Builders," in *Eleven Kinds of Loneliness* (London: Methuen, 2006, first published 1962).

2. Richard Poirier, "The Performing Self," in *The Performing Self* (New Brunswick, NJ: Rutgers University Press, 1992), 86.

3. Ibid., 88.

4. Ibid., 98.

5. Richard Yates, *Cold Spring Harbor* (London: Methuen, 2005, first published 1986), 136.

6. Blake Bailey, *A Tragic Honesty: The Life and Work of Richard Yates* (London: Methuen, 2004, first published 2003), 17.

7. Maria Russo, "The Collected Stories of Richard Yates," *Salon*, June 19, 2001, http://archive.salon.com/books/review/2001/06/19/yates/index.html, accessed May 20, 2008.

8. Ernest Hemingway, *The Sun Also Rises* (London: Vintage, 2000, first published 1926), 23.

9. Ibid., 30.

10. Richard Yates, *Young Hearts Crying* (London: Methuen, 1986, first published 1984), 281.

11. Jerome Klinkowitz, *The New American Novel of Manners: The Fiction of Richard Yates, Dan Wakefield, and Thomas McGuane* (Athens: University of Georgia Press, 1986), 16.

12. Richard Yates, *Revolutionary Road* (London: Methuen, 2001, first published 1961), 98. The details and light Yates provides in such scenes make them very reminiscent of many Edward Hopper paintings, paintings such as *Eleven A.M.*, *Summer Interior*, or *A Woman in the Sun*: shafts of light point up the stark interiors and the loneliness of the figures illumined.

13. Ibid., 115.

14. Ibid.

15. Ibid., 22.

16. Morris Dickstein, "Fiction and Society, 1940–1970," in *The Cambridge History of American Literature*, vol. 7, ed. Sacvan Bercovitch (Cambridge: Cambridge University Press, 1999), 219.

17. Since Yates's work contains many comic moments, this comment needs some clarification. What I want to draw attention to here is the unusual way Yates's narra-

tive voice, the voice of Bob Prentice, has a note of levity; it is not only a dry observational narrative perspective that encompasses in its vision some of the absurdities of human behavior, as is more usual in Yates's fiction, but it is also a voice that mocks itself.

18. Maria Russo, "The Collected Stories of Richard Yates," *Salon*, June 19, 2001, http://archive.salon.com/books/review/2001/06/19/yates/index.html, accessed May 20, 2008.

19. This is a tightrope flagged up by Henry James who wrote about the difficulties inherent in the first person narrator, for the realist writer, when he reflected on his presentation of Lambert Strether: "Had I, meanwhile, made him at once hero and historian, endowed him with the romantic privilege of the 'first person' . . . variety, and many other queer matters as well, might have been smuggled in by a back door. Suffice it, to be brief, that the first person, in the long piece, is a form foredoomed to looseness." Henry James, "Preface to 'The Ambassadors,'" in *The Art of the Novel: Critical Prefaces* (London: Charles Scribner's Sons, 1935), 320. The looseness and variety that James dislikes and wants to avoid is precisely what many of the postmodernists celebrate.

20. Yates does this also, though less successfully, within his other semiautobiographical novel, *A Good School*, a novel framed by a first person narrative.

21. Yates, "Builders," 180.

22. Ibid., 181.

23. Ibid., 215.

24. Bailey, *A Tragic Honesty*, 127.

25. Richard Yates, *A Good School* (London: Methuen, 2006, first published 1978), 169. The fact that the name Robert/Bob Prentice occurs in two of Yates's publications ("Builders" and *A Special Providence*) is indicative of the fact that he always saw himself as a *student* of the art of writing.

26. Yates, "Builders," 180.

27. Ibid.

28. Ibid., 183.

29. Ibid., 181.

30. Ibid., 183.

31. Ibid., 190.

32. James, "Preface to 'The Portrait of a Lady,'" in *The Art of the Novel*, 55. It is interesting to note that twenty-three years later James employed the same metaphor but with a negative slant in order to expose the looseness, the lack of selection or discrimination of writers such as Arnold Bennett and H. G. Wells. He talks of the lack of an "idea" in Bennett's work, the lack of anything, "but just simply of the quarried and gathered material it happens to contain, the stones and bricks and rubble and cement and promiscuous constituents of every sort that have been heaped in it and thanks to which it quite massively piles itself up." Leon Edel and Gordon N. Ray, eds., *Henry James and H. G. Wells: A Record of Their Friendship, Their Debate on the Art of Fiction, and Their Quarrel* (London: Rupert Hart-Davis, 1958), 188.

33. Henry James, "The Real Thing," in *Selected Short Stories* (Baltimore: Penguin, 1963, first published 1893), 50.

34. Yates, "Builders," 192.

35. Ibid., 193.

36. Ibid., 200.

37. Ibid., 221.

38. Ibid., 220.

39. Ibid., 221.

40. Klinkowitz, *The New American Novel of Manners*, 30.

41. James, "Preface to 'Portrait of a Lady,'" in *The Art of the Novel*, 46.

42. Ibid.

43. Yates, "Builders," 221.

44. Richard Yates, ed., *Stories for the Sixties* (New York: Bantam Books, 1963), vii.

45. Richard Yates in DeWitt Henry and Geoffrey Clark, "An Interview with Richard Yates," *Ploughshares* 1, no. 3 (1972), 70.

46. Yates, *Young Hearts Crying*, 33.

47. Ibid., 37.

48. Ibid., 35.

49. Ibid., 38. We have to link the apparently casual manner Nelson employs to produce his art with the equally casual manner in which he dresses and views his artistic performance.

50. Ibid., 37.

51. Jackson Pollock, "The Process," http://www.nga.gov/feature/pollock/process3gv.shtm, accessed September 26, 2013.

52. Yates, *Young Hearts Crying*, 38.

53. Ibid., 39.

54. Ibid., 38.

55. Ibid., 36.

56. Norman Podhoretz, *Making It* (London: Jonathan Cape, 1967), 213.

57. Ibid., 214.

58. Yates, *Young Hearts Crying*, 77.

59. Ibid., 3.

60. Ibid., 4.

61. Ibid., 389.

62. Ibid., 5.

63. Richard Yates, *The Easter Parade* (London: Methuen, 2004, first published 1976), 104.

64. Ibid., 105.

65. Tony Tanner, *City of Words: American Fiction, 1950–1970* (New York: Harper and Row, 1971), 17.

66. Yates, *Young Hearts Crying*, 30.

67. Ibid., 102.

68. Kurt Vonnegut Jr. in Bailey, *A Tragic Honesty*, 369.

69. Ibid., 167.

70. Arnold Gingrich, introduction to F. Scott Fitzgerald's *The Pat Hobby Stories* (New York: Scribner, 2004, first published 1962), xxii.

71. "The living wage is the reader's grant of the least possible quantity of attention required for consciousness of a 'spell.' The occasional charming 'tip' is an act of his intelligence over and beyond this, a golden apple, for the writer's lap, straight from the wind-stirred tree." Henry James, "Preface to 'The Portrait of a Lady,'" in *The Art of the Novel*, 54.

72. Yates, *Revolutionary Road*, 87.

73. Ibid.

74. Ibid., 123.

75. Ibid., 174.

76. Yates, *The Easter Parade*, 93.

77. Ibid., 95.

78. Ibid., 102.

79. Ibid., 94.

80. Ibid., 103.

81. Klinkowitz, *The New American Novel of Manners*, 45.

82. Yates, *The Easter Parade*, 80.

83. Ibid. This dismissal of psychiatry, a growth industry in 1950s America, is a recurrent theme in Yates's work; borne out of his own experiences at the hands of therapists, it is most fully explored in his novel *Disturbing the Peace*.

84. Ibid., 81.

85. Ibid.

86. Yates, discussing *Revolutionary Road*, explained that he felt, "a young woman dying of a self-inflicted abortion was a good fictional metaphor for the Fifties." Yates in Henry and Clark, "An Interview with Richard Yates," 73.

87. Yates, *The Easter Parade*, 80.

88. Ibid., 97.

89. Ibid.

90. Ibid.

91. Ibid.

92. Ibid., 98.

93. Ibid.

94. Ibid., 101–2.

95. Ibid., 115.

96. Yates in Henry and Clark, "An Interview with Richard Yates," 76.

97. Yates, *The Easter Parade*, 211.

98. Klinkowitz, *The New American Novel of Manners*, 46.

99. Poirier, "The Performing Self," 104.

100. Ibid., 86.

101. Lee Siegel, "Revolutionary Road (Richard Yates' Classic Work Republished)," *Harper's Magazine*, July 1, 2001, http://www.highbeam.com/doc/1G1-76134284.html, accessed September 26, 2013.

Chapter 7

1. Sharon Monteith, *American Culture in the 1960s* (Edinburgh: Edinburgh University Press, 2008), 100.

2. Ibid.

3. Ibid.

4. Stewart O'Nan, "The Lost World of Richard Yates: How the Great Writer of the Age of Anxiety Disappeared from Print," *Boston Review* (October/November 1999), http://bostonreview.net/BR24.5/onan.html, accessed September 10, 2007.

5. Richard Yates, "Builders," in *Eleven Kinds of Loneliness* (London: Methuen, 2006, first published 1962), 179.

6. Ibid.

7. Richard Yates in DeWitt Henry and Geoffrey Clark, "An Interview with Richard Yates," *Ploughshares* 1, no. 3 (1972): 68.

8. Richard Yates, letter to DeWitt Henry, July 24, 1972, Wichita, Kansas, The Richard Yates Collection, Howard Gotlieb Archival Research Center at Boston University, Massachusetts.

9. Yates in Henry and Clark, "An Interview with Richard Yates," 74.

10. Elizabeth Venant, "A Fresh Twist in the Road for Novelist Richard Yates, a Specialist in Grim Irony, Late Fame's a Wicked Return," *Los Angeles Times*, July 9, 1989, http://www.tbns.net/elevenkinds/venant.html, accessed September 22, 2013.

11. Blake Bailey, *A Tragic Honesty: The Life and Work of Richard Yates* (London: Methuen, 2004, first published 2003), 93.

12. DeWitt Henry in *Richard Yates: An American Writer, Tributes in Memoriam*, ed. Seymour Lawrence (New York: Seymour Lawrence, 1993), 31.

13. Elizabeth Cox, "Meet Richard Yates," pif *Magazine*, http://www.pifmagazine.com/2000/10/meet-richard-yates/, accessed November 12, 2007.

14. Richard Yates, ed., *Stories for the Sixties* (New York: Bantam Books, 1963), viii.

15. Leon Edel and Gordon N. Ray, eds., *Henry James and H. G. Wells: A Record of Their Friendship, Their Debate on the Art of Fiction, and Their Quarrel* (London: Rupert Hart-Davis, 1958), 136.

16. Richard Yates in Scott Bradfield, "Follow the Long and Revolutionary Road," *The Independent*, November 21, 1992, http://www.tbns.net/elevenkinds/bradfield.html, accessed April 3, 2009.

17. Yates in Henry and Clark, "An Interview with Richard Yates," 70.

18. Susan Braudy in Lawrence, *Richard Yates: An American Writer*, 21. Susan Braudy and Yates spoke on the phone every day for the last two years of his life; this comment comes from one of these phone calls and is recorded in *Richard Yates*.

19. Yates in Henry and Clark, "An Interview with Richard Yates," 69.

20. Milton Ehre, introduction to *Chekhov for the Stage* (Evanston, IL: Northwestern University Press, 1992), 11.

21. Anton Chekhov, *The Seagull*, trans. Marian Fell, in *Six Famous Plays* (London: Gerald Duckworth, 1958), 39.

22. Ibid., 46.

23. Ibid., 41.

24. Ibid., 95.

25. Treplieff angrily shouts at Trigorin and his mother, "You are the slaves of convention. . . . I refuse to accept your point of view, yours and his, I refuse!" Ibid., 76.

26. Treplieff only becomes famous or acknowledged as a writer once Nina has left him.

27. Chekhov, *The Seagull*, (Trigorin, act two), 64.

28. Bailey, *A Tragic Honesty*, 470.

29. Richard Yates, "Some Very Good Masters," *New York Times Book Review*, April 19, 1981, 3.

30. Ibid.

31. F. Scott Fitzgerald, *Tender Is the Night* (London: Penguin, 1955, first published 1939), 23.

32. Richard Yates, *Disturbing the Peace* (London: Methuen, 2007, first published 1975), 19.

33. Ibid., 20.

34. Ibid., 47.

35. Ibid., 16.

36. Ibid.

37. Ibid., 133.

38. Ibid.

39. Ibid., 61.

40. Ibid., 36.

41. Ibid., 41.

42. Ibid., 211.

43. Ibid., 60.

44. Ibid., 2.

45. Tony Tanner, *City of Words, American Fiction, 1950–1970* (New York: Harper and Row, 1971), 27.

46. Yates in Henry and Clark, "An Interview with Richard Yates," 68.

47. Mikhail Bakhtin, "Discourse in the Novel," in *The Dialogic Imagination*, ed. Michael Holquist, trans. Caryl Emerson and Michael Holquist (Austin: University of Texas Press, 1981), 288.

48. Jerome Klinkowitz, *The New American Novel of Manners: The Fiction of Richard Yates, Dan Wakefield, and Thomas McGuane* (Athens: University of Georgia Press, 1986), 155.

49. Richard Yates, "The Achievement of Gina Berriault," *Ploughshares* 5, no. 3 (1979): 41.

50. Richard Yates, *Revolutionary Road* (London: Methuen, 2001, first published 1961), 304.

51. Donald Barthelme, "Me and Miss Mandible," in *The New Granta Book of the American Short Story*, ed. Richard Ford (London: Granta Publications, 2007), 98.

52. Ibid., 108.

53. Ibid., 109.

54. Richard Gray, *A History of American Literature* (Oxford: Blackwell, 2004), 736.

55. Review of *Revolutionary Road*, *New Yorker*, April 1, 1961, http://www.richardyates .org/bib_rrnyorker.html, accessed October 12, 2006.

56. Jorge Luis Borges, "Tlon, Uqbar, Orbis Tertius," in *Fictions*, trans. Andrew Hurley (London: Penguin, 2000, first published 1998), 7.

57. Ibid.

58. I am referring to Tom Wolfe's *Esquire* magazine article from 1963 called "There Goes (Varoom! Varoom!) That Kandy-Kolored (Thphhhhhh!) Tangerine-Flake Stream-line Baby (Rahghhh!) around the Bend (Brummmmmmmmmmmmmmmmmm). . . ."

59. Tom Wolfe, *The New Journalism* (New York: Harper and Row, 1973), 15.

60. Yates greatly admired the work of Joan Didion and felt she "deserved every bit of her big success with *Play It as It Lays*." Yates in Henry and Clark, "An Interview with Richard Yates," 77.

61. Gray, *A History of American Literature*, 724.

62. O'Nan, "The Lost World of Richard Yates."

63. Wolfe, preface, in *The New Journalism*.

64. Georg Lukács, *The Meaning of Contemporary Realism* (London: Merlin Press, 1963, first published in German 1957), 48.

65. Wolfe, *The New Journalism*, 41.

66. Richard Yates, *Young Hearts Crying* (London: Methuen, 1986, first published 1984), 115.

67. Ibid.

68. Yates in Henry and Clark, "An Interview with Richard Yates," 76.

69. Richard Yates, letter to DeWitt Henry, July 24, 1972, Wichita, Kansas, The Richard Yates Collection, Howard Gotlieb Archival Research Center at Boston University, Massachusetts.

70. David Castronovo and Steven Goldleaf, *Richard Yates*, Twayne's United States Authors (New York: Twayne Publishers, 1996), 9.

71. Richard Yates, *A Good School* (London: Methuen, 2006, first published 1978), 61.

72. Bailey, *A Tragic Honesty*, 507.

73. Ibid., 508.

74. Lee Siegel, "Revolutionary Road (Richard Yates' Classic Work Republished)," *Harper's Magazine*, July 1, 2001, http://www.highbeam.com/doc/1G1-76134284.html, accessed September 26, 2013.

75. Sinclair Lewis, *Main Street* (New York: Harcourt, Brace and World, 1920), 90.

76. Ibid., 37.

77. Ibid., 86.

78. Ibid., 425.

79. Ibid., 268.

80. Ibid., 267.

81. Lionel Trilling, *The Liberal Imagination: Essays on Literature and Society* (Lon-

don: Penguin Books in association with Secker and Warburg, a Peregrine Book, 1970, first published 1950), 215.

82. Gray, *A History of American Literature*, 369.

83. Morris Dickstein, "Fiction and Society, 1940–1970," in *The Cambridge History of American Literature*, vol. 7, ed. Sacvan Bercovitch (Cambridge: Cambridge University Press, 1999), 222.

84. Yates, *Young Hearts Crying*, 17.

85. Walker Percy, "Notes for a Novel about the End of the World," in *The Message in the Bottle: How Queer Man Is, How Queer Language Is, and What One Has to Do with the Other* (New York: Farrar, Straus and Giroux, 1975), 108.

86. Ibid., 112.

87. Ibid.

88. Truman Capote, *In Cold Blood* (London: Penguin, 1966, first published 1965).

89. Ernest Hemingway, *The Sun Also Rises* (London: Vintage, 2000, first published 1926), 132.

90. J. D. Salinger, *The Catcher in the Rye* (London: Penguin, 1994, first published 1951), 184.

91. Castronovo and Goldleaf, *Richard Yates*, 21 (my italics).

92. Yates, *A Good School*, 167.

93. Yates, *Revolutionary Road*, 337.

94. Siegel, "Revolutionary Road."

95. Richard Yates, *The Easter Parade* (London: Methuen, 2004, first published 1976), 7.

96. It is interesting that our reading of Emily makes this a shock to discover; we would not be surprised if at this point Yates had told us she is seventy, so harsh and unrelentingly difficult is her life, full of the wrong choices and with so little real joy.

97. Yates, *The Easter Parade*, 224.

98. Ibid., 226.

99. Percy, "Notes for a Novel about the End of the World," 112.

100. Yates, *The Easter Parade*, 3.

101. Yates, *Disturbing the Peace*, 1.

102. While Nick Carraway's mournful and reflective beginning to *The Great Gatsby* is one example of this, Fitzgerald's opening lines to *The Crack-Up* sound extraordinarily similar to the beginning of a Yatesian tale: "Of course all life is a process of breaking down, but the blows that do the dramatic side of the work . . . don't show their effect all at once." F. Scott Fitzgerald, *The Crack-Up*, with other pieces and stories (London: Penguin, 1965, *The Crack-Up,* first published 1936), 39.

103. Yates, *Revolutionary Road*, 3.

104. Ibid., 337.

105. Yates, "The B.A.R. Man," in *Eleven Kinds of Loneliness*, 118.

106. Ibid., 119 (my italics). The italics are used to illustrate the shifts in perspective.

107. Notwithstanding April's demise in the latter stages of *Revolutionary Road*, it is not where the novel ends; her death is not the last image the reader takes away.

108. Alain Robbe-Grillet, *Snapshots* and *Towards a New Novel*, trans. Barbara Wright (London: Calder and Boyars, 1965, *Pour un nouveau roman* first published 1962, *Instantanés* first published 1963), 48.

109. Yates, *The Easter Parade*, 23.

110. Ibid.

111. Ibid., 29.

112. Ibid.

113. Ibid., 178.

114. Ibid., 188.

115. Ibid., 189.

116. Ibid., 190.

117. Yates, *Disturbing the Peace*, 130.

118. Ibid.

119. Ronald Sukenick, *In Form: Digressions on the Act of Fiction* (Carbondale: Southern Illinois University Press, 1985), 48.

120. Ibid., 68.

Chapter 8

1. Norman Podhoretz, *Doings and Undoings: The Fifties and After in American Writing* (London: Rupert Hart-Davis, 1965), 107.

2. Warren Susman with the assistance of Edward Griffin, "Did Success Spoil the United States? Dual Representation in Postwar America," in *Recasting America: Culture and Politics in the Age of the Cold War*, ed. Lary May (Chicago: University of Chicago Press, 1989), 21, quoted in Wini Breines, *Young, White, and Miserable: Growing Up Female in the Fifties* (Chicago: University of Chicago Press, 2001, first published 1992), 52.

3. Elaine Tyler May, *Homeward Bound: American Families in the Cold War Era* (New York: Basic Books, 1988), 3.

4. Richard Yates, *Revolutionary Road* (London: Methuen, 2001, first published 1961), 29.

5. Ibid. (my italics).

6. Elaine Showalter, *A Jury of Her Peers: American Women Writers from Anne Bradstreet to Annie Proulx* (London: Virago Press, 2009), 391.

7. Ibid., 392.

8. Ibid.

9. I am thinking of Virginia Woolf's *A Room of One's Own* (1929) and Charlotte Perkins Gilman's *The Yellow Wallpaper* (1892).

10. Showalter, *A Jury of Her Peers*, 393.

11. Blake Bailey, *A Tragic Honesty: The Life and Work of Richard Yates* (London: Methuen, 2004, first published 2003), 429.

12. Richard Yates, letter to Geoffrey Clark, April 16, 1978, The Richard Yates Collection, Howard Gotlieb Archival Research Center at Boston University, Massachusetts.

13. Richard Yates, *The Easter Parade* (London: Methuen, 2004, first published 1976), 211.

14. Ibid., 215.

15. Ibid., 216.

16. Ibid.

17. Blake Bailey, "Richard Yates' Real Masterpiece: What Kate Winslet Doesn't Tell You about Yates and Women," *Slate*, January 5, 2009, http://www.slate.com/articles /arts/books/2009/01/richard_yates_real_masterpiece.html, accessed April 3, 2009.

18. Yates, *The Easter Parade*, 81.

19. Kate Charlton-Jones, "Living on Revolutionary Road," *The Times*, January 24, 2009. http://entertainment.timesonline.co.uk/tol/arts_and_entertainment/film /article5573136.ece, accessed January 24, 2009.

20. Susan J. Douglas, *Where the Girls Are: Growing Up Female with the Mass Media* (London: Penguin, 1994), 9.

21. Ibid., 13.

22. Yates, *Revolutionary Road*, 110.

23. Ibid., 108.

24. Ibid., 110.

25. Ibid., 24. The notion of "belief" in the potential of the male within a relationship is an interesting one and is echoed throughout Yates's fictions. In *Young Hearts Crying*, Lucy similarly "believes" in Michael Davenport's potential as a writer. Lucy, it is clear, has fallen in love with an idea of him, as someone who "*knows* so much," as someone who writes poems and plays and has "a profound understanding of the—you know—of the human heart." Richard Yates, *Young Hearts Crying* (London: Methuen, 1986, first published 1984), 5. Like April, Lucy's path through the relationship is one that disabuses her of such belief.

26. Yates, *Revolutionary Road*, 112.

27. Ibid., 113.

28. Ibid., 114.

29. Ibid.

30. Ibid.

31. Ibid.

32. Ibid., 13.

33. Yates, *The Easter Parade*, 119.

34. Richard Yates, "Evening on the Côte d'Azur," in *The Collected Stories of Richard Yates* (London: Methuen, 2004), 408.

35. Ibid., 416.

36. The second Kinsey Report, *Sexual Behavior in the Human Female* (Dr. Alfred Kinsey, Wardell Pomeroy, and others, 1953), challenged the myth that premarital sex was not happening; it provided substantial proof that young people enjoyed several sexual relationships before they settled down and drew significant attention to female sexual desire. David Halberstam suggests that Kinsey was surprised by his findings:

"As a result of his work, Kinsey was both fascinated and troubled by the vast difference between American sexual behavior the society wanted to believe existed and American sexual practices as they actually existed." David Halberstam, *The Fifties* (New York: A Fawcett Book, Random House, 1993), 272.

37. Douglas, *Where the Girls Are*, 61.

38. Yates, "A Clinical Romance," in *The Collected Stories of Richard Yates*, 387.

39. Richard Yates in DeWitt Henry and Geoffrey Clark, "An Interview with Richard Yates," *Ploughshares* 1, no. 3 (1972): 67.

40. *A Summer Place*, directed by Delmer Daves, based on the novel by Sloan Wilson; featuring Richard Egan, Dorothy McGuire, Sandra Dee, and Arthur Kennedy (Warner Bros. Pictures, 1959).

41. *Love with the Proper Stranger*, directed by Robert Mulligan; featuring Natalie Wood and Steve McQueen (Pakula-Mulligan, 1963).

42. Douglas, *Where the Girls Are*, 74.

43. Incidental couples, such as the Nelsons in *Young Hearts Crying*, appear to live companionable lives, but not being at the center of the narrative focus, little is made of this.

44. Yates in Henry and Clark, "An Interview with Richard Yates," 68.

45. Yates, *Revolutionary Road*, 332.

46. Richard Yates, "The Best of Everything," in *Eleven Kinds of Loneliness* (London: Methuen, 2006, first published 1962), 22.

47. Ibid., 25.

48. Ibid., 22.

49. Brett Harvey, *The Fifties: A Women's Oral History* (Lincoln, NE: ASJA Press, 2002, first published 1993), xiv.

50. Breines, *Young, White, and Miserable*, 11.

51. Friedan coined the term the "fourth dimension" in her speech "The Crisis in Women's Identity," delivered in 1964 at the University of California, San Francisco.

52. We see this, for instance, in April Wheeler's desire to move to Paris where she will work and support her family; in Emily Grimes's character as she works but cannot find fulfillment in her home life; and in short stories such as "The Best of Everything," where the fact that Grace is prevented from working, "whether she wanted to or not" (Yates, "The Best of Everything," in *Eleven Kinds of Loneliness*, 21) the Friday before her wedding, acts as a metaphorical indicator of what life after marriage has in store.

53. Jessica Weiss, *To Have and To Hold: Marriage, the Baby Boom, and Social Change* (Chicago: University of Chicago Press, 2000), 53.

54. Ibid., 79.

55. Ibid., 7.

56. Ibid., 59. This seems like an unfair indictment of Friedan's work, not least for the fact that she did far more than survey women's magazines. Friedan herself acknowledges that there is much still to do when she states at the end of the introduc-

tion to the first edition that "there are many questions which social scientists must probe further." Betty Friedan, *The Feminine Mystique* (London: Penguin, 1965, first published 1963), 12.

57. Sharon Monteith, *American Culture in the 1960s* (Edinburgh: Edinburgh University Press, 2008), 164.

58. Richard M. Fried, "1950–1960," in *A Companion to 20th-Century America*, ed. Stephen J. Whitfield (Oxford: Blackwell, 2004), 80.

59. Ibid.

60. Douglas, *Where the Girls Are*, 43.

61. Martin Halliwell, *American Culture in the 1950s* (Edinburgh: Edinburgh University Press, 2007), 41.

62. Fried, "1950–1960," 71.

63. Bailey, *A Tragic Honesty*, 52.

64. Blake Bailey describes how "Ruth knocked on the Rodgers's door and was met by a man in grease-stained overalls who appeared to be Laurence Olivier blithely impersonating a laborer. The rest of her life was decided in that moment." Ibid., 43.

65. Indicating quite how closely April is modeled on Sheila, Monica Yates (Yates and Sheila's second daughter) remembers speaking to her father about the similarities between the two women: "'It's not your mother,' he said," and she came to understand what he meant. Nevertheless, "it is a portrait of her; it's not what she did with how she behaved but it's exactly how she behaves," Monica says (Charlton-Jones interview).

66. Yates, *Revolutionary Road*, 111.

67. Ibid., 65.

68. Ibid., 68.

69. Ibid., 110.

70. It has always struck me as interesting that Yates dedicated *Revolutionary Road* to Sheila Bryant even though they were divorced in 1959 and had been separated for a number of years by the time it was published in 1961. Monica Yates feels that her mother saw the book as "an apology" (Charlton-Jones interview).

71. Crude though it may be as a device, Yates often uses his protagonists' names as a very traditional indicator of their moral position.

72. Yates, "The Best of Everything," 29.

73. Ibid., 33.

74. Ibid., 23.

75. Ibid., 24.

76. Ibid., 34.

77. Ibid.

78. Ibid., 36.

79. J. D. Salinger, *The Catcher in the Rye* (London: Penguin, 1994, first published 1951), 118.

80. Yates, "The Best of Everything," 29.

81. Ernest Hemingway, "The Snows of Kilimanjaro," in *The Short Stories* (New York: Scribner, 2003), 59.

82. Yates, *The Easter Parade*, 25.

83. Ibid., 27.

84. Ibid., 28.

85. Ibid., 192.

Chapter 9

1. Richard Yates in DeWitt Henry and Geoffrey Clark, "An Interview with Richard Yates," *Ploughshares* 1, no. 3 (1972): 70.

2. Ibid.

3. Ibid.

4. Ibid.

5. Bailey includes an interesting vignette about the complexity of Yates's relationship with his mother: Once, when Yates was responding to questions about his work, a young woman commented on how *awful* the mother was in *A Special Providence*—"so careless and thoughtless and self-centered"—and asked Yates what *he* thought of her. "Oh, I don't know," he said quietly. "I guess I sort of love her." Blake Bailey, *A Tragic Honesty: The Life and Work of Richard Yates* (London: Methuen, 2004; first published 2003), 36.

6. Ibid., 17.

7. Ibid.

8. Ibid.

9. Richard Yates, *A Special Providence* (New York: Picador, Henry Holt, 1969), 14.

10. Ibid.

11. Ibid., 16.

12. A similar predicament has clearly arisen for the male child in one of his short stories. Yates's narrator, reflecting on the events of his childhood, describes the sculptures his mother had been working on: "her speciality had been . . . a life-size little boy." Richard Yates, "Oh, Joseph, I'm So Tired," in *Liars in Love* (New York: Delacorte Press/Seymour Lawrence, 1981), 3.

13. Yates, *A Special Providence*, 133.

14. Ibid.

15. Bailey, *A Tragic Honesty*, 21.

16. Yates, "Oh, Joseph, I'm So Tired," 3.

17. Ibid., 26.

18. The intertextual references between these two stories suggests to me that Yates, dissatisfied as he was with the novel, tried to salvage what was strong about that first fiction in the later short story.

19. Yates, *A Special Providence*, 220.

20. Ibid., 340.

21. Yates, "Oh, Joseph, I'm So Tired," 30.

22. Ibid., 31.

23. Wini Breines, *Young, White, and Miserable: Growing Up Female in the Fifties* (Chicago: University of Chicago Press, 1992), 41.

24. Ibid.

25. Ibid., 33.

26. Ibid., 44.

27. Elaine Tyler May, *Homeward Bound: American Families in the Cold War Era* (New York: Basic Books, 1988), 96.

28. Richard Yates, *Cold Spring Harbor* (London: Methuen, 2005, first published 1986), 34.

29. Ibid., 35.

30. Ibid.

31. Ibid., 34.

32. May, *Homeward Bound*, 101.

33. Yates, *Cold Spring Harbor*, 44.

34. Ibid., 45.

35. Yates, *A Special Providence*, 75.

36. Yates, *Cold Spring Harbor*, 48.

37. Richard Yates, *The Easter Parade* (London: Methuen, 2004, first published 1976), 6.

38. Ibid., 5.

39. Ibid., 135.

40. Richard Yates, *A Good School* (London: Methuen, 2006, first published 1978), 75.

41. Ibid.

42. Ibid., 78.

43. Richard Yates, "Lament for a Tenor," uncollected short story, *Cosmopolitan*, February 1954, 50–57, at 51.

44. Ibid., 53.

45. Ibid.

46. Ibid., 57.

47. Ralph Waldo Emerson, "Experience," in *The Heath Anthology of American Literature*, vol. 1, 4th ed., ed. Paul Lauter (Boston: Houghton Mifflin, 2002), 1589.

48. Yates, *The Easter Parade*, 42.

49. Ibid., 41.

50. Yates, "Oh, Joseph, I'm So Tired," 8.

51. Ibid.

52. Ibid.

53. Yates, *Revolutionary Road*, 52.

54. Bailey, *A Tragic Honesty*, 345.

55. Yates, *The Easter Parade*, 4.

56. Ibid., 9.

57. We see her, for instance, driving her "fist repeatedly into the pillow" at the end

of a relationship (ibid., 67) and pacing up and down her apartment after the death of her mother, "with her fist in her mouth" (ibid., 137).

58. Robert Towers, "Richard Yates and His Unhappy People," *New York Times*, November 1, 1981, http://www.richardyates.org/bib_towers.html, accessed October 7, 2007.

59. Yates, *Revolutionary Road*, 39.

60. Ibid., 65.

61. I am referring here to Blanche DuBois's "Barnum and Bailey world" where she admits, "I don't tell the truth. I tell what *ought* to be truth." Tennessee Williams, *A Streetcar Named Desire*, together with *Sweet Bird of Youth* and *The Glass Menagerie* (London: Penguin, 1982, first published 1947), 204. It is interesting that between 1947 and 1956, three major plays were written and produced in which the home is both a central character and a notable point of dissonance or absence: *A Streetcar Named Desire* (1947), *Death of a Salesman* (1949), and *Long Day's Journey into Night* (1956). They invoke images of the ideal home as much as they attack those ideals by suggesting that the harsh reality of daily life for the average American makes such high standards unattainable.

62. Yates, *A Special Providence*, 4.

63. Ibid., 10.

64. Yates, *Cold Spring Harbor*, 20.

65. Yates, *The Easter Parade*, 34.

66. Breines, *Young, White, and Miserable*, 55.

67. Ibid.

68. Yates, *The Easter Parade*, 69.

69. Yates, *A Good School*, 127.

70. Yates, *The Easter Parade*, 37.

71. Ibid., 75.

72. Ibid., 76.

73. Ibid., 215.

74. Ibid., 216.

75. Yates, *Cold Spring Harbor*, 97.

76. Ibid., 9.

77. Yates, "Oh, Joseph, I'm So Tired," 25.

78. Richard Yates, *Disturbing the Peace* (London: Methuen, 2007, first published 1975), 39.

79. Ibid., 63.

80. Ibid.

81. Ibid.

82. Ibid., 64.

83. Bailey, *A Tragic Honesty*, 86.

84. Ibid., 250.

85. Breines, *Young, White, and Miserable*, 49.

86. Ibid., 33.

87. May, *Homeward Bound*, 94.

88. Bailey, *A Tragic Honesty*, 39.

89. Ibid.

90. Susan Braudy in Seymour Lawrence, ed., *Richard Yates: An American Writer, Tributes in Memoriam* (New York: Seymour Lawrence, 1993), 21.

91. Richard Yates, *Young Hearts Crying* (London: Methuen, 1986, first published 1984), 111.

92. Richard Yates, "A Clinical Romance," in *The Collected Stories of Richard Yates* (London: Methuen, 2004), 394.

93. Bailey, *A Tragic Honesty*, 506.

94. Yates, *A Good School*, 77.

95. In *Young Hearts Crying*, for instance, Lucy Davenport's attack on her doctor and on psychiatry as a profession has the sound of Yates about it: "Your whole profession is a slippery, irresponsible business. You suck people in when they don't know where else to turn; then you seduce them into telling you all their secrets until they're utterly naked." Yates, *Young Hearts Crying*, 138. Like Yates, she despises the self-absorption and the exposure psychiatry promotes and depends on.

96. Yates, *The Easter Parade*, 64.

97. Ibid., 66.

98. Ibid.

99. Jerome Klinkowitz, *The New American Novel of Manners: The Fiction of Richard Yates, Dan Wakefield, and Thomas McGuane* (Athens: University of Georgia Press, 1986), 9.

100. Breines, *Young, White, and Miserable*, 4.

101. Ibid., 9.

102. W. H. Auden, *The Age of Anxiety: A Baroque Eclogue* (London: Faber and Faber, 1948).

103. Yates, *Cold Spring Harbor*, 168.

Chapter 10

1. C. Wright Mills, *The Sociological Imagination* (Oxford: Oxford University Press, 1959), 5.

2. Ibid., 6.

3. Richard M. Fried, "1950–1960," in *A Companion to 20th-Century America*, ed. Stephen J. Whitfield (Oxford: Blackwell, 2004), 84.

4. Norman Podhoretz, *Doings and Undoings: The Fifties and After in American Writing* (London: Rupert Hart-Davis, 1965), 107.

5. Vance Packard, *The Status Seekers* (London: Longmans, 1960, first published 1959), 4.

6. Fried, "1950–1960," 73.

7. Lionel Trilling, *The Liberal Imagination: Essays on Literature and Society*

(London: Penguin Books in association with Secker and Warburg, a Peregrine Book, 1970, first published 1950), 215.

8. Richard Yates, *Young Hearts Crying* (London: Methuen, 1986, first published 1984), 9.

9. Ibid., 11.

10. Ibid., 22.

11. Ibid.

12. Blake Bailey, *A Tragic Honesty: The Life and Works of Richard Yates* (London: Methuen, 2004, first published 2003), 232.

13. James Howard Kunstler, *The Geography of Nowhere: The Rise and Decline of America's Man-Made Landscape* (New York: Simon and Schuster, 1993), 104.

14. Richard Yates, *The Easter Parade* (London: Methuen, 2004, first published 1976), 200.

15. Kunstler, *The Geography of Nowhere*, 105.

16. Richard Yates, *Revolutionary Road* (London: Methuen, 2001, first published 1961), 30.

17. Richard Ford, introduction to *Revolutionary Road*, xvii.

18. Ibid., xviii.

19. Yates, *Young Hearts Crying*, p. 30.

20. Ibid., 45.

21. Richard Yates in DeWitt Henry and Geoffrey Clark, "An Interview with Richard Yates," *Ploughshares* 1, no. 3 (1972): 66.

22. Yates, *Young Hearts Crying*, 29.

23. Ibid., 28.

24. Yates, *Revolutionary Road*, 119.

25. Ibid., 323.

26. Ibid., 5.

27. Yates, *The Easter Parade*, 17.

28. Richard Yates, *Disturbing the Peace* (London: Methuen, 2007, first published 1975), 187.

29. Ibid., 192.

30. Podhoretz, *Doings and Undoings*, 110.

31. Sloan Wilson, *The Man in the Gray Flannel Suit* (London: The Reprint Society, 1957, first published 1955), 255; the spelling of the title was changed from the American *Gray* to *Grey* for the UK edition.

32. Ibid., 256.

33. Yates in Henry and Clark, "An Interview with Richard Yates," 66.

34. Ibid.

35. Yates, *Disturbing the Peace*, 238.

36. Ibid.

37. Joseph Kahl, *The American Class Structure* (New York: Holt, Rinehart and Winston, 1962), 109.

38. David Castronovo and Steven Goldleaf, *Richard Yates*, Twayne's United States Authors (New York: Twayne Publishers, 1996), 1 (my italics).

39. Richard Yates, "A Natural Girl," in *Liars in Love* (New York: Delacorte Press/ Seymour Lawrence, 1981), 37.

40. Maria Russo, "The Collected Stories of Richard Yates," *Salon*, June 19, 2001, http://archive.salon.com/books/review/2001/06/19/yates/index.html, accessed May 20, 2008.

41. *The Hour* (TV series), directed by Jamie Payne, Harry Bradbeer, Coky Giedroyc, and others; featuring Ben Whishaw, Dominic West and Romola Garai (Kudos Productions Ltd., distributed by the BBC, 2011/12). The series is set in Cold War–era England and centers on a journalist, a producer, and an anchorman for an investigative news program.

42. *A Single Man*, directed by Tom Ford; featuring Colin Firth and Julianne Moore (Fade to Black Productions, 2009).

43. *An Education*, directed by Lone Scherfig; featuring Carey Mulligan, Peter Sarsgaard, Alfred Molina, and Rosamund Pike (BBC Films, 2009).

44. *Mad Men*, a television series, created by Matthew Weiner, AMC TV (Los Angeles: first aired on July 19, 2007). The popularity and success of *Mad Men* is phenomenal and may be a further indication that the late 1950s and 1960s is being re-evaluated in the twenty-first century; it picked up six Emmy awards in November 2008 and won the Golden Globe award for Best Television Series—Drama in 2008, 2009, and 2010.

45. Marge Piercy describes how women's clothing of the 1950s constrained their bodies in ways that were designed to emphasize their curves: "a litany of rubber, metal bands, garters, boning, a rosary of spandex and lycra and nylon, a votive candle of elastic." Marge Piercy, "Through the Cracks: Growing Up in the Fifties," in *Parti-Colored Blocks for a Quilt* (Ann Arbor: University of Michigan Press, 1982), 120.

Conclusion

1. *Revolutionary Road*, directed by Sam Mendes; featuring Kate Winslet, Leonardo DiCaprio, and Kathy Bates (BBC Films in association with DreamWorks SKG, released December 2008 [USA] January 2009 [UK]).

2. Richard Price, introduction to *Richard Yates* (New York: Everyman's Library, Alfred A. Knopf, 2009), ix.

3. Ibid.

4. Vance Packard, *The Status Seekers* (London: Longmans, 1960, first published 1959), 8.

5. Ibid., 311.

6. David Krasner, *American Drama, 1945–2000* (Malden, MA; Oxford: Blackwell Publishing, 2006), 28.

7. James Howard Kunstler, *The Geography of Nowhere: The Rise and Decline of America's Man-Made Landscape* (New York: Simon and Schuster, 1993), 140.

8. Packard, *The Status Seekers*, 7.

9. Wini Breines, *Young, White, and Miserable: Growing Up Female in the Fifties* (Chicago: University of Chicago Press, 2001, first published 1992), 105.

10. Packard, *The Status Seekers*, 6.

11. David Castronovo and Steven Goldleaf, *Richard Yates*, Twayne's United States Authors (New York: Twayne Publishers, 1996), 53.

12. Ibid.

13. Ibid., 5.

14. Theo Tait, "Just Like Mother," *London Review of Books*, February 2003, http://www.tbns.net/elevenkinds/tait.html, accessed January 4, 2008.

15. Richard Yates in DeWitt Henry and Geoffrey Clark, "An Interview with Richard Yates," *Ploughshares* 1, no. 3 (1972): 71.

16. Ibid.

17. Martin Naparsteck, "Drinking with Dick Yates," *North American Review* (May–August 2001), http://www.tbns.net/elevenkinds/naparsteck.html, accessed August 8, 2007.

18. Ronald Sukenick's *In Form: Digressions on the Act of Fiction* (Carbondale: Southern Illinois University Press, 1985), 3.

19. Ibid.

20. Ibid., xix.

21. Richard Ford, introduction to *Revolutionary Road* (London: Methuen, 2001, first published 1961), xiv.

22. Richard Yates, *The Easter Parade* (London: Methuen, 2004, first published 1976), 105.

23. Richard Yates, *A Good School* (London: Methuen, 2006, first published 1978), 61.

24. Alain Robbe-Grillet, *Snapshots* and *Towards a New Novel*, trans. Barbara Wright (London: Calder and Boyars, 1965, *Pour un nouveau roman* first published 1962, *Instantanés* first published 1963), 57.

25. Norman Podhoretz, *Doings and Undoings: The Fifties and After in American Writing* (London: Rupert Hart-Davis, 1965), 110.

26. Ibid.

27. Carolyn See quoted in Elizabeth Venant, "A Fresh Twist in the Road for Novelist Richard Yates, a Specialist in Grim Irony, Late Fame's a Wicked Return," *Los Angeles Times*, July 9, 1989, http://www.tbns.net/elevenkinds/venant.html, accessed October 7, 2007.

28. Blake Bailey, *A Tragic Honesty: The Life and Works of Richard Yates* (London: Methuen, 2004, first published 2003), 509.

29. An important caveat to this comment has to be in his contradictory, and sometimes overly harsh, writing about women and their sexuality.

30. Venant, "A Fresh Twist in the Road for Novelist Richard Yates, a Specialist in Grim Irony, Late Fame's a Wicked Return."

31. Kate Charlton-Jones, "Living on Revolutionary Road," *The Times*, January 24, 2009. http://entertainment.timesonline.co.uk/tol/arts_and_entertainment/film/article5573136.ece, accessed January 24, 2009.

32. Ibid.

33. Dan DeLuca, "The Collected Stories of Richard Yates," Knight Ridder/Tribune News Service, June 13, 2001, http://www.highbeam.com/doc/1G1-75512763.html, accessed February 10, 2008.

34. Dina Vakil, "Return of the Enchanter," about Salman Rushdie, *The Times of India*, April 13, 2008, http://timesofindia.indiatimes.com/Review/Return_of_the_Enchanter/articleshow/2947770.cms, accessed January 9, 2010.

35. Ford, introduction to *Revolutionary Road*, xxiv.

36. Lee Siegel, "Revolutionary Road (Richard Yates' Classic Work Republished)," *Harper's Magazine*, July 1, 2001, http://www.highbeam.com/doc/1G1-76134284.html, accessed September 26, 2013.

37. *Revolutionary Road*, directed by Sam Mendes; featuring Kate Winslet, Leonardo DiCaprio, and Kathy Bates (BBC Films in association with DreamWorks SKG, released December 2008 [USA] January 2009 [UK]).

38. *Mad Men*, a television series, created by Matthew Weiner, AMC TV (Los Angeles: first aired on July 19, 2007.

39. Stewart O'Nan, "The Lost World of Richard Yates: How the Great Writer of the Age of Anxiety Disappeared from Print," *Boston Review* (October/November 1999), http://bostonreview.net/BR24.5/onan.html, accessed September 10, 2007.

40. Tony Tanner, *City of Words: American Fiction, 1950–1970* (New York: Harper and Row, 1971), 15.

41. Ibid., 19.

42. Nick Fraser, "Rebirth of a Dark Genius," *The Observer*, February 17, 2008, http://www.theguardian.com/books/2008/feb/17/biography.fiction, accessed February 20, 2008.

Bibliography

Primary Texts

Yates, Richard. *Cold Spring Harbor*. London: Methuen, 2005, first published 1986.

———. *The Collected Stories of Richard Yates*. London: Methuen, 2004, first published 2001.

———. *Disturbing the Peace*. London: Methuen, 2007, first published 1975.

———. *The Easter Parade*. London: Methuen, 2004, first published 1976.

———. *Eleven Kinds of Loneliness*. London: Methuen, 2006, first published 1962.

———. *A Good School*. London: Methuen, 2006, first published 1978.

———. *Liars in Love*. New York: Delacorte Press/Seymour Lawrence, 1981.

———. *Revolutionary Road*. London: Methuen, 2001, first published 1961.

———. *A Special Providence*. New York: Picador, Henry Holt, 1969.

———. *Young Hearts Crying*. London: Methuen, 1986, first published 1984.

Secondary Texts

Albee, Edward. *Who's Afraid of Virginia Woolf?* London: Vintage, 2001, first published 1962.

Anderson, Sherwood. *Winesburg, Ohio*. Edited by Charles E. Modlin and Ray Lewis White. New York: W. W. Norton, 1996, first published 1919.

Auden, W. H. *The Age of Anxiety: A Baroque Eclogue*. London: Faber and Faber, 1948.

Bailey, Blake. *Cheever: A Life*. New York: Alfred A. Knopf, 2009.

———. "*Revolutionary Road*—the Movie." *Slate*, June 26, 2007, http://www.slate.com /articles/news_and_politics/summer_movies/2007/06/revolutionary_roadthe_movie .html, accessed April 3, 2009.

———. "Richard Yates' Real Masterpiece: What Kate Winslet Doesn't Tell You about Yates and Women." *Slate*, January 5, 2009, http://www.slate.com/articles/arts/books /2009/01/richard_yates_real_masterpiece.html, accessed April 3, 2009.

———. *A Tragic Honesty*: *The Life and Work of Richard Yates*. London: Methuen, 2004, first published 2003.

Bakhtin, Mikhail. *The Dialogic Imagination*. Edited by Michael Holquist. Translated by Caryl Emerson and Michael Holquist. Austin: University of Texas Press, 1981.

Baldwin, James. *Giovanni's Room*. New York: Dial Press, 1956.

Barth, John. *The End of the Road*. London: A Panther Book for Granada, 1981, first published 1962.

Barthelme, Donald. *The New Granta Book of the American Short Story*. Edited by Richard Ford. London: Granta Books, 2007.

Bellow, Saul. *Herzog*. New York: Penguin Modern Classics, 2007, first published 1964.

Bercovitch, Sacvan, ed. *The Cambridge History of American Literature*. Vol. 7. Cambridge: Cambridge University Press, 1999.

Booth, Wayne C. *The Rhetoric of Fiction*. Chicago: University of Chicago Press, 1961.

Borges, Jorge Luis. *Fictions*. Translated by Andrew Hurley. London: Penguin Classics, 2000, first published 1998.

Bradfield, Scott. "Follow the Long and Revolutionary Road." *The Independent*, November 21, 1992, http://www.tbns.net/elevenkinds/bradfield.html, accessed April 3, 2009.

Breines, Wini. *Young, White, and Miserable: Growing Up Female in the Fifties*. (Chicago: University of Chicago Press, 1992.

Burkitt, Ian. *Social Selves: Theories of the Social Formation of Personality*. London: Sage Publications, 1991.

Capote, Truman. *In Cold Blood*. London: Penguin, 1966, first published 1965.

Castronovo, David, and Steven Goldleaf. *Richard Yates*. Twayne's United States Authors. (New York: Twayne Publishers, 1996.

Charlton-Jones, Kate. *KateonYates*. A blog about the work of Richard Yates, http://kateonyates.wordpress.com.

———. "Living on Revolutionary Road." *The Times*, January 24, 2009, http://www.thetimes.co.uk/tto/arts/film/article2430362.ece, accessed January 24, 2009.

Cheever, John. *Collected Stories*. London: Vintage, 1990.

———. *The Wapshot Chronicle*. Alexandria, VA: Time-Life Books, 1965, first published 1954.

Chekhov, Anton. "The Seagull." Translated by Marian Fell. In *Six Famous Plays*. London: Gerald Duckworth, 1958.

Cowley, Malcolm. *A Second Flowering: Works and Days of the Lost Generation*. London: Andre Deutsch, 1973.

Cox, Elizabeth. "Meet Richard Yates." pif *Magazine*, October 1, 2000, http://www.pifmagazine.com/2000/10/meet-richard-yates, accessed November 12, 2007.

DeLuca, Dan. "The Collected Stories of Richard Yates." Knight Ridder/Tribune News Service, June 13, 2001, http://www.highbeam.com/doc/1G1-75512763.html, accessed February 10, 2008.

Dickstein, Morris. "Fiction and Society, 1940–1970." In *The Cambridge History of American Literature*. Vol. 7, edited by Sacvan Bercovitch. Cambridge: Cambridge University Press, 1999.

Didion, Joan. *Play It as It Lays*. London: Weidenfeld and Nicolson, 1971.

Douglas, Susan J. *Where the Girls Are: Growing Up Female with the Mass Media*. London: Penguin, 1994.

Dreiser, Theodore. *An American Tragedy*. Cleveland and New York: World Publishing, 1925.

———. *Sister Carrie*. Oxford: Oxford University Press, 2009, first published 1900.

———. *Tragic America*. New York: Horace Liveright, 1932.

Edel, Leon, and Gordon Ray, eds. *Henry James and H. G. Wells: A Record of Their Friendship, Their Debate on the Art of Fiction, and Their Quarrel*. London: Rupert Hart-Davis, 1958.

Ehre, Milton. *Chekhov for the Stage*. Evanston, IL: Northwestern University Press, 1992.

Eliot, T. S. *The Sacred Wood: Essays on Poetry and Criticism*. London: Methuen, 1920.

Emerson, Ralph Waldo. "The American Scholar." In *The Heath Anthology of American Literature*. Vol. 1, 4th ed., edited by Paul Lauter. Boston: Houghton Mifflin, 2002.

———. "Experience." In *The Heath Anthology of American Literature*. Vol. 1, 4th ed., edited by Paul Lauter. Boston: Houghton Mifflin, 2002.

Fielder, Leslie. *Love and Death in the American Novel*. London: Paladin, 1966, first published 1960.

Fitzgerald, F. Scott. *The Crack-Up*, with other pieces and stories. London: Penguin, 1965.

———. *The Great Gatsby*. London: Penguin, 1950, first published 1926.

———. *The Last Tycoon*. London: Penguin, 1960, first published 1941.

———. *The Pat Hobby Stories*. New York, London: Scribner, 2004, first published 1962.

———. *The Price Was High*. Vols. 1 and 2. London: Picador, 1981, first published 1979.

———. *Tender Is the Night*. London: Penguin, 1955, first published 1939.

Flaubert, Gustave. *Madame Bovary*. Translated by Alan Russell. London: Penguin, 1950, first published 1857.

Ford, Richard. Introduction to *Revolutionary Road*, by Richard Yates. London: Methuen, 2001.

Ford, Richard, ed. *The New Granta Book of the American Short Story*. London: Granta Publications, 2007.

Fraser, Nick. "Rebirth of a Dark Genius." *The Observer*, February 17, 2008, http://www.theguardian.com/books/2008/feb/17/biography.fiction, accessed February 20, 2008.

Fried, Richard M. "1950–1960." In *A Companion to 20th-Century America*, edited by Stephen J. Whitfield. Oxford: Blackwell, 2004.

Friedan, Betty. *The Feminine Mystique*. London: Penguin, 1965, first published 1963.

Geismar, Maxwell. *The Last of the Provincials*. London: Secker and Warburg, 1947.

Gilman, Charlotte Perkins. *The Yellow Wallpaper, and Other Stories*. Edited by Robert Shulman. Oxford: Oxford University Press, 1995, first published 1892.

Goffman, Erving. *The Presentation of Self in Everyday Life*. London: Penguin, 1959.

Gray, Richard. *A History of American Literature*. Oxford: Blackwell Publishing, 2004.

Halberstam, David. *The Fifties*. New York: A Fawcett Book, Random House, 1993.

Halliwell, Martin. *American Culture in the 1950s*. Edinburgh: Edinburgh University Press, 2007.

Harvey, Brett. *The Fifties: A Women's Oral History*. Lincoln, NE: ASJA Press, 2002, first published 1993.

Hemingway, Ernest. *A Farewell to Arms*. London: Arrow Books, 1994, first published 1929.

———. *The Short Stories*. New York, London: Scribner, 2003.

———. *The Sun Also Rises*. London: Vintage, 2000, first published 1926.

Henry, DeWitt, and Geoffrey Clark. "An Interview with Richard Yates." *Ploughshares* 1, no. 3 (1972).

Holquist, Michael. *Dialogism: Bakhtin and His World*. London, New York: Routledge, 1990.

Hornby, Nick. *A Long Way Down*. London: Penguin, 2006, first published 2005.

James, Henry. *The American*. London: Everyman, 1997, first published 1877.

———. *The Art of the Novel: Critical Prefaces*. London: Charles Scribner's Sons, 1935.

———. "The Beast in the Jungle." In *The Beast in the Jungle and Other Stories*. New York: Dover, 1993, first published 1903.

———. *The Europeans*. London: Penguin, 1964, first published 1878.

———. *The Portrait of a Lady*. London: Penguin, 1963, first published 1881.

———. "The Real Thing." In *Selected Short Stories*. Baltimore: Penguin, 1963, first published 1893.

James, William. *Selected Writings of William James*. London: Everyman, 1995.

Kahl, Joseph. *The American Class Structure*. New York: Holt, Rinehart and Winston, 1962.

Kees, Welden. *The Collected Poems of Welden Kees*. Edited by Donald Justice. London, Boston: Faber and Faber, 1993, first published 1962.

Klinkowitz, Jerome. *The New American Novel of Manners: The Fiction of Richard Yates, Dan Wakefield, and Thomas McGuane*. Athens: University of Georgia Press, 1986.

Krasner, David. *American Drama, 1945–2000*. Malden, MA, Oxford: Blackwell Publishing, 2006.

Kunstler, James Howard. *The Geography of Nowhere: The Rise and Decline of America's Man-Made Landscape*. New York: Simon and Schuster, 1993.

Lawrence, D. H. *Sons and Lovers*. London, New York: Penguin, 1978, first published 1913.

Lawrence, Seymour, ed. *Richard Yates: An American Writer, Tributes in Memoriam*. New York: Seymour Lawrence, 1993.

Lewis, Sinclair. *Main Street*. New York: Harcourt, Brace and World, 1920.

Lukács, Georg. *The Meaning of Contemporary Realism*. Translated by John and Necke Mander. London: Merlin Press, 1963, first published 1957.

Lytal, Benjamin. "Reconsiderations: Richard Yates's 'Revolutionary Road.'" *New York Sun*, July 2, 2008, http://www.nysun.com/arts/reconsiderations-richard-yatess -revolutionary-road/81093/, accessed August 9, 2008.

Macdonald, Dwight. *Memoirs of a Revolutionist*. New York: Farrar, Straus and Cudahy, 1957.

Mailer, Norman. *The Deer Park*. London: Andre Deutsch, 1969, first published, 1957.

May, Elaine Tyler. *Homeward Bound: American Families in the Cold War Era*. New York: Basic Books, 1988.

Medvedev, P. N., and M. M. Bakhtin. *The Formal Method in Literary Scholarship: A Critical Introduction to Sociological Poetics*. Translated by Albert J. Wehrle. Baltimore: Johns Hopkins University Press, 1978.

Mills, C. Wright. *The Sociological Imagination*. Oxford: Oxford University Press, 1959.

Monteith, Sharon. *American Culture in the 1960s*. Edinburgh: Edinburgh University Press, 2008.

Munro, Alice. *The View from Castle Rock*. London: Chatto and Windus, 2006.

Nabokov, Vladimir. *Lolita*. London: Penguin, 1980, first published 1955.

Naparsteck, Martin. "Drinking with Dick Yates." *North American Review* (May–August 2001), http://www.tbns.net/elevenkinds/naparsteck.html, accessed August 8, 2007.

———. *Richard Yates Up Close: The Writer and His Works*. Jefferson, NC: McFarland, 2012.

Neve, Brian. *Film and Politics in America: A Social Tradition*. New York: Routledge, 1992.

O'Hara, John. *Appointment in Samarra*. New York: Vintage Books, 2003, first published 1934.

———. *Selected Short Stories of John O'Hara*. New York: Modern Library, 2003, first published 1994.

O'Nan, Stewart. "The Lost World of Richard Yates: How the Great Writer of the Age of Anxiety Disappeared from Print." *Boston Review* (October/November 1999), http://bostonreview.net/BR24.5/onan.html, accessed September 10, 2007.

Packard, Vance. *The Status Seekers*. London: Longmans, 1960, first published 1959.

———. *The Waste Makers*. London: Longmans, 1960.

Packman, David. *Vladimir Nabokov: The Structure of Literary Desire*. Columbia: University of Missouri Press, 1982.

Park, Robert Ezra. *Race and Culture*. Glencoe, IL: Free Press, 1950.

Percy, Walker. *The Message in the Bottle: How Queer Man Is, How Queer Language Is, and What One Has to Do with the Other*. New York: Farrar, Straus and Giroux, 1975.

———. *The Moviegoer*. London: Eyre and Spottiswoode, 1963, first published 1961.

Piercy, Marge. "Through the Cracks: Growing Up in the Fifties." In *Parti-Colored Blocks for a Quilt*. Ann Arbor: University of Michigan Press, 1982.

Podhoretz, Norman. *Doings and Undoings: The Fifties and After in American Writing*. London: Rupert Hart-Davis, 1965.

———. *Making It*. London: Jonathan Cape, 1967.

Poirier, Richard. *The Performing Self*. New Brunswick, NJ: Rutgers University Press, 1992.

Price, Richard. Introduction to *Richard Yates*. New York: Everyman's Library, Alfred A. Knopf, 2009.

Riesman, David, with Nathan Glazer and Reuel Denney. *The Lonely Crowd: A Study of the Changing American Character*. New Haven, CT: Yale University Press, abridged edition 1970 with 1969 preface, first published 1950.

Robbe-Grillet, Alain. *Snapshots* and *Towards a New Novel*. Translated by Barbara Wright. London: Calder and Boyars, 1965, *Pour un nouveau roman* first published 1962, *Instantanés* first published 1963.

Robinson, Edwin Arlington. *The Collected Poems of Edwin Arlington Robinson*. New York: Macmillan, 1961.

Rosen, Marjorie. *Popcorn Venus: Women, Movies, and the American Dream*. London: Peter Owen, 1975, first published 1973.

Roth, Philip. *American Pastoral*. London: Vintage Books, 2005, first published 1997.

———. *The Ghost Writer*. London: Vintage Books, 2005, first published 1979.

Russo, Maria. "The Collected Stories of Richard Yates." *Salon*, June 19, 2001, http://archive.salon.com/books/review/2001/06/19/yates/index.html, accessed May 20, 2008.

Russo, Richard. Introduction to *The Collected Stories of Richard Yates*. London: Methuen, 2004.

Salinger, J. D. *The Catcher in the Rye*. London: Penguin, 1994, first published 1951.

Samson, Leon. "Americanism as Surrogate Socialism." In *Failure of a Dream? Essays in the History of American Socialism*, edited by John H. M. Laslett and Seymour Martin Lipset. Garden City, NY: Anchor Press/Doubleday, 1974.

Scott, Ian. *American Politics in Hollywood Film*. Edinburgh: Edinburgh University Press, 2000.

Showalter, Elaine. *A Jury of Her Peers: American Women Writers from Anne Bradstreet to Annie Proulx*. London: Virago Press, 2009.

Siegel, Lee. "Revolutionary Road (Richard Yates' Classic Work Republished)." *Harper's Magazine*, July 1, 2001, http://www.highbeam.com/doc/1G1-76134284.html, accessed May 20, 2008.

Snyder, Mark. *Public Appearances, Private Realities: The Psychology of Self-Monitoring*. New York: W. H. Freeman, 1987.

Steinbeck, John. *The Grapes of Wrath*. London: The Reprint Society, 1940, first published 1939.

———. Of Mice and Men. London: Penguin Books, 1994, first published, 1937.

Styron, William. *Lie Down in Darkness*. New York: Vintage International, 1992, first published 1951.

Sukenick, Ronald. *In Form: Digressions on the Act of Fiction*. Carbondale: Southern Illinois University Press, 1985.

———. *Narralogues: Truth in Fiction*. Albany: State University of New York Press, 2000.

Tait, Theo. "Just Like Mother." *London Review of Books* (February 2003), http://www.tbns.net/elevenkinds/tait.html, accessed January 4, 2008.

Tanner, Tony. *City of Words: American Fiction, 1950–1970*. New York: Harper and Row, 1971.

Towers, Robert. "Richard Yates and His Unhappy People." *New York Times*, November 1, 1981, http://www.richardyates.org/bib_towers.html, accessed October 7, 2007.

Trilling, Lionel. *The Liberal Imagination: Essays on Literature and Society*. London: Penguin Books in association with Secker and Warburg, a Peregrine Book, 1970, first published 1950.

Updike, John. *Couples*. London: Penguin, 1969, first published 1968.

———. *A Rabbit Omnibus*. London: Penguin, 1991.

Vakil, Dina. "Return of the Enchanter," about Salman Rushdie. *The Times of India*, April 13, 2008, http://timesofindia.indiatimes.com/Review/Return_of_the_Enchanter /articleshow/2947770.cms, accessed January 9, 2010.

Venant, Elizabeth. "A Fresh Twist in the Road for Novelist Richard Yates, a Specialist in Grim Irony, Late Fame's a Wicked Return." *Los Angeles Times*, July 9, 1989, http://www.tbns.net/elevenkinds/venant.html, accessed October 7, 2007.

Voloshinov, V. N. *Marxism and the Philosophy of Language*. Translated by Ladislav Matejka and I. R. Titunik. New York: Seminar Press, 1973.

Vonnegut, Kurt, Jr. *Slaughterhouse 5*. London: Vintage, 2000, first published 1969.

———. *Welcome to the Monkey House* and *Palm Sunday*. London: Vintage, 1994.

Weiss, Jessica. *To Have and To Hold: Marriage, the Baby Boom, and Social Change*. Chicago: University of Chicago Press, 2000.

West, Nathanael. *Miss Lonelyhearts* and *The Day of the Locust*. Toronto: A New Directions Paperbook, George J. McLeod, 1962, first published 1933.

Wheeler, Mark. *Hollywood: Politics and Society*. London: British Film Institute, 2006.

Williams, Tennessee. *A Streetcar Named Desire*, together with *Sweet Bird of Youth* and *The Glass Menagerie*. London: Penguin, 1982, first published 1947.

Wilson, Sloan. *The Man in the Gray Flannel Suit*. London: The Reprint Society, 1957, first published 1955.

Wolfe, Thomas. *Look Homeward, Angel*. New York: Charles Scribner's Sons, 1957, first published 1929.

Wolfe, Tom. *The New Journalism*. New York: Harper and Row, 1973.

———. "There Goes (Varoom! Varoom!) That Kandy-Kolored (Thphhhhhh!) Tangerine-Flake Streamline Baby (Rahghhh!) around the Bend (Brummmmmmmmmmmm-mmmmmmm). . . ." *Esquire*, November 1963.

Woolf, Virginia. *A Room of One's Own*. London: Penguin, 1992, first published 1929.

Yates, Monica. *Here's Hoping*, written for richardyates.org, March 29, 2008, http://www.richardyates.org/bib_shapiro.html, accessed April 20, 2008.

Yates, Richard. "The Achievement of Gina Berriault." *Ploughshares* 5, no. 3 (1979).

———. "Lament for a Tenor." Uncollected short story. *Cosmopolitan*, February 1954, 50–57.

———. *Lie Down in Darkness*. Screenplay. Cambridge, MA: Watertown Ploughshares Books, 1985.

———. "Some Very Good Masters." *New York Times Book Review*, April 19, 1981.

———. *Uncertain Times*. Unpublished draft of a novel. The Richard Yates Collection, Howard Gotlieb Archival Research Center at Boston University, Massachusetts.

Yates, Richard, ed. *Stories for the Sixties*. New York: Bantam Books, 1963.

Other

Bluestone, George. Introduction to William Styron's *Lie Down in Darkness*, a screenplay by Richard Yates. Cambridge, MA: Watertown Ploughshares Books, 1985.

Kinsey, Dr. Alfred, Wardell B. Pomeroy, Clyde E. Martin, Paul H. Gebhard, and others. *Sexual Behavior in the Human Female*. Bloomington: Indiana University Press, 1953.

Review of *Revolutionary Road*, *New Yorker*, April 1, 1961, http://www.richardyates.org/bib_rrnyorker.html, accessed October 12, 2006.

Film

All That Heaven Allows. Directed by Douglas Sirk. Featuring Jane Wyman and Rock Hudson. Universal International Pictures, 1955.

An Education. Directed by Lone Scherfig. Featuring Carey Mulligan, Peter Sarsgaard, Alfred Molina, and Rosamund Pike. BBC Films, 2009.

Gone with the Wind. Directed by Victor Fleming and George Cukor. Featuring Clark Gable, Vivien Leigh, Leslie Howard, and Olivia de Havilland. Selznick International Pictures, 1939.

It's a Wonderful Life. Directed by Frank Capra. Featuring James Stewart and Donna Reed. Liberty, RKO, 1946.

Love with the Proper Stranger. Directed by Robert Mulligan. Featuring Natalie Wood and Steve McQueen. Pakula-Mulligan, 1963.

Mr. Deeds Goes to Town. Directed by Frank Capra. Featuring Gary Cooper and Jean Arthur. Columbia, 1936.

On the Waterfront. Directed by Elia Kazan. Featuring Marlon Brando, Karl Malden, Lee J. Cobb, and Rod Steiger. Horizon Pictures, 1954.

Rebel without a Cause. Directed by Nicholas Ray. Featuring James Dean, Natalie Wood, and Sal Mineo. Warner Bros. Pictures, 1955.

Revolutionary Road. Directed by Sam Mendes. Featuring Kate Winslet, Leonardo DiCaprio, and Kathy Bates. BBC Films in association with DreamWorks SKG, released December 2008 (USA), January 2009 (UK).

A Single Man. Directed by Tom Ford. Featuring Colin Firth and Julianne Moore. Fade to Black Productions, 2009.

A Summer Place. Directed by Delmer Daves, based on the novel by Sloan Wilson. Featuring Richard Egan, Dorothy McGuire, Sandra Dee, and Arthur Kennedy. Warner Bros. Pictures, 1959.

The Wild One. Directed by Laslo Benedek. Featuring Marlon Brando, Lee Marvin, and Mary Murphy. Stanley Kramer Productions, 1953.

The Wizard of Oz. Directed by Victor Fleming. Featuring Judy Garland, Ray Bolger, Jack Haley, and Bert Lahr. MGM, 1939.

Television

The Hour. Television series. Directed by Jamie Payne, Harry Bradbeer, Coky Giedroyc, and others. Featuring Ben Whishaw, Dominic West, and Romola Garai. Kudos Productions, distributed by the BBC, 2011.

Mad Men. Television series. Created by Matthew Weiner. Featuring Jon Hamm, Christina Hendricks, Elisabeth Moss, and John Slattery. AMC TV, Los Angeles. First aired on July 19, 2007.

Index